Sexuality & Gender Politics in Mozambique

Rethinking Gender in Africa

Sexuality & Gender Politics in Mozambique

Rethinking Gender in Africa

Signe Arnfred

Associate Professor
Department of Society & Globalization
and Centre for Gender, Power & Diversity,
Roskilde University

Nordiska Afrikainstitutet
The Nordic Africa Institute

JAMES CURREY

James Currey
is an imprint of Boydell & Brewer Ltd
PO Box 9
Woodbridge, Suffolk IP12 3DF (GB)
www.boydell.co.uk

In cooperation with
The Nordic Africa Institute
PO Box 1703
SE-751 47 Uppsala, Sweden
www.nai.uu.se

and of

Boydell & Brewer Inc.
668 Mt Hope Avenue
Rochester, NY 14620-2731 (US)
www.boydellandbrewer.com

British Library Cataloguing in Publication Data
Arnfred, Signe.
  Sexuality & gender politics in Mozambique : rethinking
  gender in Africa.
  1. Women--Mozambique--Social conditions. 2. Sex role--
  Mozambique. 3. Gender identity--Mozambique. 4. Gender
  identity--Political aspects--Mozambique.
  I. Title
  305.4'2'09679-dc22

ISBN 978-1-84701-035-3 James Currey (Cloth)
ISBN 978-1-84701-087-2 James Currey (Paperback)

This publication is printed on acid-free paper

Typeset in 10.5/11.5 Photina MT
by Avocet Typeset, Somerton, Somerset

For my daughters

Anne Julie & Katrine

Contents

List of Illustrations

Acknowledgements

The work on which the chapters of this book are based started thirty years ago, when in March 1981 I was employed as an in-house sociologist at the Maputo headquarters of the *Organicação da Mulher Moçambicana* – the OMM, the national women's organization in Mozambique. The idea was that I should assist the OMM in the preparation of an Extraordinary Conference for debating 'women's social problems'. My period of work with the OMM (March 1981 to June 1984, with a return visit for the Extraordinary Conference in November 1984) was decisive not only for development of my knowledge and my thinking regarding women in Mozambique, but also for my general political and feminist orientation. A co-worker, interpreter and personal friend during these early years was Adelina Penicela, then an employee of the OMM secretariat of Maputo province. I remained closely connected to Mama Adelina throughout my life in Mozambique, until her death in May 2008; to me she was somewhere between a friend and a mother (she was ten to fifteen years older than me) and an extra grandmother to our daughters. Mama Adelina was a remarkable woman. Born and raised in Manjakaze in the province of Gaza, she had come to Maputo where at the time of Independence she worked as a market woman. Through Frelimo she had attended alfabetization classes, thus she spoke Portuguese in addition to her native XiChangane. The OMM selected Mama Adelina as interpreter for my work in the XiChangane speaking parts of the country. My relationship with the city of Maputo is closely connected to my relationship with Mama Adelina. Thanks to her I moved with ease and confidence in the *bairro* of Chamanculo, where she lived, and where through the 1990s and 2000s – after Structural Adjustment Policies (in Mozambique the PRE, *Programa da Re-estruturação Económica*) with concomitant pauperization – not many whites would move around. Thus I want to acknowledge the memory of Mama Adelina in this book.

During my years with the OMM I was employed by the Danish Development Agency, Danida. In the second half of the 1980s I did some work in Mozambique for the Norwegian Development Agency, Norad, which made it possible for me to take leave from university and stay on in Maputo, in order to read through the material collected from all over the country during the preparation process for the OMM Extraordinary Conference 1984. These readings and subsequent analysis of the data, facilitated by a research grant from the Danish Council for Development Research (1988-1990), made me keen to return to the matrilineal north of the country, particularly to Nampula province, for proper fieldwork. Eventually the Frelimo/Renamo war came to an end, and it was again possible to travel outside the cities in Mozambique. By the end of the 1990s I again got research money, this time from the Danish Social Sciences Research Council

(1998–2000), allowing me to spend eight months – November 1998 to June 1999 – in Nampula province, mainly in Ribáuè district (inland) and in the coastal town Ilha de Moçambique.

In Ribáuè I worked with Ricardo Limua, who at that time was District Director for Culture in Ribáuè. Ricardo Limua was himself very interested in Makhuwa culture; he suggested himself as a collaborator shortly after my arrival in Ribáuè. He knew all important people in Ribáuè district: traditional healers, initiation ritual counselors, male and female chiefs. He was invaluable as a helper, friend and interpreter, and I want to acknowledge his importance for my work. Also in Ribáuè I stand in debt of gratitude to Salama, a Nampula-based NGO working with community health. The then head of Salama, Dona Michaela da Silva Sale, whom I met through friends in Nampula city, invited me to settle in Salama's small house in Ribáuè town, one of the few brick houses, which had remained standing through the war. Here I got my own room with electricity and access to water, being well looked after by Salama's cook, Esmínio. I also owe thanks to the Danish NGO MS (Danish Association for International Cooperation) from whom I borrowed a 4x4 car – very useful for getting around on the sandy trails of Ribáuè district, and also for helping informants with transport tasks. At one point my car was used as a wedding carriage for bringing the young couple to church.

In Ilha de Moçambique I worked with Maria da Conceição Amade, a friend of Flora Pinto de Magalhães, whom I met through a mutual friend, and in whose house, *Casa Branca*, I stayed through all research periods and later visits to Ilha, always in the same room with a wide view over the ocean and light curtains waving in the breeze. Maria da Conceicão was/is a native of Ilha and I got the impression she knew every one of the 13.000 inhabitants of Ilha, or at least the 8,000 men and women, who were proper islanders, those born and bred in Ilha de Moçambique – as distinct from those who had settled on the island during and after the war. Maria da Conceicão had a job as a pre-school teacher; she knew everything worth knowing about Ilha's history and culture, and she was a very sensitive, precise and poetic translator. The translation from Emakhuwa to Portuguese of Tufo songs (see Chapter 14 for some of these songs) is her work. I want to acknowledge Maria da Conceição for her importance for my work, and for her friendship.

In Maputo I have a circle of gender scholars and friends with whom I have met over the years, for discussion of my work and their work, and for coffee and gossip in Maputo cafés. Centrally placed in this group are those who are and have been connected to the Mozambique branch of the Women and Law in Southern Africa research project, such as Isabel Casimiro, Maria José Arthur, Ximena Andrade, Conceição Osório, Terezinha da Silva and Ana Loforte. It has been important to me over the years to have this circle of gender scholars as a reference group in Maputo.

From 2000 to 2007 most of my trips to Mozambique, including two shorter fieldwork visits to Nampula province 2003 and 2005, were funded by the Nordic Africa Institute in Uppsala. I was an employee of this institute from 2000 to 2007, the first six years as a research programme coordinator (the *Sexuality and Gender in Africa* research programme), the last year as Acting Research Director. The years in Uppsala gave me a lot in many different ways (see further in the

Introduction) and I want to acknowledge the generous funding from the Swedish Development Agency, Sida, which facilitated this work – including the travels to Mozambique, and to many other countries and Centres of Gender Studies on the African continent. Towards the end of my stay in Uppsala I received research funding from the Sida Department for Research Cooperation (SAREC) for final writing up on my Mozambique material. This funding was crucial for getting together the bits and pieces of this book, also because it encouraged me to concentrate on this work, rather than on all the other projects in which I tend to get involved.

Individual chapters have been written over quite a long time span. Some have been published before in different versions. Chapter 1 was first published 1988 in *Review of African Political Economy* vol. 15 no. 40; it is reprinted by permission from Palgrave Macmillan, who re-published the paper 2010 in a volume edited by Meredith Turschen: *African Women. A Political Economy*. Chapter 2 was published in 1990 in a volume of writings by colleagues from International Development Studies at Roskilde University, Agnete Weiss Bentzon (ed.): *The Language of Development Studies*, New Social Science Monographs, Copenhagen. Chapter 3 was published in 2000 by CEAN (Centre d'Etude d'Afrique Noir) Bordeaux, in *Travaux et Documents*, no 68-69. Chapter 4 was first published in 2001 in a Swedish conference report: *Svensk Genusforskning i Världen*, the Swedish National Secretariat for Gender Studies, and again in 2002 in *JENdA: A Journal of Culture and African Women's Studies*, vol. 2, no. 1. Chapter 5 was published in 2004 by CODESRIA (Council for the Development of Social Science Research in Africa) Dakar, in their Gender Series no 4: *Gender Activism and Studies in Africa*. Chapter 6 was written for *Qaderns d'Anthropologia* no 6, a special issue focusing on bodies, published in 2010 by CSIC (Consejo Superior de Investigaciones Científicas) Barcelona. Chapter 10 was published in 2010 in Alex Ezeh (ed): *Old Wineskins, New Wine: Readings in Sexuality in sub-Saharan Africa*, Nova Science Publishers. Chapter 11 was published in 2006 in *Studia Africana* no 17, CSIC Barcelona. Chapter 12 was published in 2001 in Rachel Waterhouse and Carin Vijfhuisen (eds): *Strategic Women, Gainful Men. Gender, Land and Natural Resources in Differet Rural Contexts in Mozambique*, Nucleo de Estudos de Terra (Universidade Eduardo Mondlane) and Action Aid Mozambique. Chapter 13 was published in 2007 in *Sexualities*, vol. 10 no. 2. Chapter 14 was published in 2004 in *Lusotopie*, CEAN Bordeaux. Some chapters have been changed only slightly to fit the context of the book, others have undergone more substantial changes. Their character as individual articles – written at different points in time – has, however, been maintained. The years of writing are indicated in brackets alongside the chapter titles.

The woodcuts at the chapter openings were crafted in the early 1980s by artists in Nandimba, Cabo Delgado. They were sold as postcards in Maputo 1983, published by the Mozambique Angola Committee. They are reprinted here with the kind permission of the Mozambique Angola Committee.

Acknowledgements usually include family members. In my case I have three fellow travellers, who have been close to me from day one of this project, thus having followed its ups and downs through all of the thirty years. They are first my friend and *companheiro*, and after fifteen years together also my husband, Jan Birket-Smith, and second our two daughters, Anne Julie (born 1977) and

Katrine (born 1980). Anne Julie and Jan feel as close to Mozambique as I do; the years in Maputo in the early 1980s have been very important for all of us. Katrine was very young when we returned to Denmark, thus she is less connected to Mozambique – but she has become a gender scholar, thus providing a different kind of sounding board for my ideas and concerns regarding this project.

The book is dedicated to my daughters. This book has been a key project of my life over thirty years. So have they. Only they flew from the nest before the book got going. Now it follows.

Signe Arnfred
Roskilde University, January 2011

Glossary

aldeia comunal/aldeias comunais	Frelimo-organized re-grouping of people in villages
amante	lover, male/female
amantismo	informal polygamy (usually with one formal wife and additional informal wives, i.e. *amantes)*
autoridade tradicional	traditional authority
bairro	part of town
batuqueiro/a	man/woman who beats the drum
caniço	reed; building material for houses in *bairros de caniço*
capataz	overseer, expression used in colonial times
capulana	women's clothing. An often brightly coloured piece of cotton cloth, 1.00 by 1.80 meters. In the coastal culture of northern Mozambique *capulanas* are sold in pairs, one to be used as a skirt and (part of) the other as a scarf. *Capulanas* are used by women all over Mozambique.
carrama	large festive gathering of Tufo groups
chefe da família	family head
chocalhos	rattles, used by *curandeiros/as* and during rituals
colono/s	Portuguese during colonialism
conselheira/s	woman in charge of initiation rituals; assistants to woman in charge
curandeiro/a	traditional healer m/f
erukulu	family unit at household level, literally meaning 'womb'
escudo/s	Portuguese coinage, used in Mozambique until 1980
esteira	woven mat made of grass/weeds
feitiçaria, feitiçeiro/a	witchcraft, witch (male/female)
Frelimo	*FREnte de LIbertação de MOçambique:* Mozambique liberation front, in 1977 turned into a Marxist-Leninist Party. Mozambique, since 1994, has been a multi-party country, however with Frelimo still in power.

halifa	in Ilha de Moçambique: the *xehe*'s deputy – generally a woman
ikano	chanted advice, given during initiation rituals
indígena/s	native/s
ithuna	elongated *labia minora*
kulukana	traditional healer m/f
lobolo	usually translated as 'bride price', but better translated as 'traditional marriage' in the patrilineal south of Mozambique. Without *lobolo* the ancestral spirits are not informed about the marriage, and the children do not properly belong
lobolar	*lobolo* turned into a Portuguese verb: to marry through *lobolo*
machamba	field
macuti	palm leaf thatch for houses
madras, madrasa	Quranic school
madrinha	already initiated woman, supporter of initiates during initiation rituals
makeya	finely ground flour of *mapira*. *Makeya* is used for communication with the ancestors; it is produced and administered by women.
mandioca	cassava
mapira	cereal grass with glossy seeds, something like millet or sorghum
mato	bush
mestra	woman in charge of initiation rituals
metical/meticais	Mozambican currency after 1980
miropo	yeast made of *mapira* for the production of *otheka*, ceremonial beer
missangas	glass beads
msiro	ground weed of a certain tree; used for making skin light and smooth. Also used at specific ceremonial occasions.
munumuzana, mulumuzana	man of importance, southern Mozambique
mwali, amwali	young girl(s) undergoing initiation rituals
mwene, mamwene	chief(s); in other parts of Nampula province the *mwene* is called *humu*
nakhapa	home-made briefs for use during menstruation
namalaka, anamalaka	woman/women in charge of initiation rituals
nihimo	matrilineal descent, the matriclan
nkhonsikaze	first wife in a polygamous marriage, southern Mozambique
noivo	fiancé

npichi	bush plant with oily seeds
olimiha	day of mutual work on somebody else's farm in return for *otheka* and/or food
OMM	*Organização da Mulher Moçambicana*, the national women's organization
otheka	ceremonial beer made from *mapira* and *mandioca* (cassava)
padre	Catholic priest
peneira	broad, flat winnowing basket
pilão	mortar
PLF	*Projecto da Lei da Família*: family law project
PRE	*Programa de Re-estrutuação Económica* = SAP, Structural Adjustment Programme
povoação	village, settlement
puxamento	Portuguese for vaginal lip-elongation
pwiyamwene, mapwiyamwene	female chief(s)
raínha do lar	queen of the home, housewife
régulo	Portuguese for chief, with colonial connotations
Renamo	REsisténcia NAçional de MOçambique, Mozambique National Resistance; opposition army during Frelimo/Renamo war, since 1994 elections opposition party
tariqa	way, path (Arab); Sufi order
tiquiri	Arab = *dhikr*; remembrance of God, prayer
unyango, unyago	Yao name for female initiation rituals
wineliwa	'to be danced to'. Name for female initiation in parts of Nampula province
wula	menstrual blood
xehe	Arab = *shaykh*: leader of Sufi order/respected man of learning
zauria	'woman's mosque' in Ilha de Moçambique
ziara	large religious gathering

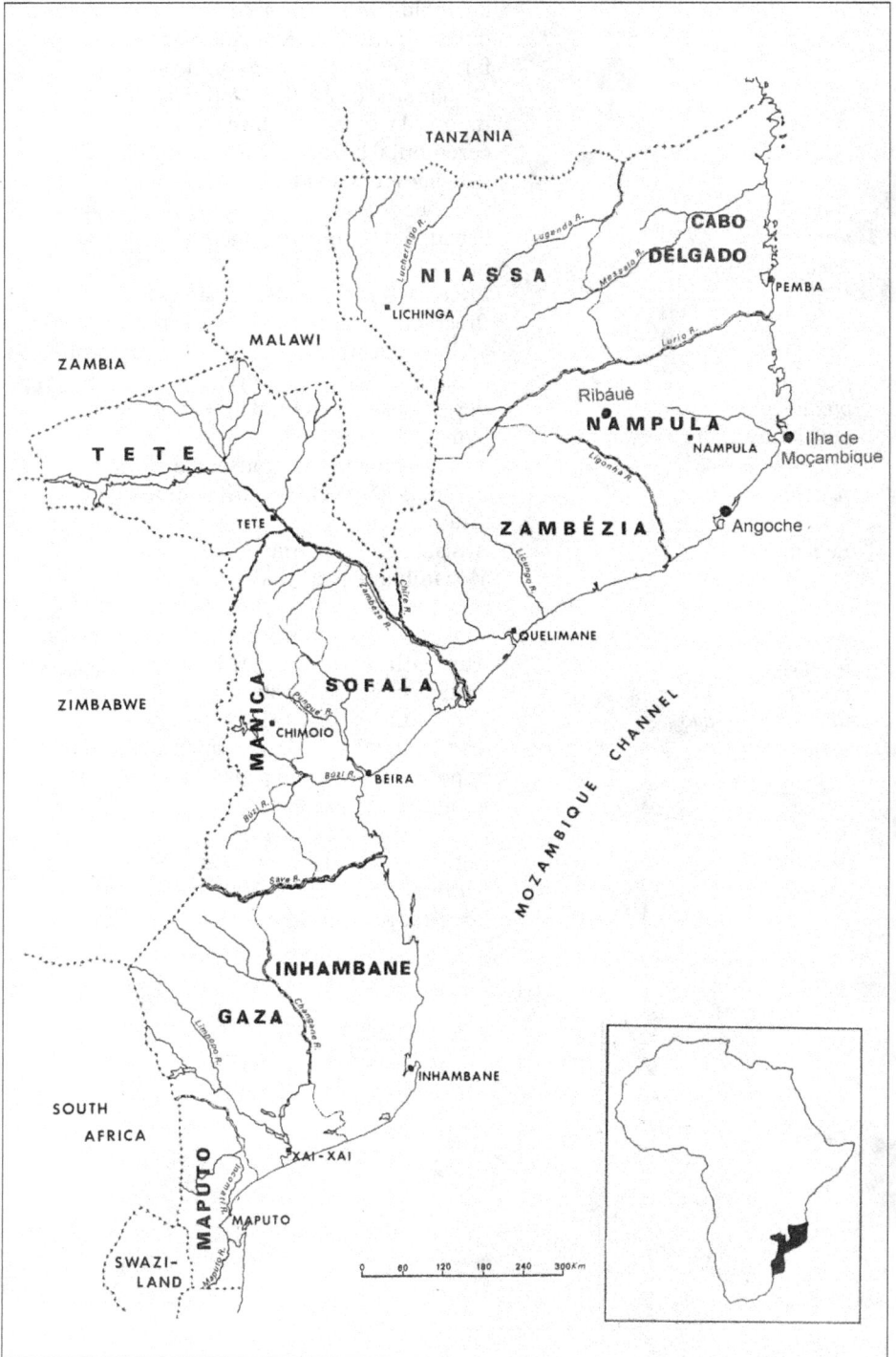

Map of Mozambique

Introduction

Woodcut by Faustino Robati

The title of this book reflects its double ambition: to make a contribution to feminist theorising by rethinking gender (and sexuality) based on material from Mozambique, and to say something about gender politics, sexuality and matriliny in Mozambique. The two ambitions are closely related. The chapters discuss sexuality and gender politics and policies in Mozambique over three decades, from Independence in 1975 to 2005. In doing so, they also investigate ways of understanding gender and sexuality. Gender policies from Portuguese colonialism through Frelimo socialism to later neo-liberal economic regimes share certain basic assumptions about women, men and gender relations. This however begs the question as to what extent such assumptions fit into the ways rural Mozambican men and women see themselves. The book is a discussion of Mozambican gender policies with a focus on the early post-Independence years, but it is also a conceptual discussion – facilitated by post-colonial feminist thinking – of how to understand gender and sexuality taking as a point of departure the lives and views of Mozambican men and women.

The discussions are based on 30 years of work off and on, in and with Mozambique, from full-time work in the National Women's Organization, the OMM (*Organização da Mulher Moçambicana*) 1981–1984, over a series of shorter and longer visits, consultancy work and teaching at the Eduardo Mondlane University during the second half of the 1980s and the 1990s, to periods of fieldwork in Nampula province 1998–1999, 2003 and 2005. The chapters were written over a span of more than 20 years, the first in 1987, the last in 2010. The organization of chapters in the book, however, is thematic, not chronological.

In Part I state gender policies are discussed as seen from below, by rural and urban men and women in different parts of the country. Post-independence state gender policy condemned polygamy and bride price (*lobolo*), but seen from local people's points of view these so-called 'traditional' customs are much more complex. Most of the chapters in Part I are rooted in fieldwork and knowledge from my work in the OMM. Part II zooms in on female initiation rituals, likewise condemned by early Frelimo policies, but very popular with rural women (and men) in northern Mozambique. Female initiation rituals are described and analysed from different viewpoints. The chapters in this section are mainly based on data material from the Makhuwa, the largest ethnic group in northern Mozambique. Part III deals with implications of matriliny. In the northern half of Mozambique the kinship systems of the dominant ethnic groups are matrilineal. This means that close to 40 per cent of Mozambique's population live under conditions of matriliny. What are the implications of matriliny for gender relations, for family structure and for ways of being women and men? In the coastal areas of northern Mozambique matriliny coexists with Islam. Parts of Part III investigate, how this mix works out in practice.

The book is concerned with empirical subject matters: gender policies and politics in Mozambique is the overriding theme, with focus points on particular – from a policy point of view – problematic areas, such as female initiation rituals and implications of matriliny in northern Mozambique.[1] At the same time the book is a discussion of different analytical approaches, mapping a

[1] Female initiation has been condemned by political powers, and matriliny – if acknowledged at all – is considered difficult.

struggle to find appropriate ways of understanding gender and sexuality in the country. In this struggle, aspects of post-colonial African feminist thinking have proved particularly helpful, thus some chapters may also be read as introductions to aspects of post-colonial African feminist thought (see Chapters 4 and 10).

Regarding gender policies/politics it is argued throughout the book that even if economic policies have shifted in Mozambique from Portuguese colonialism, over Frelimo socialism to donor-driven neo-liberal approaches, conceptions of gender and sexuality have remained much the same. Discrepancies between state policies and men's and women's lives have thus remained. Regarding female initiation rituals it is a main argument that these rituals have been systematically misunderstood as indications of women's subordination in a hierarchy of gender. The chapters show that the rituals have little to do with hierarchies of gender, but lots to do with hierarchies of age, and that female initiation is better understood as focal events for regeneration and maintenance of female community, identity and power of certain kinds. Through initiation rituals young girls are transformed into grown-up women. Sexual capacity building is an important element in the proceedings; the rituals confirm and celebrate Makhuwa femininity. Regarding matriliny it is a main argument that this kinship system – at least in the form it takes in northern Mozambique – does make a difference for women, and that the conventional anthropological position of matriliny just being a matter of uncles replacing fathers is untenable. Man/woman gender power relations differ from gender power relations under conditions of patriliny, partly because of matrilineal inheritance to land, partly because of a double-gendered system of chieftaincy: every *mwene* (male chief) has at his side a *pwiyamwene* (female chief) particularly responsible for matters regarding links to the invisible world. The matrilineage embraces the dead as well as the as yet unborn, and those in charge of such connections are mainly women.

It is an overriding argument throughout the book that development policies on gender, which do not take into account local understandings (and local realities) of gender, sexuality and gender power relations, have little chance of success. Mainstream development policy, frequently based on gender-and-development conceptualizations, sees African women as subordinated and oppressed. In matrilineal northern Mozambique such assumptions do not fit realities very well. Rather than starting off from fixed assumptions, development policies for women should take into account the actual positions of power, which women do command, and go on from there.

Periods and types of fieldwork: historical overview

When I first arrived in Mozambique in 1979, as a member of a group visit arranged by the Danish Association for Solidarity with Mozambique, I had already read about President Samora Machel's explicit concern for women's emancipation. Samora Machel had been leader of Frelimo's successful struggle against the Portuguese colonial power (Frelimo = Frente de Libertação de Moçambique, Mozambique's Liberation Front) which had led to Mozambique's Independence in 1975. He was then President of the People's Republic of Mozambique. One Samora-quote in particular from the First Conference of the National Women's Organization, the OMM, in 1973 spoke to my feminist heart. The quote goes like this: 'The liberation of women is a necessity for the revolution, a guarantee of its continuity and a condition for its success' (Machel 1973) (See photo 1.2). I wanted to work in a country where the President could talk in this way about women.

In Denmark I had been a part of the New Women's Movement since its early days in 1970. The Women's Movement had emerged as a part of the Student's Movement and of the New Left, but also in opposition to implicit and explicit patriarchal ideologies and male domination in these movements, as well as in society at large. Reading Samora Machel I understood him as being a part of this feminist struggle, and in 1979, together with my partner, Jan, and our two-year-old daughter Anne Julie, I was heading for Mozambique. Jan had his own socialist agenda. As an architect and a physical planner he had been working in Chile in the government of Salvador Allende, and he was ready for more experience of work in a socialist country. Returning to Denmark from Chile in 1973 he worked as a journalist at a left wing journal, and as such (speaking Spanish, close to Portuguese) he was sent to Portugal from 1974 to 1975 in order to cover the Portuguese anti-fascist revolution. I had finished my degree in sociology and was employed as an assistant professor at Roskilde University, but I was given research leave in order to to go to Portugal to study the involvement of women in the Portuguese revolution. In a Portuguese newspaper we read about the need for all kinds of professional competence in Mozambique – after Independence most Portuguese nationals had left the country, and the newly independent state was in desperate need of qualified labour power. We began to consider a move to Mozambique.

Before embarking on a work contract of several years, however, we wanted to get a feeling of what the place was like. This was the background for our participation in the 1979 journey to Mozambique arranged by the DK-Mozambique Solidarity Association. The result was clearly positive. Mozambique at that point, barely four years after Independence, was infused with a spirit of enthusiasm and hopes for the future. During this trip we visited ministries, factories, cooperatives and communal villages, *Aldeias Comunais*. We strongly felt the energy and enthusiasm, released by the fact that colonial oppression by the Portuguese had come to an end at last. We also saw how sometimes the political fervour of Frelimo cadres and the Soviet-inspired line of Frelimo politics – kindled by ideas of huge state farms operated by effective labour power usefully assembled in communal villages – were somewhat out of tune with lives and dreams of the rural peasant population.

We moved to Maputo with very little furniture, lots of books and our two daughters (the youngest, Katrine, only six months old) the following year. I was determined to get myself a job in the OMM (Jan had employment in a Government institute of physical planning). This, however, turned out to be complicated. The OMM was a political organization, and foreigners (*cooperantes*) would typically be working in Government ministries, not in political organizations. When finally I succeeded in arranging a job in the OMM, it was in roundabout ways through an agreement between the Danish Agency for International

Family photo, Maputo 1982; Bairro Chamanculo, where Mama Adelina lived. From right to left: Jan, Jan's mother (who was visiting from DK), Mama Adelina, who worked with me in the OMM, Anne Julie, Terezinha (Mama Adelina's daughter), Katrine. I am behind the camera. The car is our beloved Niva.
(Photo: Signe Arnfred)

Development Aid (Danida) and the Mozambican ministry for collaboration with foreign donors. A high-level official in this ministry was interested in sociology and in women; she knew that the OMM had recently been tasked by Frelimo to organize an Extraordinary Conference for discussion of 'women's social problems', i.e. issues of so-called tradition, such as lobolo, polygamy, initiation rituals etc., which Frelimo found difficult to reconcile with their modernist socialist programme. Seen from the point of view of this official I would be useful as a person who could support the OMM in this regard. She managed to convince Danida that they should pay my salary, while I was working with the OMM.

My work with the OMM, 1981–1984

My actual work situation in the National Secretariat of the OMM was weird in many ways, particularly in the beginning, when nobody really knew what I was supposed to be doing. The OMM Secretariat was housed at three floors in a high-rise building in one of the previously affluent parts of Maputo, full of large villas built for upper-class Portuguese people. The OMM building and the Frelimo building next door were (and are) the only high-rise buildings in this area, the Frelimo building taller than the OMM building (which the OMM shared with the National Youth Organization, the OJM). I got an office and a typewriter, but instructions regarding my work were unclear. Thus I set off on some initial investigations in the immediate surroundings, interviewing working women

[2] A *bairro* is a part of town; in Maputo most Mozambicans lived (and live) in the *bairros de caniço*, ie parts of town where houses are build of reeds (*caniço*).

in Maputo factories and *bairros.*[2] In the Greater Maputo area at that time there were many factories, several with a majority of women workers, such as cashew nut processing factories and textile factories. Since then Mozambique has been deindustrialized due to World Bank Structural Adjustment Policies in the 1990s. Later I also went to agricultural cooperatives, state farms and *Aldeias Comunais* in rural areas of Maputo Province, interviewing women.

In 1980, at the time of our move to Maputo, Frelimo was busy discussing an overall plan for industrialization of Mozambican agriculture. Kindled by images of Soviet-type state farms, the Party envisaged that this change could be completed within a span of ten years. The OMM 1976 Second Conference documents were full of talk of the Socialist Family and *o Homem Novo* (the new man), meaning the new human being. Frelimo meetings all over the country started and finished with the shouting of slogans such as *abaixo lobolo, abaixo poligamia, abaixo ritos de iniciação* (down with brideprice, down with polygamy, down with initiation rituals) – but clever Party officials of course were aware that ways of life of a peasant population did not change just by shouting slogans. In Party headquarters – or anywhere else – there was far too little empirical knowledge regarding ways of life in various parts of the country. After all Mozambique is quite a big place – 800,000 square kilometres, which is bigger than any single EU country, something like Germany and France together – embracing many different groups of people with different lifestyles, talking different languages. It is generally considered that 13 major African languages are spoken in the territory known as Mozambique.[3]

For all of these reasons the Party wanted the OMM to undertake grass root level investigations and discussions, leading up to an Extraordinary Conference not yet scheduled in terms of date and year. The OMM was waiting for more specific instructions on what to do. The OMM at that point saw itself as a women's organization, but also as 'an arm of the Party', whose function it was to transmit Party politics to Mozambican women, not the other way round. Thus they were waiting – and in the meanwhile I was carrying out my more or less individual investigations, however in the name of the OMM, and with travel conditions and local support (such as interpretation from local languages to Portuguese) supplied by the organization. By 1982 word came from the Party that investigations of women's lives in a core Frelimo area, the northern province of Cabo Delgado, were requested. Cabo Delgado was the province where the armed struggle against the Portuguese had started in 1964, and thus the province with the longest standing so-called 'liberated areas', areas which during the war had been captured from the Portuguese, and where – even before formal Independence – Frelimo had been the force in power.

Thus in September 1982 I set off for Cabo Delgado in order to carry out much the same form of investigations, which I had undertaken in the south of the country: In the chosen villages and cooperatives etc. ten women would be selected in each location for a life-story kind of interview; this would be supplemented with public meetings and group discussions. Selections of locations as well as selection of individuals were undertaken in cooperation with local OMM

---

[3] At Independence it was decided that Portuguese – albeit the colonial language, but also the only language potentially shared by all in Mozambique – should be the national language. Swahili, the *lingua franca* of East Africa, is only spoken by a tiny minority in northern Mozambique.

staff, with the aim of getting as much diversity (and approximate representation) as possible. This experience of interviewing peasant women in Cabo Delgado became decisive for my later thinking and analysis regarding women in Mozambique. In the reflections on analytical approaches below I shall explain in greater detail what actually happened, and why this experience became so important.

The OMM Extraordinary Conference preparation

Then again some time passed. The Party was busy with preparations for the 1983 Fourth Frelimo Congress, and only after the succesful completion of the Frelimo Congress, at long last, in August 1983, the official campaign for the Extraordinary OMM Conference (now scheduled for April 1984) was initiated.[4] Information Minister Luis Cabaço gave the opening speech, stressing the importance of going out, this time, not to teach, but to listen and learn.

The conference preparation campaign was modelled after the recently completed campaign preparing for the Fourth Frelimo Congress, in terms of an explicit bottom-up approach. Questionnaire material (i.e. loose lists of topics to be discussed) was prepared at central level – this was where I could contribute with my sociological background, by now supplemented with a fair amount of knowledge regarding living conditions and family life in south and north of Mozambique. Brigades were educated at central level, subsequently to be sent out to all ten provinces of Mozambique for instruction of local OMM staff regarding how to conduct meetings, which topics to discuss, how to take notes etc. At province level new brigades were educated for instructing OMM staff at lower levels. Administratively Mozambique at that time had ten provinces with seven to eighteen districts per province; meetings were held in every single district of the country, in cooperatives, state farms, factories, villages and *bairros*. Altogether several thousands of meetings all over the country, with an average of 200 public meetings and 200 group interviews per province. The meetings were fora for discussion of the issues at stake – *lobolo*, polygamy, initiation rituals, etc., supplemented with group interviews on selected issues conducted by local level OMM staff. The idea was to collect data not only regarding how customs worked in relation to initiation, polygamy etc. but also regarding women's and men's attitudes to these customs, and how they could possibly be changed or replaced.

The whole Conference preparation process lasted well over six months – from August 1983 to March/April 1984. During this time everybody everywhere discussed the conference issues. It was like being in the midst of a social movement. I remember one Party veteran, with whom I worked in Maputo province, saying that these were the best political meetings she had ever attended in her entire political career. For a while issues of polygamy and lobolo were topics of discussion among people queuing at bus stops in Maputo. I participated in all phases of the campaign, travelling to the provinces for participation in meetings at all levels. The public meetings at district and lower levels were particularly successful. Often you started with a smaller crowd, but as people passed and listened, they too wanted to join, and before long you ended up with big crowds

---

[4] More about this meeting and about the conference preparation process in Chapter 1.

and meetings to be continued the following day, because of the long list of issues to be debated. Different viewpoints were frequent, and heated debates between young and old, and between women and men. The meetings were organized by the OMM, but everybody was invited to take part, and Frelimo, as well as the OMM, was particularly keen that the debates should not be among women only.

After discussions and taking of reports at district level, the material/the findings were written up and analysed in preparatory conferences at district level, subsequently to be sent to the provincial level, where provincial conferences were held for discussion of the findings and deliberations on suggested policies in one field or another. Finally all data ended up at the National Secretariat of the OMM in Maputo, as background material for the OMM General Secretary's Report, to be read to the delegates of the Extraordinary Conference.

The OMM Extraordinary Conference, November 1984

At the very last minute the conference, scheduled for April 1984, was postponed for half a year, to November. Evidently the Frelimo leadership, who was used to be in control, felt uneasy regarding what was taking place in this national social movement, into which the conference preparation had developed. The postponement worked as intended: when at last, in November 1984, the OMM Extraordinary Conference took place it was indeed closely controlled. A few days before the start of the five day conference – delegates had been travelling to Maputo from all over the country – Samora Machel announced, that as the President of Frelimo and of Mozambique he was going to not just deliver the opening and closing speeches, but to preside over proceedings during the entire conference. I recall how everybody in the OMM felt very honoured by this message. However, in reality it was nothing short of a sabotage of the conference. During the OMM General Secretary's presentation of the conference document, based on analysis of the masses of data gathered in the conference preparation process, the President incessantly intervened with his own stories and interpretations. In this way the presentation of the document took much longer than expected, and fifty-one conference delegates, wanting to speak from the floor supplementing or responding to the conference document, never got a chance. Instead of a forum for discussion of the conference preparation findings, and for future politics of the OMM, the conference became yet another platform for the President's often misogynistic and moralistic points of view.

My initial respect for Samora Machel's feminist positions had long since vanished. At the OMM conference he expressed views regarding women, which were so narrow minded and out of place that even the OMM leadership – otherwise generally Party soldiers par excellence – felt a need to voice a different opinion. The issue of struggle was the theme of *mães solteiras* – unmarried mothers. When the OMM General Secretary reached this point in her report, the President jumped to his feet: 'To be an unmarried mother is a disgrace,' he exclaimed, 'the concept, the very phenomenon must be abolished. In my department I want no single mothers.' He proceeded to announce an investigation in the entire state administration for identification and expulsion of single mothers. This was where the OMM put its foot down, suggesting in very polite tones in the concluding document from the conference that unmarried mothers should be helped, rather than castigated (Arnfred 1985).

The story of the preparation of the OMM Extraordinary Conference juxtaposed with the absurdities of the President's performance at the Conference itself shows – to me – in a nutshell some of the basic dilemmas of gender politics in Mozambique: on one hand you have tremendously rich resources in a population with very diverse cultural lives, and with an interest – so clearly demonstrated in the conference preparation process – to discuss, debate and develop their ways of life; on the other hand you have a powerful ruling Party, and a President, who in spite of his Minister's opening speech regarding bottom-up approaches, proved unable to, and uninterested in, listening and learning – except from himself.

This description of the process of my work in the OMM is important for several reasons. First because my thinking about issues discussed in subsequent chapters has been influenced by these events. Decisively of course by the very experience of meeting and listening to women north and south in Mozambique, pinpointed during my trip to Cabo Delgado, to which I shall return below, but also by the entire OMM Extraordinary Conference preparation period with its political contradictions. Second, because the empirical material, on which some of the chapters in this book are based, has been produced in the course of the conference preparation process. After the Extraordinary Conference all material was archived at OMM headquarters in Maputo. At that point I (with husband and daughters) had returned to Denmark and resumed my job as Roskilde University. I managed however to arrange money for going back to Mozambique in order to read through the OMM conference material and to write on that basis. This resulted in a number of articles, some of them included as chapters in this book.

Subsequent rounds of fieldwork 1998–1999, 2003 and 2005

Other chapters draw on subsequent rounds of more normal sociological/ anthropological fieldwork. From 1984 to 1992 the war in Mozambique between Frelimo and Renamo forces (Renamo = *Resistência Naçional de Moçambique*, oppositional army, later oppositional party) made fieldwork outside major towns impossible. After official peace agreements in 1992 and general elections in 1994 (the first in the history of Mozambique) it took another few years before people in Mozambique felt confident that peace had come to stay, and that immediate post-war fears of the war starting all over again were unfounded. Towards the end of the 1990s it again became possible to do fieldwork in Northern Mozambique. Ever since the early 1980s I had been keen to return to the north of Mozambique in order to have a closer look at women's positions under conditions of matriliny. My own Cabo Delgado experience and the OMM material had pointed to interesting differences between the patrilineal south of Mozambique as compared to the matrilineal north, and I was longing to get a possibility for making investigations in the province of Nampula, the heartland of the large, matrilineal (and matrilocal) Emakhuwa speaking population of northern Mozambique. This possibility emerged when in 1998 I received a research grant, enabling me to spend eight months (Oct 1998 to May 1999) in Mozambique. During this period I undertook fieldwork in two different locations in Nampula Province, the inland district of Ribáuè, and the coastal towns of Ilha de Moçambique and Angoche. My original idea had been to compare women's lives under conditions of matriliny in social settings characterised by different religious influences: Christianity in the inland areas versus Islam at the coast. Northern Mozambique coastal areas represent in many ways an extension of Swahili culture, with specific characteristics due to colonial history and the special combination of Makhuwa matriliny with Sufi Islam. Ribáuè, on the other hand, is characterized by the Catholic church as implanted by the Portuguese, a few old-time Protestant missions, and an astonishing post-war influx of new African (Evangelical) Churches.

For various reasons I changed my mind regarding this idea, ending up putting less emphasis on religion. This fieldwork (and subsequent shorter field work periods in Ribáuè 2003 and 2005) resulted in some chapters, discussing female initiation and various aspects of matriliny in the inland setting, and in Chapter 14 investigating the unique coastal northern Mozambique combination of matriliny and Islam, seen from women's points of view.

The Nordic Africa Institute: Theoretical inspirations
From 2000 to 2006 I worked at the Nordic Africa Institute in Uppsala, Sweden, as a research programme coordinator for a programme on 'Sexuality, Gender and Society in Africa'. The stay in Uppsala gave me a unique opportunity for collaboration with gender researchers in Africa, the aims of the research programme being 'to promote and enhance conceptual and methodological discussions on issues related to studies of sexuality and gender in Africa, and to encourage research' (Sexuality, Gender and Society in Africa brochure, 2004). This new job (during which I was on leave from university) came in handy at a point when I was at a loss regarding analytical inroads for coming to grips with apparent contradictions in my data material – such as the contradiction between the ways in which initiation rituals were described by the OMM, and the ways in which they were perceived by participating women. I had a clear feeling of conceptual tools from my feminist and sociological/anthropological background being insufficient for proper in-depth analysis of my material and experience from northern Mozambique. I felt that what was at stake was not just concepts for analysis of this particular data material – but also that my data material pointed to shortcomings in mainstream understandings of gender, which it would be very important to identify, in order to enable re-conceptualizations of other issues relating to sexuality and gender – re-concep-tualizations which would be important for feminist analysis as such, not just for knowledge about women in Mozambique.

My collaboration with, and reading of works by African feminist researchers provided me with some of the conceptual tools I had been looking for. Particu-larly in terms of reconceptualizations of concepts like 'women' and 'gender'. One of the characteristics of Second Wave feminist thinking, which I found it increasingly hard to deal with, was the foundational idea of 'the universal subordination of women'. In the New Women's Movement back in the 1970s we had been convinced that male domination/female subordination was a global phenomenon. It did not occur to us that gender relations might be different elsewhere in the world, and that we could possibly learn about different, more balanced gender relations by studying other cultures. I was familiar with the work of Chandra Mohanty and a few other post-colonial feminist scholars, but it was only now I realized that also African gender scholars, such as Ifi Amadiume and Oyèrónké Oyewùmí had criticized Western feminist ways of looking at 'women' and 'gender', pointing to the impact of colonialism and Christianity in terms of introducing European gender concepts and gender power relations into African societies (Amadiume 1987, 1997, Oyewùmí 1997). In pre-colonial days, according to their analysis, conceptions of gender and gender relations in Nigeria had been very different, but with mission and colonization norms had changed.

Oyewùmí's critique of Western partriarcalizing interpretations of African cultures hit the nail on the head for me: every time Europeans saw a throne they expected a man to be sitting on it. Most Nigerian personal names, unlike most European ones, are not gender specific. Nevertheless, long lists of Yoruba rulers going back in time, were read as 'lists of kings', even if – as it later turned out – some of the rulers had actually been women (Oyewùmí 1997, 83–91). In her native Yorubaland, Oyewùmí says, the subordination of *wives* has nothing to do with the wives being women, but everything to do with their position as strangers and outsiders to the *lineage* (in this case a patri-lineage) into which they are married. Hierarchical relations are based on being inside/outside of a particular lineage, much more than on being a 'man' or a 'woman' (Oyewùmí 2002). Thus the Second Wave feminist notion of gender hierarchies (male domination/female subordination) being foundational just doesn't fit these African settings.

At this point in time, to me Ifi Amadiume, Oyèrónké Oyewùmí and other post-colonial African feminist writers were essential sources of inspiration. They not only criticized Western notions of gender, they also suggested alternative ways of thinking about issues of men and women. The Nordic Africa Institute programme was, however, not just about gender, but also about sexuality. In my data from Mozambique there was a lot about sexuality; in Cabo Delgado I had come across the unexpected importance of initiation rituals for the women, and also during the Extraordinary Conference preparations, discussions of initiation rituals were often very heated and intense. Very few of the African feminists, however, on whose work I could draw for general rethinking of concepts of gender, made any reference to sexuality.[5]

Regarding reconceptualizations of sexuality I thus had to look elsewhere. My thinking about sexuality in a post-colonial African setting sent me out on journeys into the long colonial history of European perceptions of sexualities in Africa. Supporters on this journey were other post-colonial scholars with a historical touch and focused on sexuality, such as Anne McClintock (1995) and Janice Boddy (1989, 2007) – as well as an expanding network of African gender scholars attached to the *Sexuality, Gender and Society in Africa* research programme. There were also a few important conferences, 'Sex and Secrecy', organized 2003 at Witwatersrand University, Johannesburg by IASSCS (International Association for the Study of Sexuality, Culture and Society) and a much smaller workshop convened in Uppsala by myself 2002.[6]

---

[5] The only exception at this point in time was Swazi/Zimbabwean feminist scholar Patricia McFadden, who as early as 1992 had taken up issues of sexuality (McFadden 1992).

[6] Papers from this workshop were later published in Arnfred 2004a: *Re-thinking Sexualities in Africa*.

Reflections on analytical approaches

When I started in Uppsala in autumn 2000 my search for different conceptual tools and new analytical inroads had been going on since 1982 when I had been interviewing women in Cabo Delgado.

The women of Cabo Delgado greatly impressed me by the way they recounted events during the war. These women had taken part in the war against the Portuguese colonial regime; they had transported war material over long distances, they had cooked food for the guerrilla soldiers. The war had changed their world and opened their horizons. The women had learnt new things and experienced different social relations, including relations of gender. Based on their war experience they now questioned a number of issues, which they wouldn't previously have been thinking about. Their critique of the ways in which Frelimo had changed – from guerilla warfare to running a one-party state – was devastating, as was their critique of OMM, having disappeared to the city in the south (Maputo), forgetting about the women in the north. I was very impressed by the insight and eloquence of these women. What puzzled me, was the fact that these same women defended the female initiation rituals. As far as I knew – my knowledge being based on OMM writings – these rituals were oppressive and humiliating, confirming women's subordinate position in society: 'The initiation rites implant in the woman submission and total depen-dendy of the man. The woman is conditioned to submit herself and gradually to assume self-inferiority' (OMM 1977, 90). The OMM and Frelimo campaigned against the practice of these rituals. How come then, that these very conscious and critical women would defend them?

In general terms the official OMM understanding of women's positions corresponded fairly well to my own preconceived assumptions about women in Mozambique. From my engagement in the New Women's Movement, I was well acquainted with the socialist theory of women's emancipation, which had inspired Frelimo's approach to women's issues. According to this line of understanding, women in Mozambique were oppressed under age-old patriarchal traditions, but since Independence they had a unique possibility for liberation, emancipation and development, guided by Frelimo's socialist ideas.

The contradictions in Cabo Delgado led for me to a serious destabilization of all preconceived ideas regarding women's emancipation. If these strong and eloquent women were defending rituals, which according to the general theory of women's emancipation were seen as oppressive and degrading, something had to be wrong somewhere! I felt that the very gender thinking I had adhered to – from Simone de Beauvoir onwards in the New Women's Movement – had to be reconceptualized and rethought.

The Cabo Delgado experience sent me off on two different lines of inquiry: of meanings and of interpretations. First I had to find out more about what these rituals were actually about: What happened during the rituals, and why did the women consider them so important? What was for them the *meaning* of the female initiation rituals? This was the first line of inquiry. Along the second line of inquiry I was asking questions regarding the ways in which these rituals had been *interpreted* and understood by outsiders, such as Christian missionaries, colonial administrators, European anthropologists, and the socialist state. Thus the first line of inquiry was about Mozambican women, while the second line was basically about myself, and the lines of thinking developed in the culture and history to which I myself belonged.

Inquiry line one: searching for meanings

In my search for meanings, of course I asked the women. Their answers, however, were not very helpful. Asking why they found it so important to continue performing the rituals, they gave this type of reply: 'We cannot give up the initiation rituals. They are our tradition.' 'We will have to go on with the rituals. It is an education of our daughters.' When I asked if they did not find the female initiation rites humiliating and oppressive, their faces made it evident that they did not understand what I was talking about. Oppressive? 'In these rituals there is nothing very big or very special. It is only us dancing and singing throughout the night until the morning comes.'

Searching for meanings invariably involves interpretations. On the outlook for local meanings, however, your interpretations have to be very open, flexible, alert and sensitive to context, atmosphere and emotions. What you want to grasp may very well lie beyond the words. And sometimes the odd answers, the ones that make no immediate sense, may provide the clue to understanding. This was what happened to me in Cabo Delgado. Among all the answers along the lines of 'it is our tradition', there was one woman who said: 'The drum is our only opportunity for playing.' What was this about? I had expected to hear about oppression and humiliation, and these women talked about drumming and dancing.

Eventually it dawned on me that the initiation rituals were both: the younger women are subjected to trials, while the older women have fun. For the young initiates it is all about discipline and codes of behaviour, their capabilities are tested, sometimes they are castigated and anyhow they are bossed around by the older women. At the same time, however, for the grown up women, i.e. those who have already been through the initiation rituals, for these women each new celebration of initiation rituals is an new and cherished occasion for fun and games with other women, in a special ritual space where special rules apply.

In the early 1980s the initiation rituals were supposed *not* to take place, and travelling as an employee of the OMM, there was a limit to what the women would show me. When in 1998–1999, and later in 2003 and 2005 I returned as an individual researcher, the times as well as my position having changed, I had the chance to be present during several celebrations of initiation rituals. At these occasions I got a very strong impression of the division between on one hand the subdued and scared young women with downcast eyes and on the other hand the rowdy older women, behaving without restraint.

Inquiry line two: interrogating interpretations

Interrogating interpretations is a very different activity, compared to searching for meanings. For finding meanings I had to listen to people on location, taking part in relevant activities while trying to grasp and understand their ways of life. For unpacking interpretations, however, I had to go back into history, digging into my own Western/Christian cultural baggage with adjoined stereotypes and implicit assumptions. What I found there was not very nice.

The story about European views of African female sexuality is rather grim:
Patriarchal, racist, ethnocentric and misogynist. When researching into this
field I was taken aback by the derogatory and misogynist attitudes vis a vis
African women (Arnfred 2004c), sometimes even shared by feminists (cf.
Mohanty 1991). I came to see Christian/missionary gender morals and
hypocrisy as a major factor in the whole setup. In Christian contexts, sexuality
in general and female sexuality in particular, is equivalent to sin, immorality
and so on: Eve being the carrier of primordial sin. In Mozambique the general
attitude of the Portuguese colonial power, closely connected to the Catholic
church, was a strong condemnation of the female initiation rituals, because of
their focus on the development and education of female sexuality; female initiation rites were considered 'immoral and offensive to the human nature'
(Medeiros 1995, 5). The attitude of the Protestant missions was equally dismis-
sive. An early and foundational work on southern Mozambique, first published
1912 by Henri Junod of the Presbyterian Swiss Mission, bears evidence to this.
According to Junod it is bad enough to face explicit education of male sexuality; but to confront education of female sexuality is beyond the pale.[7] There is
in some of the missionary accounts regarding female initiation an unpleasant
mixture of fascination and disgust – a mix which even today characterises some
Western attitudes to African female sexuality.

Even worse was the realization that Frelimo's attitudes to women and female
sexuality were not only rooted in socialist classics on women's emancipation,
but also very much in Christianity. Samora Machel had been educated in the
Swiss Presbyterian Church – the so-called Swiss Mission (*Missão Suiça*) – a fact
which often transpired in his marathon speeches. On several occasions, in the
long speeches in which he excelled, Machel spoke in strongly condemnatory
terms about women who have children with different men, and about prostitutes who smell like rotten meat (Machel 1982). The Christian fear of female
sexuality is barely hidden. And even if the guiding documents of the OMM do
not directly speak negatively of female sexuality, they do not talk about it in any
positive terms. In the documents from the second OMM conference in 1976
everything related to the female initiation rites is bad and problematic. On the
whole women in so-called 'traditional-feudal' society are oppressed and
exploited, and this position is seen as confirmed and maintained through
customs and rituals, among which the initiation rites loom as most hideous.
'These ceremonies and institutions, which during centuries have been practised in traditional-feudal society, placed the woman in a position of inferiority
and passivity' (OMM 1977, 90). Because of the initiation rituals 'the woman is
violated and traumatized, transformed into a passive being without capacity
for initiative' (ibid., 91). The document goes on to list the horrors and humiliations to which the girls are subjected in the course of the initiation rituals. It was
evident that the OMM/Frelimo perception of the female initiation rituals, widely
practised especially in northern Mozambique at the time of Independence, had
much more to do with the Christian view of African women and African sexuality than it had with the meaning and implications of the initiation rites as
experienced by the women themselves.

[7] Junod's work is discussed in several chapters, particularly in Chapter 3. See Chapter 2 for
Catholic/Protestant positions regarding women's sexuality.

Sections and chapters – overview

In most of the chapters in this book I discuss both meanings and interpretations, applying a reflective approach to my own conceptualizations, while also wanting to say something about the subject matters at hand.

Part I – Conceptions of Gender and Gender Politics in Mozambique

This first section consists of five chapters, which all in one way or another deal with gender policy in Mozambique, as linked to understandings of gender. Chapter 1 – 'Women in Mozambique: Gender Struggle and Gender Politics' – is also the first-written chapter in the book,[8] published in 1988. In this chapter I try to come to grips with the contradictions between Frelimo/OMM gender policies on one hand, and women's concerns as I saw them on the other, especially in the north of Mozambique. Elements in the analysis are the following: (a) As long as the OMM saw itself as 'an arm of the Party', it would not be able adequately to represent the women, who were organized in the OMM. (b) It was my feeling – corresponding to my findings – that unlike what I had expected before arriving in Mozambique, women had not only a lot to gain from the process of development/modernization – they had something to lose as well. (c) Against Frelimo's preaching that gender struggle is a characteristic of 'the petty bourgeoisie', I argued that gender struggle is not only a predictable outcome of social change – when gender power relations have been destabilized compared to previous norms, as it had happened in the north of Mozambique during the liberation war, it is to be expected that men as well as women will fight to maintain new positions, or to reestablish old positions, whatever the case may be. Gender struggle is indispensable in the process of change of gender relations. How could Frelimo, who believed in the necessity of class struggle for changing power relations of class, presume that power relations of gender could change softly and smoothly without struggle? (d) I also found that processes of development/modernization *without* concomitant gender struggle most likely would result in enhanced power positions for men, again especially in the north. The political tradition of which Frelimo was a part (socialism/communism) was/is strongly androcentric,[9] and also the state as an institution favours male power. Thus Frelimo's political programme of modernization, while seemingly gender neutral, would often in reality support male gender power.

The second chapter (written in the late 1980s) 'Notes on Gender and Modernization: Examples from Mozambique' is somehow programmatic for my later work on issues of gender in Mozambique. Actually this chapter introduces all of the themes developed in this book: it has a long analysis of initiation rituals, north, centre, south; an analysis of different economic structures in different parts of Mozambique; passages on implications of different kinship systems (matriliny/patriliny) in north/south of Mozambique , and an analysis of implications for women of the different religions: Christianity (Catholic/

[8] Previous papers had been published in Scandinavian languages only (Arnfred 1985, 1987, 1988). This paper was my first publication in English.
[9] See for an analysis of gender aspects of a the ANC – a Southern African fellow political organization at the same point in time – Raymond Suttner 2009.

Protestant) and Islam. The chapter was written on the basis of my participation in the OMM Extraordinary Conference preparation process, and also on the basis of the OMM archive, i.e. the data material gathered from all over the country during the Conference preparation process.

Chapter 3: 'Family Forms and Gender Policy in Mozambique' (written also in the late 1980s) is likewise based on a mixture of data from my own investigations and data material from the OMM archive. In this chapter I go through the OMM material related to family/marriage. Quite a lot of the topics discussed during the OMM Extraordinary Conference preparation period actually belonged in this category: lobolo, polygamy, divorce, early marriages. The chapter goes into these issues, primarily lobolo, polygamy and divorce, discussing them with a focus on differences between matriliny (north) and patriliny (south). Issues are seen from women's points of view, and in relation to the proposed New Family Law – a legal project which had been in the pipeline since very early post-Independence days, but which by this time (late 1980s when the chapter was written) had not yet got off the ground. In 2000, when the chapter was first published, the Family Law – now slightly revised – was again discussed in Parliament, backed by active lobbying from various Mozambican women's NGOs. The New Family Law was finally passed by the Mozambican parliament April 2003[10]. The guiding question in the chapter on 'Family Forms' is the following: How does a unified Family Law, based on a notion of gender equality, work under conditions of diverse realities? The chapter discusses some of the unexpected consequences of this political project, noting that in the process of modernization under the political ideology of gender equality, ideology becomes nicer to women, but reality becomes harsher. This is particularly true in the northern, matrilineal parts of the country, where the law's push for nuclear families – as opposed to the previous extended families based on sister-brother bonds and uncle-nephew relations – is likely to make women's situation more precarious and to undermine female positions of power in extended family settings.

Three different insights worked as inspiration for Chapter 4, 'Simone de Beauvoir in Africa: Woman – the Second Sex?' namely the following: (a) the similarities, from women's points of view, between liberal/capitalist and socialist/communist types of development/modernization. Economic ideologies may differ, but the outcome, from women's points of view, is much the same. (b) Simone de Beauvoir universalizes women's subordination, in ways which are duly criticised by post-colonial feminists like Chandra Mohanty, Ifi Amadiume and Oyèrónké Oyewùmí. I wanted to discuss and elaborate this kind of critique. (c) From African feminist points of view motherhood has a social position very different from the one it is given in mainstream feminist thinking – and by Simone de Beauvoir. The chapter was provoked by the fiftieth anniversary celebrations of de Beauvoir's important 1949 book: *The Second Sex*. It is one thing to see de Beauvoir as an important historical figure, another thing (in my view) to hail her as a contemporary theorist of feminism. It was the latter position, quite prevalent in the celebrations, which provoked me.

Finally Chapter 5, 'Conceptions of Gender in Colonial and Post-colonial

---

[10] See more on the Family Law in Chapter 5.

Discourse' brings together lines of thought in other chapters in Part I, connecting conceptions of gender with gender policy. A major reason for my focus on concepts and re-conceptualizations is my conviction that concepts are important, and that different lines of thinking do make a difference, also in politics. The point in this chapter is, however, that in spite of radical and dramatic changes in overall Mozambican politics, from Portuguese colonialism, over Frelimo socialism, to donor-driven neo-liberal economic policy – the concepts of gender and connotations attached to gender have remained fairly stable. Each different regime has launched its politics as a radical break with the immediate past – but seen from women's points of view (and particularly as seen from women's positions in the matrilineal North) there is a clear line of continuation from colonialism over socialism to World Bank market economy. This chapter is not based on the OMM material, but on work in the Portuguese archives in Lisbon, reading *Boletim Geral das Colónias* and other similar publications. It is also based on political documents and speeches from the socialist Frelimo period as well as from the liberal, donor driven, market-economy period, when Frelimo is still in government, but when socialism has gone.

Part II – Night of the Women, Day of the Men: Meanings and Interpretations of Female Initiation

In this section all chapters deal with different aspects of female initiation rituals, some of them written some time ago, others more recently. I struggled for a long time to find a proper analytical approach to the material. I was confused, I think, because of the widespread contamination of concepts regarding sexuality, the 'thick fog of miscomprehension, stereotypes and other misleading constructions' as Marc Epprecht has called it (personal communication). My attempts to conceptualize sexuality in African settings pushed me backwards into European theories of knowledge, and into rather nasty racist, sexist and misogynist assumptions and ideas, underpinning seemingly straightforward notions of man, woman, sexuality. I came to understand why at that point in time (early 2000s) African feminists seemed to refuse to deal with sexuality at all. The field was simply too heavily charged with an overload of colonial preconceptions, still alive and kicking long after they were presumed dead.

I have named the section 'Night of the Women, Day of the Men' after important events during my fieldwork in Ribáuè 1998–1999. On several occasions I was present during ceremonies of initiation and at other ritual occasions, during which the most intense and holy moments took place in the dark of night, lit only by a few candles, with drumming and dancing and falling into trance all headed and monitored by women. These aspects of everyday life, which generally took place at night, were never included in development programmes. It was as if, in the light of day, other rules applied and other forces governed, even in the same locations and with the same people involved. Government programmes of development take place in broad daylight. This is when the men of Frelimo, of the local government – and also of the Catholic/ Protestant churches – take over. Oyèronké Oyéwùmí says something about vision being the privileged sense in Western culture – Europeans speak of knowledge as illumination, knowing as seeing and truth as light. 'A concentration on vision as the primary mode of comprehending reality promotes what can be seen over that which is not apparent to the eye; it misses the other levels and nuances of existence' (Oyéwùmí 1997, 14). In contrast she points to hearing as the more important sense in many African settings. Her observation fits my own experience in Ribáuè. When night falls and when Europeans go to bed – this is when a different life takes over. As an example, long sections of Chapter 7: 'Moonlight and *mato*' take place at night (*mato* is Portuguese for bush). This chapter is a descriptive account of one of the sessions of female initiation in Ribáuè anno 1999, during which I was present. This chapter was written in 1999, shortly after returning from fieldwork in Ribàuè. Description was no problem. The problem was the analysis. What did all this mean – and most importantly: how could an analysis of female initiation contribute to the re-thinking of gender and sexuality, which I found pertinent and necessary?

The chapters on female initiation in this section are written (and rewritten) at different points of my struggle with analytical approaches. Three different analytical approaches have been applied. The first one is my initial analytical approach, also applied in most of the chapters in the first section of this book, with a focus on male/female gender power relations. The analysis takes a point of departure in a critical deconstruction of pre-conceived notions of male dominance/female subordination, and a conviction that gender power relations should be investigated, not assumed. Similarly – in line with the analysis of Chapters 1 and 2 – modernization and economic development are seen as part of an implicit and partly invisible gender struggle in favor of male positions of power, to the detriment of previous female positions. Further, from this point of view, the persistence of female rituals of initiation are seen as expressions of resilience *vis a vis* increasing male privilege. Chapter 8 '*Wineliwa* – the Creation of Women: Initiation Rituals during Frelimo *abaixo* Politics' is mainly based on OMM material and written with a focus on male/female gender power relations.

This analytical approach worked well, to a certain extent – but it didn't capture the aspects of embodiment and sexuality, also very prevalent in female initiation. For this reason, inspired by Judith Butler's concept of performativity and Foucauldian thinking on bodies, I decided to try out another approach: an analysis of the ritual proceedings, following a set of distinctions suggested by Sandra Bartky. This happens in Chapter 6 'Feminism and Gendered Bodies: On Female Initiation Rituals in Northern Mozambique'. To me it was an interesting experiment to look at my data from this somewhat different angle, but the approach did not really produce the breakthrough in understanding I was looking for. Thus I returned to my previous sources of inspiration, the field of African feminist research, where in the meanwhile studies of sexuality had started to emerge (Tamale 2003, 2005 a & b, McFadden 2003, Pereira 2003, Nnaemeka 2005 and others). The third approach, applied in Chapter 9 'Female Initiation Rituals and the Coloniality of Gender', is based on post-colonial feminist lines of thinking. The expression 'the coloniality of gender' is borrowed from Latin-American feminist philosopher Maria Lugones, who builds on the work of Oyérònké Oyewùmí among others. Somehow, however, she takes Oyewùmí's thinking further, in terms of saying that gender as such – the very concept, the very idea as applied in global South – is a product of colonization. In the context of this logic, such things as rituals of initiation cannot be understood with current concepts of women and gender; in the context of this logic, female initiation is not (just) about the precise and goal-oriented creation of adult Makhuwa women (as different from notions of natural biological growth) but also about the manifestation and recreation of a powerful female universe; in the context of this logic, thinking gender might be something about thinking social forces, powers and patterns, including – in the Makhuwa case – the invisible world. Chapter 10, the final chapter in Part II, 'Situational Gender and Subversive Sex?' doesn't deal directly with initiation rituals, but being concerned with reinterpretations of so-called African culture from feminist points of view, introducing and discussing the work of a number of African feminists regarding reconceptualizations of gender and sexuality, it elaborates on and puts into context the post-colonial feminist approach which (with Maria Lugones) I have called 'the coloniality of gender'.

Implications of Matriliny in Northern Mozambique

My initial experience from 1982 of gender power relations working differently in northern Mozambique was confirmed by later investigations. Because of the to me so obvious difference – from women's points of view – between patriliny in southern Mozambique and matriliny in the north, I was very surprised to find, when by the mid–1980s I returned to Denmark and to my normal life as a university teacher, that so little had been written on matriliny in Africa; very little anthropological literature, and even less from a feminist perspective. I tried to find out why this was so – and to some extent my experience in this endeavour was parallel to my experience (reported above) of asking questions regarding interpretations of sexuality. I found that pre-conceived assumptions play a very big role, even in social science, and that in studies of matriliny the asssumption of male dominance/female subordination as the 'normal' state of affairs had been the background onto which any kind of research findings had been mapped. Chapter 11 'Male Mythologies: An Inquiry into Assumptions of Feminism and Anthropology' reports these findings.

Further along the lines of investigation into meanings and interpretations, as reported in 'Reflections on analytical approaches' above, I tried to find out, particularly through my studies in Ribáuè , what life was like in this matrilineal society, from the point of view of the women. One of the findings was that patriliny and matriliny are different things (for instance depending on patterns of residence) and that gender power relations may be changing, while inheritance to land still follows maternal lines. My concern in Chapters 12 and 13 has been to identify female positions of power, in a kind of implicit polemic against the assumptions of male dominance/female subordination, which I had found dominant in other studies of matriliny. One of the early findings was that the world in Makhuwa context goes beyond the day-to-day visible world. It also includes the ancestors who have died, and the children yet to be born; men may have an upper hand in the visible world, but women hold the key to the world beyond. This double world is reflected in the double power system of the *mwene* and the *pwiyamwene*, the male and female chiefs, the hidden female power structure also making these societies resilient to change. The colonial power and later Frelimo only intervened in relation to the male power; they never saw the female counterparts. Initially my 1998–99 fieldwork had been planned to be shared between inland (Ribáuè) and coastal locations (Ilha de Moçambique and

Angoche), but I ended up spending more time in Ribáuè, because the matrilineal structures were more clear inland; at the coast the mapwiyamwene had
disappeared.

Looking for female power positions I soon found food and land. Land is a source
of food, and as such it is necessary for all men and women. Land is conceived as
plentiful: 'we people are few in numbers compared to the vastness of the land' as
they said in Ribáuè (cf. Chapter 12); land is the basis of life. For this reason land
must be provided for those who come to the community from the outside: 'They
need to produce and eat like we do'. Land is like the air you breathe; to think of
land as a commodity is an alien idea in rural areas of Ribáuè district – even if this
idea is coming closer in the vicinities of Ribáuè town. In Chapter 12, 'Ancestral
Spirits, Land and Food', I operate with a 'logic of subsistence' (with 'life' as the
ruling principle) as distinct from a 'logic of the market' (where the ruling principle is 'money'). This chapter gives examples of the ways in which the 'logic of
the market' is encroaching in the Ribáuè area (including examples from the
neighbouring district of Mecuburi), spokespersons in favour of the market logic
are not surprisingly young men. Not surprisingly, because subsistence logic and
female power seem to go well along, or put differently: Female power positions fit
well in a context of subsistence logic. This is quintessentially the case regarding
control of food as a source of female power. It thus is not by accident that both
Chapters 12 and 13 focus on food. Control of food is crucial in a subsistence
setting, and this control is in the hands of women. Women control food, women
control sex, and women control offspring; children belong to the mother's line,
and men are positioned through their relations to women. In Chapter 13, 'Sex,
Food and Female Power', I elaborate on sex – parallel to cooking – as an area of
female capacity and expertise.

In Chapter 14 the location shifts to coastal town Ilha de Moçambique – and
to a very different matrilineal setting. My interest in this chapter has been to
investigate the co-existence of matriliny with Islam; the coastal populations
have for centuries been Muslim. I found the co-existence to be very peaceful,
and Islam – in the form of Sufi orders or brotherhoods (*tariqas*) – very open to
Makhuwa gender relations. Sufi tariqas is the traditional and still prevalent
form of Islam at the coast, even if it is challenged by other, more orthodox
editions (Wahabism), boosted in recent years by funding from Saudi Arabia.
The chapter focuses on the coastal dance group culture, using Tufo dance
groups as a prism through which to see matriliny and Sufi Islam from women's
points of view. I found matrilineal male/female leadership structures to be
reflected in the setup of local Sufi orders, and this plus other aspects of Sufi
order life to be reflected in (or even taken over by) the dance groups. In the dance
groups the dancers are women, and men in leadership positions are put there
by women and/or through their relationships with women. This far the dance
group structure follows matrilineal patterns, even in the context of Islam.

Conclusion

Overriding concerns in all chapters are issues of conceptualizations, and of
seeing things from women's points of view. The two support each other, in as far

as 'seeing things from women's point of view' in all phases of the fieldwork process has pointed to the insufficiencies of existing conceptualizations, and pushed me off, as described, along two different lines of inquiry. One of these has been the searching for meanings in customs and culture, the other has focused on investigations of implicit assumptions in existing interpretations. Nevertheless, beyond and across these conceptual, and also by implication political concerns, I am also deeply fascinated with the cultural wealth, abundance and diversity of rural Mozambique. It is my hope that beyond conceptual discussions and polemics also some of this fascination will transpire, at least from some of the chapters.

Part I CONCEPTIONS OF GENDER & GENDER POLITICS IN MOZAMBIQUE

1 Women in Mozambique:
Gender Struggle and Gender Politics (1987)

Woodcut by Matias Mtundu Mzaanhoka

Women in the war: towards a new gender identity

The liberation of women is a necessity for the revolution, a guarantee of
its continuity and a condition for its success. (Samora Machel, 1973)

In his opening address to the first conference of the Mozambique Women's
Organisation (OMM) in 1973, Samora Machel, President of Frelimo, affirmed
that women's emancipation was an integral aspect of revolutionary struggle.
In 1973 Frelimo was still a liberation front engaged in armed struggle against
colonial rule. The northern part of Mozambique was a battle ground and the
first OMM conference had to be held in the Frelimo camp at Tunduru in
southern Tanzania. A photograph of the participants of this first conference
can be seen In the OMM's national secretariat in Maputo. Peasant women and
women guerrillas are pictured lining up outside the meeting hut, with Samora
Machel in battledress amongst them. The non-hierarchical atmosphere depicted
in this photograph is in marked contrast to the more formal arrangements on
similar later occasions (Photo 1.1).

The participation of women in the war was massive. In 1967, at the request
of the women themselves, a women's detachment of the guerilla army – *Destacamento Feminino* – had been formed. Part of its task was to inform and mobilize
the peasant population. To support this work, a broader non-military organization of women was needed. This was how the the OMM originated in 1973.

Between 1981 and 1984 I worked as a sociological consultant of the OMM.
In 1982 I was sent to Cabo Delgado, the longest standing war zone, to find out,
among other things, how the experience of war had affected the lives of women.
I was surprised how many of the women I interviewed had taken an active part
in the war in one way or another. Most had grown food for the army or had
transported goods and weapons. Viewed in isolation, as concrete tasks, these
do not seem very different from what peasant women normally do in their every
day lives: growing food and carrying burdens on their heads. But during the
war it had been different: women were travelling long distances, staying away
from home for many days, and they were doing so on an equal footing with
men! That was really new, corresponding to the new ideas of gender equality
introduced by Frelimo.

New also was the structure of authority within which these tasks were
carried out. In their normal daily lives, women are subordinated to patriarchal
family authority, whether it be of a father, an uncle, a husband or a brother.
Their lives are circumscribed and their gender role is defined by their position
in the family. During the war, however, the family was not the ultimate source
of authority. On the contrary, if there were conflicts between women and the
male members of their families, if their husbands would not permit them to be
absent to carry out their tasks of mobilisation or transport, women could call
in Frelimo. A new authority was at work, an authority which, when necessary
and for the time being supported women against men. This was described to me
by Habiba (in Mueda, Cabo Delgado), an impressive woman now some 50 years
old and formerly the provincial representative of the OMM:

During the war we held meetings, we mobilised women to transport war material, to
grow food and to cook for the soldiers. Women volunteered but sometimes husbands

1.1 The first conference of the OMM (Organização da Mulher Moçambicana) in Tunduro, southern Tanzania, 1973, during the liberation war. Samora Machel in battledress is standing among the women (in the second row, a bit to the right of the middle of the picture). (Photo from the archive of *Revista Tempo*)

SAMORA MOISÉS MACHEL

A LIBERTAÇÃO
DA MULHER
É UMA
NECESSIDADE
DA REVOLUÇÃO,
GARANTIA
DA SUA
CONTINUIDADE,
CONDIÇÃO
DO SEU TRIUNFO

1.2 Frelimo iconography: Young woman with gun, writing. The pamphlet contains Samora Machel's speech at the First OMM conference 1973, with the quote which brought me to Mozambique: 'The liberation of women is a necessity for the revolution, a guarantee of its continuity and a condition for its success.'

tried to prevent them from participating in the tasks of war. When that happened, we called in Frelimo. I remember a case of one man who was beating his wife. We tied his arms behind his back and took him to Frelimo. Frelimo told him that he shouldn't fight his wife for it was better to fight the Portuguese together. The man became a soldier and the woman continued her war work. During the war women were respected because we were organised. Men and women were equal. There was no division, no resentment. One week the woman was away, another the man. When the woman was away, it was the husband who did the housework and looked after the children. Men and women worked together for the same goal.

Before the war, men and women had led separate lives with a clear division of labour and different rules of conduct. During the war they came together on equal terms as Mozambicans in the struggle against the Portuguese. In this process, gender relations changed. Some women developed a new concept of themselves as women: new aspirations, new goals. A new female identity was emerging. Take the example of Cecilia, a nurse at the hospital in Pemba, provincial capital of Cabo Delgado. She had been in Destacamento Feminino during the war:

When I was a child it never occurred to me that I should be educated, that I should become a nurse. I thought I would go to school until the fourth grade, and then I would marry and stay at home with my husband and children just like my mother had done. She was always at home, working the fields and looking after the house and the kids. That was what she did. But since I was in the armed struggle, everything has turned out differently for me. I have been to places which otherwise I would never have visited. I have come to know many different people and I've seen other ways of life in other provinces. These are things that I would never have known. All of this has been very important to me and it has changed my life. Formerly, although practices varied in each province, men kept women at a distance: men and women worked separately. Now we work together. My husband doesn't prevent me from working outside the home, or from participating in OMM meetings. But he was in the war like myself and that of course is important. You still find many men who do not understand the necessity of women's liberation and who won't allow their wives to work outside the home.

Another example was Maria, now an agricultural worker on the state farm at Nguri, Cabo Delgado:

During the war I was in Destacamento Feminino which sent me to a medical centre. I married but my husband left me. After the war, I knew that I could not be satisfied by going back to the village and living the life of a peasant woman. So when I heard of this state farm being started, I came here at once to enlist as a worker. After work I go to school at the factory. I want to continue my health education and become a nurse.

Three points emerged from my discussions with these veterans of the war. First, the conditions of war had challenged the relations between women and men and created the possibility for new gender relations and new female identities. Second, these new relations had been established through women's gender struggle: through confrontation with the male members of their families. Third, Frelimo had supported women engaged in this struggle.

After the war: abandoned by Frelimo and the OMM

After the war, Frelimo found itself in a totally new situation for which it was badly prepared. Independence came sooner than expected as a result of the overthrow of the fascist regime in Portugal. Portuguese soldiers and officers had, in fact, learned about democracy and people's power (*poder popular*) from the African liberation movements they were fighting, putting these lessons into practice in their home country. Portugal withdrew from its colonies in 1974, and in 1975 Frelimo gained power in Mozambique.

Fighting a liberation war is very different from building a nation state. The political centre moved from the bush in the north to the capital city in the south. It was a confusing situation: how was Frelimo to manage the complex tasks of creating a new nation? Rather than popular mobilisation and collaboration with the peasantry, the focus now was on the creation of national institutions and the structures of economic and political power. In this process, different people and new ideas had to be relied upon. Most of the guerrilla fighters had been illiterate peasants, barely able to speak Portuguese. Habiba and others like her were removed as representatives of the OMM and replaced by girls educated at the mission schools, literate but without political fervour or experience. The idea of people's power that had been developed during the war was insufficient as a political base in this new situation. Shortly after Independence, at the third Frelimo Congress in 1977, the Liberation Front was transformed into a Vanguard Party in the Marxist-Leninist style and ideological/theoretical tradition. Similar changes took place in the OMM. At its second Conference in 1976 policy towards women was restructured along the lines of the classical socialist theories of women's emancipation (for a discussion of this see below).

What happened to the women in the north who had been active in the war but had not had the opportunity, like Cecilia or Maria, to establish a different life? Habiba explained:

> During the war, Frelimo had said: 'Women have always suffered: we must fight for women's emancipation: women too must be liberated'. But it seems that all that mobilisation was just to fight the Portuguese, for now it has all gone. During the war, women's problems were discussed but now nobody talks about that kind of thing. At that time we struggled to change the division of labour between women and men. Men and women worked together. But now men behave just as they did before the war. Nowadays nobody respects women. There are OMM representatives at all levels of the state, but they do nothing. Formerly the OMM was important, it had influence, but this is no longer the case. Nobody defends our lives and our needs. Our Mother doesn't protect our interests any more. Previously, when a quarrel was brought to the people's court, our Mother would deliver the judgement. But today our Mother [i.e. the OMM], doesn't even appear in the people's court. It is the men who make the judgements. The daughter is in prison, but the Mother doesn't care. I think the Mother is dead. But where did she die? Was it in the District or in the Province, or did she die far away in the capital? I ask because I do not know. The daughter is suffering because the Mother died.

In the rural areas of the north, gender relations returned to the situation before the war. Men took back what they had lost of patriarchal power. According to the women, they took back even more than they had had. Cabo Delgado is an area of matrilineal descent. In the case of divorce, for example, women remained in the house with their children while the husband left. Goods and household utensils were divided between them. By 1982 these practices were changing. As a peasant from Mueda explained:

> During the war Frelimo said all those things about women's emancipation, but today a husband can divorce his wife for no reason at all, and he'll stay in the house and keep all the goods that they have acquired together, even the capulanas (a piece of cloth used as a skirt) of his wife. She will have to leave the house with nothing at all. These days no woman is respected. We are at the bottom and the men are sitting on top of us.

The insight and anger of these women was impressive. They clearly felt that men had taken the upper hand in the gender struggle and that women were losing out; that women had been forgotten by their one-time supporter, Frelimo, and even by their own organisation, the OMM. They felt that the OMM, their own organisation, had ceased to exist.

Women defending the initiation rituals

I was impressed, but I was also puzzled, for these same women were defending the traditional initiation rituals for women. Indeed, a focal point of their reproach to Frelimo and their anger with the OMM was the political campaign to repress these women's rituals. This appeared to me an outright contradiction. As far as I knew – and this was certainly the position of the OMM – women's initiation rituals were the supreme expression of male dominance and female subordination. In these rites performed at puberty, I had been told, young girls were submitted to various humiliations in the course of which they learned to adopt a subservient attitude appropriate to their subordinate position in a male dominated society. How then could it be that these strong and politically conscious women would defend them?

The explanation of this apparent contradiction emerged slowly and indirectly through my conversations with the women. My direct questions didn't help me very much. When I asked about the humiliating and oppressive aspects of these rituals, the women did not seem to grasp what I was talking about; and when I asked why they wanted to continue practising them, I found their answers useless: 'because it is our tradition, because we have always been doing it.' One answer however was different. One woman said: 'the drum is our only opportunity for playing.' During the initiation rituals there is a lot of drumming and dancing. The girls who have reached puberty stay for weeks in a hut outside village territory where they are visited by adult women, but which no man may approach.

I gradually came to see the importance of the initiation hut as a kind of free space for the women: a gendered space for them to meet on their own without men. I was never present at an initiation ceremony,[1] but on some occasions during my work in Cabo Delgado in all-women meetings arranged for the sake of my visit, issues of marriage, divorce and love were discussed and the atmosphere could reach unexpected heights of hilarity, with dancing and sexual pantomimes and jokes about the men. What I saw was a collective female

---

[1] This statement refers to the time of my work with the OMM, 1981–84. Only fifteen years later, during fieldwork in Ribáuè 1998–99, I was invited to attend female initiation, cf Chapters 6–9.

gender identity, strong, self-confident, full of laughter. In their daily lives with men these women might be subdued and oppressed, but here, among themselves, they were not. Thus I began to understand why women who had experienced the war defended the initiation rites. The rituals instruct young women in the rules of decent female behaviour: self-control, downcast eyes, respect to men and elders, always ready to provide a husband with food and hot water for his bath. But the rituals also provide adult women with the opportunity to get together under circumstances that permit a very different behaviour: disrespectful, non-subservient, mocking men.

I came to see the initiation rituals as the ritual celebration of a shared female gender identity. A focal point of the rites is the confirmation of the sexual maturity of the girls. Having passed the rituals they should be familiar with their own potentials for sexual care and pleasure. This sexual self-confidence seems to be an important base for the strength of these women. Its existence and reproduction depend on the initiation rites. No wonder that the women saw them as important and indispensable, especially when traditional women's rights, such as divorce, were under attack.

During the war the initiation rituals had been infrequently performed, partly because social life had been completely disrupted, but also because women had needed them less in the war situation of changing gender relations and new demands. In their new gender organisation, the OMM, women had been on the offensive in the gender struggle, seeking to establish new gender relations and a new gender identities, with gender equality as the ultimate goal. The idea of gender equality in this context is new, new not as a contrast to oppression, but because the traditional construction of gender identity did not rest on any notion of equality but rather on ideas of complementarity between women and men and the separation of male and female spheres, whether this be in the sexual division of labour or in the concept of different capacities.

In pre-war Cabo Delgado it seemed to me, gender dimensions of society had been fundamental, men and women performing different tasks and inhabiting different spheres. This division had been the basis of such power as the women had held. This situation had, however, been changed and challenged by the war, the gender spheres broken up, men and women had been set on the move for new identities and new relations. But the war came to an end. The political atmosphere changed. The support to women's struggles disappeared, whereas men were able to take advantage of the new situation. The women continued fighting, but now their struggle was a defensive one, aiming to maintain at least their traditional rights and the sources of power they had had in the past. The important point is that in this political context the past is not simply one of 'oppression', nor is the future an obvious 'progression'. Women in northern Mozambique may have a lot to gain, as the experience of war demonstrated, but they have something to lose as well.

Matriliny

The initiation rituals are not the only example of what women have to lose. Women's defence of these rites is stronger in the north of the country than in the south. In the south, the rituals have virtually ceased. This seems to have happened for two reasons: first, the south is more involved in the money economy; men have been wage workers for generations, predominantly as migrant workers to the South African mines; second, in the north (roughly north of the Zambezi River) matrilineal systems of kinship prevail, while the southern societies are patrilineal. Matrilineal societies are not, of course, matriarchal. Authority in the family is the prerogative of men, as uncles and brothers. But this also means that women are primarily defined in their roles as sisters rather than wives. As a sister, a woman is surrounded by her own kin; at marriage a man comes to live with his wife, and he is only accepted as a husband if he behaves well and has shown that he is capable of making her pregnant. Divorce is easy for both partners, but at divorce a woman stays in the house with the children while her husband must leave.

Matriliny and matrilocality is a source of social authority for women. But this is not how Frelimo and the OMM see it, and they do not defend it. In fact, Frelimo and OMM promote patriliny, not explicitly but as a product of their general policy which is centred on the promotion of the nuclear family. Ever since the second OMM Conference in 1976 the 'family as the basic cell of society' has had a central position in OMM policy. It is conceived as a monogamous unit in which parents – not a woman and her brothers – have authority over their children. A woman is expected to be closely attached to her husband and, for example, to follow him if he is transferred to another job. Matriliny does not meet the requirements of this policy. It doesn't produce the small, mobile, nuclear family functional to a modernizing society.

Frelimo and OMM are equally opposed to divorce. But to women, access to divorce is crucial. In the matrilineal areas women's right to divorce is one of the ways in which they avoid a polygamous marriage. When a husband starts to consider taking a second wife, the first wife will often initiate divorce proceedings. In the northern matrilineal areas, polygamy is less common than in the south. Under the new family law,[2] divorce is in principle available to women, but Frelimo and the OMM preach against it on the grounds that it disrupts family life. When women use their traditional rights to divorce, they are blamed for lack of respect for the institution of marriage and for being altogether loose and promiscuous. This angered the women in Cabo Delgado:

> Attitudes towards divorce began to change after Independence because Frelimo doesn't want 'unjustified' divorces. They say that the children won't know their father. The village Party Secretary doesn't like divorces; he punishes people who want to divorce. They have to do community service in the village. For instance, the Party house was built in this way. In the old days women divorced much more easily. The men are like the *colonos*. They want everything. They marry two women. Then the first one says: 'Look my friend, I don't want to put up with this'. But the husband doesn't listen. He brings everything to the other woman's house. You say that this is too much, and go to the Party Secretary in order to get a divorce. But he says: 'No, you cannot have a divorce. Go back to your home, you must not disrupt your family.'

---

[2] At this point in time the new family law, drafted in 1980, was still not passed as law, but it had been decided that *Projecto da Lei da Família* (PLF) should be used as guidelines for the tribunals. More on the Family Law in Chapters 3 and 5.

It is invariably women who want to divorce who get the blame, not the polygynous husband. Polygamy, of course, is against the policy of Frelimo and the OMM, but men are rarely rebuked for it and the Party often turns a blind eye.

The gender policy of Frelimo and the OMM

During the war Frelimo and the OMM supported peasant women in the promotion of their gender interests. Since the war they have either failed to provide support, or they have directly opposed the gender struggles of women.

Frelimo is a vanguard party based on a worker-peasant alliance. It represents the interests of peasants and workers at the level of the state. The state is the people's state. The OMM is 'an arm of the Party, a link for communication between the Party and the people' (Jorge Rebelo 1981). Class struggle is an important concept in Frelimo ideology. It is seen as the struggle of the people, united under the leadership of the Party against 'internal enemies', 'aspirants to the bourgeoisie' (Frelimo 1983) and other similar opponents of nationalist socialist interests. Class struggle does not mean the struggles of peasants and workers against the state. This kind of struggle is not conceivable, as the state and the Party themselves represent the interests of the labouring classes. The function of trade unions is not to formulate the specific interests of their members. Strikes are not allowed. The role of trade unions in the socialist state

1.3 OMM's emblem is Communist Party iconography with an African touch. A Communist star, and (women) workers and peasants united: the hammer and the hoe. This book of documents from the 2nd OMM Conference 1976 was the Bible during most of my years with the OMM.

is to 'organise work, practice discipline, promote increased productivity and encourage creativity and innovation' (Frelimo 1983). The trade unions are seen as democratic mass organisations and their function – rather like that of the OMM – is to be a link for communication between the Party and the people.

Similarly, specific gender interests are not acknowledged: 'the antagonistic contradiction is not found between man and woman, but rather between women and the social order, between all exploited women and men and the social order' (Machel 1977b). The necessity of struggle between women and men is not acknowledged; women's demands are condemned as the 'radicalism of the petty bourgeoisie' (Machel 1977a). This conception, however, fits facts rather badly. Specific gender interests do exist. You cannot miss them when you listen to peasants and workers. Gender struggle is a fact of women's lives, especially in the period of social and political turmoil in Mozambique during the war and since Independence. The previous structure of gender relations has been shattered: women as well as men are fighting to defend their old rights and privileges or to gain new ones. The problem is that while Frelimo and the OMM do have women's emancipation and the construction of new gender relations on their agenda, they do not acknowledge that these will not emerge without struggle. Gender struggle is not (just) disruptive and destructive. On the contrary, it is the means through which gender relations change, as class struggle is the means through which the relations of production are transformed. Women do not gain liberation without struggle, nor can they gain it as a gift from above. Women's liberation can only be achieved through their struggles as gender and class subjects. It is, therefore, much to be lamented that women do not have their own organisation through which to voice their own interests and concerns. The OMM is an arm of the Party, and the movements of the arm are decided in the head, in the all male leadership of Frelimo. Particularly since the 3rd Frelimo Congress 1977 the politics of OMM are the politics of Frelimo.

The socialist project of women's emancipation – like the socialist project in general – is a project of modernisation. It is based on the rational, industrial exploitation of the riches of the earth; the small-scale peasant farmer must be turned into a wage worker on a state farm or maybe into a member of an agricultural cooperative. The emancipation of women is to arise as a consequence of their integration into new forms of social production on equal terms with men. The two initial paragraphs of the 1976 OMM programme for action reflect this project. It is stated that the OMM must: first, ensure that all women become engaged in production (in the factory or in the agricultural cooperative), in the planning and organisation of work and social life, in the creation of *o Homem Novo*, the new man (sic) and the new society; and second, organise the struggle against the old ideas which constitute the obstacles to the full participation of women in public and social life as citizens, in economic life as free producers and in family life as true companions and revolutionary educators (OMM 1977, 78).

In Mozambique both of these tasks are problematic. I shall begin with the second task. The basic problem here is that emancipation is seen as a unilinear process. In the past, according to this understanding, there has been nothing but the oppression and enslavement of women. The OMM describes their role in 'the old society' as being 'to serve men – as an object of lust, as a procreator of children, and as workers without pay' (OMM 1977, 89).

Emancipation lies in the socialist future. This gives no recognition to the degree to which women in the 'old society' maintained spheres of autonomy and collective gender identity. The defence of these sources of strength in the past must, therefore, be condemned as reactionary, against modernisation, an obstacle to progress. It does not acknowledge what women know in their bones: that the process of modernisation favours male power. This may or may not have to be so but it certainly has been so. Through wage labour, however arduous it has been, men have gained access to money income denied to the vast majority of women and this has increased their power in the family. In the process of urbanisation, many women have lost such sources of economic independence as they had previously had, and have become financially dependent upon men. The nuclear family, advocated as the basis of women's emancipation, is the site of the dissolution of collective gender identity for women, the erosion of women's previous rights in marriage and the individualisation of male power. These tendencies correspond marvellously to the Christian mission morality of father right and female subordination, opposition to initiation rituals and to women's control over their sexuality.

The political programme of modernisation and the exclusion of gender struggle often amounts to a tacit support for male power, whether intended or not. If women are to gain at all from the processes instituted under socialism, continued gender struggle is indispensable.

The first task stated in the 1976 OMM programme for action, the OMM's obligation to ensure women's participation in production – is largely beside the point in the Mozambican context. The vast majority of women are already engaged in social production; indeed, the number of 'economically active women' exceeds that of 'economically active men' in Mozambique.

Here again the most important struggle is rather a defensive struggle in order not to become marginalised in the modernisation process. It has not been women's lack of engagement in productive labour but rather patriarchal authority which has confined women to domestic life. The emancipation of women in Mozambique must lie in breaking the boundaries of patriarchal authority as well as the confines of domestic life.

This is important, since the family[3] remains the dominant social and economic institution in Mozambique despite the inroads of capitalism. It is far from becoming merely a unit of consumption and reproduction. According to the 1980 National Census, more than 75 per cent of the economically active population are working in family agriculture, 94 per cent of all economically active women work in a family context, predominantly as farmers but including some 10,000 – 20,000 traders and artisans. Thus the vast majority of women are engaged in family production and spend their entire lives in the sphere of the family.

The socialist policy towards women described above is characteristic of other Marxist-Leninist vanguard parties and their women's organisations. But the particular way in which Frelimo and the OMM have implemented these strate-

---

[3] See Chapter 3 regarding the diversity of family forms in Mozambique.

gies in the Mozambican context need explanation. Why in particular did Frelimo withdraw its support from those women who had fought the war? These women were, by their very example, 'fighting old ideas'; they were engaged in social production; they were following the route to emancipation defined by Frelimo. Why were they abandoned?

The answer seems to lie in the changed relationship between the party and 'the people' and the focus on the construction of the state. During the war, Frelimo stressed the need for daily collaboration with the people. Following Independence, however, the priority was to extend the authority and control of the Party and the state. This change took place, in most cases, without any overt alteration in political rhetoric as may be understood from the following illustration of the ways in which the meaning of the expression 'the principal task (*tarefa principal*) of the revolution' as a strategy for women's liberation has been transformed.

In his opening speech to the second OMM Conference in November 1976, President Machel said:

> The decisive factor for the emancipation of woman is her engagement in the principal task, the task which transforms society. At that time [i.e.during the war], it was the struggle for liberation. What then constitutes the principal task in the present phase of the revolution? The principal task of the present phase of our process is the following: the construction of the material and ideological base for building a socialist society. Thus for the implementation of this strategy, which has as its objective the construction of socialism, the principal task is production and the principal form of action is class struggle. (Machel 1977a)

Production, in its turn, means fulfilling the plan. This is how it was put by the Secretary for Ideology of the Central Committee, Jorge Rebelo, when talking to the OMM in 1981. He advised the OMM to: 'concentrate its activity on what constitute at this moment the two principal tasks of all citizens – male and female – of the RPM (*República Popular de Moçambique*): the increase of production and productivity so as to fulfil the plan for 1981 and participation in the defence of our country' (Rebelo 1981).

More specifically the OMM was advised to investigate how women could participate in voluntary labour and in the maintenance of public buildings. In addition, women were asked to be active in the control of the new ration system, in the fight against contagious diseases, and for education, hygiene and cleanliness. Finally, it was stressed that the role of women as mothers and educators in the family was fundamental. These activities, no matter how useful and necessary they may be from the point of view of the state, have little potential for altering gender relations. They constitute no challenge to male family authority. They provide no grounds for gender struggle.

The Extraordinary Conference of the OMM, 1984

In 1983 the preparation for the fourth Frelimo Party Congress revived, for the time being, the old Frelimo ideals of popular democracy and peoples power. Political debate was held throughout the country and people participated enthusiastically. The Party Congress itself became a forum for critical interventions

1.4 The Extraordinary Conference of the OMM, 1984, in the newly-built parliament building in Maputo. It is a conference of the women's organization, but men of the Frelimo leadership occupy the front row (with a sprinkling of women: Graça Machel, who is Minister of Education, and Salomé Moiane, General Secretary of the OMM). Samora Machel, speaking, took up most of the time during the conference.
(Photo from the archive of *Revista Tempo*)

and discussion and radical policy measures of various kinds followed. Frelimo decided that an extraordinary OMM Conference should be held in 1984 to discuss women's social situation as a basis for the revision of current policy on women's issues. The conference was to be preceded by a nation-wide campaign to collect information and views on women's lives and problems, especially in relation to family structure and customary practices important to female gender roles. The instruction issued by the Frelimo Central Committee to inaugurate the conference preparation campaign marks the policy shift very clearly: 'being a matter of concern to the whole society, the liberation of women is, in the first place, the task of women themselves. No one can liberate a woman. Women must take over the struggle for emancipation themselves'.

For the first time since the war, women were mentioned as the subjects of their own emancipation. A Secretary of the Central Committee (then Minister for Information), José Luis Cabaço, presided over the OMM national meeting at the start of the campaign. He criticized the *abaixo* (down with) policies which had prevailed hitherto: abaixo lobolo[4], abaixo polygamy and abaixo initiation rites, which had been the catch words of OMM/Frelimo gender politics since Independence. This kind of campaign, Cabaço said, is of no use when nothing else in society is changed. Polygamy and bride price are parts of a social struc-

---

[4] *Lobolo* is the local term for brideprice, customary in southern Mozambique.

ture; you cannot just do away with things like that without understanding their context and if there is nothing to replace them with. Before embarking on a policy of social transformation at least one must understand the society which has to be transformed. He stressed how important it was that the OMM brigades being sent out in preparation for the conference should listen and learn and not, as had become increasingly the practice of Frelimo agents, tell the people how they ought to behave.

What resulted were intense and very lively discussions which involved the whole country for months, even in the midst of war, drought and famine. Once again it was demonstrated that when people, in this context mainly women, are allowed to speak out on the basis of their own felt needs and concerns, not in isolation but as part of a national movement and with the prospect of changing their own lives, amazing reserves of social energy are let loose. Thousands of discussion meetings and group interviews were held (I took part in the whole process at central level in the OMM and as a member of brigades at other levels). The preparation for the conference allowed discussion of the traditional sources of female strength to be linked to new perspectives on breaking down women's confinement to the family. Women grew in strength and confidence during these months and the OMM learned a lot.

Shortly before the national conference was to be held – a conference delegation from a remote province had already arrived in Maputo – the Party Central Committee postponed it for six months. They had obviously become nervous about what was going on: things seemed to have gone out of control. When the OMM Extraordinary Conference was finally held, in November 1984, it was indeed well controlled. The President himself presided over all the plenary meetings with the Party's second in command, Marcelino dos Santos, at his side. The only two women in the front row of the platform were the OMM General Secretary, Salome Moiane, and Mozambique's only woman Minister, Graça Machel (the President's wife). The rest were all men of the Political Bureau or the Government (Photo 1.4).

Few delegates from the floor got a chance to speak at the plenary sessions. Only during the one day of group discussions (the Conference lasted for five days) were the keen atmosphere of discussion and the fervour of the preparation period felt. The intense preparation could have produced guidelines for a powerful movement for social change, but this was not the case. The final resolutions of the conference are neither radical nor precise. In retrospect, the aspects of gender struggle at the conference seemed quite clear. The men, feeling threatened, had mobilised what they could in terms of dark, solemn suits to carry the paternal authority of the Party.

The General Union of Cooperatives in Maputo (UGC)

In striking contrast, women are organising elsewhere though not in association with the OMM and not along the lines of classical socialist theory of women's emancipation. An organisation of agricultural cooperatives in the Maputo Green Zones (*Zonas Verdes*) consists mainly of women. It is not a women's organisation; for that there is only the OMM. But more than 95 per cent of these cooperative farmers are women. They produce vegetables for the local market. The UGC (*União Geral das Cooperativas*) was created in order to fight for the interests of the cooperatives as productive units and the interests of the cooperative farmers as people and producers, but the cooperative members don't hesitate to put forward their views on women's emancipation. The striking thing about these views is that they combine the defence of women's traditional economic position with the struggle for a new gender identity. They understand women's situation from their own points of view and not from that of the state.

The growth of the agricultural cooperatives in the Maputo Green Zones is impressive. Initiated in 1980 following the establishment of the *Gabinete das Zonas Verdes* (GZV, under the Ministry of Agriculture), the number of cooperatives has increased from 7 to 181 in 1987, with 10,500 members, 9,500 of whom are women. This growth arises from a clear policy directive from the GZV to support cooperatives without patronizing them and to cater not just for the needs of production but also for the needs of producers by ensuring their access to social services, such as crèches. In this process, democratic structures have been built up in each cooperative which, in 1982, formed a Union – the UGC. This enabled them, some years later, to leave the GZV and to establish an independent organisation. According to the President of the UGC, Celina Cossa, herself a cooperative farmer, the UGC has from time to time been in fierce confrontations with Frelimo, the Ministry of Agriculture and other government institutions which have tried to intervene and control their activities. But because of the Union's autonomy and democratic structure, they have been able to resist these external pressures. For these reasons, the women in the UGC are very conscious of their achievements and very clear about the basis of them. A document they prepared for a seminar in Maputo in 1986 states:

> In the first place it is important to be aware of the fact that the majority of these thousands of women (i.e. the women who joined the agricultural cooperatives) were people without any kind of prospect for the future; they had no paid employment and they had been deprived of the opportunity of contributing to the upkeep of their families by farming their family land because of the shortage of land in the city since the vast influx of population. These women were, thus, condemned to live in a state of complete economic dependence on their husbands which, in any part of the world but especially in Africa, is a bad thing for a woman.
>
> In colonial and pre-colonial days, women could only achieve social recognition in their capacity as members of their families, and in the last analysis, as the property of their husbands ... but in the cooperatives and in the Union, women are working, women are taking part in the decision making process, women are running the cooperatives themselves, and enjoying the fruits of their own labour in total equality and democracy. In this way, the cooperatives are breaking definitively with the social basis of women's traditional subservient status.
>
> All this creates new relations in the family because a woman, contributing to the upkeep of the family in an equal or even more important way than her husband, and in a way that is socially recognised, stops being just *um ser familiar* (a family being), she becomes *um ser social* (a social being) (UGC 1986).

The women of the UGC take their point of departure in what used to be their strength: a certain degree of economic self-sufficiency, their importance in maintaining the family at least in terms of producing food. This economic

strength is essential to women and they do not want to lose it; to be economically dependent on a husband is 'a bad thing for a woman' because a husband's
power over his wife thereby increases. Taking part in cooperative production,
however, serves not only to maintain a degree of economic independence. It
also means that part of a woman's productive life is now spent outside the institution of the family. Here she makes decisions and directs: in the family this is
the privilege of men. She achieves a social existence as a person in her own
right, not merely as a member of a family. In the cooperatives, women are
producers, not wives. This in turn creates new gender relations in the family.

The cooperative women thus combine the defence of old gender positions
and rights, threatened by development and modernization, with a struggle to
break the confines of traditional women's lives. The experience of the UGC
women provide a basis for reflections on the possible combination of gender
struggle and gender politics in Mozambique, as did the example of the women
in the war. In both cases, the women are acting as subjects, collectively and
organised, for changing their own lives. On the other hand, when this is not the
case, gender politics and gender struggle seem to fall apart.

2 Notes on Gender & Modernization   (1988)

Woodcut by Matias Mtundu Mzaanhoka

In an essay from 1976 the feminist historian Joan Kelly sums up her work in women's history as follows:

> Indeed, what emerges [when the study of history is approached from the vantage point of women] is a fairly regular pattern of relative loss of status for women precisely in those periods of so-called progressive change. ... Our notions of so-called progressive developments such as classical Athenian civilization, the Renaissance, and the French Revolution, undergo a startling re-evaluation. (Joan Kelly 1984, 2)

On the basis of my work in Mozambique between 1981 and 1984, and afterwards through the analysis of extensive data on women and gender relations[1], I will extend this statement to include the so-called development process in Africa, as I have seen it unfold in Mozambique. Mozambique is governed by a political power, Frelimo, which since the onset in 1964 of the armed struggle against Portuguese colonialism until the acceptance of Structural Adjustment Policies in the late 1980s battled to structure the development process into a socialist mould. Sadly, however, seen from the vantage point of women's lives, initial socialist and later neo-liberal development policies have made no great difference; the 'fairly regular pattern of relative loss of status for women' still holds true.

I have reached these conclusions the hard way. It was not at all expected. On the contrary, when in 1981 I started to work as a sociologist in the OMM, *Organização da Mulher Moçambicana*, the Mozambican national women's organization, I was an enthusiastic supporter of a socialist women's politics, seeing the introduction of women into socially organized production (cooperatives, state farms, factories) as the main route leading to a break with women's traditional confinement within the family (and under patriarchal power), thus paving the way for gender equality and women's emancipation.

An uneasy feeling of things not being that simple crept up during my years in the OMM. But it is really only since 1984, after I left Mozambique and my daily work in the women's organization, and embarked on a research project to analyse the mass of data collected in between 1982 and 1984 in preparation for the Extraordinary Conference of the OMM (see note 1), that a more general pattern has taken shape of interrelations between, on one hand, processes of development/modernization, and on the other hand, changes in male/female gender relations. In the following I shall look at such interrelations in the fields of (a) female initiation, (b) systems of kinship (matriliny/patriliny), (c) structures of production and (d) predominant religions (Christianity/Islam).

Female initiation rituals, north to south

Two interconnected discoveries emerged in the process of analysing the OMM conference data. First: what in different parts of Mozambique people referred to

[1] The data material was collected as a part of the preparation for the Extraordinary Conference of the OMM (*Organização da Mulher Moçambicana*) in 1984. The provenance of the material is diverse, and the quotes have been marked accordingly. 'SA iw' indicates material gathered by myself in 1981–82 and later in the conference preparation process; 'OMM iw' is data from direct transcriptions of interviews or oral contributions collected by others; 'OMM rep' (report) is OMM data from compilations made at district or province level. For more on the OMM Extraordinary Conference preparation process, see the Introduction.

as female initiation rituals were not, or were not any longer, the same thing; second: presumably partly because of this, a marked and systematic difference from north to south in Mozambique could be noted, in the attitudes of women and men to female initiation rituals.

I am convinced that previously female initiation rituals were more or less similar all over the country. This comes through from the OMM material, where people refer to what the rituals were like in the old days, e.g. in the southern provinces of Gaza and Inhambane, where now these rituals have virtually disappeared, as well as from other anthropological sources.[2] I should therefore like to suggest that the present differences in Mozambique, as they emerge in the OMM data material have been produced by processes of modernization over the last 100 years, affecting different parts of the country in different ways. These involve a mixture of external influences (of which two major ones: money and missions, shall be investigated here) and internal structures within local societies, i.e. different potentials for adaptation or resistance.

The northern region: shared socialization and female sexual self-determination
In the north of the country[3] female initiation rituals (like the male ones) were an important community event before the liberation war. The rituals represented a public announcement of the fact that the daughter/son of so-and-so had now passed from childhood to womanhood/manhood. During the liberation war, which was fought precisely in these northern provinces, predominantly in Cabo Delgado, Niassa and Tete, normal peasant life had been uprooted to such an extent as to stop the traditional celebrations from being continued in their proper form. After Independence Frelimo stamped female initiation rituals as being backward and woman-oppressive, and political campaigns were organized against them: 'down with the initiation rituals', *abaixo ritos de iniciação.*

When in 1982 I was interviewing in Cabo Delgado, women everywhere complained about the political ban on initiation rites. This is what one peasant woman said:

> I see just one problem in Frelimo: Frelimo doesn't want you to do what you like with your child. In the old days, when I was a child, we had ceremonies, we were dancing and beating the drums. The whole population would know that now the daughter of so-and-so is in the initiation rituals, that she is now a woman. I have eleven daughters, but nobody knows about it, because I didn't send them to the initiation rites. Now I don't feel like arranging marriages for my daughters, since they haven't been through the initiation rituals. (SA iw)

In the northern provinces the frustration caused by the political ban on female initiation rituals was very evident, and an indication that until recently the rituals had been practiced more or less in their traditional form. Many people

[2] Anthropological data about female initiation rituals in other parts of Mozambique: H.A.Junod (1912/1974) on Gaza and Inhambane in the 1930s; Dora Earthy (1933/1968) on Gaza in the 1920s. On female initiation rituals in neighbouring countries: Audrey Richards (1956/1982) on Northern Rhodesia (Zambia) in the 1930s; Terence Ranger (1972) on Southern Tanzania in the 1920s and 1930s; Marja-Liisa Swantz (1970/1986) on Eastern Tanzania in the 1960s.
[3] Included in the northern region are here the provinces of Cabo Delgado, Niassa, Nampula, Zambézia, and the northern part of the province of Tete.

continued performing the rituals secretly, but had been forced to hide important aspects. Thus the shared community celebration and the public announcement of a daughter's maturity were getting lost.

In the proper course of events the women's initiation rituals would be preceded by the small girls (some 8–10 years) learning how to manipulate the small lips of the vagina, in order to pull them longer. This preparation previously was an integrated aspect of becoming a woman all over Mozambique. Here is a description from Gaza province:

> Groups of girls would go to the dense bush about 3 o'clock in the morning, each of them carrying a capulana to be used as cover once the work would start, because they would be sitting like somebody giving birth to a child. On the first day they would be given instructions by the *madrinhas* [older women in charge] about how to proceed, and after that each of the girls would continue on her own, using a certain pomade to facilitate the process. In the course of this work the madrinhas would control each one of the girls in order to see if they had been pulling satisfactorily, at the same time verifying that some of them had been doing too little work. It was strongly prohibited for a man to appear at the place where the girls went to pull their vaginal lips. If some man should happen to pass the place he would be driven back by handfuls of sand thrown at him, after which the place would be moved to somewhere else. (OMM iw)

When the girls reach the time of their first menstruation, after the fulfilling of various rituals, they would be secluded for a certain period. Normally the seclusion would take place in a ceremonial hut constructed for the purpose. While they were in seclusion the whereabouts of the girls would be strictly controlled, and only adult women and small girls would be allowed to visit them in the hut. For the adult women the initiation rites seem to have had a double function. Besides being the initiation of their daughters into womanhood, they also provided a kind of free space where women could get together on their own, without interference from men. This was the place where women had fun and games among themselves. Two Portuguese anthropologists, working in Cabo Delgado in the years immediately before the Liberation war, report what they saw at such occasions:

> The married women come and go with their babies tied to their backs. They speak loudly and livelily. Their behaviour is clearly different from the kind of behaviour they maintain in front of men. Evidently they feel free, being among themselves, and there is no lack of juicy jokes that make everybody laugh. ... The comic elements mostly used would be stylized sexual movements, repeated in the dance again and again, and always received by everybody with the greatest exaltation. Apparently these women, who in the presence of men always behave with dignity, delicacy and self-control, were determined on this occasion to compensate, and temporarily shake themselves free from all the burdens society had laid upon them. (Dias & Dias 1970, 220, 231)

The whole thing is contradictory, however, because at the same time as the older women have a great time with sexy jokes and lots of fun, they are very stern with the young ones, they give them trials and beat into them self-control, submissiveness and obedience to men. Dias and Dias also noted the difference between older and younger women: 'In contrast to the merry women, the young candidates for initiation stay very serious, with downcast eyes, as if nothing went on around them. During long hours we never saw them fall out of this role' (Dias & Dias 1970, 220). Clearly there is a relation of authority and dominance from the older to the younger women; this is evident from all of the OMM material. But women run women's matters, and men have very little to do with the female initiation rituals, apart from acting, occasionally, in roles prescribed by the senior female head of ceremonies. But even if the young initiates learn obedience to men, they also learn how to take charge of their own sexuality. In continuation of the vaginal lip elongation, the girls would be taught how to go about married sexual life (as distinct from the childish sexual activities, in which they may have engaged beforehand), how to please the husband, as a means to pleasing themselves, altogether for joyous sexual relations.

Appreciation of the female initiation rituals

The OMM material provides rich evidence of what these rituals meant in the northern provinces. The women (and the men as well) were very happy about the female initiation rituals, and insisted on their continuation. Here are just a few examples from statements made in the many meetings with discussions on this topic:

> Regarding the elongation of the vaginal lips, it is the general feeling that this custom should be continued, as it has the advantage of working as a brake on the penis at the time of sexual intercourse, that is it secures the slow entrance of the penis, tightly fitting around it, so as to let the man as well as the woman feel aroused. The vaginal lips are a great stimulation for the man; before starting sexual intercourse he will become excited by pulling the lips of the vagina. If the civilized way of having sexual intercourse is kissing and embracing, this is what we are doing with the lips of the vagina. (OMM rep, Zambézia province)
>
> This thing [elongation of the lips of the vagina] is practiced simply in order to have sexual pleasure with your husband. The women who don't have these elongated vaginal lips, who haven't pulled them, are not well liked. In addition to this, the elongated lips of the vagina have another quality of making the penis rise faster. it is well known that some men have difficulties in getting an erection. For this type of man it is important to begin by caressing the woman's vaginal lips, in order that he should be able to feel himself more like a proper man. (OMM iw, Nampula province)
>
> The initiation rites must continue, because people get pleasure from them. Through the initiation rituals, the man will know everything about how to treat his wife, he even will have learnt how to burn this fruit called *npichi*, which is used to smear the vagina in order to avoid sliding during the sexual act. I am an old woman, but when I apply this pomade, I am turning young, and which ever man grabs me would be satisfied sleeping with me. He would be so satisfied that next morning he would pick up the hoe and go to the field, working to his heart's content. (OMM iw, Zambézia province)

The vaginal lip-elongation (*puxamento* in Portuguese) gets the girl acquainted with her own sexual potential at an early age, and the convention of the man having to play with the elongated lips of the vagina before intercourse ensures proper foreplay, pleasing both sexual partners. Furthermore, during the period of seclusion, the girl will start having tattoos made on her body. These tattoos are folds of skin filled with charcoal powder; when healed they give an uneven body surface. Cut in pretty designs the body tattoos are/were considered to have an aesthetic value, as well as important sexual functions. Of course it hurts a bit to have it done. But it is worth it:

> The tattoos as well as the *missangas* [a string of glass beads worn round the hips] serve to motivate the man, as certain men do not know how to arouse the woman sexually; when they feel the need of having sexual relations they take the woman by

surprise, and under such circumstances she has little chance of reaching full orgasm, that is sexual pleasure. However, if the woman has tattoos on her body, wears missangas and has the elongated lips of the vagina, the man has to start by playing with these things. By his doing this the woman becomes prepared for the sexual act, resulting in satisfaction for both parties. (OMM iw, Zambézia province)

The central region: individualized preparation in order to please the men

In the central region (the provinces of Sofala, Manica and Southern Tete) the situation of the female initiation rituals differs from the north; in the central region (south of Zambezi river) kinship relations follow patrilineal lines. Here the expression 'initiation rites' does not seem to refer to any community cele-bration. On the contrary, the so-called 'rites' seem to be a very private, practical and non-ritualized affair just dealing with the preparation of the individual girl for marriage. What was previously a collective, shared socialization to female sexual self-determination, has here turned into individualized prepa-ration:

> After what I know and what I have seen here in Beira the preparation will start when the girl is 10 years old. When the mother can see that the child has reached this age, she will tell her to get up at five o'clock in the morning in order to go to the bathroom to prepare herself. But as the mother cannot herself control if the child is really doing as she has been told or if she is not, she will arrange some woman of the family to go there and check that the girl is actually pulling her small lips of the vagina.[4] (OMM rep, Beira)[5]

The so-called 'initiation rites' in this part of the country seem to be little more than this, combined with other individualized teachings of sexual movements to please the man. There is no sense of a community event to mark the passage of the girl from one phase of life to the next, nor much sign of the self-confident female sexuality of the north. Here the driving force behind the 'preparations' seem to be a certain fear that the men would not be pleased, and that the girl thus will stay unmarried.

> A girl of 12 has to be submitted to this work. If a girl has not been through this, the man will not like her. Only if she has been properly prepared with the help of the old women, the man at marriage will be able to say: 'Now certainly I have got myself a wife!' (OMM iw, Sofala province)

By comparison with the north, the girls from the central region are prepared to be sexual objects rather than sexual subjects. And this of course makes for inse-curity: Will the men prefer them like this or like that? This indeed is not an easy question in times of change, as some men prefer the girls 'prepared' in the tradi-tional way (which includes body tattoos and elongated vaginal lips, as well as the ability to move in specific ways during intercourse), while others consider all of this old fashioned and shameful; they just want modern girls without any sexual preparation at all. The dilemma is stated in the concluding report from a meeting in Beira:

> The men want prepared women, because they give more sexual pleasure. The man does not have to struggle so much during the sexual act. When the woman has not been prepared, the man gets tired too quickly, he loses his appetite. According to the

---

[4] It is always another woman, never the mother herself, controlling the daughter in this respect.
[5] Beira is the second largest city in Mozambique.

men the movements of the girls from the countryside are better than those of the city girls. On the other hand, today in the cities you find men that do not want the women 'prepared'. Some men furthermore demand of their wives that they should use a night-dress or pyjamas, even when they have never been accustomed to do so. All of this creates a certain anguish and anxiety in the women, who see their husbands disappear in search of younger women that have not been 'prepared'. (OMM rep, Beira)

Accordingly in these parts of the country the women (and men) are not so sure that they want the female initiation rites (or rather: what is left of them) continued; it is all really just creating problems. The tides of change are very evident in some of the statements from the various meetings where these things were discussed:

The body tattoos are already in the process of extinction. The girls that were born towards the end of the 1950s have not got them. Tomorrow they will be considered a disgrace. (OMM iw, Sofala Province)

Southern region: no sexual preparation at all
Moving further south there is very little remaining of anything that might reasonably be called initiation rituals. In the province of Maputo few people seem to know what 'initiation rituals' are supposed to be. In the provinces of Gaza and Inhambane people have long stories of how it was in the past. The dilemma of the central region is felt here too: If the man expects the girl to be 'prepared' and she is not, it is no good (this was the problem of the old days), and if he does not expect her to be, and she is, it is no good either (this is the problem of today). Thus the conclusion reached in a communal village in Gaza is widely shared:

The population of the village propose to finish with this tradition, because it has created many problems in the families. In the old days whoever did not have these elongated lips of the vagina would be thrown out by her husband; and today whoever continues to have them is rejected by the men. (OMM rep, Gaza province)

Matriliny versus patriliny

The OMM material, as related above, suggests a relation between matriliny/ strong traditions of female initiation rituals, and patriliny/fading female initi-ation rituals. Yet the relation is not direct nor simple: 50 to 60 years back there were strong female initiation rituals even in the patrilineal South (cf. Junod 1912/1974 and Earthy 1933/1968). The different kinship systems seem to have reacted differently to external modernizing influences, affecting economic as well as ideological structures. The different implications of matriliny as compared to patriliny struck me as being very important from women's points of view, when I interviewed and talked to women from north to south.

In the north: matriliny
Seen from a patrilineal point of view an important fact of matriliny would be that inheritance to land follow female lines. When in interviews this was never mentioned, it is presumably because matrilineal inheritance was not threat-ened; they did not see land following female lines as anything specific. This was

just the way things worked. What the women did mention, however, were the terms by which women obtained a divorce (currently in a process of change, divorce becoming more difficult). Traditionally in these areas marriage is not a very solemn celebration and divorce is easy for both partners. However after divorce it is the man who moves out; the woman stays in the house with the children. This is linked to the fact that marriage is largely matrilocal, which is to say that the newly married couple settles on the land of the woman's family, surrounded by her kin (uncles and brothers, mothers and sisters).

This pattern of settlement gives the woman in matrilineal areas considerable advantages. She is the one at home, the husband is the stranger who is evaluated by his in-laws: Is he good enough for their daughter/sister/niece? Does he treat her well? Does he work well? Is he likely to beget offspring for the family? Significantly, what is tested here on the wedding night is *not* the virginity of the woman, but the virility and fertility of the man: The old women keep an eye on his performance in bed, and they will gather some of his semen, examining it to see if it gives good promise for procreation. In a matrilineal setting there is no brideprice (*lobolo*) involved, the lobolo being tied to a patrilineal and patrilocal system, as a compensation for a daughter who is given away. However, in places of matriliny you frequently find brideservice: the husband-to-be will be working for a certain length of time on the land of the mother-in-law. This is the period when his work is evaluated and supervised: does he work well?

Furthermore, paternal authority and control of the offspring rest with the uncles (the mothers' brothers) not with the father. The close and important relation is not from father to son/daughter, but rather from uncle to nephew/niece, i.e. to the sister's children. Paternal authority was another issue frequently debated during the OMM conference preparation discussions, especially because it clashed so sharply with the modern ideal, politically promoted, of a nuclear family: husband, wife and kids. What a mess then, what an unbearable disorder, to have the uncles, and not the proper father, the *Chefe da Família*, controlling the kids! (Significantly it would be men voicing these points of view).

Patriliny in the centre and south of Mozambique

The women living under terms of patriliny tend to be much worse off in many respects, compared to their sisters of the north. First and foremost, marriage is much more binding and divorce much more difficult, seen from women's points of view. This is linked to lobolo. Lobolo is a transfer of values from the husband's to the wife's family, enabling the latter to get hold of another woman (as a wife for one of their sons), thus filling the empty space left by the daughter being married away.

In the south of Mozambique it is the woman who leaves her family in order to settle with the husband's kin in the first years of marriage. The young wife is literally in the house of her parents-in-law put under the authority of the husband's mother for whom she works as a maid until she herself becomes a mother, and sometimes for longer than that. There are many tales of hardship in the houses of the mothers-in-law, especially in the not infrequent cases in southern Mozambique, when the husband has left for South Africa as a migrant worker, staying away for years. His young wife is then stuck with her in-laws, unable to leave because of the lobolo.

For a woman to divorce, she must persuade her own family, receivers of the lobolo, to return it to her husband. As very often the lobolo has already gone, this is no easy task. Consequently there will be pressure on the woman to stay and endure even a bad marriage. For the man divorce is easy. He just sends the wife away, back to her own parents; he stays in the house, with the kids (excepting the very young ones, who follow the mother) and with the couple's belongings.

Generally in the patrilineal part of Mozambique, virginity is an issue of concern; the girl will be controlled in various ways to make sure that she avoids sexual intercourse before marriage, and on the wedding night the vigilance of the old women will be directed towards this issue: is she, or is she not a virgin? The former condition will produce joy and pride, the latter will bring shame upon her family. If it turns out that no children result from the marriage, the blame is automatically put on the woman, the fact being a perfectly accepted reason for the husband to claim divorce and return the wife to her parents – or to demand a second wife from the same family, without additional lobolo.

In the OMM discussions women spoke out against lobolo, lobolo being seen as a reason for the precarious situation of the married woman, who was at the mercy of her husband and his family. Previously, however, the woman most pitied was the one for whom no lobolo had been paid, as this signified a lack of respect on the part of the husband, and consequently a lack of status for the wife. Furthermore in the old days, judging from early sources (Junod 1912/1974, Earthy 1933/1968) even under conditions of patriliny women did have a space, a strength and a sexuality of their own. Women's lives under patriliny did not seem so different from matriliny-women's lives, as they do today. It appears as if the conditions for women nowadays are more different north/south, and the consequences of matriliny/patriliny more pronounced than they previously have been. Why? It is my hypothesis that this might be due to the different kinship systems being different vehicles for modernization. This should be investigated taking into consideration the fact that the modernizing influences, both economic and ideological, have also been different in different parts of the country.

Economic modernization

Economic modernization in Africa has often been about transforming subsistence economies into (more easily exploitable) money economies.[6] This also happened in Mozambique, with taxes, cash crops and wage labour being introduced by the Portuguese, and by the concession companies ruling large parts of the country up till 1940. Cash crops and wage work signify economic coercion: in order to pay the taxes you have to produce a marketable surplus, or to make money by selling your labour power. Frequently however, the Portuguese colonial power was not that sophisticated: it simply used direct physical coercion in order to make people work, by violent recruitment to obligatory labour (*xibalo*) on roads and harbours, and/or by forced cultivation. Forced cultivation was

[6] The sections on Mozambique's economic history draw on Marc Wuyts 1978, Centro de Estudos Africanos 1979, and Malyn Newitt 1981.

supervised cultivation of specific crops (cotton, rice) on one's own fields with forced delivery of the produce. Actually, by these crude measures of exploitation, the Portuguese delayed the modernization process; because of this in large parts of the country a money economy was not really effectively introduced.[7]

The southern region: wage labour in South African mines

The part of Mozambique where the money economy first penetrated daily life, was the southern region. Here wage work has been a part of peasant life for more than hundred years, not because of the Portuguese but because of the need for labour power in the neighbouring South African economy.

In 1850 the first Mozambican workers were recruited to the Natal sugar fields, and later on, with the opening of gold mines in the Rand in the 1890s, the number of Mozambican wage workers was multiplied. From 1900 to 1970 an average of 80,000–100,000 Mozambicans were yearly working in the mines, on 12 to 18 months contracts (*Centro de Estudos Africanos* (CEA) 1979). From 1940 to 1970 this represents an average of 25 per cent of the active male population south of the Save river. More than double this number would at some point in their lives have had a mining contract (CEA 1979). In limited areas as many as half of the men of working age would be away at any one time (Newitt 1981). The Save river is the northern border of the Gaza and Inhambane provinces, and close to the northern limit of legal recruiting to the South African mines. The Portuguese colonial government had made this agreement with the Rand mine administration, in order to protect the interests of the plantation owners north of the Save river, who were also in need of labour power.

Mine work is wage work proper. It is not compulsory (except to the extent that people were migrating in order to escape *xibalo*), and the wage is reasonably high, at least when compared to the wages offered internally in Mozambique. Young men from the southern region were proud to go to work in the mines (this was still the case up to early 1980s). Somehow wage work – and mine work par excellence – had become a symbol of manhood. The majority of the men in the southern region do not see themselves as peasants; cultivation is what women do, men should be wage workers!

Mine work is industrial work; it does not depend on the seasons or the rains. When contracts were of 12 to 18 months, the cycle of peasant work was broken; the men came home at odd times, seen from an agricultural point of view. The women had to take responsibility for all farm work, even ploughing, if there were no young sons or other available male labour power around. Thus even if migration work gave men the advantage of control over money and greatly added to the workload of women, it also challenged the gender divisions of labour. Women could transgress traditional limits of the female gender sphere and build female self-confidence on a new basis.

Mine work brought Mozambican men into contact with a different culture. Many miners learned English, and acquired new visions of life, investing the money they brought home in farming implements like plough and oxen, and maybe another wife, for purposes of accumulation.

[7] Newitt puts it like this: 'The phase of development through which other colonies passed were delayed in Portuguese East Africa. ... The evolution of a wage-earning, cash-oriented society had only imperfectly taken place at the time of Independence' (Newitt 1981, 147, 95).

In addition the miners would often be the first to bring a knowledge of Christianity back to the home village, missionaries having been at work in the mineworkers' compounds. The brand of Christianity coming into Mozambique this way was largely Protestant (baptist, methodist), and even today, the majority of the African Independent Churches thriving in Maputo come from South Africa and are of Protestant/Evangelical origin.

Modernization / individualization

The spread of the money economy and wage work bred individualization: an undermining of traditional kinship hierarchies and authority structures. In southern Mozambique the process can be seen in what happened to *lobolo*. In the old days marriage and lobolo were family issues, controlled by the linage head. He decided who should marry, when and with whom. He was the one to enter the lobolo negotiations, the lobolo at this time typically being a number of heads of cattle.

However, with so many young men working in the mines, this changed. Lobolo gradually came to be paid at least partly in money, and the young man played a greater part in the decision. The money he had earned enabled him to jump the kinship hierarchy and maybe marry before his elder brother, or get himself a second wife of his own choice.

Thus money meant that traditional kinship authority structures crumbled, and authority was increasingly placed at the level of the nuclear family, and with the male family head, the *chefe da família*. This however also meant increasing the husband's powers vis-à-vis the wife/wives. Gender relations too become individualized. Previously men and women had lived in different spheres, men with men and women with women. The close-knit kinship structures and extended family networks made sure that groups of women, and groups of men, could work and spend leisure time together. These networks now are dissolving; women increasingly find themselves on their own, with no other women in the household, only their husband. As a general rule, the women's room for manoeuvre has been narrowing, even if under specific circumstances (such as the men being away in the mines) the women would be pushed into new situations, developing new skills.

The money economy and individualization can bring freedom from subjection to extended family/lineage authority to women as well as to men. But most frequently the men are in a much better position to take advantage of this freedom than are women. To women, these same developments often mean loss of extended family gender networks, and more immediate exposure to husband-power. The men, of course, lose their traditional extended family gender networks too. But as wage workers they find new ones: Comradeship in the compound, and dancing groups, maybe; in Mozambique a very popular male dance, the *Makwaela*, originated in the compounds as a miners' dance.

The woman's situation becomes even more precarious if the family moves to town. To the social dependency on the husband is now added an economic dependency. Bereft of her traditional means of subsistence, the land through which she used to feed the family, she now becomes dependent on the husband's income.

In a context of patriliny, the individualization caused by economic modernization transforms the traditional extended family by contracting the authority structure to a unit of just two generations: parents and offspring in the nuclear family. The transformation has taken place rather smoothly; after all the nuclear family was already there, just embedded in the larger family structure.

In a context of matriliny, however, this kind of transformation is not so easily achieved. Matriliny and modernization do not go well together. The values of traditional kinship clash with the nuclear family-ideal promoted in the modernization process; paternal power in the nuclear family does not combine with the matrilineal tradition of strong uncle/nephew relations. Matriliny thus, to a certain extent, means greater resistance to modernization.[8] But it also means greater vulnerability. When economic modernization really takes over, most likely matriliny will have to yield.

Modernization places women in a difficult situation, but modernization also brings literacy, education, new and wider horizons, thoughts and ideas, to women as well as to men. And it helps combat illnesses, it gives shelter and clothes (to some), and it provides technical wonders of many kinds. Modernization breaks down, at least partly, the restricted gender spheres. Women now (to some extent) may do and learn what was previously within the male preserve, and *vice versa*. This is potentially positive, and does hold promise for women as well as for men.

The way modernization has come about, however, in Mozambique as elsewhere, has promoted male gender power at women's expense, and gender hierarchies have been erected where previously they hardly existed. A key to an understanding of this development, as I see it, is to follow what has happened to female sexuality. This is where developments regarding female initiation become important, as do the developments that have contributed to change of morals, feelings and conceptions of sexuality, such as the imported 'religions of the book': Christianity and Islam. Below I shall elaborate on the religious changes in different parts of Mozambique. But first, in broad outline, I shall look at the economic changes of the central and northern regions during colonialism.

The central region: seasonal wage work on local plantations

Analyzing the material on people's attitudes to female initiation rites, the three regions north, central and south, suggested themselves, the Zambezi river marking the division between north and centre, the Save river between centre and south. In terms of economy, however, the central region becomes larger and includes also northern Tete, and most of Zambézia. Thus defined, the central region becomes heterogeneous in kinship terms (patriliny in the south and matriliny in the north).

From the 1890s the central region was occupied by concession companies. The Mozambique Company (until 1940) ruled in what are now Manica and Sofala provinces, whereas the so-called *Zambezi Prazos* (political domination of trading territory) was the system in the provinces of Zambézia and Tete, part of the *prazos* later being transformed into the Zambezi company. Portugal, being

---

[8] For another example of incongruence of 'development' with matriliny, see Barbara Rogers 1980 about the World Bank's problems with its Lilongwe Land Development Program in an area of matriliny in Malawi.

too weak a colonial power to run its territory on its own, leased out the land to these companies, leaving it to them to exercise governmental power, and to exploit the inhabitants as best they could, through taxes, recruitment of labour power for plantation companies, subleasing of land, and control of trade with peasant surplus production. This arrangement really resembled feudalism more than capitalism, taxing the surplus production of the inhabitants rather than controlling the means of production, and deriving virtually all its funds from fiscal income, not from profits from capital investment (Newitt 1981).

However, a number of plantations (sisal, copra, sugar, tea) did operate in the region, most of them with foreign capital (British, German, French, Swiss), and some of them with considerable success. In 1928 as many as 138,000 workers were recruited for plantation work on six months' contracts, only in the Mozambique Company territory. This is to say that the peasant population in this area had wage work experience as well, but of a different kind (compared to the southern region) and with a much more limited cultural impact. The plantation workers were employed locally, or at least not too far from their places of origin, for seasonal, agricultural labour: the work they were doing was of the same kind, more or less, as the work they knew from the family farm, and the work cycle followed the agricultural year. Frequently, of course, peak work at the plantation would coincide with peak work at the family farm, this causing various problems. But seen from a cultural, ideological point of view the world of these wage workers did not change as much as was the case for the migrant miners of the South.

Furthermore, the salaries of these plantation workers were much lower than that of the mine workers, kindling no dreams of personal economic prosperity, and changing no means of production on the family farm. The backbone of peasant economy was here still the family plot, tilled in traditional ways with hoe and machete.

The northern region: family farming

The northern region (in this economic context approximately covering the provinces of Cabo Delgado, Niassa and Nampula) is still another story. The economic history of this region bears a certain resemblance to the centre, in so far as a concession company, the Niassa Company, from the 1890s to 1930 was master of all of the present provinces of Cabo Delgado and Niassa, promoting even less economic activity here than had been the case in the central region. In the north, the Company's profits derived almost exclusively from taxes on peasant production. The peasants were left to themselves, one of the reasons being that the northern parts of the country were thinly populated and hardly even colonized until after the First World War,

In the 1930s, however, the Portuguese introduced a new form of exploitation, which was practised all over the country but which weighed heavily on the northern region, especially the province of Nampula: forced cultivation of cotton. Areas were measured out, seeds distributed, and the cultivation was strictly supervised. Cotton cultivation is highly labour intensive, some 150 workdays a year per cotton field. Clearly this was devastating for the food production of the peasants. They had to adopt the easily grown but less nutritious cassava as a food staple in order to make ends meet. At its height in 1944, the forced cotton cultivation is estimated to have involved as many as 790,000 peasants (Newitt 1981), many of them women, as the men would have been dragged off for xibalo (forced labour). The forced cotton cultivation was thoroughly hated by the peasant population, to an extent that has made it very difficult for the Frelimo government to persuade people to continue cotton growing after Independence. But unlike the various types of wage labour which in different measure were changing peasant social structures, cotton growing took place in a family setting; it was an unbearable coercion of peoples' lives, but it did not disrupt kinship authority structure.

Thus, to conclude this highly generalized overview of Mozambique's economic history: The social and cultural effects of the money economy and wage labour were strongest in the south, weaker in the central region, and almost absent in the North, this presumably being one of the reasons for the persistence here of matrilineal kinship structures, and of female initiation rituals.

Religious changes

Besides economic changes and demands, another major modernizing factor has been active in the same areas and in the same period of time: the Roman Catholic and Protestant Missions. Their activities to some extent have been demarcated by the contemporary expansion of Islam. If economic modernization had an impact on gender relations (through individualization and promotion of nuclear families) so also have the Missions; on gender relations, on morals and on female gender identity. But first, I'll look at Islam.

Islam
In the northern part of the Mozambique coast, in Cabo Delgado, Nampula and Zambézia provinces, Arabs have been present for centuries; in some places Swahili is the spoken language. But Islam is not just a coastal phenomenon; as far inland as Niassa province people see themselves as Muslims. The expansion of Islam to the northern interior seems to have happened in the end of the nineteenth century, according to Edward Alpers (1972), roughly from 1890 to 1930. In the early 1890s António Enes, the Portuguese Governor of Mozambique, reported the situation like this: 'If Christianity only vegetates like an exotic plant, Mohammedanism is spread out like dog's grass. ... It is gaining by its proselytization all the northern districts of the province of Mozambique.[9] [The Islamic communities] react against Christian influences, and in certain hypothetical situations [they] will be capable of a common action' (quoted in Aplers 1972, 189).

The Portuguese saw Islam as a potential threat, surely something unwanted: a Christian population could be more easily controlled. According to some theories regarding the why and how of the spread of Islam in Eastern Africa, the strongest inroads have been made by Islam in times of crises (Alpers 1972), and certainly the imposition of Portuguese colonial rule from 1890 onwards

[9] In colonial days the whole country was called the Province of Mozambique, conceptualized as an overseas province of Portugal. What are now provinces were called districts.

must have been experienced as highly critical by local chiefs – and by the population at large. Islam was seen by the chiefs as an agent of modernization: Islam meant literacy. According to a contemporary observer (another Portuguese official):

> One of the perceptible results of Islamic influence is precisely the spread of instruction, and the necessity that all the chiefs have today of being ... instructed in writing and reading, for which purpose they frequently call in men of the coast. They commonly maintain relations among themselves and with the authorities in writing, which is not the case in the south of the province [i.e. Mozambique] where the chiefs are completely illiterate. (quoted in Alpers 1972, 190)

As for the influence on social structure and on the values and norms of the societies, Islam seems to have mingled rather well with what was there beforehand. According to I.M. Lewis: 'As long as traditional beliefs can be adjusted in such a way that they fall into place within a Muslim schema in which the absoluteness of Allah remains unquestioned, Islam does not ask its new adherents to abandon confidence in all their mystical forces (Lewis, quoted in Alpers 1972, 173).

This fits well with my own impression of Islam in Mozambique being extremely adaptable, the further away you get from the coast. As opposed to Christianity, the demands that Islam has made on the local population seem to have been few. This may be due to a greater congeniality with values and orientations in traditional African society. According to Edward Alpers, who have specifically studied Yao society (the Yao is the major ethnic group in Niassa): 'Every manifestation of 'ancestor veneration' among the Yao emphasized communal rather than individual values, in common with virtually all traditional African religions. [This, together with other factors] seem to have favourably predisposed the Yao for the spread of Islam among them' (Alpers 1972, 176).

Unlike the Christian missions Islam did not condemn the initiation rituals. Instead the rituals were Islamized (the female as well as the male ones), apparently without making any changes whatsoever in the rituals as such, or in the case of the women, the related customs of extending the vaginal lips, making tattoos and wearing missangas. In the OMM material from Niassa, the female initiation rituals are described pretty much like anywhere else in the north, the custom of ritual defloration[10] being mentioned more frequently here than elsewhere. But the rituals are explicitly referred to as being Muslim: 'Our Islamic religion taught us the initiation rites, and we follow this Mahometan principle' (OMM iw, Niassa province). 'The children that have not been through the *unyango* [the initiation rituals] have no respect for their parents, or for other adults. Furthermore they cannot enter the Mosque' (OMM iw, Niassa province).

The eastern parts of Nampula province are also largely Islamic, as is the southern part of Cabo Delgado and the northern part of Zambézia provinces, all places inhabited by Makhuwa. Especially in Cabo Delgado the Makhuwa are keen to define themselves as Islamic, as opposed to the Makonde in northern Cabo Delgado, who have been Christianized by Catholic missions. However, in the OMM data material from these places there is no mention, and certainly

[10] See Chapter 8 regarding ritual defloration.

not as explicit as in the Niassa case, of the initiation rites being seen as Islamic. Nevertheless, Islamicized or not, the female initiation rituals are still surviving strongly among the Makhuwa , as is the matrilineal kinship system.

According to Moroccan muslim and feminist writer, Fatima Mernissi (1975/1985) Islam, patriarchal as it may be in terms of social organization, accepts and recognizes active, subjective female sexuality. The Islamic control of women is an external one (e.g. in Mozambican Islamic areas, if the young girl is not married immediately after the initiation rites, her seclusion will be continued, until a suitable suitor emerges and she can get married). Mernissi quotes George Murdock as saying that societies fall into two groups with respect to the manner in which they regulate sexuality: One group enforces respect of sexual rules by a 'strong internalization of sexual prohibitions during the socialization process'; the other enforces that respect by 'external precautionary safeguards such as avoidance rules'. These societies, according to Murdock, have failed to inter- nalize sexual prohibitions in their members. Further according to Murdock, Western society belongs to the first group, while societies where veiling exists belong to the second (Murdock 1949, quoted in Mernissi 1975/1985). Mernissi adds to this distinction the difference of the very concept of female sexuality in these two types of societies: 'In societies in which seclusion and surveillance of women prevail, the implicit concept of female sexuality is active; in societies in which there are no such methods of surveillance and coercion of women's behaviour, the concept of female sexuality is passive' (ibid., 31).

This of course does not mean that Islam is not patriarchal and woman- oppressive, but it is so in a different way from Christianity. Mernissi gives this characteristic of Western/European Christian culture, which I find quite fitting:

> In the western Christian experience sexuality itself was attacked, degraded as animality and condemned as anti-civilization. The individual was split into two anti- thetical selves: the spirit and the flesh, the ego and the id. The triumph of civilization implied the triumph of soul over flesh, of ego over id, of the controlled over the uncon- trolled, of spirit over sex. (ibid., 44)

Islam, Mernissi says, took a different path. In Islam 'sexuality per se is not a danger' (ibid.). On the contrary, it has a series of positive, vital functions, among them the fact that sexual satisfaction is seen as necessary to intellectual effort. This line of thinking is remarkably different from the position of Sigmund Freud, who saw intellectual effort as a result of diverted, sublimated sexual ener- gies; to Freud culture is achieved as a result of (painful and costly) *transforma- tion* of sexual energies (Freud 1917). Sex as such is seen as opposed to cultural achievement, the sexual energies must be sublimated, or chaos will prevail. Much to the contrary, according to Mernissi, 'the Muslim theory views civi- lization as the outcome of satisfied sexual energy' (ibid., 44). Sexuality should not be repressed or transformed, but it must still be controlled, and Islam controls sexuality by controlling women: 'What is attacked and debased is not sexuality but women, as the embodiment of destruction, the symbol of disorder' (ibid.). The result in both cases works against women, but in different ways.

The Mozambican data material suggests that the Muslim way has been less devastating than the Christian one, and less destructive to the Mozambican 'concept of womanhood' (cf. T. O. Ranger below) and to female gender identity and the ways it was and is maintained.

Christianity

Christianity is suspicious of any sexuality that does not directly serve procreation, and somehow female sexuality is feared the most. Another feminist scholar writing on Africa, Nici Nelson, has made observations about Christianity very similar to Mernissi's above:

> Christian philosophy has always made a separation between body and spirit: things of the body are valued less than things of the spirit. ... Fear of women's unbridled sexuality has continued through the Christian era and permeated the work of philosophers and psychologists until the 20th century. ... In Africa, this division of the flesh and the spirit into immoral and moral does not seem to exist. (Nelson 1987, 235)

That is also to say that when this division of flesh/spirit equal to immoral/moral exists in Mozambique, as it certainly now does, it is very likely to have been implanted by Christian missionaries. To the Christian mission at large the initiation rituals, female as well as male, were seen as immoral and obscene. Terence Ranger quotes a German Protestant missionary, writing in 1934, following a Freudian logic: more sex = less civilization.

> The decisive period in the life of an African youth is the time of the initiation rites, the *khoma* or *unyago* ... This period, however, is poisoned by so many excrescences of pagan superstition and unbridled sensuality that many friends of the negro think that the abrupt break and arrest of the intellectual and moral development of many young boys and girls at the age of 13 or 14 is the outcome of such orgies. (Ranger 1972, 238)

Accordingly, Ranger adds, most missionaries waged relentless war on the idea of initiation. Ranger reports in this context of a rare attempt by a Christian mission (*in casu* the UMCA, Universities Mission to Central Africa) in southern Tanzania to Christianize the initiation rituals. As for the male rituals the attempt more or less succeeded, but with the corresponding female rituals the missionaries made no headway. Presumably because the distance between the female sexuality of the rituals, and the sexuality known to the white women, who had to effect the Christianization, was just too big. Ranger reports: 'Women's rituals were much more 'obscene' than the male ceremony ... In any case, the missionaries did not approve of the concept of womanhood in Masasi society, regarding Yao and Macua marriages as defective and matrilineal institutions as a hindrance to the establishment of the Christian family (ibid., 237). Here we have again the incompatibility of matriliny with development and modernization.

In this same context Ranger quotes an African woman, interviewed in 1963, about what the initiation rites used to be. I will copy the quote because it fits so nicely into my own observations:

> The girls were prepared for their future lives as wives in extending their lower parts in preparation for sex during their married life. The instructors also made certain that the girls should know all sorts of manners ...The girls' bodies were washed with wet husks to make their skin lighter and beautiful and it was lovely to see them coming out looking so beautiful. The girls were given a proper bath in the morning of the day of coming out; they were also given new clothes and their bodies oiled and veiled. At the end of the ceremony each girl with her helper would have to do a 'belly dance' and this was a great amusement, especially for the boys, who usually came and chose the best dancers to be their future wives. ... Today the missionaries have changed all this ... what we are left with now is the memory of the good old days. (Ranger 1972, 327)

The Roman Catholic Mission

Both Catholic and Protestant missions have operated in Mozambique. The Catholic missionaries coming from different orders: Fransiscans, Dominicans, Jesuits etc., and the Protestants from the Anglican Church, Swiss Mission, Baptists, Methodists etc. The Catholics boast of an early start, the first Catholic church being built 1505 in Sofala, at the time when early Portuguese explorers were building fortresses along the East African coast. But effectively the Catholic Mission only started in the 1890s, at more or less the same time as the first Protestant missions.

Up till 1930 the two types of missions worked on comparable terms, neither of them with state funding, and they expanded at approximately the same rate, in the early 30s having some 30–40 mission stations each (Moreira 1936). The Protestant ones were conspicuously clustered in the southern region, with just a few outposts further north, the UMCA Mission at Lake Niassa being the most renowned. The Catholic Missions were more evenly distributed, still however with a heavy weight in the south and next to nothing in the far north (*Anuàrio Católico de Moçambique* 1974).

This state of affairs changed dramatically in 1930. Salazar came to power in Portugal and introduced his *Estado Novo*, the new state. In the ideology of *Estado Novo* the African colonies were no colonies but *Províncias Ultramar* (overseas provinces). Consequently, the Mozambicans should be taught to see themselves as Portuguese, and this great civilizing task was put on the Catholic Church, from now on subsidized by the state. According to government instructions to the missions in 1930 the 'rudimentary primary education shall have as its aim to civilize and nationalize the natives of the colony, disseminating among them the Portuguese language and customs' (Hedges 1985). This means that from now on 'all teaching and writing must be in Portuguese. Any reading or writing in the native language is absolutely prohibited' (Moreira 1936).

This in effect was a severe blow to the Protestant Mission, which had had as a principle to teach in the respective native tongues. The Protestant missionaries, being non-Portuguese, always made the effort to learn the local language, and the Protestant Mission had done a great work constructing a written language and translating parts of the Bible to Tsonga, one of the languages of southern Mozambique (Biber 1987). But from 1930 onwards the Catholic Mission expanded, heavily supported by the Portuguese state. The Protestant Mission survived, however under difficult conditions, constantly harassed by the colonial government.

The expansion of the Catholic Church in the following decades looks impressive on a map and in the church's own statistics; many so-called elementary schools were erected all over the country. But what you learnt there, according to Adelina Penicela of the OMM Maputo province secretariat, was 'só Ave Maria e capinar' ('just Ave Maria and weeding'). The 'schooling' was compulsory for children between seven and fourteen years, living in a radius of three kilometres from the bush school. Adelina Penicela, who went to such a school herself, tells about it:

> The *régulo* called for my father, saying that now there had been constructed a school on his land: 'Go and call your children and tell them to come to the school.' The parents would send their children, but only the small ones. The ones of fifteen years

could not go. You needed money in order to go to the school: we only had cashew nuts and products from the field for payment. When I was a child there was not much money around. The boys went to school in the morning and the girls in the afternoon. Thus I started studying, but really it was only learning to pray and to sing: 'Ave Maria, Santa Cruz, nome do Pai, nome do Filho, Espirito Santo, Amen'. That was all you learned. Nobody bothered to teach you reading or writing. When you knew this dogma, you had passed school. The teacher would say to the *Padre* (at the mission station a thirteen hour walk away): 'Now I have X number of children to be baptized'. The Padre would come from the mission in his car and he would start baptizing the children. You had to pay 150 escudos for each child to be baptized. The Padre said that you could not marry somebody that was not baptized, and that no marriage could be made without the Padre. For marriage you had to pay as well: 150 escudos. On Thursdays there was no school, just work in the field of the teacher. On other days the teacher would count ten girls to go and fetch water, four to pound maize, four to fetch wood for fuel. At the time of the harvest of cashew each child had to bring a twenty-litre tin of cashew nuts as a gift for the teacher. Many children fled from the school, but then the teacher would tell a group of boys to go and find them and when they were found they would be beaten. Anybody who had passed fourth grade could become a teacher.

The proper schools run by the mission, and certainly secondary schools and high schools, were almost exclusively for Portuguese children. No wonder that among Mozambicans the Catholic Mission had a bad reputation, and was seen as a part of colonial oppression.

I have not been able to find much material on how the Catholic Church in practice reacted to people's traditional customs and rituals, as for instance the initiation rituals. Doubtless in principle it was against it, following the general ideology of Christianity – and of the Portuguese government in this statement from 1940: 'To us Portuguese, colonization is essentially to lift the indigenous populations to our own level of civilization, by teaching them our religion, our language, our customs. ... It is our mentality that we want to transmit to the people of the colonies, we are not intending to take away their riches' (quoted in Hedges 1985, 14).

Nevertheless I suspect that mostly in practice it worked the other way round: exploitation first, 'civilization' after. In the following observation from Nampula province it looks as if the concern of the Padres has been the tax on the initiation rites, rather than the content of the ceremonies:

> In the time of colonialism, in order for the initiation ritual ceremonies for boys as well as for girls to take place, the *régulo* had to inform the colonial administration that in his zone X number of young people stood before initiation. The administration would give its authorization against payment of a certain sum of money (tax). Likewise it was necessary to ask authorization from the Padres. Normally the requests would be authorized for the period just after the harvest in order not to interfere with the forced production of cotton and other crops. (OMM rep, Nampula province)

On the other hand, exactly this slackness seen from a Christian point of view, may have been fortunate from the point of view of the women: to some extent they were left on their own, and their rituals could survive.

The Protestant Mission
In contrast to the Catholic Church, the Protestant Mission stands in high esteem in present independent Mozambique and for good reasons. As opposed to the

Catholics, the schooling given by the Protestant missions was much better and was continued up to secondary level. The Protestant missions offered the only possibility for proper education for Mozambicans, and they were not compromised by the colonial regime. It is therefore no coincidence that many later Frelimo leaders have roots in the Protestant Mission schools. Frelimo's first president, Eduardo Mondlane, was educated in the Swiss Mission. And Samora Machel – Frelimo's second president, and the first president of Mozambique – all of his life thought very highly of the Protestant Mission, as is evident in his speech in 1982 at a large public meeting in Gaza:

> The Protestants helped us a lot. They educated us in order for us to know the value of a human being. Ever since the Portuguese effected the total domination of our country, the Protestants constructed churches, and there they taught us about our history, our value as human beings, our identity. They taught us that we were Mozambicans, Africans and not Portuguese. They never betrayed our land like the Catholics did; the Catholics wanted to convince us that we were Portuguese. For all of this: *obrigado protestantes* (thank you, Protestants). ... When the Catholic Church spread as a close ally of Portuguese colonialism, thus uniting the cross and the sword, making religion an instrument for the consolidation of foreign oppression, it was in the Protestant churches to a large extent that the spirit of resistance and the fight against the oppressor could seek refuge and become organized. (Machel 1982, 40

The Protestant missions seem to have been somewhat more zealous, as compared to the Catholic ones, in schooling as well as in 'civilizing'. They really saw to it that new values and norms of conduct were adopted by the Mozambican converts, the concept of 'discipline' having an important standing: 'In the Presbyterian communities in Mozambique 'discipline' plays an important part ... being in Mozambique principally: the mode of dressing (proper suit instead of sacs, capulanas worn in a decent way), ban on alcoholic beverages, on polygamy, on free unions [i.e. non-sacramental marriages], and also on divining bones, ancestor veneration, and participation in ritual dances' (Biber 1987).

The above quote is from an internal source in the Swiss Mission, but it is confirmed, at least at a general level, in the previously quoted speech by Samora Machel, where he goes on to praise the Protestant Church for its contribution to the instalment and maintenance of moral norms like individual and collective hygiene, the dignity of marriage and of the family, and the fight against alcoholism and prostitution: 'The Protestant Church developed some of these values. We want publicly to acknowledge this contribution that the Protestant Church gave to the Mozambican people' (Machel 1982, 40).

Thus the Protestant missions seem to have had an impact, and in spite of their smaller size maybe a greater impact, in changing peoples' ways of life. The impact was reinforced, presumably (a) by the Protestant missions being localized predominantly in the south of the country where the modernizing effects of the money economy and wage work were felt most, and (b) by the close relationship between the Protestant Mission and Frelimo leaders. Significant Frelimo leaders and presidents of Frelimo/Mozambique – Eduardo Mondlane, Samora Machel, Joaquim Chissano – all come from Gaza province, the Protestant Mission stronghold par excellence.

Protestantism, socialism and Frelimo

In this final section I'll outline a theme that could be developed much more fully: The (partial) overlap between Frelimo and Protestant morals, and Frelimo's use of the Protestant ethic to build socialism. In the 1982 speech quoted above, Samora Machel gave a list of moral norms, including 'the dignity of marriage and the family', and 'an organized life, rejecting the impure burden that capitalism drags with it of idleness (*vagabundice*), alcoholism, prostitution, marginality' calling it all *'a ética socialista'*, the socialist ethic (Machel 1982).

In his analysis of 'the Protestant ethic' Max Weber points to idleness as a major sin: 'Waste of time is thus the first and in principle the deadliest of sins' (Weber 1920/1930, 157). Weber also noted how Protestantism is even fiercer than Catholicism in its ban on sexuality; Catholicism decrees celibacy for priests, monks and nuns, but there is no interference with sexual life in general, as long as it is practiced in matrimony. Under Protestant puritanism, however, 'sexual intercourse is permitted, even within marriage, only as the means chosen by God for the increase of His glory, according to the commandment "Be fruitful and multiply"' (Weber 1920/1930, 158). Samora Machel in countless speeches (including the 1982 Gaza one) comes down hard on 'prostitutes'; sometimes one could have the feeling that what he was really after was uncontrolled female sexuality as such.

The Frelimo/Protestant coincidence of values regarding marriage and the family has already been hinted at. Furthermore, the Protestants, just like Frelimo/the OMM, by propagating the nuclear, patriarchal family see themselves as fighting against women's oppression. First the Protestant vision, in the words of the Swiss Mission historian quoted above: 'Convinced that there existed just one model for the Christian family – monogamy, indissolubility, faithful love, social priority of the man over his wife, but equal dignity in front of God – the missionaries in the young Presbyterian churches would fight against polygamy, against lobolo, against all reduction of the woman to an object of possession, but also for equal education for girls and boys' (Biber 1987, 64).

In the concluding document from the OMM Extraordinary Conference 1984, Frelimo's/OMM's political vision of the family is very similar: 'The OMM Extraordinary Conference emphasized very specifically the vital importance of the coherence, stability and harmony of the family, because this is the basic cell of our society, the foundation of the Mozambican Nation, and the basis for the consolidation of our State' (OMM 1984).

On this background the OMM Extraordinary Conference recommends that every family should make an effort to create a new equilibrium, based on the equality of rights and duties, and on the fulfilling of the tasks of each one of its members, as father and *chefe da famlia*, as wife, mother and *dona da casa*, and that they together should be responsible for the education of their children. The achievement of this family is part of the programme for women's emancipation supplemented, of course, with the fight against polygamy and lobolo, and against initiation rituals. Even if the OMM as a consequence of the debates during the conference preparation achieved a less straightforwardly condemnatory attitude to the female initiation rituals, than previously it had had, the rituals are still seen as 'inducing concepts and behaviours of submission and inferiority of the woman in front of the man' (OMM 1984).

Actually, the whole socialist vision of woman's emancipation, drawn from Friedrich Engels, and expressed in OMM's programme from 1976, is still in force: (1) the road to women's emancipation is their integration in production side by side with men, and (2) the OMM should struggle against old customs and ideas, obstacles to the full participation of women in social and political life. This vision does not differ markedly from Protestant statements on women's issues.

The entire plan for socialist development, in economic terms, rests on transforming the whole economy into state farms and industries. Within just one decade millions of small scale peasants would be turned into wage workers (as was wishfully imagined in the early 1980s). This neatly follows the general path of modernization: technical development and economic rationalization. A socialist path may differ from a capitalist one in terms of state as opposed to private control over the means of production, and in terms of a moral obligation to democracy, access to literacy, health etc. Socialist politics also may be more insistent on pushing women into wage work, as in the case of Mozambique, which even if it expands the women's work load may provide a base for new female self confidence (parallel to what was described above regarding the miners' wives). Nevertheless, in terms of the central aspects of modernization here under discussion: (a) the gender biased effects of the money economy and wage work, (b) the preference for a nuclear family headed by the man, and (c) the moral views on female sexuality – in terms of these aspects, capitalist and socialist modernization follow the same path – there is no difference at all.[11]

The necessity of independent women's organizations

I have ventured to assess processes of modernization as they have occurred in Mozambique 'from a vantage point of women'. The main conclusion is that the greater the impact of modernization, the less life there is for women, with women's sexual self-determination seen as a cardinal point. Does this imply that Frelimo/the OMM should abandon development/modernization? Certainly not! As I have already pointed out, modernization does hold promises for women as well as for men. Criticizing the way modernization has taken place does not imply a glorification of the 'good old days'. This is not a simple dichotomy of good and bad.

The critique of the process of modernization, as it has happened in Mozambique and elsewhere, should not point back to a glorious past (which never existed). Rather it should raise awareness as to possible alternatives: how can modernization with literacy, education, better health, new ideas and larger horizons be promoted in a way that does not at the same time undermine female sexual self-confidence and promote male gender power? As it happens now, 'development' almost everywhere takes place on men's terms, marginalizing women, with no or very few possibilities for women to defend themselves in the process.

In order to be able to fight back, women must act together. Democratically working organizations are indispensable; in order to collectively develop actions

[11] This line of thinking is further pursued in Chapter 5.

and ideas you must be organized. At rare historical moments, the process of change has been dynamized not by missions and money, but by the movements of men and women themselves, women have been able to give voice to their own felt needs through a gender organization – as in Mozambique during the liberation war, the OMM at that time working very differently from what later became the case. At such historical moments the male gender bias in the development process has been much less pronounced, women being in a position to take advantage of new possibilities offered by economic and political change: new experiences and new skills – without losing the strength of their traditional gender identity in the process. Another Mozambican example, as I see it, is the organization since 1980 of peasant women of the Maputo Green Zones, in the *União Geral das Cooperativas*, the UGC.[12]

Typically these kind of developments are either short lived or marginal, or both. But instead of being exceptions or sidelines, these experiences should be considered foundational. They should be points of departure for women's development policies led by strong women's organizations. Women need independent and democratic gender organizations through which to promote women's interests, to fight marginalization, and to insist on modelling modernization on women's terms. Why should development not be possible combined with matriliny? With female sexual self-determination? Of course it is possible – but it takes a host of very strong and independent women's organizations to fight for such visions to come true.

[12] See more on UGC in chapter 1.

3 Family Forms & Gender Policy in Mozambique 1975–1985 (1989–1990)

Woodcut by Matias Mtundu Mzaanhoka

Introduction

In 1982 a pioneer article was printed in the new bulletin of the Mozambican Ministry of Justice, *Justiça Popular* (Dagnino, Honwana & Sachs 1982). The article dealt with the diversity of family forms in Mozambique, thus establishing an anthropological overview that to my knowledge had not been there before, and on that basis discussing the difficult task of making a unified legislation function on such a diverse social base. The article pointed out (at least) five different family forms, or rather marriage systems existing in Mozambique: 1) The traditional matrilineal system of marriage, which is the most frequent one in the northern part of the country; 2) the traditional patrilineal system: marriage with *lobolo* (bride price) dominating in the south; 3) the traditional Muslim system; 4) marriage according to Christian rites (Catholic or Protestant); and 5) civil marriage at the civil registry, the marriage form promoted (although without any great success) by the new Mozambican state.

This diversity is important. The first two forms of marriage, matrilineal and patrilineal, are especially important as they indicate two different sets of rules, norms and morals governing not only kinship relations but the very structures of society as such, structures according to which the lives of men and women have been formed for ages. Compared to the importance of the matrilineal/patrilineal diversities the other differences – of religious vs civil marriages – are minor. But of course they must be taken into consideration in an article aimed at discussing the legal base of marriage, because it is to this existing traditional/legal diversity that attempts to create a new Mozambican family law have been addressed.

In 1982 this insight into the diversity of family forms was new and much needed. However, it is not nearly profound enough. In this paper, based on material that was collected by myself and by the OMM (*Organizaçao da Mulher Moçambicana* – the Mozambican Women's Organization) between 1981 and 1984, I shall discuss in greater detail some of the – unexpected – consequences of imposing a uniform legislation – based on an abstract principle of gender equality – on social realities as diverse as the ones found in the different parts of Mozambique.

The new legal framework: the proposed family law[1]

A few years after Mozambique's Independence in 1975, after the important post-independence conference of the national Women's Organization (the Second OMM Conference, in November 1976), and after the very important post-independence Party Congress (the Third Frelimo Congress, in March 1977), work was initiated regarding a new family law to replace the Portuguese *Código Civil* and create a unified legal basis regulating the family lives of all Mozambicans, irrespective of race, colour, religion, etc. A draft of such a new family law was finished in 1980, and there was a plan that it should be put out for public discussion, as everybody was well aware how

[1] For a follow-up on the Family Law, see Chapter 5.

difficult a task it is to interfere with norms and rules that have been governing marriage arrangements and family life for generations. These discussions never happened. Neither was the proposed family law released and codified as a law, apparently because at higher political levels there were disagreements as to parts of its content. Thus the family law project remained a project for years, in Mozambican legal circles, named the PLF *(Projecto da Lei da Família)*. Like other parts of new Mozambican legislation, prominently the Constitution, the proposed family law was based on the three basic principles that follow:[2]

First, uniformity – that every Mozambican citizen should be subject to the same laws, thus doing away with the legal diversity of colonial days, with one set of law for the Europeans and *assimilados*, another one for the natives *(indígenas)*, different laws for the Muslim communities, etc.

Second, equality – that everybody, women as well as men, should be equal before the law. This marks a difference from the 'traditional laws' of the *indígenas*, as well as from the *Código Civil* of the Portuguese: in both cases women were subject to different rules and morals from men. This principle of gender equality is rightfully a source of pride to the Mozambicans. In the Constitution, §§ 17 and 29 it reads: 'The emancipation of woman is one of the essential tasks of the state. In the People's Republic of Mozambique woman is equal to man in rights and duties, this equality being extended to political, economic, social and cultural fields' (§ 17). 'In the People's Republic of Mozambique women and men enjoy the same rights and are subject to the same duties. This principle governs all of the State's legislative and executive acts. The State protects marriage, family, maternity and infancy' (§ 29).[3]

Third, secularism, i.e. the dissolution of any previous tie between civil law and the Catholic Church. People are free to belong to any congregation of their choice, but a religious marriage shall have no legal status. You may marry according to any faith, but in order to give legal validity to your marriage you must marry at the civil registry as well.

In spite of political hesitation regarding the law as such, it was agreed in 1982 to release some basic points of the PLF as guidelines for the tribunals. These guidelines were issued in the Directiva n° 1/82 of February 27, 1982.

There was an acute need for unified guidelines for the resolution of family conflicts, especially as the colonial *Código Civil Portugues* would still be in force as long as there was no new law. These points thus represent the aspects for which there was political support in the Party.

Principal issues of the *directiva* of 1982 are rules regarding divorce, de facto marriage, and polygamy.

---

[2] The following is based on a series of documents prepared by the *Departamento de Investigação e Legislação* (DIL), *Ministério da Justiça*, for an internal seminar. They were given to me in 1986 by Albie Sachs, at that time Director of Investigation in the DIL.

[3] *Constituição da República Popular de Moçambique*, Instituto Nacional de Livro e Disco, Maputo 1978.

Nas Forças Populares há homens
e mulheres.

A mulher, tal como o homem,
participou na luta armada.

Viva a emancipação da
mulher moçambicana.

37

3.1 Frelimo iconography: Gender equality, Frelimo style. This is from an adult literacy textbook. The text reads: 'In the Armed Forces there are both women and men. The woman, just like the man, took part in the armed struggle. Long live the emancipation of women.'

Divorce

Divorce is a central issue in the PLF, as well as in the 1982 *directiva*. But it is an issue replete with inherent conflict. On one hand the possibility of divorce is a *sine qua non* of a progressive family legislation in Mozambique, important among other things to mark the break with the laws of Catholic marriage. On the other hand the stability of the family is guiding principle number one of Frelimo morality. This ambiguity comes forward clearly in the first article of the section on divorce in the proposed family law, which more than the subject of the divorce deals with its undesirability (seen from the state/society's point of view):

> The stability of the family is essential for the realisation of its functions in relation to its members, and in relation to society. It is the interest of the State to defend and preserve the relation of marriage. However, factors exist that may provoke a crisis in the married relation, and which may lead to its destabilization, to such an extent that the family no longer fulfills either the aspirations of the married couple, nor its obligations in relation to society. In such circumstances the dissolution of the marriage will be justified...[4]

The ambiguity continues all way through, not only in the text of the law, but in its practice as well. Consented are two kinds of divorce: 'Normal' litigious divorce, and divorce by mutual consent. The litigious divorce (the only type known from the *Código Civil*) like any criminal case operates with an 'offended' and a 'guilty' party, an 'accuser' and an 'accused'. According to the PLF in case

[4] *Projecto da Lei da Família, Ministério da Justiça* (dated 821223) art. 33.

7 de abril de 1981

10° aniversário da morte da camarada
Josina Machel
símbolo da mulher moçambicana combatente

Mulher moçambicana: cumprir as metas de produção
é garantir o sucesso da luta contra o subdesenvolvimento.
Participemos activamente na defesa da nossa Pátria Socialista!

3.2 Frelimo iconography: Seventh of April is Mozambique Women's Day. This was the day of the death, in 1971, of Josina Machel, Samora Machel's first wife (before Graça, who later married Nelson Mandela). Josina Machel took part in the war of liberation, *a luta armada*; after her death she was turned into an icon of new Mozambican femininity. The figure in the centre of the star is Josina, surrounded by images of womanhood: Mother, soldier, student/teacher, peasant, industrial worker.

of 'grave violation of the rules and duties of marriage and family life' either of the spouses can put in a plea for divorce. This is an important step forward compared to indissoluble Catholic marriage, and an advantage in relation to *lobolo*-marriage of southern Mozambique, which gives the woman and the man incomparable possibilities of divorce – in northern Mozambique the situation is very different, as shall be shown below. But a plea for divorce has to be taken to the court, thus giving the court a possibility for attempts of reconciliation.

Divorce by mutual consent – the proposed possibility for a couple to agree to divorce, simply because they want to, even if the rules and duties of marriage have not been violated by either party – has been considered a very radical proposal, too radical for some people who have maintained that this possibility would make divorce too easy, thus leading to promiscuity among young people and diminishing respect for marriage. As a consequence, in the edition of the Family Law project referred to in the 1982 *directiva*, divorce by mutual consent is preceded by a series of preconditions: it can only be granted after three years of marriage and one year of separation, and even so the tribunal should attempt reconciliation. Altogether the atmosphere around divorce is that it is legal, certainly, but politically disapproved, the political goal being the stable, harmonious nuclear family.

De facto marriage, i.e. traditional marriage

The proposed recognition of de facto marriages is another of the points in the Family Law project that has been frowned upon. It was seen as counteracting the political request for registered marriages. In actual fact, however, what in the law are called de facto marriages, is just another name for the vast majority of all marriages in Mozambique, now as before contracted according to tradition, depending on the kinship system, customs and rules of a particular area/ethnic group.

In spite of political campaigns aimed at getting people to marry at the *Registo Civil*, only a small percentage of the marriages actually in force have in fact been registered. In 1981–1982 (according to the above-mentioned article in *Justiça Popular*) the number of officially registered marriages was estimated to be just 10 per cent of all newly established marriages during those two years. Thus in fact there was not much choice: in order for no less than 90 per cent of the married population not to stay out of reach of the family law, the only thing to do was to legalize de facto marriage. As a result the section in the PLF on de facto marriages is included in the 1982 *directiva*:

> A de facto marriage as considered by this law is a relation between one man and one woman, who, being both legally eligible for marriage, establish between themselves a community of material and affective life with the character of sincerity and stability fitting for a family. They shall thus be considered by society as such.[5]

This means that all the rules regarding divorce, division of goods in the case of divorce, inheritance rights of children and spouse etc., are applicable in principle to these de facto marriages just as they are to the officially contracted ones. Thus the marriage contracted through *lobolo* is accepted as a legal marriage, even though lobolo as such is campaigned against; in a different paragraph of the same family law proposal it is stated that 'the state in particular combats the handing over of any values or goods, be they called lobolo, gratification, *anelamento* (*anel* = engagement ring) or compensation'.[6]

Polygamy

Dealing with polygamy at the level of the law has been uncontroversial, in so far as there has been political unanimity regarding the proposal in the PLF that:

- a polygamous marriage cannot be registered as such, because an already married person cannot enter a new marriage (before the first one has been dissolved);
- whoever wants to leave a polygamous union should be helped in doing so (assisted by the courts in questions of parental rights, division of goods, rights of alimony etc.). (That the latter point is not always followed in practice is a different issue, to which I shall return later.)

This then was the principal legal framework put in place on the diversity of the Mozambican family systems and issues.

[5] *Projecto da Lei da Família*, art. 23.
[6] The list of 'cover names' for *lobolo* reflects popular attempts to pretend that they – in response to the political request – had given up marriage by *lobolo*, when in fact they had not, just hiding the exchange of *lobolo* by giving it other names.

Family forms in Southern Mozambique

I shall now take a look at family diversities in the northern and southern parts of the country respectively (starting with the south). After a description of the state of affairs in 'the old days' (an expression frequently used by Mozambicans) [7] I shall investigate how things changed in the so-called process of modernization. Major factors in this process of change are mission, money and colonial administration. It is important to note that even if Mozambique at Independence was relatively backward compared to other countries in Africa because of inefficient Portuguese colonialism (cf. Newitt 1981, 95, 145) it was not unchanged, especially not in the south. Processes of change were taking place, in people's everyday lives and in their conceptions of it, induced by economic changes, by Christian missions and by colonial rule. Finally I shall show how the new norms regarding family structure formulated in the new legislation of Independent Mozambique were put into practice (in the early 1980s) and how they worked.

Southern Mozambique in 'the old days'[8]

Under conditions of patriliny[9] the children of a married woman belong to her husband's family. Most frequently patriliny goes along with patrilocality, which means that at marriage the woman has to move away from her own family and settle with the family of the husband. In southern Mozambique, this was considered (with good reason) a period of crises for the young newly wed woman, especially as during the first year of marriage she was obliged to live and work more or less as a servant in the house of her parents-in-law, i.e. without a home or house, essentially without a *fogueira* – a fireplace – of her own (Junod 1912/1974, 179).[10]

Marriage as a whole was anticipated without enthusiasm by the young women, or by their families. This is an ancient wedding song from Southern Mozambique (it goes along with a particular wedding dance) :[11]

[7] In most cases the expression 'the old days' (*os tempos antigos*) refers to a particular state of affairs rather than to a particular point in time. Nevertheless the expression 'the old days' has, I think, a certain advantage compared to the expression 'traditional society'. It does not invite dichotomous thinking to the same extent, and it tends to be more indeterminate, open and blurred at the edges – just like the phenomena it is supposed to name.

[8] The section on southern Mozambique is based on data collected in investigations conducted by myself in 1981–1982 in the city of Maputo and in Maputo Province, as well as on the data gathered in the OMM Extraordinary Conference preparation period from August 1983 to March 1984. As in the previous chapter 'SA iw' indicates material gathered by myself in 1981–82 and later in the conference preparation process; 'OMM iw' is data from direct transcriptions of interviews or oral contributions collected by others; 'OMM rep' (report) is OMM data from compilations made at district or province level. For more on the OMM Extraordinary Conference preparation process, see the Introduction.

[9] Patriliny dominates in southern Mozambique, south of the Zambezi River.

[10] Henri-Alexandre Junod (1863 – 1934) was a Swiss missionary of the Presbyterian Church, working in southern Mozambique, first from 1889 – 1896 and again from 1913 – 1920. His two volume anthropological study of the people of Southern Mozambique, *The Life of a South African Tribe* (1912–13) was published in English and later translated to Portuguese with the title: *Usos e costumes dos Bantos*. The Portuguese edition from 1944 was re-published in Lourenço Marques in 1974, and again in Maputo in 1996.

[11] This wedding song was recorded by myself in Maputo province in 1982.

Go away my daughter go away
you do not know to where you are going
weep my daughter weep
you will suffer in the house of your husband
you will have to work a lot
may not even sit down when you are eating
you will be everybody's servant
fetching the water
chopping the firewood
washing the clothes for everybody else
you will have to heat the water
preparing the bath for your husband
for his father, for his mother, for his aunt
the water is not enough
you must go to the river for more
working, working
your husband will beat you
your mother in law will call you a thief and a liar
you who never stole nor lied
weep my daughter weep
you will suffer in the house of your husband.

There is certainly no vision of a 'romantic wedding' here! And yet, marriage is the way to fulfillment for a woman (the only way, the best way). It is through marriage that you get access to land and to socially accepted motherhood. Frequently the young woman would not know her husband before marriage, and even more frequently he would not be a man of her own choice. However, if a young girl objected very strongly to a suggested husband, she would be listened to, according to Junod (1912/1974, 106).

In a society structured by kinship relations, marriage arrangements are no individual affair, concerning only the two people who actually get married. By marriage the whole family group becomes related to another family group, and the kind and character of these relations are essential for power, influence and sometimes even survival of the families in question. Thus marriage arrangements are far too important to be left to young, inexperienced members of the family groups. Marriage arrangements are essentially the business of the fathers, the heads of the family groups, the patriarchs. Marriage arrangements and *lobolo* negotiations are their principal means of exercising power and influence.

Accordingly, following the accounts of Mozambican women (of middle age) the fact that their husbands were not of their own choice has no great importance in their tales of their lives. A series of newspaper debates in Mozambique in the early 1980s[12] point in the same direction: The whole concept of courting, falling in love etc. is new, it has no history in southern Mozambique. Young people of today wondering about what is expected of them seek advice in the newspaper debates on how to behave. The tradition for individual pairing as a prelude

[12] The Maputo weekly *Domingo*, April/May 1982.

to marriage is very young. However, moving away from one's own family, becoming a part of a strange and alien family group – that of the husband – was a strain, and most of the women recounting their lives to me in 1981–2 dwelled on this period as being particularly difficult. The problem is not the husband, but his family, and more particularly his mother. The husband is only a problem in so far as his solidarity, as it appears, is more with his family/his mother than with his (miserable) wife. For the men who went to the mines it was normal to send money to their mothers, not to their wives; the mother could then give a hand out to her daughter-in-law if she wanted to. Sometimes she didn't.

A former miner's wife (she later ran away and is now working in a Maputo cashew factory) talks about her married life:

> When he came back from South Africa he only stayed in his mother's house, and only gave money to her. Then it would be her, my mother-in-law, who would take me to the shop and allow me to choose a capulana. Just one. She herself had many capulanas. (SA iw, Maputo)

Many are the tales of harsh relations between mothers and daughters-in-law. Those who were in power were the older women; there was no doubt about that.

Especially precarious was the situation of the younger woman if the husband went to South Africa, to the mines – and stayed away, for years on end, or maybe forever. This of course was not the norm, but it did happen. In that case his wife was stuck: she was married, she belonged to the husband's family – but because she was abandoned she was bound to stay the underdog. It was even worse if the husband disappeared before she had got pregnant and borne a child.

I met a number of women who told this story. I met them in the factories of Maputo, those that were there had fled the unworthy life as a married but single woman in the husband's family and had gone to town on their own. Obligation number one in those circumstances was to repay the lobolo. This is the story of one of them. Let us call her Maria:

> I was born in Inhaca.[13] I also married there. The marriage was decided by my father and my husband, we never had a period of courtship. My husband didn't treat me well. He was working in Maputo. I stayed in his parents' house. I got pregnant, but the baby died. My mother-in-law didn't like me. I got pregnant again, this time also I lost the child. I was suffering and I called my family, I said: 'My husband doesn't treat me as his wife. He doesn't even buy me clothes, nothing. I want to get out of this marriage'. But my mother and my uncle said: 'Your father has died. Where do you think we could get hold of money to pay back the lobolo? You had better stay with your husband.' (SA iw, Maputo)

The husband returned to Inhaca, but the situation didn't change. At last Maria decided to flee to Maputo, in order to earn money to be able to pay back the lobolo herself.

> I took the boat to Maputo all on my own, without telling anybody. I started to work in people's houses. When my escape was discovered, my parents-in-law went to see my mother and my uncle, saying: 'We want our daughter-in-law'. But they answered: 'No, she will not come back. You'll have to go to Maputo to look for her, she has to pay back the lobolo'. So my parents-in-law came to Maputo, they found me and took me to Inhaca. I gave them the money that I had already made: 1,500 escudos (the whole

[13] Inhaca is a small island a few hours boat journey from Maputo.

lobolo was 2,500 escudos). I asked for permission to go to Maputo once more in order to get hold of the rest: 1,000 escudos. I returned, I paid. (SA iw, Maputo)

In Maputo Maria was living in the house of a married sister. Another husband turned up. He was willing to pay lobolo, but Maria said no: 'I didn't want to have anything more to do with lobolo'. Still she didn't get pregnant. The husband said: 'You'd better go to the hospital, it isn't good to stay without children.' She had some treatment at the hospital, but it only resulted in stomach ache, and a halt in menstruation. 'This husband is good. He doesn't reproach me, he never beats me, he never has lovers. As soon as he is off from work, he'll be home.'

Lobolo: Kinship relations

Lobolo is to be found widely in southern Africa. It is even called the same all over: lobolo or lobola. In the recent tradition of southern Mozambique lobolo was heads of cattle. Before that, according to the women, it had been a series of other things: bunches of firewood, the hide of a leopard, a number of hoes. According to Junod (1912/1974) history went like this:

> The *lobolo* first was *esteiras* (i.e. straw mats) and different kinds of baskets. That was in the ancient times when the whites had not yet appeared. After that, big rings of iron were used; they came in by trade with the sailors visiting the coast. ... Also heavy rings of copper were used in the old days. ... For a long time cattle were used for the lobolo. ... The lack of cattle, probably caused by the wars with the Zulus, surely is the reason for cattle being substituted by hoes for lobolo. Thus hoes were in use, all over, from 1840–1870 along with cattle when available. Ten hoes was the normal amount for lobolo. Later parents started demanding twenty, thirty or fifty hoes. ... Hoes in their turn were substituted by pounds sterling. ... In the beginning one pound sterling was equal to ten hoes, and the lobolo was settled at eight pounds for chiefs. ... Later the amount rose to twenty pounds for an ordinary girl, and thirty pounds for the daughter of a chief .(Junod 1912/1974, 265–7)

Thus lobolo has been many different things. What matters is not what lobolo is, because it is first and foremost a symbol, a token exchange. On the other hand, the amount, the value of lobolo, has mattered. It has always been higher for the highest (the chiefs). And generally it has gone up and up. Presumably because of this, lobolo is often called a price. But lobolo in the old days had nothing to do with buying and selling. Thus the European name 'bride price' is misleading. Lobolo is an exchange, but not a price. It is a token of a new or reinforced relation between two family groups.

Lobolo creates relations. Between families and between men, just as much as between a man and a woman. Very often lobolo is not fully paid at once, and complicated relations of debt, dependence and dominance result. Sometimes I have had the feeling that the importance of lobolo could not be overestimated. It seemed to be the very glue holding society together. I will quote two very different sources to support, or rather to illustrate, this point of view.

One is from Junod (1912/1974), in an appendix to his book where he discusses how, from a Christian point of view, to deal with the pagan habit of lobolo. An old man has been baptized, but he is still tied up in 'pagan customs' (as Junod says). The problem is the following: Does he have to demand a lobolo that someone owes to him, in order to pay a lobolo that he owes to somebody else? As a Christian he should not demand lobolo; on the other hand how can he escape the obligation of paying the lobolo to a pagan creditor? And in order to fulfill this second obligation, he has to demand the lobolo himself. Another Christianized Mozambican, Zebedeus (later a well-known opponent of Portuguese colonialism, eventually murdered by PIDE, the Portuguese secret police) explains it to Junod like this:

> These debts of lobolo are like strings that go from the neck of one man to the neck of another. Even if your father dies, this string will keep you fettered, you are tied to the bones of your father by this blasted chain. Others are pulled into its knots, and you will stay imprisoned in its loops. Cut it, and you are free. (Junod 1912/1974, 109)

This is what lobolo is really about: relations and obligations in the kinship network. From a 'modern', i.e. Western/European and/or Christian point of view, such kinship relations are chains and fetters, limiting the freedom of the individual person. From a different point of view, these are the strings of a network that keeps people alive. The Portuguese anthropologist José Fialho (1982, 1998) is my second source, representing this different point of view. Southern Mozambique is very dry. In great parts the soil is sandy, the rains are irregular, droughts are not infrequent. Floods are not infrequent either, the big rivers (Limpopo, Incomati) are a blessing but they are dangerous neighbours. Agriculture in these conditions necessitates a dispersed habitation, and an expanded network of social relations of rights and obligations: If your own area is struck by drought or failure of crops, it is essential that you have relatives and allies in different areas, with different natural conditions and thus with chances of a luckier harvest. They will support you when you are in need. The following year it may be vice-versa. Such an expanded network of kin and allies is created by the lobolo. If the father and his brothers have taken their wives from a particular set of families in a particular place, these families are taboo to the sons' generation. They must go elsewhere in search of their wives. Their sons however, pick from the same families as the grandfathers did. This system secures (a) a wide range of allies, (b) good relations between the co-wives of the same man, as they will be recruited from the same group of families; frequently they'll be cousins, or even sisters. Thus lobolo is not just lobolo. It creates relations for the exchange of other goods and services as well. There are lots of different rules about what should be given when to whom by whom:

> The relations between the allies in this system are egalitarian; the relations are symbolically expressed, and they are also expressed in circuits of exchange of particular goods seen as feminine from the party that supplied women, and another set of goods, seen as masculine from the party that supplied lobolo. Thus it is the institution of lobolo that guarantees the functioning of this whole system. (Fialho 1982, 16)

Thus in the old days the exchange of X heads of cattle was more than just a token. The token exchange is material, in so far as it creates social relations, i.e. channels along which goods and services can flow. The lobolo of the old days had, however, on top of this the very practical effect of enabling the family that gave away a daughter to get hold of another one. As a head of family A, you marry away a daughter to a son of family B. Family B in exchange provides you with X heads of lobolo cattle. These lobolo cattle are subsequently passed on to family C, who have a daughter, suitable as a wife for your eldest son. A group of cattle has changed hands, and two women have changed families, not in direct exchange, but with the cattle as intermediary. Of course in order for everything to fit so neatly all families should have an equal number of sons and daughters. Which clearly is not the case. Nevertheless, this exchange of women and cattle is the basic principle of lobolo. Lobolo is a particular kind of compensation that enables you to replace the woman lost.

Consequently in the old days the lobolo cattle were 'earmarked' for lobolo. You could not receive X heads of cattle as exchange for your daughter, and then sell the cattle or exchange it for something else. Lobolo cattle were for lobolo only. If there were no more sons in a family group in need of wives, the cattle could wait for a while. New generations of sons would grow up, and they too would have to get married. Far into this century, when lobolo had turned from cattle into money (sometimes cattle *and* money) the air of *not* being a 'general equivalent' stuck to lobolo money.

Mozambique's first female academic lawyer, Gita Honwana Welch, wrote in 1982 her *Tese de Licenciatura* on lobolo, based among other things on an interview with her father, Raúl Honwana. This is part of her father's tale, illustrating the complication of lobolo-relations, as well as the 'ear marking' of lobolo money:

> I'll tell you the story of my mother, your grandmother, Vulande. Vulande who was an only daughter was lobolo'ed by an Indian. At that time the Indian tradesmen did not bring their families with them when they came to do business in Africa. Vulande had a daughter, but in the meantime her husband died, and she returned to her parents' house. Some time later Vulande was lobolo'ed by a man by the name Massinga, with whom she had two sons. These sons died however, and as she did not get on well with her husband, she returned once more to her parents' house. In the meantime Vulande's father, Mutxeketxa Hunguana, who was a resistance fighter, was in Gaza where he participated in the battle at Magul together with the troops of Gungunhana against Portuguese domination [this was in 1895]. After this battle Mutxeketxa went home to his land in Marracuene, but as he found everything destroyed by the Portuguese – the fields ruined, the cattle killed – he decided to go and found a new settlement near the beautiful lake Malongotiva, thus restarting his life. Vulande, wanting to alleviate the sadness of her father, lobolo'ed a wife for him, a widow named Mi Hambene, who already had a daughter from her previous marriage. However, Mutxeketxa died without having fathered yet another child. Following the laws of lobolo, Mi Hambene was inherited by Mwa Massangalane, Vulande's cousin on her father's side, and with him she had a daughter, Babalala. Later however, Mi Hambene left the home because Mwa Massangalane maltreated her. In this way Vulande was left with the rights over Babalala, because Babalala was born as a consequence of the lobolo paid by her. Later again Mi Hambene started living with another man, named Nwa Vilanculo, but she refused to be lobolo'ed by him, as long as the bond of lobolo with the Hunguana family had not been undone. Mi Hambene had children with Nwa Vilanculo. When the first daughter Hlonipane was lobolo'ed, for 35 pounds sterling, it was Vulande who according to her rights received this lobolo.
>
> When Vulande died, the person who inherited this money was her only proper son, myself, who had been born in a later marriage with Manuel Honwana in 1905. However, when I married for the first time in 1927, the father of my wife who was a dignitary of the [Protestant] church [just like Zebedeus, quoted above, SA] did not want any lobolo, for which reason I used the thirty-five pounds sterling to build myself a house in which to live together with my wife.[14] (Honwana Welch 1982, 36)

---

[14] This first wife died; Gita is a daughter of Raúl Honwana's second marriage in 1940 with Nely Nhaca.

This story further illustrates lobolo's consequences in relation to children, and to levirate marriages. Levirate marriages are less common nowadays. Seen from the point of view of families and relations a levirate marriage is nothing strange: it creates a way for the widow to remain a member of the family group to which her children belong. It is an arrangement that allows her to go on with her life as before. Frequently her new husband will have another first wife, and especially if the widow is aged this may be a good solution to the problems raised by her husband's death. It is seen as such by Raúl Honwana: 'To the woman who became a widow, when she was no longer very young, it was comforting to feel protected and to be guaranteed a *companheiro*; and to the kinsmen of her deceased husband this was a duty of honour' (ibid., 16). If the widow is young of course things might look different. But even in the old days the inherited marriage would not normally be carried out if the woman was very much against it. The lobolo's effects on the rights to children, however, are valid even today, even in the judgments of the courts of independent Mozambique, as says the *Juiz Presidente* (presiding judge) of the tribunal of Sabié (Gaza Province), interviewed by Gita Honwana Welch:

> In cases of separation when there are small children, they will stay with the mother until they are seven or eight years old. After this, and especially if the mother marries again, the children will go to stay with their father or with his family, because of the strong sentiment (of the mother as well as of the father) that the child belongs to his father's family. Also because a man who marries a woman who already has children, is not very likely to accept to bring up these sons and daughters of another man (ibid., 17).

To be sure, everyday Mozambican life follows the same rules, even though in some cases it is very hard on the women to have to leave their children. The way for the woman to keep the children is to pay the lobolo back, as in the following case, recorded in one of the cashew factories of Maputo:

> My husband had gone to the mines, but he never sent home anything from South Africa. I had to go fishing for shrimps at night and then in the morning go to the market to sell them. It was very hard, I was worn out. I went to the *régulo* (the chief) who said that I was right, it would be OK if I left my husband and took the kids with me, but I had to repay the lobolo. So I went to Maputo and started working at the cashew factory. (SA iw, Maputo)

As a general rule, when lobolo has been given, the woman as well as her offspring will belong to the family of the husband. The woman, however, keeps her own family name. This is an indication that even if she belongs to the husband's family, her ties with her own family continue to be strong. The children get the surname of the father. In cases when no lobolo has been paid, the children as well as their mother belong to her family group, they stay with her family (frequently in the settlement of the mother's uncle) and take her family name.

In the old days (before the influence of the Christian church and the politics of Frelimo), not paying lobolo was disrespecting the woman and her family. Again, let us listen to Raúl Honwana:

> In the old days there was no such thing as a 'civil marriage' for us [i.e. at the *registo civil*]. Lobolo – that was our way of marrying. Even at that time we had to have some-

thing that distinguished a proper wife from a mistress (*amante*). To start living with a woman without lobolo, without anything, that was abduction. That could only be excused if the man, when the two were living together (it might be many years later) eventually did pay the lobolo to the woman's family. Otherwise this marriage would not be regarded as a marriage. It had no value. The woman's family had no regard for their son-in-law. And the woman did not feel protected; she had no guarantees. The man could tell her to leave at any moment. If she was lobolo'ed it wasn't like that. The matter had to be talked over very thoroughly before there could be a divorce, which meant that the goods handed over by the husband should be handed back, i.e. returning of the lobolo. (Honwana Welch 1982, 35)

Thus there is no sense in talking of lobolo as such as woman-oppressive. On the contrary lobolo can be seen as a tribute to women – as a recognition and indication of their value and importance. Without women there is no continuation of society, nor of a particular family group. Women indeed were very valuable (as also recognized by Meillassoux 1975/1981) and the lobolo may be seen as recognition of this value. This was how it was seen by the women themselves – in 'the old days'. An unhappy lot was bestowed on the women for whom no lobolo had been paid. In the province of Gaza the women describe the situation as follows:

A woman that had not been lobolo'ed had no value in society, she was not respected, either by her husband, or by her own family, and she could not take part in certain specific and secret ceremonies in the house of her own parents, as they had not received lobolo from her husband. A woman in these conditions was to be pitied. When she was pounding or doing other domestic work, she would sing sad songs about her sorrowful fate of not being lobolo'ed. (OMM iw, Gaza province)

When a woman was not lobolo'ed she was not taken into account. For example when a meeting was held in the family she could not participate because she had not been lobolo'ed. Or when some ceremony was held she was not invited because the spirits of the ancestors of the house did not know her. Nor would she herself have any self-esteem. An example of this is that when she was pounding or grinding millet she would invent sorrowful songs about the fact that she hadn't been lobolo'ed. Furthermore, as she hadn't been lobolo'ed , she wouldn't bear any children, because the spirits of the ancestors did not know her. (OMM iw, Gaza province)

The connection between lobolo and offspring is mentioned many times in the material resulting from the OMM conference preparation discussions, particularly in the provinces of Maputo and Gaza. It confirms the general impression that lobolo indeed was an integrated part of the kinship structure. And it shows the importance of the spirits of the ancestors that are alive in people's minds, even today. This is a report to the preparatory OMM conference of the city of Maputo from one of the urban districts:

The populations of some neighbourhoods say that lobolo must continue, because it is through lobolo that the ancestors are informed about the fact that the girl is leaving for the house of her husband. Without lobolo the ancestors will not know of the departure of the girl, and as a consequence she will not be able to become pregnant, and because of this the husband will have to get himself another wife. (OMM rep, Maputo)

Similarly the conception of lobolo as a valuation of the woman, and lack of lobolo as a de-valuation, holds true even today to some extent. When interviewing women workers in Maputo, I noticed that a great many of the factory workers who had started working when they were still young girls, i.e. before marriage, (a) were girls who had grown up without fathers, or (b) were girls that had become pregnant without marriage, with a big overlap between the two. Which means that a girl who works as a wage-earner will very often be a fatherless girl (having to help her mother to support any brothers and sisters), and a girl who has no father is accessible, you can treat her in any way you like. You don't have to respect her or to marry her, you just seduce her. In other words, there is felt to be no lobolo-obligation on fatherless girls, and thus they may be maltreated[15].

During the OMM conference preparation discussions in Gaza province it was expressed like this: 'The women who weren't lobolo'ed had no value whatsoever; any man could get at her, which is to say that she was everyman's woman.' 'Lobolo is a way of respecting the woman – without lobolo she will be considered a prostitute'(OMM iw, Gaza Province).

Polygamy: Everyday life

Lobolo has to do with the structures of kinship: which other family groups you are related to by marriage and how these relationships work. Polygamy has to do with everyday life: how family life is organized, how work is divided, how the days are spent. And basically it has to do with production.

Like lobolo, polygamy is not just a fancy custom that you can finish off with a political declaration. Like lobolo, you might call polygamy an aspect of a particular system of reproduction. However, in the economy of pre-colonial and early colonial Mozambique production and reproduction are so closely interlinked that it hardly makes sense to make a distinction. Thus in this economy, lobolo and polygamy, each in its own way, are really relations of production.

In a farming economy, like Mozambique's, based on very simple technology (the plough was only introduced in the 1920s, and only in limited areas of southern Mozambique), the major means of production besides the land itself is human labour. And apart from occasional ploughing and clearing of new land, which is a man's job, all other aspects of farming depend on women. The more women in one family group, the more land can be taken under cultivation, the more food can be produced and the more prosperous the family head will be. Land in Mozambique has always been plentiful. The country as such is sparsely populated. Of course all land is not the same. Some land is better than other land because of soil quality, rains, proximity to rivers, etc. Sites may be of different desirability for other reasons as well. But basically the impediment to wealth in old-time Mozambique would not be land so much as people, human labour power, which means wives and daughters to do the cultivation, and sons to look after the cattle.

Thus until the system of production has been altered you cannot expect polygamy to disappear. Of course not all men had two (or more) wives. But the important ones – like chiefs (heads of family groups) and *curandeiros* (traditional healers) – were sure to. They were the *munumuzanas*:

---

[15] In the 1982 investigation of women workers in Maputo, I found that the women who had started working as girls were a minority. The women factory workers would mostly be previously married women, who for some reason or other had left their husband or had been abandoned/ divorced by him. Very few women workers would be married.

The man with just one wife couldn't associate with the *munumuzanas* with many wives, as he himself was not yet a *munumuzana*. (OMM rep, Gaza Province)

The number of wives was considered a sign of virility and prosperity. To be polygamous was the desired state of manhood. As a southern Mozambique proverb, quoted by Junod says: *Uma única mulher não constitui uma povoação,* which is: One single woman does not make up a village. (Junod 1912/1974, 276)

All subsequent marriages would be contracted like the first one, through lobolo, and the new wife would settle in the husband's village (*povoação* = family-settlement) – if he wasn't the head himself, the head would be his father or his elder brother – in a hut of her own (built for her by the husband) next to the hut of the first wife. A typical old-time settlement (as described by Junod ibid., 299 ff) would be a ring of huts surrounded by a circular fence, with just one broad entrance, opposite which you would find the hut of the first wife of the village head, the huts of the subsequent wives next to it on either side. After these huts, completing the circle you would find the huts of younger brothers' wives and the huts of wives to married sons.

It is the men's work to construct the huts, but the number of huts is deter-mined by the number of women. The man's quarters will be in the hut of his first wife, but being polygamous he is obliged to sleep regularly, at fixed intervals in the huts of each of the other wives. Unmarried young men would share a special hut near the entrance, not too far from the similar hut of the unmarried young women. And in the middle of it all you would find the corral for the cattle, and smaller pens for goats and chickens, maybe pigs. A special shaded area on the left hand side of the entrance is the *bandla*, the meeting place of the men. This is where the men receive visitors, talk and eat. At meal-times each of their wives brings their husband's food to this place, and the married men share the food between themselves, the young men and any visitors. Many women means rich varieties of food.

In the outdoor kitchen of her hut each woman will cook the maize [i.e. the basic stiff porridge, made of finely pounded maize flour] and the sauce [various vegetables, occasionally meat or fish, cooked with ground peanuts] in two different pots. ... From everywhere dishes with food are brought to the men's meeting place. Not all of the plates come with just plain millet porridge; some are filled with *mandioca* (cassava), sweet potatoes, etc. The men plunge into the first dish, all of them eating with their fingers. Then they go on with the next one, and so forth until everything is finished. (Junod ibid., 305).

Another proverb on polygamy, quoted by Junod, refers to this: *Não basta um só dedo para meter os graus de milho cozido na boca* which means: One finger is not enough to put the cooked maize into your mouth (ibid., 276).

The husband with many wives must take care to treat his wives according to the rules. No one must be neglected, and he must sleep with the wives in turn. But the wives are not equal. The first wife has a special status. She is the 'big wife' as compared to the subsequent 'little wives'. She has special ritual duties and rights. And if and when the husband wants to marry another wife, the first wife must be consulted. She may very well suggest that the husband take a second wife herself. A second wife can alleviate her workload and she herself will still be the one in command.

> Often polygamy will arise when the man, after having married his first wife agrees with her to marry a second one, because she has loads of work in the field, and she cannot manage to do it all on her own. ... There was a habit that, when possible, the married woman would always take her younger sister from her parents' house to the house where she herself was married, and then this sister would be called a *xlapswa*, thus becoming the new wife of the *régulo* (chief) or *curandeiro* in question... Other important cases that have brought about polygamy in this area are the men with big farms who, because of the quantity of work in the fields, have considered it a necessity to acquire another wife in order to have more help with the work. ... Frequently the husband (*munumuzana*) only considers his first wife (*nkhonsikaze*), the remaining ones being persons that have to subordinate themselves to the *nkhonsikaze*. Sometimes even she will be the one responsible for the distribution of food and clothes to the others. At times this will be taken to the extent that she is considered the mother of the other wives of her husband, and grandmother of their children. (OMM rep, Gaza Province)

Even when the two (or more) wives of the same man were not actually sisters, they would often be related, and in any case they would consider each other as older and younger sisters, a relationship combining the emotional affiliation and solidarity with hierarchy. Altogether, emotional *and* hierarchical human relations seem to me to be the norm in this society, as opposed to today, when the general pattern seems to be on one hand unemotional and hierarchical (for the relations of production) and on the other hand emotional and egalitarian (at least as an ideal!) for the relations of reproduction, i.e. family life.

Many of the women I interviewed in the south of Mozambique had no complaints about polygamy. On the contrary: it was nice to be two, workwise and emotionally. Actually it is a macho-fixed way of thinking that brings Westerners/Europeans to automatically suppose that two wives to the same man must by nature be rivals to his favours. Why should they? It might as well be the husband having a hard time faced with two women. Jealousy was mentioned as a possibility when I asked the women what polygamous life was like. But for polygamy in a rural setting this is not the rule. What seems to be much more important is the companionship, especially in the areas where the husbands are away a lot of the time, and when the whole burden of running the farm thus falls on the women. In those cases it was very nice to be two. And in fact in many of the rural households even today, when the big proud family settlements of Junod's accounts have largely and for a variety of reasons disappeared, you still find more than one woman.

When interviewing in a remote locality in the Maputo province in 1981, on one of my very first interviewing trips, when I still did not know very much about women's lives in Mozambique, I remember how impressed I was to find that the majority of the ten households randomly selected for investigation were headed by women (because the husbands were away in the South African mines, in Maputo, in other places, working). Furthermore, in eight of the ten households there would be *two* adult women running the place together. There was always a clear hierarchy, as they would be first and second wives, mother and daughter or (most frequently) mother-in-law and daughter-in-law. But still women were working together all over the place.

Five of the ten women interviewed in this locality of the district of Magude, Maputo province, were or had been parties in a polygamous marriage. When asked what they thought of polygamy this was what they said:

'I don't like to be alone.' 'I like it because I can rest now – the second wife does the work.' 'I liked it because it was my own sister who was the first wife.' 'In the old days I liked it, we could help each other. Today I don't like it.' 'I was married [to a polygamous man] so I had to like it.' (SA iw, Maputo province)

Another illustrative story of happy polygamy is cut from the weekly magazine *Tempo* (no. 454, 1979). It is told by Joana Massimbo, fifty years old and a worker at Cajuca, one of the Maputo cashew factories. Evidently the interviewer expects polygamy to mean suffering for the woman, but Joana tells a different story:

When I was born our neighbours had a boy, five years old at that time. We grew up and everybody treated us as a couple, until he started going to the mines in South Africa. The first time he went away I was thirteen years old, and when he returned he wanted to *lobolar* me. My parents, however, thought that I was too young, and in a meeting between the two families it was agreed that he should get himself another wife. So he did. After the feast of lobolo his wife was introduced to me as my older sister to whom I owed respect. To her they said that I was like her younger sister and that she should look after me and take care of me.

Our husband continued to go to the mines, and meanwhile we planted sweet potatoes and sold them, and thus we could tend to our own needs as well as pay the taxes, if the time for taxpaying came before he had sent the money. Years passed like this, and then it was my turn to be *loboloed*, after which the three of us started living together. We always lived in an atmosphere of understanding and happiness with our husband and our children. But this happy life was interrupted thirteen years ago when our husband died. My sister by now had reached an advanced age. I left it to her to take care of the children and went to Maputo myself in order to start working here at Cajuca. In this way it is possible for us to keep our children studying.... As you can see, not all wives of a polygamous husband would have to be rivals. Very often it would be the intervention of the mother-in-law creating rivalry between the two, as she would whisper with one behind the back of the other, talking ill of her, and vice-versa. (Tempo 1979, 46)

Altogether it is my impression that polygamy in the context of southern Mozambique in 'the old days', apart from being deeply integrated in the structures of that particular society and its system of production, had many advantages from the women's point of view. I do not say that men and women were equal. This was not the case; moreover the mere posing of the question in that way tends to lead thinking regarding women's issues in that society off on the wrong track. Men and women belonged to different gender groups with different tasks and responsibilities. Men had some positions and women had others. True enough, those who were heads of villages were always men. Those who led the negotiations on lobolo were men. Those who administered the structures of kinship thus were men. But those who ran the everyday life of farming and cooking were women. Those who produced life and food were women.

Generally it is my impression that men and women respected each other, and if the women felt offended they would fight back! I found a nice example of this in Junod (1912/1974, 277). He is discussing the incidence of jealousy among the wives in a polygamous marriage:

What gives rise to this feeling? A husband shows preference for one of the wives, giving her better presents than the ones he gives to the others, staying in her hut more nights than he does in the huts of the others, or giving her, on his return from the hunt, the best piece, for instance a leg of gazela. This creates *bucuéle* (jealousy) in the hearts of the others, and when he continues in that way, a straw is enough to light the fire. How then is this feeling expressed?

By mutual insults between the wives ... ; by insults and threats against the husband; by refusal on the part of the abandoned woman to cook for him or to look after his harvest; by acts of violence directed towards him – a woman may get to the point of grabbing the husband in front of the hut of the rival and making life so intolerable for him that he'll flee to South Africa just to find peace....

Junod, as a Protestant missionary, naturally sees polygamy as essentially immoral, and he is trying to induce this feeling in the congregation surrounding the mission station of Rikatla in southern Mozambique, where he lived and worked in the late nineteenth and early twentieth centuries. Regarding changing people's attitudes to polygamy, however, his success was limited. The above description of cases of jealousy in polygamous households actually orig- inates from a small enquiry that Junod made at one point among his adult pupils (all male of course) of the missionary school. He received some twenty written answers listing the arguments in favour of and those against polygamy, seen from the pupils' points of view. And in fact the point about jealousy is the only genuinely negative aspect of polygamy that the pupils can think of. The arguments in favour of polygamy are the following:

1) Quotation of the proverb: 'One single wife does not make up a *povoação*.'
2) To have several wives brings glory to a man.
3) A polygamous man may be generous and hospitable as his wives cook lots of food.
4) If the first wife dies he is not left alone.
5) If the first wife falls ill, he will not be in need of food.
6) There are lots of people to do the work of the household. The women help one another.
7) The polygamous man has many children.

The arguments against polygamy are not very convincing. All but 1), the above mentioned one about jealousy – which surely can create unpleasant situations for the man – are seen as if with the eyes of the mission:

2) Polygamy makes it easier to get drunk, because of the great quantities of beer that can be produced by so many people.
3) It makes pride swell in the heart of the polygamous man.
4) Polygamy is expensive because the husband has to pay one pound sterling in taxes for the hut of each of the wives.
5) It saps the man's strength because of the sexual excesses that he has to perform.

This last point, Junod has to admit, as presented by one of the pupils, 'seemed to have little value in the eyes of the others, as in fact it made them laugh' (1912/1974, 277). On the whole Junod cannot hide his disappointment at the outcome of this inquiry: The pupils do not really see the immorality of polygamy, he complains, and: 'Not a single one mentioned the great principle of equality between man and woman in front of the law of sexual purity' (ibid., 512). Junod's comments are interesting because they show some of the areas of conflict between the norms and ways of the 'old days' Mozambique on one hand, and on the other hand the modern European standpoint (although in a very moralist edition) that Junod himself represents. In the following sections I shall investigate what happened to these characteristics of the southern Mozambican social network and everyday life: lobolo and polygamy, in the subsequent process of social and economic change.

Southern Mozambique: Impacts of colonization, mission and money

Basically what happens in the so-called process of modernization is that the social structure based on extended kinship relations and intricate *lobolo*-debt links is broken up. This break-up gives larger room for maneuver for the individual, or rather for some individuals. In a certain way you can say that the individual as such is created in the process.

This is Marx's point of view. In the introduction to *Grundrisse* Marx criticises Adam Smith and David Ricardo for taking the human individual (whom they call 'economic man') as the point of departure in their analysis of society. But the individual, Marx points out, is not history's starting point, on the contrary 'the indvidual' is a product of history.

> The single, individual hunter and fisherman, with whom Smith and Ricardo begin, belong in the unimaginative visions of the eighteenth century Robinsonades ... The eighteenth century prophets, on whose shoulders Smith and Ricardo are standing see this individual of the eighteenth century as an ideal, not as an outcome of a historical development, but as the starting point of history. This is wrong, because ... the further we go back in history, the less independent the individual becomes, the more he seems a part of a larger whole. (Marx 1858/1939, 5–6)

To me it makes a lot of sense to admit a gradual but radical break in the ways society is working, a break that took place in Europe more or less at the end of the so-called Middle Ages, later named the 'Dark Ages' in contrast to the following 'Age of Enlightenment'. The 'Age of Enlightenment' was indeed structurally different, with science and rational thought in central positions, initiating the gradual marginalization of religion. Conceptions of gender and general morality, however, are still firmly rooted in Christianity.

In Mozambique this process of so-called modernization was initiated in the late nineteenth century with more effective Portuguese colonization, with the introduction of money and paid work and with the work of the Christian missions. The process was, however, gradual, multiple and diverse, with built-in incongruences of time. The new introduces itself in the guise of the old, and may stay so for a long time.

Transformations of the lobolo: Commercialization
Just as the first motor cars in the USA were shaped like stagecoaches (think of an old Ford T), so in the beginning when lobolo turned into money, the money behaved like cattle. It was 'ear marked' for lobolo, and it could be used for nothing else. But once lobolo has turned into money, there is a risk that it will start behaving like money. And the characteristic of money – again following Marx – is *not* to be ear-marked, but to be a 'general equivalent' exchangeable

with anything else. And thus lobolo over the years – parallel to other changes in society likewise initiated by missions and money – increasingly *did* become a 'bride price': a sum of money paid by the husband to the father for the delivery of his daughter. Lobolo became a price; marriage became commercialized. And lobolo's implication for women shifted to the opposite of what it used to be. From being a sign of dignity and respect it turned into a means of oppression.

The Mozambicans are well aware of this shift. Time and again in the OMM conference preparation discussions it was emphasized that in the old days lobolo was a symbol of exchange, an alliance between families, whereas nowadays... I quote from the OMM district report from Chokwe, Gaza province:

> Lobolo doesn't mean buying. ... Lobolo in the old days was very different from what it is today. The handing over of various objects was a sign of respect, it was a ceremonial act, and had nothing to do with buying. At a certain stage, however, lobolo totally lost this quality. Money was introduced, from 500 escudos to 2,500 escudos. And in addition to the money you would have heads of cattle ... At this time, however, cattle were not very expensive, they only cost 400 to 1,000 escudos. So at this stage of the process, lobolo could not be said to be expensive. However, since 1975, the year when we reached national Independence, lobolo has started climbing to very high values, varying from 10 to 80 contos [a conto is 1,000 escudos, or 1,000 *meticais* after 1980] and cattle. But today cattle is very expensive, from 15,000 to 30,000 meticais. And furthermore you have to provide engagement rings, earrings, clothes, food, drink, etc. ... In this way lobolo has stopped having this ceremonial character of respect, of indication of commitment of the young man to the girl. It has turned into a commercial process, and a very expensive one, as if it were about buying a car or another item of luxury goods. (OMM rep, Gaza province)

There are two things in this report worth noting. One is the awareness that something important happened when lobolo turned into money. And the other is the concern about the elevated amount. This concern is shared by everyone (with perhaps the exception of men with daughters of marriagable age). As a general rule people like lobolo because of what it meant in the old days, and they do not object to the fact that lobolo has turned into money. What they see as the problem is the way lobolo has gone up, the very elevated price that today (i.e. in the early 1980s when this data was collected) you have to pay in order to get married. The interconnection, however, between lobolo-turned-money and the price rise should not be missed. Once lobolo has turned into money the whole business may be seen as a commercial transaction. It is no longer a recompense for a daughter lost, enabling you to get hold of another 'daughter', but as a compensation for expenses you incurred in raising this daughter – which is a totally different thing. As if the daughter was a commodity, the value of which is calculated by the cost of its production!

In the old-time lobolo-compensation what counts is *use value*: women are precious and indispensable; in letting one woman go you must be assured of having access to another. The 'rationale' of new-time lobolo however is *exchange value*: expense X must be replaced by income Y. This argument is very frequent in the lobolo debate. I will quote once more from the abovementioned Chokwe report:

> The rise of lobolo is speculated as being the result of the price-rise of consumer products. ... When a person thinks of the cost of raising the daughter, of sending her to

school, to hospital, when calculating the lobolo he stipulates very exaggerated prices, with the aim of being compensated for the expenses he has incurred. Generally it is modern civilization and the price-rise of consumer products which is the principal reason for the rise of lobolo. (OMM rep, Gaza province)

In any case, lobolo amounts have risen greatly in recent years. From the district of Chibuto in Gaza province the situation is reported like this:

Aldeia Comunal Ngungunhana: 60,000 meticais, as well as three to four heads of cattle, and clothing for the parents. Locality of the district administration: 15,000–20,000 and engagement ring, watch and clothing for the parents. Aldeia Comunal Acordos de Lusaka: 40,000 meticais and two heads of cattle. Locality Chipadiap: 20,000–50,000 meticais and five liters of wine. (OMM rep, Gaza province)

In more remote places, as for instance in the vast and sparsely populated district of Chicualacuala (still the province of Gaza) apparently the habit of paying lobolo mainly in cattle is still in use. But if the cattle is calculated into money the end result remains much the same:

Aldeia Comunal Maconguele: 1,500 meticais and eight heads of cattle. Aldeia Comunal Obrigado Tanzania [Thank You Tanzania]: 1,500 meticais and eight heads of cattle. (OMM rep, Gaza province)

And this is what they say in Xilembene, a small town in the district of XaiXai, Gaza province: 'The actual lobolo has turned into an illegally performed commercial transaction. Lobolo today is nothing but *candonga* (black market trading)' (OMM rep, Gaza province).

As a thread through all the discussions of lobolo runs the proposal of a legally defined ceiling of the skyrocketing lobolo prices, and the suggested maximum is very frequently mentioned as 2,500 meticais. This was, it turns out, what it used to be in the later years of colonialism. Raúl Honwana tells how it came about:

In the beginning of this century the Portuguese didn't interfere directly [with the lobolo] but in the 1930s Augusto Cabra, who was Head of the Department for Native Affairs *(Negócios Indígenas)*, ordered that the price of lobolo should be 2,500 escudos, and 4,000 if the girl was the daughter of a chief. This was because they [the Portuguese] were of the opinion that there was too much disturbance among the natives because of matters of lobolo.

Furthermore they wanted to control the movements of cattle, and enforce the use of money. In the colonial administration they had a veterinarian whose job it was to control the cattle of the region. Thus in the cases of lobolo still being made in cattle, you had to report it to the native register at the colonial administration, saying who provided the cattle and how many heads. (Honwana Welch 1982, 36)

I suspect that this official limit to lobolo set by the colonial administration was the main reason for the (reported) rocketing of the price after Independence. Since Frelimo came into power, it has campaigned against lobolo, but that has not had much effect apart from driving lobolo underground and changing the name of what was seen at the surface. In Frelimo in the beginning there was no understanding of the importance of lobolo in people's minds. This understanding actually only came with the preparation of the OMM conference.

Transformations of lobolo: Individualization

In 'the old days' lobolo was an aspect of the kinship system, commanded by the father, the head of the family-group living together. In the normal order of things, the lobolo obtained for the marrying away of one daughter would be used for getting a wife for the eldest son, and so forth. The sequence of marriage would be according to age, and it would be the father who ran the show and administered the lobolo. By the turn of the century, however, and increasingly in the following decades, young men from southern Mozambique started going off to the gold mines of the Rand in South Africa, near Johannesburg which is not very far from the Mozambican border. In doing so they earned their own money. In the beginning, they would hand most of it over to their parents; for a while the fathers were still in control. But their power was not as unquestioned as before. With the money from the mines, an alley had been opened for the young men to escape kinship hierarchy and order. If they didn't want to wait for sisters and elder brothers to be married, they could arrange their lobolo themselves! For a while two kinds of lobolo, the old and the new, coexisted side by side. This is how the situation is described by Junod:

> Today you have two kinds of lobolo: (1) The lobolo that is obtained by the marriage of a sister, and which the young man, with the acceptance of the family, can use to get himself a wife. This, according to the old customs, is the way to get married. (2) The lobolo that is acquired as money earned by the young man who has worked for this purpose and who thus owns the money himself. This second type of lobolo is much easier to obtain with the new conditions of life, especially as a stay of a year or two in Johannesburg is sufficient to accumulate the money needed for the purpose. The young men that don't have a sister, or who for some reason have been disfavoured in the past, now may dream of marrying even three or four women. (Junod 1912/1974, 267)

Increasingly the power and authority of the family heads were broken, and the young men took the matter into their own hands. Very different social relations resulted. The old *povoação*, the extended family settlement, was broken up. This happened for other reasons as well. Increasingly in the 1930s and 1940s the Portuguese made raids on the settlements of the Mozambicans for labour power. The very conspicuous *povoações* were obvious targets. People dispersed and hid in the bush. Men now went to Joni (Johannesburg) in order to escape *xibalo* (forced labour).

The driving force behind the change from natural economy in a kinship network to a money economy based on paid work and cash crops, was the colonial power's desire for exploitation and profit. A natural economy, just producing for people's needs, cannot be exploited. Nevertheless the change did bring some advantages, especially to the young men. They gained a freedom they had not previously had: they could earn money and they could get wives. They didn't have to depend (as much as before) on fathers and older brothers. They went off to foreign countries, learning new things. Even if the mine work, as such, must be terrible (it is underground, hard, dangerous, off-work living in crowded compounds) in the minds of Mozambican males in the 1980s, there was a splendour about it. Going to the mines was considered very attractive. Young men crowded outside the WENELA recruiting office in Maputo, waiting for days and weeks, hoping to get a contract. Going to the mines had become a sign of manhood.

However, seen from the point of view of the women, this same change in the social set up had very different consequences. The men became liberated. The women became imprisoned, to put it in the extreme. From being part of a larger kinship network, living in extended families with lots of other women for help and support in work and leisure, women increasingly came to depend on one man only, their husband, and they lost their close contacts with the other women of the kin group, even though women today very often succeed in arranging their daily lives together with at least one other woman.

With changing society, the implications of lobolo as such were radically changed. Not all of this had a direct link with the commercialization of lobolo. The implications of lobolo changed because the preconditions for it were changing. Perhaps the men stayed away in the mines. Perhaps the women wanted divorce. And then, seen from the point of view of the women, lobolo appeared to be the thing that prevented them from enjoying the same type of freedom as the men. As married women, they could not just go to town and earn their own money – because of the lobolo that obliged them to stay with their husband's family, even if he himself was away, and even if they were suffering.

Lobolo prevented divorce where divorce was needed (seen from the woman's point of view). In most cases a woman would have preferred to go home to her parents', i.e. to her own family/land/kin group, because this was what you would normally do in this situation. However, with the parents not able to return the lobolo to the husband, the woman would have to arrange the money herself. This is the story that a lot of (now) middle-aged Maputo women factory workers can tell. In the cashew factories – which as the first factories employing women started in the 1950s – in the early 1980s, judging from my interviewing experience, this kind of woman was in the majority. Not surprisingly this kind of woman does *not* like lobolo. She has felt enslaved by it and says so. This is a transcription from a typical woman's intervention at an OMM discussion meeting in a cashew factory of Maputo:

> As for the woman she does not like lobolo, lobolo makes her a slave. In case of divorce, no matter how many years the woman has lived with the husband's family, when she wants to divorce they'll demand all the money of lobolo back. Very often it is not possible [for the woman's family] to raise the money, so she has to go to work in the factories. This is my own situation. (OMM iw, Maputo)

Furthermore, even when the issue is not divorce, the new type of lobolo and the changes in society as a whole have produced a new type of attitude of the husband vis-à-vis his wife. The commercialization and individualization of lobolo makes the husband think that he has bought the wife and thus has a personal right over her – something which was unknown before. These are reports from Maputo and Gaza provinces about how lobolo works nowadays, in the husband/wife relationship:

> Lobolo has created great problems in the families, as in certain cases the man may humiliate and oppress his wife, maintaining that she is not allowed to utter any opinion because she was lobolo'ed, i.e. bought. In this way the man may hurt and insult his wife as much as he pleases, saying that this only corresponds to the value of the money or the cattle that he had to pay for the lobolo. (OMM rep, Maputo province)

> Really a woman is despised and exploited in marriage because she is lobolo'ed. I say this, because concerning any problem or issue that may a rise in the home related to the wife, the husband will always talk of the money that he has now lost by getting himself this hopeless wife who doesn't know how to do this or that in the house. (OMM rep, Maputo province)
>
> Men will beat their wives because of lobolo, saying: 'I am not beating my wife, I only beat my money.' (OMM rep, Maputo province)
>
> Both newly-wed women and the young men of the age for getting married, reject the practice of lobolo, because a lobolo'ed woman is considered by the husband merely as an object that he has bought for various uses, depriving her in this way of her rights to participate in political and other activities. As a consequence of lobolo the husband doesn't think of appreciating what work she does in the house, as she was lobolo'ed just in order to do all this. (OMM rep, Gaza province)

Whereas lobolo in the old form indicated mutual respect in the relationship between husband and wife, lobolo in the modern form seems to have the possibility of turning any discord between the spouses into a reminder of the fact that he was the buyer and she the object bought. Thus from being an indispensable mechanism in the intricate functioning of an extended kinship system, lobolo has turned into a means of male dominance, in the form of husbands' dominance and control over wives.

Lobolo and the rise of husband-power

I have the feeling that this is a major reason for the rise and spread of lobolo in later years: Lobolo works excellently as a vehicle for male dominance in the guise of *husband power* – a characteristic of gender relations in so-called modern society. Previously, gender relations were about the group of men versus the group of women, the men's domain versus the women's. The relation between husband and wife was hardly an issue; actually husband and wife did not have all that much to do with each other. This is how Junod describes the gender relation between husband and wife in the old days:

> What then are the relations between husband and wife after the honeymoon? Of course this varies a lot according to the individual persons. But generally they are not very intimate with one another; the man stays with the pals at the *bandla*, the space in the *povoação* that serves as the men's meeting place, and he only seldom comes to the *ndango*, the enclosure of *caniço* (cane, reed) where you find the fireplace and which is the true domain of the wife. (Junod 1912/1974, 179)

But all this is changing. With so-called modernization, extended families break up, and nuclear families little by little become the norm: just one husband, just one wife, individualized relations. The structure of gender relations has changed, from relations of gender groups to relations between individuals. And at the same time, promoted by the changes introduced with paid work and greatly supported by the patriarchal ideologies of the Christian missions, male dominance has increased.

An aspect of this pattern is the spread of lobolo to places where it was not known before, such as the northern matrilinear parts of Mozambique where there used to be no *lobolo*. Lobolo in its whole conception (exchange, recompensation) belongs to patriliny. It makes no sense if the wife does not move away upon marriage. Conversely in these areas the future husband had to stay for a while working on the fields of his parents-in-law, in order for the wife's family to see if he worked well. But even here lobolo is increasingly adopted! Lobolo in the modern form: individual payment of money. This was clearly evidenced by the results of the OMM conference preparation inquiries and discussions. And in the areas where lobolo is new, as might be expected, the men are in favour, while the women are against. These are extracts from a discussion in southern Zambézia, just north of the Zambezi river:

> Man: The woman for whom no lobolo has been paid is not likely to respect her husband. Woman: The lobolo'ed woman is considered a slave to the husband and she is subordinate to the husband's family. When problems arise, she cannot take the initiative to leave the husband because she was paid for. And when she goes to her uncle's house, he refuses to help her because he already has eaten up the lobolo money that he received. What happens then is that the woman is obliged to stay where she is, suffering. (OMM iw, Zambézia province)

According to sources in the OMM, lobolo is now found in all provinces of the country, especially in the cities where the influence of modern life is strongest. Lobolo isn't exactly modern, but it goes along well with other trends of rising male dominance as a result of modernization.

Lobolo as an issue between generations

I have dealt with lobolo as indicating and influencing a new husband/wife relationship. But modern commercialized high-price lobolo has another consequence as well. It is very hard on young people, who cannot get married because the young men cannot raise these exorbitant amounts of money. This aspect is also mentioned frequently, and very strongly objected to, in the OMM discussions. 'Modern' lobolo, which started as a liberation of young men from the power of their fathers, has ended up putting a heavy burden on many a young man for years on end, making it impossible for them to get married and thus to start their own lives. Now, not just Joni-goers, but everyone, including students with no income, are expected to pay the lobolo themselves. A group of young people from Gaza have this comment:

> The lobolo undermines all of our principles, as before anything else we'll have to solve the problem of money, clothing, and various other articles for the lobolo, and only after that can we start thinking about the problems connected to the establishing of a home.(OMM iw, Gaza province)

When at last the lobolo has been paid the young people are absolutely broke, with no money to start living as a family. All this lobolo-business was especially severe in the early 1980s when all sorts of commodities were extremely scarce in Mozambique. At that time, getting hold of engagement rings, watches, suits, dresses, etc. for the lobolo demanded more than the usual skill and endeavour (most of it had to be obtained by smuggling from neighbouring countries). Amassing the lobolo under those circumstances could easily take years.

Traditional polygamy in the countryside

What about polygamy under the impact of modernization? In the countryside it has stayed largely the same. The men may go to the mines or do other migrant work, but the farming goes on as before. This is a major point in colonial exploitation: the peasants-turned-workers stay linked to the land; they are only semi-proletarianized. While the men are away working, the women are farming on the land. This arrangement keeps the wages down. First the wage doesn't have to cover the sustenance of the worker's family: wife and kids. The wife looks after that. And second, the wage of a seasonal worker doesn't even have to cover the survival of the worker himself when he is off work. The wife looks after that. The wage is thus not much more than food and board while working, and pocket money.

A Mozambican wage-earning husband was expected to send money home for *capulanas* and for clothes for his wife (and kids). Not for food. Food for the family is the responsibility of the woman. Under conditions of male paid work the demand on the woman for farming is intensified because she is now on her own, without the help from her husband that she previously would have had. Under such conditions polygamy may be very useful, as was shown above in the example from Magude district. In Gaza province they blame polygamy on the miners. They come home from Joni with their pockets filled with money, and they need wives to run their farms.

> Nowadays we are witnessing an increase in polygamy because of the situation of our country in this initial phase. Generally the major part of the polygamous men have been workers in the South African mines, as until now they have at least had minimal living conditions [i.e. they are less poor than anybody else] and thus they succeed in getting women. (OMM rep, Gaza province)
>
> Previously polygamy was encouraged by agriculture because the men wanted to have many wives in order to be able to grow lots of cotton and ground nuts. Today it is encouraged by the *majoni* (men who go to Johannesburg), as they have a lot of money and many goods that attract the attention of the girls. Many parents also need clothes and blankets. (OMM rep, Gaza province)

As I see it, there is no less reason for polygamy today in the countryside than before. And if there is more money (with the *majoni*) one should expect more polygamy. Unfortunately I have no statistics to show if this is the case. The church, of course, has been against polygamy all along, but apparently without much result. As long as the relations and means of production in the countryside (family farming based on female labour with hoes) do not, polygamy cannot really be expected to change.

Polygamy of the city: amantismo

The situation in the towns is clearly different. Here you cannot expand production by getting more wives. Land is of course very scarce. Many women do manage to make a small *machamba* in the backyard, along the road, or in the countryside a long way away. But the household economy in towns is much more explicitly based on wage labour. This means that economically women are much more dependent on men than they used to be in the countryside. The household pattern of nuclear families aggravates women's dependence.

Polygamy is no exception to this. The two wives rarely live together; rather it is two nuclear family setups with the husband going to and fro. Or to be more precise: polygamy in towns is what in Mozambican Portuguese is called *amantismo*: a married man has an *amante*, a mistress, somewhere else. A very common pattern is that the first wife is a 'traditional' housewife/peasant, cultivating a small plot of land somewhere. The 'second wife' however is a wage-earner. And she is not a proper wife. There was never a marriage, no lobolo has been paid. The 'second wife' is just an amante, a mistress.

When interviewing working women in Maputo in 1982 in one of the cashew factories, *Caju de Machava 1*, and in a biscuit factory, *Compania Industrial de Matola*, of the twenty women interviewed (randomly selected), fourteen were this kind of amantes: living on their own, in their own houses, but with an amante (a man) who had a first wife somewhere else. He would come and stay with them time and again, and they would often have children together. Many of these women suffered from not being proper wives. Some of them would be informally officialized, i.e. they would have been introduced to wife number one, and to the family of the husband. This is the desired situation, because this looks most like proper (polygamous) marriage. One woman complained:

> I don't know the other wife. She does know about me [this relation has lasted for two years, and has produced one child] but we have never met. I am not happy because I don't know if the other woman is happy. I wish our husband would introduce us. At the moment I feel on the road, I cannot be happy and relaxed yet about having a husband. (SA iw, Maputo)

Many first wives do accept the amante and treat her like a sister, as you are supposed to do in a proper polygamous setup in southern Mozambique: 'She is my sister because we share a husband'. But in other cases there is conflict and *barulho* (quarrels): hostility between the wives, jealousy, competition for the favours of the husband, etc. In other words, much more of the two-women-one-man situation that from a Western/European cultural background you would expect:

> Certain women-amantes do compete. When the husband turns up in the house of the amante he'll find hot water in the bathroom for his bath, a perfumed bed, etc. The amante can cook better food – chicken, fish – because she has money. The wife back home, who is waiting for the husband to come home, can only cook vegetables, she has got nothing else. (SA iw, Maputo)

Amantismo: Who benefits is the man

The situation of amantismo thus very easily turns into a man's privilege. It is he who profits from the setup and from the competition between the wives. He can play one woman off against the other, and he does so. In the 'polygamy of the city' there is no shared daily life and no work relation between the wives. They do not live together; they do not help each other. They may know (of) each other, but only indirectly, through the husband. They are not related as closely and importantly as are co-wives in the countryside, and thus the main advantage of polygamy seen from the women's point of view, has gone. 'In the countryside the women are united', the factory women said. This is not the case in towns. It seems to me that, much more than in traditional rural polygamy, the 'city polygamy'- women are exploited by men.

Accordingly the amantes/ 'second wives' feel insecure. Today is all right, but what about tomorrow? In marriage at least you do have certain guarantees: lobolo has been paid, divorce must be negotiated by the families. But in relations of amantismo the husband is bound by nothing. Any day he may disappear, leaving the 'second wife'/amante alone with kids and everything. It is certainly not by choice that she is not a proper wife:

It is my destiny not to marry, but it is not of my preference. How could it be? Destiny made it so. I have got three sons with three different men. I feel embarrassed because they don't have a father. It would have been better if the father had been dead. I never was lucky. If I succeeded in meeting a man that would marry me, I would marry right away, putting an end to this life of amantismo. (SA iw, Maputo)

If the amantes could marry, most of them would do so right away. Marriage is the known form of a proper, dignified, and reasonably secure woman's life. These women are economically independent. They work and are self-supporting, often with a number of children, and a sister or mother or cousin in the house to do the housework. In town you see the two-woman household with an absent husband, just as you do in the countryside. But socially they are not independent: they feel that in order to be a decent woman, they should be married, they should have a husband. And sexually/emotionally they need a man.

When I asked the working women/amantes, who were dissatisfied with their lives, why they preferred to have an amante-husband instead of living on their own, these were typical answers: 'The blood is running.' 'The blood demands sexual relations, I have to get myself a husband.' 'I am still young, I need a husband' (SA iw, Maputo).

Very few of the working women had come to a different conclusion: that they were better off without a man: 'I am not going to marry again. I don't want it at all. What did I gain from marriage? I can't see what would be the advantage of marriage.' 'Marry again? No, never. Having a husband just creates problems.' 'I like living on my own together with my children. The work to earn a daily living is enough for me' (SA iw, Maputo).

What are the trends for the future? A new identity is emerging among these wage-earning women. But so far it is kind of passive, withdrawing from men rather than fighting for a new type of gender relations, which are more on women's terms. The major trend of the change from traditional polygamy to 'modern' amantismo is a change in the gender balance clearly in direction of more male dominance and female dependence and submission. Again, the men seem to have gained by the change, whereas the women have lost.

The new family law put into practice in southern Mozambique

From the point of view of the law, lobolo doesn't exist. This means that the legal attitude applied to lobolo is *ignorância deliberada*, deliberate ignorance, as explained by Albie Sachs in an interview in the weekly Newspaper *Domingo*: 'One consequence of deliberate ignorance is for example that the courts cannot recognize any obligation of either payment or return of the lobolo' (Sachs 1984). So seen from the point of view of the law, lobolo is simply ignored. It is not criminalized and it is not legalized.

Lobolo – 'deliberate ignorance' which is: lobolo goes on
Campaigns against lobolo have always been on the political level. In the early 1980s *abaixo lobolo* (down with *lobolo*) was one of the basic slogans, used for warming up and finishing off almost any political meeting – along with: *abaixo*

polygamia; *abaixo ritos de iniciação*; *viva o Presidente Samora Moises Machel*; *a luta continua*; etc. Thus for a long time lobolo was considered one of the major indications of male dominance and female subordination in old-time Mozambique.

The introductory passage to the political resolutions resulting from the Second OMM Conference 1976 reads like this:

> ... Besides this system of [colonial] exploitation and oppression shared by the whole people, the Mozambican peasant woman is victim of a second form of oppression, originating in the traditional-feudal ideology. This ideology conceives of woman as having the role in society to serve the man, as an object of pleasure, as a procreator of offspring and as a worker without salary. ... This position of woman in society is reinforced through ceremonies and institutions such as initiation rituals, and the whole system of marriage: lobolo, premature and forced marriages, polygamy. (OMM 1977, 89)

Lobolo was plainly seen as *um mal social*, a social evil (OMM 1977, 95) and thus to combat lobolo was considered an important part of the fight for women's emancipation. The efforts, however, had little success. For a while lobolo went underground and/or changed name to *gratificação, anelamento* (gratification, putting on the ring) and others, but the content remained the same. And as mentioned above lobolo even spread to areas of Mozambique where previously (because of matrilineal kinship systems) there had been no lobolo. I see this spread as a consequence of increasing modernization: transformed, individualized lobolo supports expanding male dominance and husband power in gender relations. And these trends, combined of course with the esteem of lobolo from the old days, are stronger than ideological campaigns.

Compared to the early OMM conception of lobolo, and of the women's question as a whole, the nation-wide exchange of information and the discussions raised by the OMM Extraordinary Conference preparation campaign 1983–1984 caused a significant rise in political knowledge and consciousness about these matters. It was only now that it was realized (a) that lobolo was not the traditional way of marriage all over the country but only in the patrilineal South, and (b) that previously lobolo had had a different meaning, i.e. it was not just a commercial transaction with oppressed women as the traded goods. Compare this quote from the OMM Second Conference documents, expressing the early OMM conception of lobolo:

> Lobolo. This praxis exists in the whole country. ... It places the woman in a situation of total dependence on the man who – because he paid for her – may use her and discard her like a simple object. (OMM 1977, 94)

Consequently, the issue which, at the start of the OMM Conference preparation campaign was labelled lobolo, towards the end of the campaign was renamed *casamento tradicional* (traditional marriage). This term covers the whole country – in the south 'traditional marriage' is lobolo, in the north it is something else – and furthermore the term 'traditional marriage' is not derogatory, as lobolo had become with all the *abaixo*-campaigns. Compared to the Second Conference – quote above, what is said about lobolo in the *Resolução Geral* of the Extraordinary Conference (November 1984) is very sensible:

> About traditional marriage: Regarding traditional marriage the conference notes that this is the way in which the family is constituted for the majority of our people. ...
> Nevertheless, the Conference considers it necessary to combat with efficiency those

aspects of traditional marriage that reflect and transmit inequality between men and women and the subordination of the woman in the home and in society, such as: the aspect of commercialization which in the last decades and in some regions of the country has characterized the lobolo.(OMM 1984)

An overall result of the Extraordinary Conference preparation discussions was that now people – or at least the political structures – viewed 'old customs', such as lobolo and polygamy, much more as something linked up with particular ways of production and with the structure of society as such, i.e. that you could not change those things merely through a political campaign. This of course is an important insight.

However, this attitude has had the effect of nothing being done politically about lobolo. The law system continues to be 'ignorant', and as the *abaixo*-campaign has stopped (as a consequence of a higher level of knowledge and insight, showing that things are not as simple as that) the result, at least in the mid–1980s was that lobolo was flourishing. When I visited Maputo in the years shortly after the OMM Extraordinary Conference (in 1985 and 1987), when talking to women in the *bairros* and in the cooperatives I found a broad disappointment that no firm guidelines regarding the lobolo had resulted from the OMM Conference. From all over, it had been suggested that lobolo should be politically accepted, but with an upper limit of 2,500 meticais. But no action was taken by the OMM.

Polygamy. Ideology: Nuclear family with gender equality. Reality?

One major point in Frelimo/OMM policy and in the new family law, is the promotion and protection of the monogamous, nuclear family – man, wife and kids – as the 'basic cell of society'. Obviously 'the recognition of monogamous marriage is a way of combatting, albeit indirectly, polygamy' as Albie Sachs said in the interview in *Domingo*, October 1984. In the mid–1980s this monogamous, nuclear family – or 'socialist family' as it has also frequently been called by Frelimo and by the OMM – was in focus for political mobilization regarding women's issues. In the first years of Independent Mozambique Christmas was not a public holiday, as the State has no religion (however, if you declared yourself a Christian you were allowed to take December twenty-fifth off work). But in the early 1980s December twenty-fifth was made a public holiday, named *Dia da Família*, day of the family.

This nuclear family was expected to be based on 'freedom of choice, reciprocity and equality in the relation between the spouses' (Sachs 1984). In a small nice-looking pamphlet handed over to newlywed couples it is explained why the state protects marriage and the family and how married life should be:

> The family is the basic cell of our society. It is in the family that man and woman in the most profound and total way share all aspects of life, helping one another, respecting one another, understanding one another. It is in the family that the parents educate the new generations in an atmosphere of human warmth, love and care. ... Marriage is a union between a man and a woman with the intention of constituting a family, thus creating a community full of life, in equality of rights and duties between the two. Marriage is an act that is based exclusively on the free will of the two getting married. (Undated pamphlet: *casamento* (marriage))

The new nuclear family was expected to be everything that the old extended family had not been. Politically the old family was seen as a centre for exploitation and oppression. Suddenly and miraculously the new family was supposed to be exactly the opposite. There seems to be no end to the series of nice words attached to this vision of a new family. This is from the *Resolução Geral* of the Extraordinary OMM Conference 1984:

> The extraordinary OMM conference specifically emphasizes the vital importance of the cohesion, stability and harmony of the family, as this is the basic cell of our society. ... It is the forge of the new type of man, guaranteeing the interiorization of the new political, moral and civic values. ... The family should be a cell that educates to love, understanding, mutual respect and reciprocal help.(OMM 1984)

In actual fact, however, nuclear family life seems to increase gender conflicts. Previously in the 'old' kind of family setup men and women had had little intimacy (cf. Junod 1912/1974, 179), living each in their world together with other men/other women respectively. Husband and wife were not to any great extent directly exposed to one another. When the family structure changes with modernization (paid work, money economy, break-up of extended families, individualization, etc.) gender relations change as well. Husband and wife become much more directly exposed to one another, and in various ways in the modernization process men have gained the upper hand. All of this creates conflicts. As an example: Lobolo was not previously an issue of husband-wife contradictions. Now it is. Wife-beating is not uncommon. According to my sources it was much less frequent in the old days, if it occurred at all. In the new *aldeias comunais* (community villages, with nuclear family life) the women complain that they have many more quarrels with their husbands than before. Thus there seems to be a discrepancy, and quite a serious one, between the glossy ideology of family life and the realities. Ideology as expressed in the law stresses gender equality, mutual help, reciprocity, etc. In reality, however, very different things are going on. In talking about polygamy, a similar discrepancy can be observed. Polygamy is illegal. A man cannot officially and legally marry two wives. What does he do? He marries one of them legally, keeping the other one as an amante. This is certainly no better seen from the women's point of view. It looks as if, with modernization and promoted by political ideology and the new family law, ideology becomes nicer to women, whereas reality becomes harsher.

The law was intended as a tool to protect women (among others), but it cannot do the job alone, without an organization to put it into practice. As a matter of fact the women in the *bairros* of Maputo, when I interviewed them in early 1982, were very interested in legalizing their marriage relations, because they saw it as a protection in disputes with their men. Generally, however, the men didn't want to – and so the women were stuck. An article in *Justiça popular* makes the same observation: 'There is a tendency for the women to want a marriage certificate as a guarantee for the future, whereas the men see the same thing as an obstacle to their liberty' (Sachs & Uate 1984).

A similar thing is true of the rights of unwed or divorced mothers to get alimony for their children, paid by the fathers. This is done by the State withholding a part of the man's salary and handing it over to the woman. Many of the women, however, do not know how to approach the court or how to present their case. Some do not even know their rights. And in some cases, even when the woman succeeds in putting her case to court, in the meantime the man has quit his job, thus escaping payment.

To sum up: family law supports an ideology of gender equality, reciprocity and freedom of choice as basic principles in the establishing of a family, that is a monogamous nuclear one. By promoting the nuclear family the law pulls in the same direction as the economic, political and religious changes in the process of modernization. By stressing gender equality, the law marks a difference from old-time Mozambique where gender equality was not an issue. Men and women were different, linked in complementary interdependence, but not to be measured with the same rod. By stressing gender equality, however, the law also marks a difference from the social consequences of contemporary economic and other trends, which are making women still more dependent on and subordinate to men. This second difference results in a quite remarkable discrepancy between the law and adjacent ideology on one hand, and women's realities on the other. The law is supposed to support women, but it does so only to a limited extent, because a network or an organization to support women in practical matters is lacking (like helping them to bring their case to court, or putting effective social pressure on men to legalize their marriage-like relations). The OMM, officially the women's organization, has not been doing this kind of thing, because even though it supports the ideology of gender equality, it does not recognize gender conflicts as being unavoidable on the way to this goal. Neither does it recognize women's need of practical support in such gender conflicts.

Family forms in northern Mozambique

South and north in Mozambique are in many ways two different worlds, for two major reasons. First: the traditional kinship systems are different: patriliny in the south, matriliny in the north (as a general rule).[16] And second: the impact of modernization (so far) has also been different. Money economy and paid work have been integrated into daily life in the south much more than they have in the north. In discussing family forms the differences are striking: Matrilineal and patrilineal family structures are different to start off with, and furthermore they have reacted differently to the modernizing impact – which in itself has also been different in the north as compared to the south (cf. Chapter 2). As a consequence the intended gender equality of the new family law has had very different impacts, in the north as compared to the south.

Traditional marriage by bride service: Pette
An important characteristic of matrilinity and matrilocality – in most places in northern Mozambique they go together – is the fact that when two young people marry it is the woman who stays with her family: her parents and her mother's

---

[16] Two of the important ethnic groups of northern Mozambique are the Makonde and the Makhuwa. Both are matrilineal. The Makonde live in northern Cabo Delgado (and in Tanzania). The Makhuwa cover a vast area from southern Cabo Delgado, all over Nampula and northern Zambezia. The Makhuwa are by far the largest of the Mozambican matrilineal ethnic groups. The third important matrilineal group in Mozambique is the Yao living mainly in Niassa.

brothers and sisters, whereas the man has to move. He has to build a house for his wife on her family's land, and that is where the couple will live after marriage. Marriage is unceremonial, at least compared to the complicated ceremonies of lobolo in the south, and it may be easily dissolved by the husband or by the wife, whoever feels dissatisfied by the relationship. After divorce the woman stays on in the house, near her family, with the kids (who belong to the mother's lineage and are under the tutelage of her eldest brother). The man is the one to move out. In this family structure there is no lobolo to be paid back as a condition of divorce. Before marriage it is customary, in parts of the north, for the husband-to-be to stay one year with his parents-in-law, working on their land. This is called *pette.*

This is how is was explained in Zambézia:

> Here the lobolo is found in the following way: Every young man who thinks of marriage must construct a hut close to that of the parents-in-law and accept that he will be used by them as cheap labour. He also must accept that the girl is supervised by her parents, so as to avoid maltreatment by the husband. The newlyweds do not have anything for their survival, so they need help. They can only leave from there when they have had a child. The man is obliged to live at the parents-in-law's place, working with them until the young couple succeed in having a child to hand over to the parents-in-law to help them in the home. Thus the parents-in-law will choose a piece of land for the son-in-law to construct his hut and make his own life, for now they have the opportunity of seeing what he is like. And if the man is lazy or a bad guy, or haughty, the parents-in-law will simply send him away. (OMM rep, Zambézia province)

Pette is therefore not a 'bride price', but a *bride service.* In both cases it is the man-to-be-married who must render something, but the 'bride price' gives him rights to the offspring from marriage, and rights to a new wife from the same family if no children result from the first relationship, while the bride service gives nothing of this. Nor does it represent a value to be returned to the husband upon divorce. The pette is just the new son-in-law helping his parents-in-law, and while he is doing so they have an opportunity to see if they like him and if he works well. This aspect of trial is found at the marriage ceremony as well. The old women will collect the sperm from his first ejaculation, testing it to see if it promises procreation. For the first year or so of marriage the newlywed couple lives close to the woman's family for them to see if the new in-law behaves well and if they get on well together. If there is dissatisfaction the marriage may be undone. Otherwise the young couple moves to a different place somewhat further away, starting their own life together.

This structure is indeed very different from the patrilineal one. It is simpler, because the women are placed at the centre. Biological fatherhood doesn't matter all that much. The children belong to their matrilineage in any case. The major function of husbands is as procreators. Where men exercise male authority is not in relation to their own offspring, but in relation to their sisters' children, their nephews and nieces. There is a rationale of placing women at the centre of an agricultural society, based on women's work in production as cultivators and in reproduction as the ones that bear the children. Mozambican anthropologist Eduardo Medeiros explains:

> As agriculture was based principally on female work, in matrilineal society it would be the group of sisters who constituted the stable, productive centre, in direction of

which the men had to move. Consequently, in these societies there was no need for an organized and non-violent circulation of women for marriage reasons. The marriage ceremonies were very simple, and divorce also more frequent. Anyhow, the young man had to prove that he was a good worker and that he would be a good husband. ... In return the young man acquired the status of a married man, a father, etc. (Medeiros 1985a, 22)

For good reasons in this society, girls are seen as more precious than boys. Meillassoux (1975/1981) has some interesting observations about matriliny *vs.* patriliny. I quote:

In the first case [matriliny] women live in their original communities, to which men are invited to procreate and eventually live. Such a system could be classified as gynae-costatic: the reproduction of the group rests entirely on the reproductive capacities of the women born within the group. In the second case [patriliny] women, exchanged on a reciprocal basis, do not procreate within their community but in an allied community which recovers the progeny. Reproduction depends on the political capacities of the communities to negotiate an adequate number of women at all times. These two kinds of circulation are not equally efficient since they play on the different reproductive functions of the two sexes. Man's ability to inseminate is practically unlimited, but any man can do, while woman's procreative potential is only equal to the length of her fertile period divided by the length of the periods of gestation and breast-feeding – frequently extended by cultural restrictions.

During this gestation period the symbiosis between the mother and her child creates an entity which is strictly *sui generis*. In other words, in terms of procreative capacities, men are expendable; each pregnant woman is unique in her kind (Meillassoux ibid., 24–25).

Meillassoux goes on to explain how this difference in relation to the absolutely essential procreative capacities: men expendable, women unique – is the reason for the transformation of original matrilineal societies into patrilineal ones. He may be right, or he may not. In any case, matriliny is not his concern; what interests him is patriliny, based on the political capacities of men (as subjects) to negotiate exchange of women (as objects).

Even in the matriliny of northern Mozambique, however, men are the masters. The big bosses here are the matrilineal chiefs, the powerful masters of large groups of sisters and nephews and their offspring. Preferential marriage, at least for the eldest son, is with his cross cousin, i.e. with the uncle's daughter. So the big man lives with his daughters married to his nephews around him.

Poligamia errante: Travelling polygamy
According to Medeiros, who has studied in particular the matrilineal Makhuwa of northern Mozambique, polygamy here, in the old days, was uncommon, except for these chiefs, who then would break the general rule of matrilocality and have their wives gathered around them. This was 'the polygamy of the chiefs, to whose houses every allied or subordinated lineage would send a wife' (Medeiros 1985a, 24). Polygamy for commoners typically would have the form of *poligamia errante,* travelling polygamy: the polygamous man would have a wife here, another there, the wives living in their family-villages, and he himself would travel from one to the other, spending some days in each place, helping the woman on her *machamba.* It is a strict rule for polygamy in the north that the wives must be treated equally. Here you don't have the system of the first wife

as the big one, the following being lesser wives. On the contrary, the husbands' failure to treat all of their wives equally was – and is – a cause of bitter complaint from the women.

Polygamy over the years has become more frequent than it used to be (Medeiros 1985b, 32). When I was interviewing women in Cabo Delgado in 1982, polygamy was not at all uncommon in the north of the province (with the Makonde) and more frequent than in the south of the province (with the Makhuwa). Of 231 recorded marriages dispersed all over Cabo Delgado, 78 were polygamous (34 per cent). In 1979 the Centre of African studies (CEA) at the Eduardo Mondlane University was studying four aldeias comunais in the province of Nampula and found a polygamy-rate from 5 per cent (most frequently) to 28 per cent (in one of the villages) (CEA 1980, 19).

The women of the north dislike polygamy ...
As a general rule the women of the north do not like polygamy at all. Unlike in the south under conditions of patriliny, where polygamy may ease women's lives, as they get a companion with whom to share work and leisure, in the north, where the women live dispersed they cannot profit in this way from polygamy. Not only can they not profit from polygamy. They detest it. This was really my impression when I talked to the women in Cabo Delgado. They were all complaining about polygamy and divorce (issues of divorce will be discussed later). These are typical women's interventions from Cabo Delgao discussing polygamy:

> Polygamy is much more frequent now than it used to be. Now men consider it normal to marry two-three women; but for the wife this means suffering, as she'll get nothing. The husband's money must be divided, and his time as well. A man who has several wives may stay away for five or six days without appearing in the house of one wife. He stays somewhere else. (SA iw, Cabo Delgado province)
>
> Polygamy hurts. The man marries three-four women, but you only have a real marriage in one of the houses. The others are just to show off. (SA iw, Cabo Delgado province)
>
> Yes, we suffer. The husband buys meat, he buys capulana, and you feel that this would be for you, if it weren't for this other wife. All these goods that he has bought go to the other house. (SA iw, Cabo Delgado province)
>
> The husband goes to the other house while you are cooking the food you should eat together. He stays away all day. This is what I don't like. My husband prefers this other woman, he has stopped eating the food I cook. (SA iw, Cabo Delgado province)
>
> My husband got himself a wife from another village. I had a white capulana, but my husband snatched it one night and gave it to her. And on the following day he went to the field to cut peas for this other woman. When I arrived in the field all the peas had gone. My husband is still staying with this other woman. The house I have got here is no good, it is falling to pieces, but my husband doesn't care [Keeping the house in order is the job of the man]. (SA iw, Cabo Delgado province)

... but the men defend it
The men, however, see matters very differently. They like polygamy and as usual, they have got a series of arguments in favour of it. What if the wife falls ill? Who then is going to cook for them? Or what if she dies? Besides, there is always the argument of women being more plentiful than men. This may be so to a very limited extent – according to the 1980 census the masculinity-rate is 94.5

– but certainly not enough to justify polygamy. Nevertheless the idea of a strong female surplus is a very persistent myth, presumably because it makes the men feel benevolent and self-sacrificing when they are polygamous. They just do it to help the poor women who otherwise wouldn't have had a husband. In the patrilineal south the (supposed) infertility of the first wife is a standard argument for getting a second one. This argument for obvious reasons is less frequent in the matrilineal north.

In several of the public discussion meetings during the OMM conference preparation period that I myself attended in the north, the audience would be clearly divided on this issue into men *for*, and women *against* polygamy, and fierce arguments would fly from one group to the other. Men in the provinces of Nampula and Zambézia argued like this:

> Polygamy to us is like an ulcer which is an incurable illness. Whenever we see a single woman from our region, our heart jumps and we feel a necessity to conquer her, and that is the way we become polygamous. (OMM iw, Nampula province)
> The reason for polygamy in this area is that the men are keen to get hold of more women to love them more intimately and also because the men want to experience the differences between one woman and another one. Because there are woman who wear *missangas* (a string of glass beads), who have got tattoos, and who have elongated lips of the vagina. (OMM rep, Nampula province)
> Reason for polygamy: The men have ambitions with other women, are attracted by the tattoos they have on their legs. (OMM rep, Zambézia province)
> When a woman has given birth and during the whole time she is breastfeeding the child she cannot have sexual relations with the husband. This is two years. And as the husband must satisfy his biological needs, he'll have to get himself another wife. (OMM iw, Nampula province)
> It may happen that the wife is ill and in this case the man will have nobody to fetch his water or to prepare his meals. It is in this situation that he comes upon the idea of getting himself another wife in order to avoid suffering.(OMM iw, Zambézia province)
> To marry two women is like having two arms or two legs, because if one is damaged or ruined the other one can work. To marry more than two women, that is what is bad for society.(OMM rep, Tete province)
> Polygamy shouldn't be exaggerated. It should be limited to just two women.(OMM rep, Zambézia province)

But the women know how to answer. Their opinion is a different one:

> Polygamy should be opposed. Whoever wants polygamy should make sure they have one penis for each woman.(OMM iw, Zambézia province)
> We should bring an end to polygamy because the man has got just one penis.(OMM rep, Zambézia province)
> Those who support polygamy are the men, because they want to annoy the women. For instance: A woman will wake up in the morning, she will go and fetch water, she will cook, the husband will eat well and sleep well, but anyhow, the following day he will marry another wife. This really is a pain in the ass.(OMM iw, Zambézia province)
> If it really was a question of helping the other wife who is ill, why do we women not demand the same thing? Some of us do have husbands who are ill, but we have never done the same thing as the men, nor would we ever think of doing so.(OMM iw, Zambézia province)

This last argument is very interesting because it takes as the point of departure a possible equality between women and men: the men do so and so. What if we, as women, did the same? Why is it an argument on their side, for polygamy, when it doesn't count for us, for women? I see this way of thinking as new in Mozambique and I suspect that previously it would have occurred to no one to argue like that. But actually this type of argument, based on a notion of gender equality, did appear now and again during the conference preparation discussions, all over Mozambique, in the countryside as well as in the cities.

Another argument is interesting too, because it uses the very process of modernization as a cause for polygamy. The man feels more developed than his backward wife, and this forces him to take a second wife, a more presentable one. It is a man speaking, of course:

> It is the wife herself who forces a man to become polygamous. The man may not want to be so. But if the woman is filthy and lazy ... you may buy her a dress, she doesn't put it on, she stays in the dirt, she doesn't even wash, nor does she wear a bra; when she is pounding her breasts almost fall into the mortar. The husband will want to escape from all of this; he will go to the other woman. There he'll find a clean house, a fragrant woman, food that is well prepared. He'll go there with his friend, and he'll be very pleased. This is the reason that the man forgets about his first wife. Sometimes it will be because the wife does not know how to embrace her husband in bed and give him that kind of caresses that makes him feel like making love. (OMM iw, Zambézia province)

In spite of women's protests, however, polygamy is becoming more frequent in the north of Mozambique. Maybe because modernization as such tends to favour male positions?

Women losing traditional rights: Divorce

Another area where women in the north are losing out is in the field of divorce. Previously divorce was easy for both parties. The making and unmaking of marriage did not matter that much because affiliation followed the mother. Thus, if for some reason a marriage went wrong, or was less pleasing to the husband or the wife, it would be abolished without much ado. This wasn't considered a tragedy, and it didn't have any very negative consequences for the children either, as Dias & Dias (1970) point out:

> Contrary to what happens in Western society, divorces [by the Makonde] are far from having serious consequences for the children of a discordant couple. Life in an extended family creates an atmosphere of tranquility and joy that will extinguish the consequences of any divorce. The children have many other women and men whom they are used to considering as mothers and fathers. All the other children of the village are their playmates and life goes on without the children of a divorced couple feeling any consequences of the dissolution of their parents' marriage. (Dias & Dias 1970, 267)

And actually the facility of divorces is one obvious reason for the low rate of polygamy in Nampula and elsewhere under conditions of matriliny. It is very simple: The men like polygamy, the women don't. When the man starts arranging a second wife, the first woman opts out of the marriage, i.e. she tells the man to stay away. She will be the one to remain in the house and with the children anyway.

The inverted relation between polygamy and divorce emerged very clearly from the data I gathered in Cabo Delgado 1982. In the area where there was the lowest rate of polygamy (in the southern part of coastal Cabo Delgado), the divorce rate was the highest. And vice versa. Accordingly, the most common reason for the women to want divorce was that the husband had taken another wife. In the course of 120 interviews I asked the previously married women about who had taken the initiative to divorce, and why. In 33 per cent of the cases of divorce registered in the entire data material (from the whole province), the women would state the man's inclination for another woman as the cause for divorce. Other major causes for the women to want divorce would be that the man did not treat them well, that he didn't work well, or that there was no love in the relationship. This is what some of the women said regarding polygamy and divorce:

> If the husband has got another woman that he would like to marry, he'll let the first one suffer to such a degree that at last she'll want divorce, saying 'Go then and stay with that other woman'. (SA iw, Cabo Delgado province)
> Divorce is a major problem, as the husbands like to have two wives. The new one will be the better one [seen from the husbands point of view], and the first one will ask for divorce. (SA iw, Cabo Delgado province)
> Divorce in fact is often linked to polygamy in that the husband starts living with another woman. Sometimes the first wife will want her husband to return home to her, but often she'll want to get rid of him. However, she wants to be sure of her rights to keep the house. (SA iw, Cabo Delgado province)

The current problem in this context, and one of the reasons why polygamy has increased, is that this traditional attitude to divorce is being opposed by the new legal authorities. Frelimo wants to protect the family and is not at all fond of divorce. This is complicated: According to the PLF, divorce is a legal right, but the general political position of Frelimo is *for* family stability and *against* divorce. Frelimo is also against polygamy – but in a situation (as in southern Cabo Delgado) where women use divorce to fight polygamy, Frelimo supports the polygamous men, castigating the women who want divorce. A strict line against divorces and permissiveness in relation to polygamy was what was presented to me, when in 1982 I interviewed the *Juiz Presidente* in Pemba (i.e. the top judge of the provincial court):

> Marriage is very easygoing here, this is because of the way the women are brought up, they don't see marriage as something very important. These old women *conselheiras* tell them 'you do not have to stay with a particular husband if he is no good (in bed). If things go badly, just leave your husband'. By thirty years of age these women may be on their third or fourth marriage. This is because of the woman; it is not because of the man. For example, if a new capulana appears in the market and the husband hasn't got the money to buy it, this is a reason for divorce! Divorces here are caused by the women. ... The attitude of the court to polygamy depends on economy. If the man has the possibility of supporting two women, we don't see polygamy as an evil. (SA iw, Cabo Delgado province)

The position of the *Juiz Presidente* is obviously male. He himself doesn't see it as such, however. He embodies Frelimo. The women are described as immoral and unreasonable, selfish, spoilt, demanding, etc. The major critique seem to be that they are brought up not to put up with an unhappy marriage. Certainly these women do not know their place! That they might have good reasons for wanting divorce does not occur to the *Juiz Presidente*, and even less that polygamy should have anything to do with it. On the contrary, according to the *Juiz Presidente*, polygamy is acceptable if the man can afford it. Officially this is the voice of the law. It is also the voice of male power.

In addition to polygamy, divorce was the big issue in the group discussions with women in Cabo Delgado in the 1982 investigation. The women were concerned and enraged because of the Frelimo line against divorce, which they rightly saw as a serious limitation of their room for manoeuvre. They did not hesitate to interpret it as male gender struggle, and it had not started with Frelimo either. The present line was a neat continuation of developments under Portuguese colonial rule. But it had worsened since Independence.

This is how it was explained to me by women in meetings in Montepuez, in Ilha de Ibo and in Mueda, i.e. all over Cabo Delgado. The statements are made by different women, supporting one another:

> In the old days divorce was very easy. Most divorces were caused by the men. The man went to stay with another woman, his wife asked him questions, and when he didn't answer, the wife got furious and at once asked for a divorce. At that time it was you, the woman, who would remain in the house; if the man wanted to go, he could go, he would make himself another house. For the married woman it was very easy. She would stay in her house, with her family, personal belongings would be divided and the man would leave. (SA iw, Cabo Delgado province)

> In colonial time, when a woman wanted to divorce, she would go to her family, and then the woman and her uncle would go to the *régulo*. He would say: 'Call for your husband'. The husband would bring a chicken and a goat for the régulo, so that the divorce would not be complicated. And then the régulo would say: 'All of the things in the house go to the husband'. If the woman's family was one of great power the woman's uncle would go to the régulo with a goat etc. and so the régulo would tell the husband to divide the things of the house with the woman. The régulo liked people to marry because whenever that happened a tax had to be paid to him. (SA iw, Cabo Delgado)

> In colonial times it wasn't as bad as it is now. If the woman left the marriage in a decent way, the couple's belongings would be divided between the two. But today the men exploit the women more and more. The woman is thrown out of the house, in compensation she just gets money, and what is she supposed to do with that? The woman doesn't know what to do, she doesn't know how to cut bamboo, she doesn't know how to cut poles, she doesn't know how to build a house. She sits there with the money [This was in the period of extreme scarcity of goods and abundance of useless money]. (SA iw, Cabo Delgado province)

> The court passes judgments in the husband's favour. When it is the men who ask for divorce the court will accept it right away, and the men do not have to go to re-education. But if the man beats his wife and she then goes to the court to ask for a divorce, she will be sent to the village prison for three–four months, after which she is told to go back to her husband. When the man leaves the woman, he will take with him all of the things in the house, even the capulanas of his wife. She is left with nothing. (SA iw, Cabo Delgado Province)

> This type of divorce got worse after Independence. If it is the man to divorce the woman the man will not be punished. But if it is the woman who starts, she will be given rough treatment, they will bind her by the arms, and she will be ordered to do forced work in the village. I think that when it is the man who leaves the woman he too should be punished and go to prison, but this doesn't happen. (SA iw, Cabo Delgado province)

> We women just cannot tolerate the way men behave. When we had Independence, Frelimo prohibited polygamy, but judging from the way men behave, it looks as if Frelimo was giving orders to continue with polygamy. The first among them are the Secretaries of the villages and bairros, they are the ones who take the lead, marrying three, four, five women. We women are growing thin and haggard of all these problems with the men. (SA iw, Cabo Delgado province)

Of course you can doubt the objectivity of these statements, which were all given at meetings where no, or very few, men were present and where the women could thus freely support one another. But you cannot doubt that this is how the women feel. They very clearly and undoubtedly feel that their conditions of life and their position vis-à-vis the men have changed for the worse since Independence, and quite seriously so.

The impact of the new family law in the north and in the south

Taken together, the consequences of the implementation of the new family law turn out to be very different from the intentions. The law is supposed to promote gender equality and women's emancipation. Nevertheless, the ways in which it is put into practice tend to support male power and to undermine what power positions women might have had in matrilineal contexts (such as the facility of divorce). In actual fact the very promotion of the nuclear family supports the men vis-à-vis the women. 'The children should know their father' as the argument goes. Nuclear families with husband, wife and children in a stable unit break up the extended families based on matrilineal relations, with women in central positions. Women have central positions in matriliny, among other things because the male chiefs owe their positions to their relationships with women. The pivotal male/female relationship is brother/sister, not husband/wife. Where brother/sister relationships are central, the women tend to have a stronger social position than where husband/wife relationships are the important ones (Sacks 1979). In a nuclear family, however, the brother/sister relationship has little importance; what matters is husband/wife.

In the south of Mozambique, where the women have all sorts of difficulties if they want to get out of a particular marriage – the lobolo that must be paid back, etc. – the new law is, or at least it may be, an improvement. The women in the patrilineal south are in a weaker position than the men. With the new law their position may be strenghtened, but not automatically. Even when the letter of the law talks about gender equality, it often happens that the women come out as losers. Not because the law is on the side of the men, but because men often know more about how to behave in court, e.g. how important it is to get proper witnesses to speak on your behalf. The women are socially weaker than men, and this may easily undermine the nice intentions of the law[17] – as long as the women are not organizationally supported. Thus, even in the patrilineal south where the law is of potential advantage to the women, in actual practice the women often come out as losers.

In the north the situation of the women vis-à-vis the law is even worse. In the matrilineal north the law itself contributes to the undermining of women's social positions, and even more so does the way in which it is administered. In the north, because of matriliny and matrilocality the women did have social and economic positions – as family elders, as controllers of food, as the ones

---

[17] In 1983, at one point while working in the OMM, I made an analysis of divorce suits in the Provincial Courts of Maputo province. It was striking how frequently the women lost the case just because the men were smarter and more experienced in dealing with a public authority such as a Provincial Court.

with access to land – that could compensate for the political power of the men. There are several advantages in women's position in the north as compared to the south: upon marriage the woman stays with her own people, it is the husband who is the newcomer and the stranger – and who is treated as such. If no children result from the marriage, the first assumption is that it is the man who has the problem. Accordingly he will be sent back to where he came from and replaced with another man.[18] All of this has produced a certain gender balance in the matrilineal north – potentially, one should think, a very good basis for further work for women's emancipation – i.e. the development of women in new directions, mastering new skills, looking to new horizons.

This, however, is not what happens. On the contrary, the women are pushed back, squeezed into the 'stable, nuclear family' where on the level of political ideology the genders are supposed to be 'equal', while in actual fact it is taken for granted that the *chefe da família* is the man. This is clearly stated in the *Resolução Geral* from the extraordinary OMM conference 1984: 'The family should be based on the equality of rights and responsibilities, and on the fulfillment of the functions of each of its members, the father as head of the family, the wife as mother and housewife...' (OMM 1984). Presumably the authors of the resolution don't even see the contradiction. The duality of an ideology of gender equality combined with taken-for-granted male supremacy is similar to conceptions of gender in Christian ideology, as put by Charles Biber: 'Woman is equal to man before God. But on Earth, man is the master' (Biber 1987, 30).

The OMM as well as Frelimo are unable (or unwilling?) to see women's stronger positions under conditions of matriliny. To them the norm and the point of departure for talking about 'gender equality' and 'women's emancipation' is patriliny – as a matter of course. Family law was also created with patriliny in mind. Even if half the country was known to be matrilineal at the time when the major principles of the family law were codified as guidelines for the courts, the consequences of this difference were not considered.

Presumably and unfortunately, however, this is not just a question of lack of knowledge. Modern law anywhere is based on assumptions of patriliny. The process of modernity itself promotes patriliny and undermines female power. The nuclear family is a central factor. Wage earning is another one. In a place like Mozambique, the wage earners (with a few exceptions) are men, while the ones who remain on the land growing food are women. The increased importance of the money economy means increased male power. Christian ideology talks nicely of women's liberation, but in practice it supports male dominance. Socialist ideology does the same. And thus, notwithstanding a new family law with the best intentions of gender equality and women's emancipation, what in actual fact happens – because of the implementation of the law, not in spite of it – is increasing male dominance, especially in the northern parts of the country. The ideology may sound better for women but reality does indeed become harsher.

[18] The matriliny of northern Mozambique is beautifully documented and analysed by Christian Geffray (1990) in his book *Ni Père, Ni Mère*. I only came to know this book after having finalized the chapter.

4 Simone de Beauvoir in Africa: Woman – the Second Sex?

Issues in African Feminist Thought   (2000)

Woodcut by Matias Mtundu Mzaanhoka

In an interview in 2000, Toril Moi, a distinguished figure in the contemporary relaunching of Simone de Beauvoir, confirms that there are two major ideas in de Beauvoir's *The Second Sex*. One idea is that 'one is not born, but rather becomes, a woman'. The other is that 'in all known societies, woman has always been looked upon as 'the other'" (Larsen 2000, 82). This paper sets out to question and investigate the second statement. Is it really true that in all known societies woman is and has always been looked upon as 'the other', the second sex? Looked upon – by whom? Does it have to be so forever? That 'woman equals the second sex' is a firmly grounded idea in the Western world is not up for discussion. But what about other parts of the world? What about Africa? The point of the discussion is not empirical. The point is not to show whether places do exist where this a priori othering of women does not occur. The point is to open the mind to different ways of thinking about gender, and for different ways of analyzing gender relations. Freeing ourselves from old mindsets will allow us to envision new kinds of gender relations as we look toward the future – both the future of Africa and the future of ourselves as Western women (and men).

Post-Enlightenment thinkers have described women's position in all ages and in all places according to their own androcentric models, models which subordinate women. In this way, concepts rooted in the time and space of the thinker him/herself have been universalized. In mainstream Western feminist thought and in Gender-and-Development policies, the idea that women are universally subordinated is still very strong. The argument in this chapter is not that subordination of women does not take place. Of course it does, and increasingly so, and clearly, subordination and oppression of women should be fought against. The argument concerns lines of thinking and analysis: how and from which vantage points, in what kinds of theoretical/conceptual contexts, are women's lives conceived and conceptualized? And what consequences does this have for strategy and politics?

When I take my point of departure in Simone de Beauvoir's work, is it (a) because she very early and very decisively hammered the point of woman as 'the other', and (b) because in the last few years Simone de Beauvoir's work has been enjoying a revival, which I find most undue. It is one thing to honour de Beauvoir for her brave and pioneering work in 1949. It is quite another to exalt her as a model thinker and source of inspiration now, fifty years later, when so much has happened in the world *and* in the field of feminist thought, including the rich influx of non-Western feminist thinking.

In her paper 'Histories of a Feminist Future', Elizabeth Grosz (2000) provides some lines of thinking which run parallel to my own. Where I want to introduce new lines of thinking in order to allow for reanalysis of African (and other) gendered realities, she talks about the need for feminist reinterpretations of history, in order to be able to develop perspectives for different futures. It is all about interpretations. Reality exists, but the ways in which this reality is interpreted are decisive for the ways in which strategies for the future can be developed. According to Grosz:

> It is the present that writes the past rather than – as positivist historiography has it – the past that gives way to the present. This is not to say that the present is all that is left of the past; quite the contrary, the past contains the resources to much more than

the present. Rather, it is only the interests of the present that serve to vivify or invigorate the past. (Grosz 2000, 1019)

Grosz is writing about 'positivist historiography', but she could be describing classical social science, including structuralism and Marxism, where 'traditional societies' are seen exclusively as pre-stages for 'modernity'. When non-Western societies are interpreted afresh, they can be seen to 'contain resources to much more than the present', that is to much more than the notion of Western-style modernity as the only possible goal of development. I propose to investigate this idea specifically in the field of gender relations.

Grosz too deals with gender relations. Inspiration for imagining different gender relations may be found in the past, she says: 'The past – a past no longer understood as inert or given – may help engender a productive future, a future beyond patriarchy. ... Feminist history ... enables other virtual futures to be conceived, other perspectives to be developed, than those that currently prevail' (Grosz 2000, 1018–19). Such inspiration may be found in the past – or in Africa, or elsewhere. It all depends on ways of seeing – which again, of course, depend on language and concepts and on relations of power. Nevertheless it *is* possible – and necessary – to develop alternative lines of thinking. Grosz again: 'I am interested in clearing a conceptual space such that an indeterminable future is open to women ... A future yet to be made is the very lifeblood of political struggle, the goal of feminist challenge' (Grosz 2000, 1017).

I am also interested in 'clearing a conceptual space' so that other futures become possible. A future yet to be made is the very lifeblood of political struggle. The point of the following critical discussion regarding 'woman – the second sex?' is to open the imagination for different and more liveable feminist futures than the ones now on offer, embedded in the notions of modernity and development.

The gaze of modernity: Woman as the other

Just like positivist historiography, which interprets the past in its own image, so in a similar way modernity – including modern social science – has interpreted gender relations in non-Western (pre-modern) societies as *lacking* and *incomplete* as compared to the edition of 'gender equality' which Western society sees as the apex of development as far as gender relations are concerned.

Modernity has many faces. For instance, in a country like Mozambique, the modernity of Portuguese colonialism by independence in 1975 was replaced by the modernity of Frelimo socialism, this again in the late 1980s being replaced by the World Bank-monitored neo-liberal market economy, which is still in vogue in the new millennium. These different editions of modernity – in spite of their evident divergences – nevertheless share a number of basic assumptions, three of the most important ones being the following:

(a) They share the firm position of the male subject. A human being is a man, the male position is believed to be gender neutral. In this context woman becomes 'the other'.

(b) They share the basic paradigm of a uni-linear development from 'tradition' to 'modernity', with the Western so-called 'developed world' serving as the model for achievement.

(c) They share the conception of African women (and third world women in general) as being particularly oppressed and subordinated – and thus potential and hopefully grateful receivers of the blessings of modernity.

Thus, embedded in the uni-linear and pre-packed notion of development is a pre-packed conception of gender relations: Woman as *the other*, as universally subordinated, and third world women as subordinated par excellence. The general idea is that women's subordination belongs to tradition and to the past, whereas women's emancipation – or gender equality, as the current terminology has it – belongs to modernity and to the future.

Simone de Beauvoir and 'the gaze of modernity'

Simone de Beauvoir's thinking fits into this pattern. She protests against female subordination – but nevertheless she thinks along these very lines, interpreting the past in the light of the present, and casting women's future in the model of men's. When in the following sections I present a reading of Simone de Beauvoir's *The Second Sex*, my concern is not Simone de Beauvoir's thinking in its own right, with its ambivalences and tensions, as much as it is Simone de Beauvoir as a spokesperson – a clever and very insightful spokesperson – for points of view rooted in the basic assumptions listed above. I do not say that all of de Beauvoir's work represents commonplace modernist thinking. De Beauvoir is a sophisticated and original thinker, and her work is anything but commonplace, especially considering the time when it was written. My point is that several of the unspoken assumptions on which her work is based are shared by other lines of thinking of her time, and even of today. Thus by digging out implicit assumptions of her work, points may be made regarding otherwise hidden aspects of the general assumptions taken for granted in broader trends of 'modern' and 'development' thinking regarding gender.

Simone de Beauvoir writes from and into a socialist tradition. By 1949, when *The Second Sex* was published, the United States had replaced the Soviet Union in her view as the land of hope and glory for women's emancipation. *The Second Sex* was written partly while the author was romantically involved with the Chicago writer Nelson Algren. De Beauvoir's visits to the United States are reflected in the book, especially in the last part, where she talks about the promising prospects of modernity as most developed in the US: wage work and contraception (de Beauvoir 1949/1997, 689, 705). Regarding women's emancipation, according to de Beauvoir, 'things have begun to change only recently' (de Beauvoir 1949/1997, 21). With implicit reference to the United States she proclaims that 'the free woman is just being born' (de Beauvoir 1949/1997, 723). The line of thinking is as follows: Woman is enslaved by being 'a victim of the species' (de Beauvoir 1949/1997, 52). This enslavement is expressed most clearly and inescapably in her capacity for procreation (de Beauvoir 1949/1997, 57, 705). Furthermore she (or the European middle-class women whose lives as described in literature and social science de Beauvoir draws upon for illustration of her points) is dependent on husbands and fathers for economic support. Emancipation thus presupposes control of procreation as well as economic independence. This is an agenda for women's liberation/equality, which is promoted by socialism and neo-liberalism alike.

Man the model: On transcendence, immanence, and equality

The transcendence/immanence line of thought, which de Beauvoir takes over from Jean-Paul Sartre, is an obvious illustration of assumption (a) above: The male subject at centre stage. 'Transcendence', according to de Beauvoir, is all that is fun and worthwhile, creative, productive, and essentially human: transcendence is what distinguishes humans from animals and culture from nature. Transcendence is however, in Sartres' and de Beauvoir's edition, inherently male. De Beauvoir is aware of this, even if she does not seem to be aware of the excessively male, and even phallic, metaphors of her language when describing transcendence as the human condition par excellence: 'Homo faber has from the beginning of time been an inventor: the stick and the club with which he armed himself to knock down fruits and to slaughter animals became forthwith instruments for enlarging his grasp upon the world ... he set up goals and opened up roads toward them ... he burst out of the present, he opened the future' (de Beauvoir 1949/1997,95). This movement of bursting out of the present, and of opening the future is always a movement forwards, upwards 'given that the basic image of the project remains male erection and ejaculation' as acknowledged by Toril Moi (1994, 152).

As against this creative activity of the archetypical modern hero, 'immanence' is described as passivity and repetition, the drudgery of daily housework in which giving birth, breastfeeding, and motherhood are included: 'The woman who gave birth ... did not know the pride of creation; she felt herself a plaything of obscure forces, and the painful ordeal of childbirth seemed a useless and even troublesome accident. But in any case, giving birth and suckling are not activities, they are natural functions; no project is involved; and that is why woman found in them no reason for a lofty affirmation of her existence – she submitted passively to her biological fate' (de Beauvoir 1949/1997, 94). Women's work is nothing but repetition and stagnation, not interesting at all from de Beauvoir's point of view; motherhood is naturalized and trivialized, a passive submission to nature and biology. This is motherhood as seen by (European) men; not motherhood as seen by (African) women. The value hierarchy as established by de Beauvoir – or rather, the value hierarchy of male modernity, explicitly accepted and condoned, and even elaborated by de Beauvoir – leads her to proclaim that 'it is not in giving birth but in risking life that man is raised above the animal; that is why superiority has been accorded not to the sex that brings forth but to that which kills' (de Beauvoir 1949/1997, 95).

Even Toril Moi, who generally shows a great talent for eking interesting feminist interpretations out of de Beauvoir's text, gives up on this one: In The Second Sex she says,

> the idea of immanence appears as an irresistible magnet for an astonishing range of obsessional images of darkness, night, passivity, stasis, abandonment, slavery,

confinement, imprisonment, decomposition, degradation and destruction. There is no appreciation here of the positive aspects of passivity: rest, recollection and tranquility are words that fail to emerge from Beauvoir's pen. (Moi 1994, 154)

Regarding de Beauvoir's praise for killing as more human than giving birth, she calls it 'perfectly logical – and utterly absurd' (Moi ibid., 154).

Obviously, to de Beauvoir, the way forward for women is to become as much as possible like men. Gender equality is explicitly defined in male terms: 'The 'modern' woman accepts masculine values. She prides herself on thinking, taking action, working, creating on the same terms as men; instead of seeking to disparage them she declares herself their equal' (de Beauvoir 1949/1997, 727). Similarly, in much modern thinking on gender, including Gender-and-Development lines of thought, man is the model.

The female body a handicap

However much de Beauvoir is quoted for her opening sentence to book two of *The Second Sex*: 'One is not born, but rather becomes, a woman', her work is in contradiction with itself on exactly this issue. On one hand she believes – and shows – how the conditions of women are socially determined. When women are squeezed, torn, and suffering, it is not because of menstruation and menopause, but because of the ways that society deals with womanhood. This is her official and conscious position:

> I am convinced that the greater part of the discomforts and maladies that over-burden women are due to psychic causes, as gynaecologists, indeed, have told me. Women are constantly harassed to the limit of their strength because of the moral tension I have referred to, because of all the tasks they assume, because of the contradictions among which they struggle. This does not mean that their ills are imaginary: they are as real and destructive as the situation to which they give expression. But the situation does not depend on the body; the reverse is true. (de Beauvoir 1949/1997, 706)

On the other hand there is her whole attitude to and description of the female body. Its capacity for pregnancy, childbirth, and lactation is *never* seen as a positive potential, as a source of pleasure or pride, but only and always as a curse, a drag, and a burden. Toril Moi (whose reading of 'The Second Sex' at this point corresponds to my own) gives a poignant summary:

> For Beauvoir women are the slaves of the species. Every biological process in the female body is a 'crisis' or a 'trial', and the result is always alienation. Her list of troubles and pains experienced during menstruation is impressive, to say the least, ranging from high blood pressure, impaired hearing and eyesight to unpleasant smells, destabilization of the central nervous system, abdominal pains, constipation and diarrhoea (*Second* Sex, 61). But the discomfort of menstruation pales in comparison to the horrors of gestation. ... Pregnancy, childbirth and breastfeeding all undermine the women's health and even put her life at risk: 'Childbirth itself is painful and dangerous ... Nursing is also an exhausting obligation; ... the nursing mother feeds the newborn at the expense of her own strength' (Second Sex, 62–63). (Moi 1994, 165)

The fact of the female enslavement to the species is a recurrent theme, especially of the first part of 'The Second Sex'. The human male is free to create and transcend, whereas

> the female feels her enslavement more and more keenly, the conflict between her own interest and the reproductive forces is heightened. Parturition in cows and mares is much more painful and dangerous than it is in mice and rabbits ... The woman is adapted to the needs of the egg rather than to her own requirements. From puberty to menopause woman is the theatre of a play that unfolds within her and in which she is not personally concerned (de Beauvoir 1949/1997, 57, 60).

The idea conveyed here is 'woman against her body'; from these descriptions it is abundantly clear that for women and their urge for transcendence the female body is a handicap. Obviously de Beauvoir cannot subscribe to Freud's idea that 'anatomy is destiny'. Thus she tries to convince herself that women's situation does not depend on the body, and that the reverse is true – as indicated in the quote above. There is a shadow of doubt, however, as in the same context she confesses that 'it is difficult to determine to what extent woman's physical constitution handicaps her' (de Beauvoir 1949/1997, 706).

In my reading, de Beauvoir is insincere at this point. In her entire analysis, the female body remains a handicap which can only be overcome by minimizing it, which (fortunately) is increasingly possible thanks to (a) industrial development and suitable wage work opportunities for women, supplemented with child care facilities, and (b) contraceptives and other types of reproductive technology. If the contemporary possibilities of in vitro fertilization had been available, or even imaginable, in her time, I am sure de Beauvoir would have embraced them as further steps on the road to female freedom. It is all contained within the logic of the female body as a handicap.

Regarding this model of female emancipation, socialism and liberalism by and large agree, as do large parts of the women's movement. The notion that the female body is a handicap is as persistent and pervasive as the idea of woman as other. This whole line of thinking is based on the assumption that the model body is male. But what if it isn't? I assert, as do others with me, that it is time for feminist thought to overcome the phallocentric as well as the ethnocentric biases in this line of thinking.

Critical feminist voices, 1: Challenging phallocentricity

Judith Butler's attitude to de Beauvoir is critical, but also accepting. I see this ambivalence as reflecting the ambivalence in de Beauvoir's own writing. I shall here focus on Butler's critique of de Beauvoir, which supports and adds to my own. Being a philosopher herself, Butler places de Beauvoir in the context of European philosophy, focusing on the mind/body divide and its gendered connotations:

> It appears that Beauvoir maintains the mind/body dualism, even as she proposes a synthesis of those terms. The preservation of that very distinction can be read as symptomatic of the very phallogocentrism that Beauvoir underestimates. In the philosophical tradition that begins with Plato and continues through Descartes, Husserl and Sartre, the ontological distinction between soul (consciousness, mind) and body invariably supports relations of political and psychic subordination and hierarchy. ...

> The cultural associations of mind with masculinity and body with femininity are well
> documented within the field of philosophy and feminism. (Butler 1990/1999, 17)

Having accepted this implicitly hierarchical line of thinking, de Beauvoir also
accepts the male/female hierarchy, setting man as the universal norm, and
female as other. 'For Beauvoir the "subject" within the existential analytic of
misogyny is always already masculine, conflated with the universal, differen-
tiating itself from a feminine "Other" outside the universalizing norms of
personhood, hopelessly "particular", embodied, condemned to immanence'
(Butler 1990/1999, 16).

Butler pinpoints the mechanism of this implicit manoeuvre as *disavowal* and
projection: the body, in Western thought, is disavowed – and at the same time
projected onto women. Much of the emotional load of female subordination
has its roots in this mechanism of disavowal and projection. '[The abstract,
masculine, epistemological] subject is abstract to the extent that it *disavows* its
socially marked embodiment and, further, *projects* that disavowed and dispar-
aged embodiment on to the feminine sphere, effectively renaming the body as
female' (Butler 1990/1999, 16). Disavowal and projection, as Butler points
out, are crucial parts of the mechanism in constructing *others*. 'Others' are not
there as produced by nature; 'others' are constructed. This is true of 'woman as
other', as well as of 'third world as other' and of 'third world woman as other'.
And, as pointed out by Chandra Mohanty (1984/1991, 74), constructions of
otherness go along with constructions of self.

Critical feminist voices, 2: Challenging ethnocentricity

In her important paper 'Under Western Eyes', Chandra Mohanty takes issue
with the ethnocentricity of much Western feminist thought. Ethnocentricity
is produced when

> third world legal, economic, religious and familial structures are treated as
> phenomena to be judged by Western standards. It is here that *ethnocentric universality*
> comes into play. When these structures are defined as 'underdeveloped' or 'devel-
> oping' and women are placed within them, an implicit image of the 'average third
> world woman' is produced. This is the transformation of the (implicitly Western)
> 'oppressed woman' into the 'oppressed third world woman'. (Mohanty 1984/1991,
> 72)

As shown by Mohanty the 'sexual difference' – i.e. the basic assumption
regarding universal female subordination – is exacerbated by what she calls the
'third world difference':

> The 'third world difference' includes a paternalistic attitude toward women in the
> third world. Since discussions of the various themes (kinship, education, religion,
> etc.) are conducted in the context of the relative 'underdevelopment' of the third
> world (which is nothing less than unjustifiably confusing development with the sepa-
> rate path taken by the West in its development as well as ignoring the directionality
> of the first world / third world power relationship), third world women as a group or
> category are automatically and necessarily defined as religious (read 'not progres-
> sive'), family-oriented (read 'traditional'), legal minors (read 'they-are-still-not-
> conscious-of-their-rights'), illiterate (read 'ignorant'), domestic (read 'backward') and

sometimes revolutionary (read 'the-country-is-in-a-state-of-war; they-must-fight!').
This is how the 'third world difference' is produced. (Mohanty 1984/1991, 72)

Western women, Mohanty says, succeed in staging them/ourselves as modern
and developed, equal and free, exactly by constructing the mirror image of the
third world woman as 'other': 'Universal images of 'the third world woman'
(the veiled woman, chaste virgin, etc.) images constructed from adding the
'third world difference' to 'sexual difference' are predicated upon ... assumptions about Western women as secular, liberated and having control over their
own lives' (Mohanty 1984/1991, 74). Because the images of self and other
are so closely interlinked, the patterns are hard to break by 'the self' who
constructed 'the other'. Seen from the vantage point of the other, however, the
matter looks different.

Mid-way summing-up

What I have said so far is the following: Much mainstream modern thinking
on gender shares at least three implicit assumptions: (a) man is posed as the
subject and woman as other (phallocentricity), (b) development is conceived as
an unilinear move from 'tradition' towards 'modernity' – the measure for
achievement being the Western world (ethnocentricity), and (c) third world
women are conceived as subordinated and oppressed. In order to illustrate ways
in which these assumptions work, even in feminist writings, I have highlighted
aspects of the thinking of Simone de Beauvoir in her classic and recently
relaunched work *The Second Sex*. My analysis of de Beauvoir's text aimed to
show how some of the implicit assumptions listed above work in her writing, to
a certain extent against her conscious intentions. That man is the model and
subject is abundantly clear, in explicit writing as well as between the lines. This
further implies that the female body, as measured against a male norm, is a
handicap. Aspects of contemporary feminist thinking have, however, bypassed
de Beauvoir and the kind of modernist thinking which she represents. I quote
two feminist thinkers, who particularly challenge the phallocentrism (or phal-
logocentrism) and the ethnocentrism of de Beauvoir and others: Judith Butler
and Chandra Mohanty. According to them, 'otherness' is never given, it is
always constructed: Woman-as-other, 'woman – the second sex' is not a fact of
nature. But what is the point of knowing that this is the case, if otherness keeps
being reconstructed even in feminists' analysis of women's conditions? If
woman-as-other is embedded in the very concepts and notions of gender,
making it impossible to see what else might be there?

In the remaining part of the chapter, I shall introduce concepts and lines of
thinking launched by African feminist thinkers contradicting the notion of
woman-as-other. In the work of these feminist writers, there is a refusal to see
women as 'others'; their own societies do not give rise to such ideas. The feminists in question have the courage to produce theoretical ideas based on knowledge of their African societies, even if such ideas may contradict standard
assumptions of Western knowledge. Ifi Amadiume on this basis puts 'the
mother-focused matri-centric unit' centre stage, while Oyèrónké Oyewùmí
questions the relevance, in an African context, of the very notion of 'woman'.

This may sound strange, but I shall explain. Before doing so, however, I shall provide some observations on kinship terminology. The point of this is to show the difficulties in thinking beyond the habitual concepts of everyday language.

Kinship terminology

In Western family structure the most important of women's positions in the family context are captured by the terms: Mother/daughter/sister/wife. Additional terms include aunt, cousin, niece, grandmother, and granddaughter. In Western languages, the commonly used kinship terms are normally gendered. Of the nine terms listed above, eight are gendered; only one (cousin) is not. In African languages, however, kinship terms are often 'gender neutral'. Based on her study among the matrilineal Kaonde in Zambia, British anthropologist Kate Crehan lists eight kinship terms as being the most important. Of those only two are gender specific, the six are gender neutral, like cousin, or like the English terms parent, sibling, spouse. If you need to indicate the sex of a person, you do it by other means (Crehan 1997). Furthermore, the Kaonde terms have different significance and do not translate directly to Western kinship terminology; the relationships lifted forward for naming are different from those used in the West. Often in matrilineal societies there are no fathers, and no mothers, as pointed out by French anthropologist Christian Geffray in his work on the Makhuwa of northern Mozambique:

> The kinship term *apaapa* refers to the group of men who are in-married strangers to the lineage to which the speaker belongs. The term fits all in-married men in the domestic group, among them the speaker's own 'father'. But this also means that 'the pronunciation of the word *apaapa* does not, in the minds of a Makhuwa speaker, evoke an image comparable to the one that emerges when we pronounce the word 'father' ... Actually our social figure of 'a father' is not symbolized, not verbalized and not even thinkable as such in Makhuwa country ... (Geffray 1990, 154)

Similarly, in Kaonde, the person we would identify as biological mother is not distinguished with a kinship term of her own. She is called by the same term used for all of the speaker's female matrikin in the first ascending generation (Crehan 1997, 90).

According to Crehan, and also to Oyewùmí, seniority (older than/younger than) in African contexts is often more important than sex/gender. In a Western context the first thing you want to know about a person is the sex (or gender) of the person. Generally it is given by the language – by the name, or by the titles Mr/Ms, and by the pronouns he/she when you talk about the person. There are few ways of referring to somebody without indicating in the very reference the sex/gender of the person. Compare the awkwardness of referring to a transsexual person – is s/he a she or a he? In Yoruba, however, Oyewùmí's native tongue, 'most names and all pronouns are ungendered.... [Thus] it is possible to hold a long and detailed conversation about a person without indicating the gender of that person, unless the anatomy is central to the issue under discussion, as with conversations about sexual intercourse or pregnancy. There is, however, considerable anxiety about establishing *seniority* in any social interaction' (Oyewùmí 1997, 40, emphasis added, SA). An important difference between sex/gender and seniority is that sex/gender is *absolute*: you are or are not a man/woman (the marginal case of transsexuals being the only exception). Seniority, however, is *relational:* You are older than or younger than, depending on the context and the situation. 'Seniority is relational and situational in that no one is permanently in a senior or junior position; it all depends on who is present in any given situation. Seniority, unlike gender, is only comprehensible as part of relationships. Thus it is neither rigidly fixated on the body nor dichotomized' (Oyewùmí 1997, 42).

Western feminism, Oyewùmí says, takes its point of departure in woman as wife and as daughter (2000, 1094). Simone de Beauvoir's work is a good example of this: Woman is identified and described in relation to a man in position of authority: the husband, the father. In Africa, however, Oyewùmí says, the most crucial position of a woman is her position as mother. 'Mother is the preferred and cherished self-identity of many African women' (Oyewùmí 2000, 1096). The position of mother is in itself a position of authority. Motherhood, however, is largely neglected in mainstream feminist thought (and certainly not supported in de Beauvoir's lines of thinking). Similarly in Western societies, to be a mother is often to live in a perpetual dilemma between your own emotional priorities and the economic and work-related priorities of the society of which you are a part.

Introducing African Feminist Thought, 1: Oyèrónké Oyewùmí

Even if I find Oyewùmí in some ways more radical than Ifi Amadiume in her critique of mainstream feminist thinking, Oyewùmí largely remains in the critical position, whereas Amadiume, as I see it, goes further in terms of suggesting alternative paradigms for analysis. Oyèrónké Oyewùmí and Ifi Amadiume are both Nigerian women, one of Yoruba and the other of Igbo background. Both live and work in the United States.

Oyèrónké Oyewùmí is trained in sociology. For thinking about African gender relations she draws upon her childhood and upbringing in the house of a Yoruba chief:

> In 1973, my father ascended the throne and became the *Sòún* (monarch) of Ogbómòsó, a major Òyó-Yorùbá polity of some historical significance. Since then and up to the present, *ààfin Sóún* (the palace) has been the place I call home. ... I cannot overemphasize the contributions of the conversations I had with my parents, older and younger siblings, the many mothers and fathers in the palace, and the family in general in the course of the many years of this research. (Oyewùmí 1997, xvi)

In her book, 'The Invention of Women. Making an African Sense of Western Gender Discourses' (1997) Oyewumi offers a series of very radical and very critical observations of Western feminist thought, one of them being her critique of 'woman' as a social category.

Critique of 'woman' as a social category
In 1996 the Network for Women's Studies in Nigeria organized a national workshop in order to discuss the applicability in Africa of basic concepts such as

'woman', 'gender' and 'feminism'. In her introductory speech, Amina Mama, at that point the coordinator of the network, said:

> The experience of African women across the region indicates that we cannot just passively import terms and concepts that have been developed elsewhere, under different social and political conditions. ... The task we face as African intellectuals is that of developing our own applications of given theories, and more radically, of taking our own realities as the starting point for articulating perspectives, or even entirely new theories that emanate organically from our particular conditions and concerns. (Mama 1997, 4–5)

Oyèrónké Oyewùmí did not participate in the workshop, but she took up the challenge. 'I came to realize,' she writes in the preface to her book, 'that the fundamental category 'woman' – which is foundational in Western gender discourses – simply did not exist in Yorùbáland prior to its sustained contact with the West. There was no such pre-existing group characterized by shared interests, desires or social position. ... Gender was simply not inherent in human organization' (Oyewùmí 1997, ix, xii). Thus in Yoruba society, there was no such thing as 'woman' being 'the other'. A male would not, just by virtue of his body-type, be considered superior to a female. 'Yorùbá cultural logic did not use the human body as the basis for social ranking. ... Yorùbá society was hierarchically organized, from slaves to rulers, but the ranking of individuals depended first and foremost on seniority, which was usually defined by relative age' (Oyewùmí 1997, xiii). 'Social identity' Oyewùmí sums up, 'was relational and was not essentialized. ... Man and woman are essentialized. These essential gender identities in Western cultures attach to all social engagements, no matter how far from the issues of social reproductions such undertakings may be' (Oyewùmí 1997, xiii). The Western gender categories are pervasive, however. 'Merely by analyzing a particular society with gender constructs, scholars create gender categories. To put this in another way: by writing about any society through a gendered perspective, scholars necessarily write gender into that society. Gender, like beauty, is often in the eye of the beholder' (ibid., xv). It is along this line of reasoning that Oyewùmí talks of a 'process of patriarchalizing Yorùbá history and culture' (ibid., 29) through Western social science, the patriarchalizing gaze.

The patriarchalizing gaze invents *women-as-other*, and introduces what Oyewùmí calls 'body-reasoning' (ibid., 5): a biological interpretation of the social world, resulting in hierarchies based on bodies: male/female, white/black. Oyewùmí challenges the commonly shared belief that biological determinism is dead and gone in Western thought. Not at all, she says; on the contrary, 'the cultural logic of Western social categories is based on an ideology of biological determinism; ... biology provides the rationale for the organization of social life' (ibid., ix). In the Western context, physical bodies are always also social bodies: A priori, ranking depends on gender. To make her point, Oyewùmí quotes Canadian sociologist Dorothy Smith: 'A man's body gives credibility to his utterance, whereas a woman's body takes it away from hers' (ibid., x). Biological determinism, Oyewùmí says, is a filter through which all knowledge about society is run (ibid., 5). A mind/body hierarchy is embedded in Western thinking. Bodies are disavowed, but nevertheless they are always there, as social markers. According to Oyewùmí, Freud's dictum still holds true: What he said about 'anatomy is destiny' was nothing exceptional. He was just being explicit (ibid., 7, 8).

Because of this body-focused thinking (cf. the mechanisms of disavowal/ projection as shown by Judith Butler) with bodies as social markers (e.g. male/female; white/black) the concept 'woman' carries connotations which are irrelevant and distorting in an African context. To talk about 'men' and 'women' in a Western sense creates ideas which do not fit Yoruba realities. Nevertheless, according to Oyewùmí, 'men' and 'women' are created in Nigeria by the Western patriarchalizing gaze. An example: In Yoruba *oba*, which means 'ruler', denotes a social position to be occupied by a man or by a woman. But in translation to English, *oba* has come to mean 'king'. (ibid., 30). In European minds, maleness and political power were interlinked.[1]

Introducing African Feminist Thought, 2: Ifi Amadiume

Ifi Amadiume is a social anthropologist. Her first book: *Male Daughters, Female Husbands*, based on fieldwork conducted in her own home town, was published in 1987. She initiated that study on the background of her anger and frustration over the ways in which gender issues in Africa were portrayed first by British social anthropologists and later by Western feminist scholars: 'It was not enough to shout out in anger at conferences or to get into heated debate with friends. I decided it was best to go home and, with the help of Nnobi people themselves, write our own social history, especially from the women's point of view' (Amadiume 1987, 9). In her second book *Reinventing Africa*, published in 1997, she further develops some of her leading themes.

One of her key points is similar to the one made by Oyewùmí on the 'rulers' who may be men or women, and only when seen by European eyes turn into 'kings'. Similarly, in Igbo society, many social positions may be taken up by either men or women. For example, the Igbo term for husband, *di*, is not gendered; both a man and a woman can be a husband (1997, 128). Daughters may step into positions of sons, and women may act as husbands for other wives. Thus, she says, there is 'in African gender systems a flexibility which allows a neuter construct for men and women to share roles and status' (1997, 112).

> In indigenous Nnobi society ... the ultimate indication of wealth and power, the title system, was open to men and women, as was the means of becoming rich through control over the labour of others by way of polygamy, whether man-to-woman marriage or woman-to-woman marriage. The Nnobi flexible gender system made either possible. (Amadiume 1987, 42)

The point here is that power is not masculine per se, power may be male or female – unlike in the West, where women who successfully manage to wield power in the public sphere have to take on 'an outward appearance of maleness such as deepened voices and tailored suits' (Amadiume 1997, 113). Thus in Nnobi context *woman-as-other* just does not occur. The place from which one views woman-as-other doesn't exist.

[1] See Chapter 11 for further elaboration of this point.

The importance accorded to motherhood

Another key point is the importance accorded to motherhood. Here again the patriarchalizing gaze is a major complication. Just as the Western meaning of 'woman' – i.e. woman-as-other – is assumed for women everywhere, so is the Western meaning of 'motherhood' (which carries a lot of very specific connotations) projected onto females with offspring everywhere. What is at issue, however, is not mothering as a physical fact, but the social position and importance given to motherhood, the *meaning* of mothering. As put by Mohanty: 'That women mother in a variety of societies is not as significant as the value attached to mothering in these societies. The distinction between the act of mothering and the status attached to it is a very important one – one that needs to be stated and analyzed contextually' (Mohanty 1984/1991, 60).

The challenge thus is to find out what motherhood in Africa is about. This will reveal the differences between motherhood in Africa and in the West where motherhood has no high status, being *naturalized* and *trivialized*, as demonstrated so eloquently by Simone de Beauvoir. Ifi Amadiume points to African women's power being based on 'the logic of motherhood', i.e. the notion that motherhood is empowering and not disempowering:

> In my research I have found that the traditional power of African women had an economic and ideological basis, and derived from the sacred and almost divine importance accorded to motherhood. This has led me to argue that the issue of the structural status of motherhood is the main difference between the historical experiences of African women and those of European women. (Amadiume 1997, 146)

However, she also realizes that 'the very thought of women's power being based on the logic of motherhood has proved offensive to many Western feminists. It is easy to see why this is so since in the European system, wifehood and motherhood represented a means of enslavement of women. In the African system of matriarchy it was women's means of empowerment' (ibid., 114). Amadiume plays with the idea of reintroducing the concept of matriarchy as a counterweight to the Western patriarchy, which tends to be taken for granted.

The motherhood paradigm / the matricentric unit

Trying to derive theoretical implications from her important insights regarding motherhood in Africa as compared to the West, Ifi Amadiume speaks of 'the motherhood paradigm'. The point is, by talking of the motherhood paradigm, to raise awareness regarding the often implicit *patriarchal paradigm* in social science: 'The recognition of the motherhood paradigm means that we do not take patriarchy as given, or as a paradigm' (ibid., 21). A consequence of this move is 'a shift of focus from man at the centre and in control, to the primacy of the role of the mother/sister in the economic, social political and religious institutions' (ibid., 152).

It is in this context that Amadiume (re-)introduces the term 'matriarchy'. She talks about 'a missing matriarchal structure in African studies' (ibid., 19), meaning a lack of awareness of the centrality of motherhood, or (which amounts to the same) an implicit application of Western gender terms with Western connotations, such as a priori gender hierarchies defining women as 'others'. When she takes up what she calls 'the vexing concept of matriarchy'

(ibid., 71) – and the concept of matriarchy certainly has a long and complicated history in European social science – it is not, however, in order to apply it
as an overall matrix to cover all aspects of society. She wants to use it 'not as a
totalitarian system – that is the total rule governing a society – but as a structural system in juxtaposition with another system in a social structure' (ibid.,
71). Amadiume has developed this model for analysis from her studies of Nnobi
society: 'The ideology of gender had its basis in the binary opposition between
the *mkpuke*, the female mother-focused matricentric unit, and the *obi*, the male-
focused ancestral house' (ibid., 18). These two systems, the mkpuke and the
obi, co-exist. If social science analysis only takes its point of departure in
concepts deriving from the obi, important aspects of the ways this society functions will be lost. Theoretical awareness of this co-existence of mkpuke and obi
points to the need for different and more specific concepts than the ones rooted
in a patriarchal system. 'The mkpuke as a female gendered, paradigmatical
cultural construct demolished the generalized theory that man is culture and
woman is nature in the nature/culture debate in anthropology' (ibid., 19). This
is an indirect reference to de Beauvoir: A central paper in this debate, Sherry
Ortner's 'Is Female to Male as Nature is to Culture?' (1974) draws heavily on *The
Second Sex*, and is dedicated to Simone de Beauvoir.

The point of Amadiume's suggested paradigm for gender studies is, as I read
it, (a) to be critical of the usual Western gender concepts, which often carry an
implicit male bias, and (b) to craft concepts particularly fitted to deal with motherhood; not with abstract motherhood – here the risks of the nature/culture
Western connotations hanging on is too great – but with the concrete sociological phenomenon of 'the mother-focused, matri-centric unit'. Amadiume is
trying to create a model for a kind of dialectical analysis, shifting the focus
between the obi, the male-focused ancestral house (this aspect often having
been the sole concern of the classical social anthropologists, cf. Amadiume
1997, 29 ff), on one hand, and on the other the mkpuke, the mother-focused
matri-centric unit. The implication is that this kind of double-focus analysis
would be applicable also elsewhere in Africa.

Winding up: Inspiration for feminist futures?

I have introduced Oyèrónké Oyewùmí and Ifi Amadiume as brave and determined feminist scholars who have had the courage to go against established
power structures and current fashions in feminist thought. Nevertheless I find
them too timid, in one particular aspect: they tend to limit the scope of their
analysis to Africa, which in one way is fine – concrete, rooted studies with
concepts which are sensitive to empirical particularities are always a good thing.
In another way, however, this approach tends to consolidate a difference
between Africa and the West – a dichotomization which I find unproductive
and also unjustified. Both Amadiume and Oyewùmí make explicit distinctions
between African and Western realities, talking about motherhood in the
African context being such and such, and thus needing different concepts, as
compared to analysis of Western realities, where motherhood and femininity
are different. I agree that realities may be different, particularly in the past –

both researchers draw their conceptual inspiration from things as they were *before* the impacts of colonialism, Christianity, and continued contact with the West. But to me the point about empirical differences between Africa and Europe is not that concepts developed for Africa are useful in Africa only, but rather that the 'African difference' may be a source of inspiration for developing concepts which make it possible to think differently about gender in Western contexts as well.

Thus I see Oyewùmí's and Amadiume's contributions as important to feminist theory as such, for two interconnected reasons. First, they manage to think beyond woman-as-other as taken for granted, which is a major theoretical achievement. With woman-as-other being embedded in the very concept of 'woman', imagining futures with woman *not* as 'the other' becomes an impossible task. Second, in their analysis they produce images – of human relations, of motherhood – which open the mind for different ways of thinking about gender, thus 'enabling other virtual futures to be conceived, other perspectives to be developed' (Grosz 2000, 1019). I find the rethinking of motherhood particularly pertinent. The ways in which Western patriarchal thought has managed to naturalize and trivialize motherhood are appalling. And even worse is it that feminist thought has done very little about it. Motherhood remains an under-researched and under-conceptualized area in Western feminist scholarship. In contemporary trend-setting feminist thought, as for instance in Judith Butler's work, thinking about motherhood is absent. One consequence of such blank spots in feminist thinking – and of implicit phallocentric and/or ethnocentric assumptions still going strong – is that strategies for the future remain flawed. In the lines of thinking underpinning global feminist documents such as the Beijing Platform for Action, informing current Gender-and-Development thinking, the vision of gender equality has not moved very far from Simone de Beauvoir's visions of 'wage work and contraception', i.e. feminine futures on male terrain, with man as the model. Inspiration and conceptual imagination which may help to push feminist thinking beyond those limits are greatly needed. This is the important contribution of African feminist thought.

5 Gender in Colonial & Post-colonial Discourses (2003)

Woodcut by Jose Tangawizi

Introduction

Seen in terms of conventional political science, and also as experienced by Mozambican men and women, the recent history of Mozambique has been very dramatic. There have been several changes of political regimes and almost three decades of war, from the onset of the armed struggle in 1964 to the Rome peace agreement in 1992. There have been two remarkable political shifts during this period. First there was the rapid transition in 1975 from Portuguese colonialism to political independence and Frelimo socialism. Second, in the late 1980s the government moved from Frelimo socialism to neo-liberal economic policies and a Structural Adjustment Programme (SAP, in Portuguese: PRE – *Programa da Re-estruturação Económica*) under World Bank leadership. This time the name of the government did not change. Frelimo remained in power, but with a some- what different political and economic agenda after its fifth Party Congress in 1989.

The point I want to make in this chapter has to do with the contradiction between on the one hand the ways in which each of these different politics of government have seen themselves as radical breaks with the immediate past, and on the other hand the ways in which these different political regimes (in theory as well as in practice) have approached issues of gender. Examined through a gendered lens these apparently radically different political lines have much in common. Considered from this angle the political continuities seem much more dominant than the radical breaks.

From one point of view these decades of history include dramatic changes in government. The process has moved all the way from colonial dominance and economic exploitation, to socialist politics and (attempts at) a planned economy in a one-party state, to multi-party democracy and neo-liberal economic struc- tures. From another point of view the dramatic changes are overshadowed by persistent continuities. With regard to the field of politics and policies on gender, the lines of thinking of each new period can be shown to build heavily on the previous one. This is the case in spite of the fact that for each of the decisive breaks, first Independence, and later the neo-liberal turn, part of the very profile of the change has been its gender policies. Frelimo Socialism boasted a high profile regarding women's emancipation, as in the famous words of Samora Machel: 'The liberation of women is a necessity for the revolution, a guarantee of its continuity and a condition for its success' (Machel 1973). Similarly the present period of donor-dominated development stresses the importance of gender mainstreaming in all political spheres.

This chapter examines political documents – political speeches, official reports and so on – from these three major periods: first, Portuguese colo- nialism, second, Frelimo socialism, and third, the SAP/PRE period of donor- dominated development. I shall focus on lines of thinking and implicit assumptions, but also on actual policies on gender issues in the respective periods.

Portuguese colonialism

Portuguese colonial documents and political speeches make for interesting reading for their ideological bluntness: 'To us Portuguese, colonization is essentially to lift the indigenous populations to our own level of civilization, by teaching them our religion, our language, our customs. ... It is our mentality that we want to transmit to the people of the colonies, we are not intending to take away their riches' (Ministro das Colónias, in *Boletim Geral das Colónias* 1940). Colonization for the Portuguese, according to the Archbishop of Lourenço Marques, is about civilization, Christianization and *aportuguesamento* – Portugalization – of the indigenous population (Hedges 1985).[1]

Gender issues are rarely mentioned in these political statements. In the colonial context, gender relations matching a Christian ideal are taken for granted as an aspect of the civilizing, Christianizing and Portugalizing mission. The conception of gender embedded in the civilizing mission only becomes explicit when it is challenged. One example is the difficulties Portuguese observers encountered in coming to terms with the matrilineal societies of northern Mozambique.

It is pathetic to see how the writers of colonial reports[2] struggled to make the position of women in the matrilineal north[3] fit the pre-conceived image of oppressed subordinated African women in need of liberation. According to da Silva Rego (1960) in the north it is the woman who dominates the family. The husband must leave his own village in order to marry. If the marriage does not work out he must leave, and the woman can remarry (ibid., 85). This is naturally unacceptable by Christian standards, but women take pride in the system, and they fight against change. This matriarchy (i.e. matriliny) might even look like women's emancipation, da Silva Rego says, hastening to explain that in actual fact this is far from the case. First because the individual dignity of the woman is not respected – women are subordinated to the clan. Second, true emancipation of the woman is for her to be part of a Christian family, with the man as the natural head of the family (*chefe natural da familia*) and the woman at his side (ibid., 86, 25).

Measured against Christian marriage – monogamy, indissolubility and the man as head of the family – everything was wrong with family relations under conditions of matriliny. Marriages are not particularly stable and worst of all, the husband/ father has no entrenched position. Men's positions are derived through women (not the other way round) and men are important as uncles (mothers' brothers), not as fathers/progenitors. To the colonial administration, matriliny – or matriarchy (*matriarchado*) as it is called in contemporary texts – is unacceptable, presenting 'indisputable inconveniences' (Rita-Ferreira et al.

---

[1] Portugalisation in practice was among other things forced use of Portuguese as language of instruction in mission schools, to the great annoyance of the Protestant missionaries, who were not of Portuguese origin, and who preferred to teach in local languages, cf. Chapter 2.

[2] The two reports under consideration here are A da Silva Rego 1960: *Alguns problemas socio-missionárias da Africa Negra*, and Antonio Rita-Ferreira et al 1964: *Promoção Social em Moçambique*. Both reports are published by *Junta de Investigações do Ultramar* in Lisbon.

[3] Major ethnic groups, all matrilineal, in northern Mozambique are Makhuwa, Makonde and Yao. According to the data collected in *II Recenseamento Geral da População e Habitação* in 1997, almost 40 per cent of the Mozambican population speak Emakhuwa or Elomwe (closely connected languages spoken by Makhuwa people), Shimakonde or Ciyao.

1964, 78) for a series of reasons. Apart from family life being less stable, and the father not head of the family, 'it is an acknowledged fact that patrilineal societies are better suited than the matrilineal ones for adaptation to rapid social and economic change' (ibid., 78). Matriliny conforms neither to the demands of Christianity, nor to the demands of development; and furthermore these societies are irritatingly resistant to change.

The difficult matrilineal societies in the north are described as primitive and backward. Women were embedded in demeaning traditional customs. They enjoyed less access to schools and they were burdened by heavy workloads. Thus defined, women were now positioned in the usual subordinate situation, and Christianity and civilization could come to their rescue with offers of dignity in Christian marriages, courses in sewing and hygiene (sewing was considered important as the semi-nudity of women was perceived as offensive), and men taking over agricultural work (ibid., 79).

There is an interesting relation between work and gender in this colonial discourse. As for men, inducing (or forcing) them to work was part of the civilizing mission. The image of the lazy African is the point of departure; work as such has a civilizing effect, and the repression of idleness is a goal in itself 'dignifying and uplifting the native through the work' (Governador Geral de Mozambique, in *Boletim Geral das Colónias* 1948). This line of argument seems only valid for men, however. As for women, the opposite seems to be the case. For women a heavy workload is an indication of subordination, the civilizing mission being to lift it off her shoulders, in order to enable her to devote herself to housework. 'Development goes in the direction of leaving the bulk of agricultural work to the man. Also in Africa the woman shall become the queen of the home: a *Raínha do lar*' (ibid., 26).

Civilization thus also included the well known division between public and private spheres, with the husband 'the natural head of the family' as worker and breadwinner, and the wife and mother as 'queen of the home'. This is how things worked – or were supposed to work – at the level of ideology. In practical terms Portuguese colonialism was indeed based on women's productive work in family agriculture, feeding the family while the men were away on forced or contract labour. Colonial exploitation of Mozambican wage labour was conditioned by salaries being kept very low, as male workers' families were supported through women's work on the land. Also the forced cotton cultivation in the north depended heavily on women's labour. According to Allen Isaacman (1996) the physical burdens of the cotton regime – forced cultivation on family plots, usually one hectare for husband and wife, and half a hectare for a single woman – fell disproportionately on women's shoulders. 'Women were forced to help their husbands clear new fields and, in men's absence, to cut trees and remove heavy stumps and even plough – strenuous tasks that in the past had been performed almost exclusively by men' (ibid., 53). At the same time, of course, women retained the principal responsibility for food production and household work. The colonial regime, thus, depended on women's double workload: In the official ideology they were (or ought to be) housewives; in actual fact they were major producers.

An additional problem with the 'Rainha do lar' ideology is that it naturalized women's procreative capacity, and restricted their role as mothers to the private sphere. In this way, the carpet was pulled from under the feet of women in northern Mozambique taking pride in their role as mothers, not in the private context of nuclear male-headed families, but in powerful positions as lineage elders. Power based on maternity and fertility is not recognized in the civilized Christian context, however, where fertility is trivialized as a function of nature, and maternity is reduced to the education of children in the seclusion of the patriarchal family. Yet another aspect of women's lives, also not accepted in its own right in Christian/colonial thinking, is sexuality. The general attitude of the Portuguese colonial power was a strong condemnation of female initiation rituals, because of their focus on development and education of female sexuality.[4] Female initiation rituals were considered by the colonial administration as well as by the Catholic church as 'immoral and offensive to the human nature' (Medeiros 1995, 5). The attitude of the Protestant missions was no more permissive. In the writings of Henri-Alexandre Junod, a clergyman of the Swiss Mission[5], customs relating to female sexuality were so 'vile and immoral' (Junod 1912/1974, 176) that he could only speak of them in an appendix for 'doctors and ethnographers' written in Latin.

Similarly, Terence Ranger reports from Masasi district in Southern Tanzania, populated by matrilineal Makhuwa, Maconde and Yao peoples immediately north of Mozambique, how 'the missionaries did not approve of the concept of womanhood in Masasi society' (Ranger 1972, 237). Ranger's discussion relates to Protestant missionary attitudes to female initiation rites, which were considered as 'much more obscene than the male ceremony'. 'It was difficult', writes Ranger, 'for the missionaries, perhaps especially for the white laywomen who had most to do with female initiation, to see the rites as Africans saw them. .... There was a constant tension between the mission view of the role of women in Masasi, and the women's view of their own role' Ranger ibid., 237, 247). On the 'civilized' background of the Victorian ideal of female passionlessness (Cott 1978) and 'the Angel in the House' (a Rainha do lar) – as opposed to the demonized and demeaning image of the sexualized woman as prostitute and whore – it is not surprising that explicit celebration of female sexuality should be considered obscene and repugnant. According to this logic explicit female sexuality is indistinguishable from prostitution.

In the analysis of colonial attitudes to gender I have focused on the matrilineal societies in northern Mozambique, because here the clashes between Christian 'civilization' and African realities were most explicit. In actual fact, however, the situation was very similar in other parts of Mozambique, even if, to the missionaries and colonizers' relief, thanks to patrilineal kinship systems in southern Mozambique, the man and father was the 'natural head of the family', and thanks to the bride-price (lobolo) marriages would tend to be more stable. Nevertheless, it is interesting to see that Rita-Ferreira, pointing to the preponderant and prestigious position of women in 'traditional' society, also remarks that women's powerful positions in the south of Mozambique, instead

---

[4] Female genital cutting or mutilation is *not* a part of initiation rituals in Mozambique. As opposed to cutting, the rituals, particularly in northern Mozambique, focus on female sexual capacity building.

[5] Only in the 1960s did the Swiss Mission (*Missão Suissa*) change its name to *Igreja Presbiteriana de Moçambique*. (Cruz e Silva & Loforte 1998, 43).

of disappearing in fact had been increasing in recent years, due to the absence of many men for prolonged periods (six to eighteen months) on work contracts away from home (Rita-Ferreira et al., 1964, 76). But this is a limited power, Rita-Ferreira adds, as the women continue to be more traditional and backward, less educated than the men. Thus the analysis ends up with the expected conclusion of subjugated women in need of civilization and education.

Summing up the colonial attitude in terms of work, family, maternity and sexuality, the situation looked as follows:

Work: According to colonial ideology the men were lazy and the women overworked.[6] Men were urged, if not forced, to work more, with the legitimation that work in itself is a civilizing activity. In the case of women, however, nondomestic work was an indication of oppression and subordination. At the level of ideology women should remain in the private sphere and devote themselves to housework as 'Rainhas do lar'. At the level of practical policies, however, the colonial economy was based on women's productive work in agriculture, partly to feed their families, but also to secure agricultural output for export, as in the case of cotton.

Family: At the level of ideology the family in colonial politics should follow the Christian model, a goal for which the missionaries (Catholics and Protestants alike) were perpetually struggling. This ideal family did not correspond very neatly to family structures anywhere in Mozambique. The ideal family was monogamous, stable (divorces not tolerated) and with the man and father as family head. The missionaries spoke of equality between man and wife, but it was an kind of equality for which the natural superiority of the man was a precondition: with woman as man's companion (and subordinate) but 'with equal dignity in front of God', as put by a Swiss Presbyterian historian (Biber 1987, 64). Also at the level of families, however, colonial realities were different from colonial ideology. Families were broken up and dispersed by migratory work and by forced labour. Struggling to keep family networks intact was one of many forms of resistance to colonial oppression.

Maternity: Women's roles as mothers were located in the private sphere, as one aspect of their positions as 'Rainhas do lar'. Since the Christian family structure is unwaveringly patriarchal, and since motherhood in addition to being privatized is also naturalized and trivialized, no (or very little) potential female power is embedded in the role of mother.

Sexuality: Female sexuality was considered a tool for procreation and nothing more. The civilized norm for women is passionlessness – 'Close your eyes and think of England' – allegedly the Victorian advice given to young women facing their sexual debut. To acknowledge the existence of female sexuality, to focus young women on their sexual potential, educating them in the area of sexual pleasure was considered vile, immoral and offensive to human nature.

Frelimo socialism

Unlike colonial times, when gender was not a policy issue in itself, for Frelimo, gender, or rather *women's emancipation*, became a goal in its own right. During

---

[6] Cf. Ann Whitehead 2000 for contemporary versions of similar ideological presumptions.

the armed struggle against Portuguese colonial power, issues of gender equality had been put on the agenda by women themselves, demanding the creation of a women's wing of the Frelimo guerilla army. In addition to the important female support to the guerilla struggle in terms of transport of weapons and other material, production and preparation of food etc., women claimed the right to become soldiers and to fight along with men (Casimiro 2001). The *Destacamento Feminino* was created in 1966, and a few years later (1973) was supplemented by the creation of a non-military women's organization, the *Organização da Mulher Moçambicana* (OMM) in order to facilitate the mobilization of peasant populations in support of the guerilla war. In one sense the OMM was a political organization, created to support Frelimo; in another sense it was a politization of female gender networks which had always been there, creating a link from these networks to political power, i.e. Frelimo. As I was told by women in Cabo Delgado in 1982: 'During the war we held meetings, we mobilized women to transport war material, to grow food and to cook for the soldiers. Women volunteered, but sometimes husbands tried to prevent them from participating in the tasks of war. When that happened, we called in Frelimo. ... During the war women were respected because we were organized'. Interviewing in the north of Mozambique in 1982–83, I realized that in daily talk 'OMM' was often synonymous with 'women'.

During the war it seems that women were still in command in the OMM, and even supported by Frelimo. After Independence in 1975 however, Frelimo took over. Matters as important as development of a policy for women's liberation could not be left to women – and certainly not to the largely uneducated peasant women who had struggled with Frelimo in the north of Mozambique. Centrally positioned in the Frelimo political line was the fight against 'traditional society' and the whole array of 'habits and customs', *usos e costumes*, around which the daily lives of most Mozambicans were constructed. The performance of customary ceremonies was not directly criminalized, but strong political campaigns were waged against them. These were the years of what has later been termed the *abaixo* politics. *Abaixo* means 'down with', and slogans of 'down with lobolo, 'down with polygamy', 'down with initiation rites' were shouted at every political meeting. Frelimo's socio-historical analysis was put forward in the documents for the 2nd OMM conference in November 1976. This conference preceded the 3rd Frelimo congress in March 1977 by only a few months, and these two events together mark the transformation of the previous political front Frelimo into a socialist party. The fingerprints of a communist party's socio-historical analysis are very visible in the 2nd OMM conference documents. 'Traditional society' was seen as 'feudal' and it was analyzed in terms of exploitation and oppression, not just by colonialism, but in equal measure by indigenous power structures. Any customary beliefs and practices were considered obscurantist, oppressive and an obstacle to progress and modernity. Central in all of this was the alleged oppression and humiliation of women.

Regarding the understanding of women's position in 'traditional society', Frelimo's analysis was not very different from the colonial one. Women were constructed as humiliated and oppressed. The analysis goes as follows: All Mozambicans, men and women alike were exploited and oppressed by the colonial system, but in addition to this the Mozambican peasant woman is victim of a second form of oppression which is linked to the traditional-feudal ideology. This ideology conceives of women as having the role in society of serving the man – as an object of pleasure, producer of children and worker without a salary. ... This position of women is reinforced through institutions and ceremonies such as 'initiation rites', as well as the whole system of marriage, including lobolo, premature and forced marriages, and polygamy. (OMM 1977, 89)

Just as in the colonial writings, however, a certain ambiguity may be discerned. In some writings produced by the colonial power, even if the image of the oppressed and overworked woman was maintained, it had been conceded that 'women in traditional settings enjoy a considerable preponderance and prestige' (Rita-Ferreira et al., 1964, 75). Similarly, in some OMM/Frelimo documents, even if also here the dominant line was the one about the oppression of women in 'feudal-traditional' society (this being one major legitimation for Frelimo's push for modernization), here and there a different understanding can be felt, indicating that women's positions might also be threatened, and not improved, by modernization. This understanding, which from my point of view, is much more precise, remained however an undercurrent, only popping up here and there in OMM/Frelimo writings, as in the following passage from the 2nd OMM conference documents: 'In the countryside, where in reality it is the woman who make plans, who organize and who has since immemorial times been the main producer, we nevertheless see her relegated to the role of simple workforce in our cooperatives and communal villages' (OMM 1977, 58).

Anyhow, in the dominant OMM/Frelimo view the way to women's emancipation goes through her participation in the principal task – *tarefa principal* – of the revolution. As put by Samora Machel in his speech to the 2nd OMM conference in November 1976:

The decisive factor for the emancipation of woman is her engagement in the principal task, the task which transforms society. At that time [i.e. during the liberation war] it was the struggle for liberation. What then constitutes the principal task in the present phase of the revolution? The principal task of the present phase of our process is the following: the construction of the material and ideological base for building a socialist society. Thus for the implementation of this strategy, which has as its objective the construction of socialism, the principal task is production and the principal form of action is class struggle'. (Machel 1977a, 23)

Whereas participation in the war of liberation in many cases *did* bring about changes in male/female gender relations, strengthening the position of women vis-à-vis men at a local level, participation in production or, as it was later rephrased, participation in 'the increase of production and productivity so as to fulfill the economic plan' (Rebelo 1981) did not hold similar promise for women. In post-independence Frelimo politics women were instrumentalized as a workforce for the state and nation building. In Rebelo's 1981 speech[7] to the OMM national council, the focus was on the state and the economic plan, not on women. Women were requested to work hard in production, which in fact they had always been doing, and doing increasingly during the colonial period, and in addition to this were not to forget their tasks as wives and mothers. Nevertheless, this kind of politics was launched as 'women's emancipation'.

In fact what happened was just that the double workload for women –

---

[7] Jorge Rebelo was at that point Secretary for Ideology of the Frelimo Central Committee.

production as well as domestic work – was maintained, only with a different emphasis compared to the colonial ideology. Where during colonialism the lead image had been the 'Raínha do lar', while women's productive role was maintained and even increased, the lead image now was the woman soldier and the woman producer – the image of a woman state farm tractor driver was very popular in Party contexts – but with the domestic roles as wife and mother maintained. In the socialist theory of women's emancipation, from which the Frelimo women's politics drew inspiration, the emancipatory effect of 'women as wage workers' was conditioned by state organized alleviation of domestic tasks in terms of creches, kindergartens etc. Such conditions were not in place in Mozambique.

The Frelimo ideology regarding gender equality was also characterized by a certain ambiguity, however of a different kind, more like double standards, similar to the colonial double standards of the 'social priority of the man over his wife, but equal dignity in front of God' (Biber 1987, 64). In OMM/ Frelimo contexts the position of the man as family head was taken for granted, and the gender equality aspect amounted to woman being seen as man's companion, not his subordinate. Unlike the colonial writers, however, the Frelimo leadership was not troubled by matriliny, presumably because they knew nothing about it. Most of the programme-writing party cadres (the educated intellectuals) came from the patrilineal South. Matriliny was only 'discovered' in Frelimo contexts in the course of the preparations for the extraordinary OMM conference in 1984.

The man as family head/the woman as man's companion were standard ingredients in the so-called 'socialist family' strongly supported by Frelimo as well as by OMM. Just like the Christian family model, the so-called 'socialist family' should be monogamous, stable and indissoluble. Women's easy access to divorce in the (matrilineal) north was frowned upon by the Party (cf. chapters 1 and 3). In the concluding document from the OMM Extraordinary Conference in 1984, the OMM (as always) toed the Party line: 'The OMM Extraordinary Conference emphasized specifically the vital importance of the coherence, stability and harmony of the family, because this is the basic cell of our society, the foundation of the Mozambican Nation, and the basis for the consolidation of our State' (OMM 1984).

In a speech during his travels in Gaza province in 1982 Samora Machel acknowledged the similarity between Frelimo and Christian morals: 'We have the same ideas regarding the combat of alcoholism and prostitution, but we differ regarding the ways of interpreting phenomena in the world' (Machel 1982, 42). In this speech Samora Machel specifically paid homage to the Protestant missions in southern Mozambique. The Protestants, like the Frelimo militants, had their reasons to be opposed to the Catholic colonial regime, enforcing *aportuguesamento* and greatly impeding Protestant missionary work. Thus an alliance developed between the Protestant church and the Frelimo militants[8], as expressed by Samora Machel in the Gaza speech: 'Here, in the province of Gaza, the Protestant church, which was a centre for the struggle against colonialism, cultivated some

[8] Cruz e Silva (2001) highlights the importance of the Swiss-Presbyteran mission in southern Mozambique for the formation, particularly from 1930 onwards, of an educated, politically conscious (i.e. nationalist and anti-colonial) elite.

of these values. ... The Protestants helped us a lot' (ibid., 40). The values to which Machel refers are those regarding the importance of monogamous and stable marriages, based on love, and the rejection of 'idleness (*vagabundice*) alcoholism, prostitution and marginality' (ibid.). Machel also spoke of the values of individual and collective hygiene and cleanliness, of clean nails and well-combed hair, and of the dignity of the family. Here as elsewhere he came down hard on women having children with different men, i.e. children without fathers, 'children of the bush': 'Such children are born like goats, coming from the bush, without knowledge of their father' (ibid., 39). To be human in Samora's eyes was to live in a patriarchal, monogamous family: 'We are human beings, we have family, we have parents, we have sons and daughters, we have husbands and wives, we form a cell of society. For this reason we condemn adultery, for this reason we condemn 'children of the bush'' (ibid., 40).

Even worse than 'children of the bush' were prostitutes, 'women who transform their bodies into shops. ... A prostitute is a rotten person with a foul stench' (ibid., 33). A particular kind of prostitute, according to Machel, was a 'girl of twelve to sixteen years' who hunted down adult men in political power. Interestingly, the President's blame was laid exclusively on the girls, and not on his fellow Party members, the powerful politicians letting themselves be seduced.

I am quoting the Frelimo (and Mozambique) President at length, because I find the similarities between Frelimo and Christian/Protestant morals sadly striking. In spite of all talk of 'women's emancipation' Frelimo's moral worldview was strictly androcentric and even patriarchal. In the speeches of Samora Machel this whole moral package was termed 'socialist ethics' (Machel 1982, 40). In actual fact, however, it was very similar to the 'Protestant ethic' outlined by Max Weber in his famous work (1920/1930). Even Machel's critique of *vagabundice* belongs here. According to Weber, for Protestants, the 'waste of time is the first and in principle the deadliest of sins' (Weber ibid., 157). Weber also notes how Protestantism even more fiercely than Catholicism bans sexuality. The Frelimo approach has many similarities with the Protestant line. Female initiation rites were considered, if not explicitly as vile and immoral, then certainly as oppressive and humiliating, and they were centrally positioned among the *usos e costumes* considered social problems for women, and which should become extinct. The 1976 2nd OMM conference documents, just as later the 1984 OMM Extraordinary Conference documents, refer to initiation rites, *lobolo*, polygamy etc as 'women's social problems'. Seen from my vantage point, however, these customs and traditions were not women's problems as much as they were Frelimo's problems. These so-called 'women's social problems' pointed to aspects of Mozambican social life that did not conform to Frelimo's strongly Christian /Protestant-inspired version of modernity and development – aspects which Frelimo struggled to change and to control.

Still, however, in the denunciation of 'traditional-feudal society', *lobolo*, polygamy and the rest of it, there is an interesting ambiguity in Frelimo's line. Samora Machel in the 1982 Gaza speech was, as usual, strongly against 'traditional-feudal society', but he was also against young people who wanted to marry without a specific ceremony and without consulting the parents: 'They think that this is Independence', the President snorted, 'they behave like animals, and they say that this is Independence!' (Machel 1982, 34). Furthermore these youngsters, when reproached by their parents, called them old-fashioned and outdated, *ultrapassados*. In this dispute the President was on the side of the parents, who were instructed to maintain their authority vis-à-vis the misbehaving offspring. Thus traditional marriage was bad, but no marriage at all was even worse, and the parents, much more rooted in 'tradition' that the younger generation, were given support.

One aspect of women's lives, which was not considered a social problem and thus did not figure in the OMM/Frelimo list of 'women's social problems' was motherhood. Frelimo had policies on work, family and (female) sexuality, but regarding maternity OMM merely advised a two year period between births (which conformed more or less to prescriptions of 'tradition'), and projects for *saude materno-infantil* – mother-child health /reproductive health were established. Like 'gender' in colonial days, to Frelimo 'motherhood' was uncontroversial. As long as women produced the necessary amount of children for the Nation, all was well. Mozambique is fairly sparsely populated, so the Frelimo government welcomed a population increase. Talk of family planning was in terms of spacing births, less of limiting families. Also in this aspect, thus, women were instrumentalised and subordinated in relation the Nation's needs.

Summing up, I have characterized Frelimo ideology as follows:

Work: The model is the Soviet-socialist inspired 'women in men's jobs': The woman soldier, the woman tractor driver. Tacitly however, it is presumed that women also take care of domestic tasks. In actual reality women work a lot, particularly in agricultural production, as they have always been doing.

Family: The 'socialist family' is put forward as the ideal. This family model however is indistinguishable from a Christian, particularly a Protestant, ideal.

Sexuality: Female sexuality is dealt with only in negative terms (as prostitution, blaming the woman). Campaigns are waged against female initiation rites.

Maternity is taken for granted.

I have focused critically on Frelimo ideology, because of its deplorable lack of understanding of the actual conditions of male/female relations in Mozambican daily life, and because of its unsavory (to my taste) mix of socialist/communist ideology with Protestant puritanism, both of these lines of thought being strongly androcentric and patriarchal, if not outright misogynist. Nevertheless, in actual political practice in the post-Independence years, much did happen that was also beneficial to for women. There were wide-ranging programmes of education and mobilization and political participation at local levels, to name just some of many important changes in the early years of Independence. Before long, however, the Frelimo – Renamo war paralysed political and economic change, and the Mozambique that emerged from the war in many respects was very different from the Mozambique of the immediate post-Independence period.

Donor-dominated development

The Mozambique of Frelimo socialism was a very particular country with a very particular colonial past and an equally important history of struggle. The Mozambique of SAP and PRE is just another poor African country. From the late 1980s onwards Mozambique became integrated in the 'normal' development setup under the neo-liberal auspices of the IMF and the World Bank, with donor agencies pouring in and with masses of international NGOs. Maputo's bumpy streets were flooded with donor agencies' expensive cars, and the previously empty shops were filled with goods for those who could afford them.

These transformations also brought changes in the field of gender. With the first UN Women's conference in 1975 in Mexico City and a further series of UN conferences on women, population and human rights, a globalized approach to 'women' and 'gender ' in development contexts was created. In a strange kind of dialogue between struggling women and accommodating/coopting state and donor bureaucracies, a standardized language and approach to gender issues were developed. Gender policies in this era greatly depended on gender struggles from below. The ideas of 'women in development' and later 'gender and development', were invented by women's groups and introduced into development language through lobbying and advocacy. Most frequently the government and donor agencies – in a general climate of neo-liberal politics – have done their best to co-opt and integrate WiD and GAD into their liberal economic strategies, thereby de-politicizing the gender language that they have felt obliged to apply.

The very language of *gender* is a case in point. When the vocabulary of gender-and-development was introduced into the development debate in the 1980s, it was advocated by feminists, who wanted to criticize the dominant women-in-development (WID) approach for dealing only with integration of women into existing development policies, with no critical analysis of development as such, and with no criticism of the unequal power relationships between men and women. Nevertheless, in spite of the good intentions, which were to politicize the WID debate through gender-and-development (GAD) thinking, the opposite seems to have happened. Instead of speaking about women, which implied an awareness of women's specific and often marginalized positions, the term gender came into use as a neutral term, referring to both women and men.

Because of the overall standardization of development approaches in neo-liberal economic contexts, the situation in Mozambique is not very different from development approaches to gender elsewhere. The specificity is provided, not by the donor-and-government approaches themselves, but by challenges to government and development machineries from lobby groups of women activists, women's NGOs and intellectual women. During the Frelimo era Mozambican civil society organizations were almost non-existent, and OMM had been the one and only women's organization. With the political changes in the late 1980s – the introduction of PRE (*Programa de Re-estruturação Economica*), later re-named PRES (*Programa de Re-estruturação Economica e Social*) – NGOs emerged all over the place, including a series of local women's NGOs. An umbrella organization, *Forum Mulher*, was created, embracing national and international NGOs, government institutions working with women's issues, as well as women/gender-aware individuals from trade unions and political parties (cf. Arthur 2000). Over the years *Forum Mulher* has become a focus for debate on women's issues and quite an important lobby group, pushing women's issues where and when it is felt needed. After the 1995 Beijing Fourth World Conference on Women, *Forum Mulher* was active in the setting up of a so-called operative group (*Grupo Operativo*) led by the Minister for Co-ordination of Social Welfare, and incorporating representatives for fifteen different ministries, as well as in the drafting of a Post-Beijing National Plan of Action (da Silva & Andrade 2000, 81). The planning in this case took place at a very general level, but nevertheless it could be used as a tool for putting further pressure on the government.

The PROAGRI Programme

That pressure is needed is obvious. The development of a unified, donor financed and supervised plan for the ministry of Agriculture, the so-called PROAGRI: National Programme for Agrarian Development, may in this context serve as an example. The PROAGRI process started in the mid-1990s and since then a series of plans were elaborated and a series of joint donor evaluations took place. From the side of the donors there was a more or less steady insistence regarding consideration of gender factors in the PROAGRI planning process, and various gender focal points internally in the Ministry of Agriculture as well as in the Directories for Agriculture in the provincial governments were established. Nevertheless the push for gender awareness in PROAGRI contexts was all the way an uphill struggle.

As expressed by Wenke Adam, who was involved at an early point in the PROAGRI process, all the talk about 'gender awareness' is in actual fact very simple:

> Actually it is nothing revolutionary, it is just simply to acknowledge the fact that in agriculture men and women generally perform different tasks, complementary and socially defined, and that when somebody plans to make an intervention in this sector, it will be a good idea to make an analysis regarding who does what and why, in order to be able to direct the support to the proper persons, in the most adequate form, for the best effect. ... An important aspect, in this context not to be forgotten, is that in Mozambique, for historical reasons, the major part of the actual work with the crops in the field is done by women, as their regular and permanent work. The men will clear the bush, and they may participate in the sowing and the harvesting, but for the rest of the time they will often be on the lookout for waged employment in order to be able to buy such non-agricultural products as the family needs. The men also deal with the cattle. If we consider the fact that the family sector produces around 95 per cent of the country's basic agricultural products, it becomes abundantly clear that is the Mozambican women who feed Mozambique with grain, potatoes, groundnuts and vegetables. Any support to the family sector should thus be directed to this group. (Adam 1997, 9)

This indeed seems very simple and straightforward. That the main producers in family agriculture are women is a well known fact, and since in Mozambique the family sector in agriculture is by far the largest one[9] in terms of persons engaged in production, as well as in terms of produced goods, women obviously are centrally positioned. How then is this reflected in the plan?

The answer is that it is not reflected. The PROAGRI Master Document,

[9] According to the 1997 census (*II Recenseamento Geral da População e Habitação* 1997) 79 % of the Mozambican population are 'peasants', i.e. family farmers. Among these two-thirds are women.

containing the 1998–2003 plan, is a masterpiece in deliberate gender blindness. The family sector figures fairly prominently. It is acknowledged that this sector comprises some 3,000,000 families occupying a total farming area of 3,500,000 ha of land. It is also acknowledged that about 55 per cent of the total farmed area is concentrated in the three northern provinces of Nampula, Cabo Delgado and Niassa. But gender aspects are not mentioned at all. In the text of the document neither men nor women are agents; the way it is put is as follows: 'the family sector grows commercial crops such as ....', 'the family sector engages in the cutting and sale of firewood.' (Ministry of Agriculture 1998, 29). To be noted here is first that the 'sector' as such is the subject, neither men nor women, and secondly that what are mentioned are commercial crops and firewood for sale. That women in the family sector produce food to feed the vast majority of the Mozambican population outside the market economy is apparently of no concern. Also not mentioned is the fact that the three northern provinces are populated by Makhuwa, Makonde and Yao peoples, all matrilineal.

That this fact is not mentioned comes as no surprise, however, especially as the general strategy of the whole PROAGRI endeavour is defined as 'the transformation of the subsistence agriculture into one that is more integrated in the functions of production, distribution and processing, in order to achieve the development of a subsistence agrarian sector which contributes with surpluses for the market and the development of an efficient and participatory entrepreneurial sector' (Ministry of Agriculture 1998, 37). The gender effects of this strategy are not investigated, perhaps for good reasons. Transformation of subsistence agriculture into more market-oriented production will, especially in the matrilineal areas where generally women control not only food production but also the distribution of food, imply the transfer of social power from women to men (cf. Chapters 1, 2 and 12). And as for the development of 'an efficient and participatory entrepreneur sector' – one may wonder if these 'entrepreneurs' in their majority will be women – or men?

Thus the PROAGRI plan is full of gender, but it is all implicit, and the strategies advocated will be to the advantage of men. Perhaps this is the reason for consistent gender blindness? No wonder that the 2002 coordinator of the Gender Unit in the Ministry of Agriculture was frustrated: 'We have difficulties in getting the leaders within the Ministry to take gender seriously. Some within the Ministry say that we are doing this work related to gender because it is the wish of the donors, and that we are doing it in order to ensure that we get the funds' (personal communication from a November 2002 review team).

In the Post-Beijing period Gender Units were created in several ministries, however without a clear mandate and outside the hierarchies of power. A 1998 review requested in the PROAGRI Master Document has this to say about the Ministry of Agriculture Gender Unit:

> It is placed in a situation where it has neither sufficient authority nor autonomy for doing what it ought to do. ... At the moment the coordinator of the Gender Unit in the Ministry of Agriculture does not participate in the management group meetings, nor does she participate in the counseling group. In this way there are few possibilities of letting the women's views be heard in these fora, or for introducing and promoting gender perspectives in the Ministry's policies and plans. (quoted in Arthur 2000, 14)

The situation in the Ministry of Agriculture may be extreme, but it is not unique. In a critical evaluation of the Mozambican governments gender politics and programmes Post-Beijing, from 1995–1999, commissioned by *Forum Mulher*, Maria José Arthur gives several similar examples. Summing up regarding the ministerial Gender Units she says: 'If these units are not given capacity to make interventions, power to take decisions and means to carry them out, they will remain no more than symbols of an intention which will never get beyond dead words on paper' (Arthur 2000, 14).

The new Family Law

At a very formal level all looks well. Male/female equality is guaranteed in the constitution, and the government, as in most African countries, has ratified the CEDAW convention. At the level of political practice, however, things work very differently. An example here is the long struggle for a new family law. Very early in the immediate post-Independence period, a Family Law project was developed, in order to replace the Portuguese *Código Civil* of 1967, containing several clauses which contradicted the constitution. The Family Law project contained clauses regarding acceptance of 'de facto' unions in order legally to protect the majority of women who were married 'traditionally' and not according to any written law; the concept of a 'male family head' was eliminated, divorce was facilitated and polygamy was made illegal. Perhaps for these reasons the Family Law project did not result in a new law. In 1982 a directive was issued, by virtue of which parts of the Family Law project could be used as guiding principles for juridical decisions. But in 1992 this directive was annulled, with the implication that it was now again the patriarchal values of the Portuguese *Código Civil* which ruled family relations. As an aspect of the post-Beijing mobilization women's groups have since 1997 been pushing for parliamentary action regarding the Family Law. The law has been on the parliament's agenda several times, but has been repeatedly and systematically postponed. At long last in April 2003, the new Family Law was finally discussed and passed in the Assembly of the Republic (AIM April 29, 2003). That this new law has not constituted a regression with regard to any of the radical suggestions brought forward in the first draft of 1980 is remarkable, the general political situation taken into consideration. As far as I can see the explanation for this is to be found in one particular fact: the perpetually active Maputo lobby groups of researchers and activists regarding women's issues, who have been feeding the Frelimo Minister of Justice with facts and arguments, and also, of course, the minister's willingness to listen. As noted in local media: 'The parliamentary debate showed that this is one of the few issues where the government is to the left of the Frelimo parliamentary group. While every speech broadly welcomed the bill, they usually contained reservations' (AIM April 29, 2003). According to the new bill the husband will no longer automatically represent the family; either partner may do so; 'de facto' marriages will be recognised, which means that children of this type of union will have the same protection and recognition as children of any other form of marriage, and that the father, if the marriage breaks down, will be obliged to pay maintenance. Polygamous unions are not outlawed, but they are also not recognized, except at the time of the man's death, in order to safeguard the inheritance rights of his wives and children.

I shall leave the SAP/PRE period here, with these examples, one rather negative (the PROAGRI case) and one surprisingly positive (the new Family Law) from the point of view of women's activist groups. Now for a brief summing up regarding the four aspects of work, family, sexuality and maternity.

Work: Women's work in the market sector is considered an indication of gender equality. This is not much different from the socialist vision of the woman wage worker and tractor driver: that is to say, women in men's work. What women have to deal with apart from this kind of work, in terms of housework and caretaking, seems more invisible than ever.

Family: The position regarding the 'family' is ambiguous, due to the recent passing of the new Family Law. In a Government programme proposal for 2000–2004, Frelimo flags its old preference for Christian family values, stating that 'the Frelimo government will ... guarantee the continuation of the Fatherland and stability of the family, the basic cell of our society' (Frelimo Comité Central 1999, quoted in Arthur 2000, 11). Women's groups have been struggling for different visions of family life, more on women's terms. Now the women's groups' visions have been turned into law. Of course realities still do not change overnight, but obviously this is an important step in the right direction.

Sexuality: Female initiation rituals, which were a burning issue in colonial times as well as during Frelimo socialism, are a non-issue nowadays. People are free to perform any ritual they wish, and initiation rites are now again openly taking place, particularly in the northern part of the country. Because of the HIV/ AIDS pandemic, which is widespread also in Mozambique (the prevalence rate of HIV infected on a national level is currently 12 per cent (Danida 2002)) sexuality is often being associated with risk and danger. The strong moral tone of previous politics has eased, but it has been replaced by a discourse of risk and danger.

Maternity: Motherhood is only an issue in practical terms, as for example in the contexts of health (where women's reproductive health is integrated in the Family Health section), and of maintenance payments. The *Raínha do lar* has disappeared, but motherhood as a basis for female power receives no political recognition.

Conclusion

In spite of the overall conclusion that examined through a gendered lens the political continuities during the latest fifty years of turbulent Mozambican history have been more apparent the radical changes, some changes *have* taken place. One of the more important ones is the appearance of civil society lobby groups for women's rights, gender equality and the promotion of women's perspectives (Loforte 2000, Casimiro 2004). But these groups fight an uphill battle. First they must fight just to keep women's issues on the agenda, and second they must fight on the issue of *how* women's issues are integrated into the political process. But by their actions, they might, with time, be able to integrate the forms of female power which are still embedded in the social systems of the vast and populous matrilineal societies in the north of Mozambique into the mainstream of the nation's life.

Part II
NIGHT OF THE WOMEN, DAY OF THE MEN: MEANINGS OF FEMALE INITIATION

6 Feminism & Gendered Bodies:
On Female Initiation in Northern Mozambique   (2008)

It might have been expected that coming-of-age rituals such as the female initi-ation ceremonies in northern Mozambique would have disappeared as a conse-quence of the increasing commodification of agricultural production,[1] expanding electrification of rural towns and villages, general proliferation of mobile phones and other indications of economic changes and modernizing lifestyles. Such is, however, not the case. To a certain extent what has happened is the opposite. Initiation rituals, male and female, are practised today with more vigour and zeal than 20–30 years ago. Frelimo was squarely against 'tradi-tional customs' like initiation rituals, which they found deeply backward and woman-oppressive.[2] During the 1970s and the first half of the 1980s Frelimo and the OMM (the National Women's Organization, *Organização da Mulher Moçambicana*) campaigned consistently against initiation rituals and other customs and practices, such as *lobolo* (bride price) and polygamy. At the end of every political meeting people would shout, waving their clenched fists towards the ground: *abaixo ritos de iniciação, abaixo lobolo* (down with initiation rituals, down with lobolo). During these years initiation rituals were less frequently practised, and if practised at all they took place in secret – which to some extent was a violation of the very idea of these coming-of-age rituals. The initiation rituals are social celebrations, and part of the point of the celebration is the announcement to the world that NN's son/daughter has now been through the initiation rituals and thus counts as a grown up man or woman. As told by a Cabo Delgado[3] woman, whom I interviewed during 'prohibition times' in 1982:

> In the old days, when I was a child, we had ceremonies, we were dancing and beating the drums. The whole population would know that now the daughter of so-and-so is in the initiation rituals, that she is now a woman. I have eleven daughters, but nobody knows about it, because I didn't send them to the initiation rites. Now I don't feel like arranging marriages for my daughters, since they haven't been through the initiation rituals.

The introduction in Mozambique of Structural Adjustment Programmes in the late 1980s indicated a political turn on the part of Frelimo (which was, and is, still the ruling party). The strict socialist ideology was given up, and the 'abaixo' politics were loosened. So-called traditional authority – which during the socialist ideology period had been frowned upon by Frelimo – was legalized in 2000, and people were left to do more or less as they pleased regarding customs and traditions. During the first half of the 1990s, when the civil war had come to an end, [4] the celebration of male and female initiation rituals was taken up again in rural Mozambique, particularly in the northern provinces. Even before Frelimo, initiation rituals had been stronger here, compared to the south of the country, now they resurfaced. When in the late 1990s/early 2000s I under-took fieldwork in Ribáuè district, Nampula province, female initiation rituals were celebrated all over the place during the dry season (roughly from

---

[1] The World Bank Structural Adjustment Programme (SAP) was introduced in Mozambique in the late 1980s. In Portuguese SAP is PRE (*Programa de Re-estruturação Económica*)

[2] Frelimo's perception of female initiation rituals is discussed in the Introduction, and in chapters 1, 2, 8 and 9

[3] Cabo Delgado is the northernmost province of Mozambique, bordering to Tanzania.

[4] The civil war between Frelimo and Renamo started in the early 1980s. It was formally ended 1992, but it took some years before – after close to three decades of almost continued war (first the liberation war against the Portuguese, and soon after the civil war) – people could really trust peace to be genuine and real.

November through February) and there were often two, three or more celebrations at weekends in the vicinity of Ribáuè town where I was living.

In the following I'll be concerned only with female initiation rituals. Male initiation rituals are also celebrated in northern Mozambique, but less frequently than the female ones. In the old days this had been different, but at the time of my fieldwork many people seemed to think that initiation rituals for boys were not that important. Initiation rituals for girls were another matter. I did not get any good explanations for why this was so. My own guess is that while modernizing life is offering men new possibilities for reinforcing their status and self respect as men, this has not to the same extent been the case for women. Most of the changes brought about by modernizing life in rural Mozambique are favouring male power, and disfavouring women. In my interpretation female initiation rituals in northern Mozambique are valued and maintained as a means of reinforcing women's collective identity as women, vis a vis men.

In my early writings on initiation rituals, based on fieldwork from the 1980s (Arnfred 1988 and Chapters 1, 2 and 8 in this volume) my approach to analysis took a point of departure in male/female gender power relations. In this chapter I'll approach the analysis of female initiation rituals from a different angle. I investigate the ritual proceedings from a point of view of feminist theorizing regarding gendered bodies. Initiation rituals deal with preparation of bodies as well as of minds. They are full of instructions regarding dos and don'ts, for hours the initiates sit listening to chanted advice and instructions, impossible to remember and understand after just one session. An important aspect of the rituals is repetition; once a young woman has herself been initiated, she'll participate again and again in initiation rituals of friends and relatives. The female initiation rituals are festive occasions for all initiated women of the community. This also means that under normal conditions any woman will have many times the possibility of listening to these complicated series of advice and instructions. For the purpose of this chapter, however, I'll focus on bodies.

This focus is inspired by strands of feminist theory, which have put an emphasis on denaturalizing bodies and on claiming that gendered bodies are not given by nature, that there is no such thing as a 'natural' body, and that both 'biological sex' and 'social gender' are socially produced. Male/female is not something you are but something you do and confirm by repeated re-enactments. In my view female initiation rituals make a very good case for this type of analysis. In the following I'll first briefly introduce the strands of feminist thinking relevant in this context: Post-structuralist feminist thinking as developed particularly by Judith Butler, and post-colonial feminist critique, where I'll use the work of Oyèrónké Oyewùmí (1997, 2000, 2002). Having paved the way for an approach to thinking about bodies, which takes circumstances and social relations into account, I'll present what I consider in this context to be relevant aspects of the ritual sequence of female initiation rituals as I have seen them practised in northern Mozambique. In the subsequent analysis I'll draw on these rather general conceptualizations, also introducing some more specific categories regarding bodily disciplinary practices, as developed by Sandra Lee Bartky (1988/1998) by inspiration from Michel Foucault. Finally I'll wind up in a general summary and conclusion regarding what a theoretical focus on bodies may tell us about female initiation rituals in northern Mozambique.

Feminist thinking beyond the sex/gender distinction

The analytical distinction between 'sex' and 'gender' – theoretically very productive in the early years of Second Wave feminist theorizing – has from the 1990s onwards been thoroughly debunked. The sex/gender distinction – inspired by Claude Levi-Strauss and based on the same kind of nature/culture dichotomy, which he takes for granted (Rubin 1975) – was a useful tool in arguments against 'biology is destiny' lines of thinking, which explained women's position in society in terms of their bodies. The sex/gender thinking, by inserting a separation between biological 'sex' and socio-cultural 'gender', located the dynamics of male dominance/female subordination in the socio-cultural realm, and thus as a historically produced fact, open to change through political struggle. But the sex/gender line of thinking also had limitations, such as taking a male/female binary and heterosexuality for granted. In her seminal book *Gender Trouble* (1990) Judith Butler argues against the nature/culture dichotomy as well as against sex/gender lines of thinking. There is no 'natural' sex, she says, on which socio-cultural 'gender' is inscribed; 'biology' and 'sex' itself are social constructions, and the distinction between 'sex' and 'gender' turns out to be no distinction at all (Butler 1990, 11). In Butler's view it is the socio-culturally established 'heterosexual matrix', which produces 'men' and 'women' in pre-supposed relationships of domination/subordination. Much Second Wave feminism has been thinking along such lines, but this is, according to Butler, 'a colonizing epistemological strategy', extending Western conditions of male domination/female subordination to the rest of the world, or, more precisely, misinterpreting different configurations of power hierarchies as patriarchal domination (ibid., 46). This hint is later taken up by Oyèrónké Oyewùmí, cf. below.

Judith Butler suggests very different ways of thinking about gender and about gendered bodies. Gender is not the expression of as 'essence' (as in sex/gender, nature/culture lines of thinking); it is rather the other way round: 'the various *acts* of gender *create the idea* of gender, and without those acts there would be no gender at all' (ibid., 178, emphasis added, SA). Gender should not be seen as a stable identity, or a locus of agency from which acts follow; rather 'gender is ... instituted in an exterior space through a stylized repetition of acts' (ibid., 179). Following this thinking gender is produced through repeated bodily acts. 'As in other ritual social dramas' Butler writes, 'the action of gender requires a performance that is repeated. This repetition is at once a re-enactment and a re-experiencing of a set of meanings already socially established' (ibid., 178). Repeated performance of stylized acts creates the idea and the social reality of gender. Brought to bear on initiation rituals as the ones in northern Mozambique, this line of thinking suggests that rituals such as these are constitutive not just of womanhood as a collective, shared identity but constitutive of womanhood and gender as such; it suggests that these rituals are constitutive, in the local context, of what is a woman.

As a queer theorist Butler is at odds with mainstream feminist thinking, which, according to her, is based on implicit acceptance of 'the heterosexual matrix' and 'regulation of sexuality within the obligatory frame of reproductive heterosexuality' (ibid., 173). Nigerian sociologist Oyèrónké Oyewùmí produces another line of critique of mainstream feminist thinking, focused in her case on the concept of 'woman' and on the implicit, taken-for-granted notions in Western feminism of male dominance/female subordination. Unlike Butler, Oyewùmí doesn't anchor her critique in notions of compulsory hetero-sexuality (actually Oyewùmí hardly deals with sexuality at all); she is critical of fixed male/female binaries, but from a different vantage point, and in her analysis of gender power relations, she focuses on implications of motherhood (an aspect of gender on which Butler is silent). From each of their different posi-tions Butler and Oyewùmí raise critique of mainstream feminist lines of thinking; as a queer theorist Butler finds herself misrepresented in mainstream feminism, and similarly Oyewùmí finds Western feminist concepts inadequate for understanding social relations in Nigeria. To Oyewùmí a fixed male/female opposition doesn't make sense; the idea of a 'woman' which in mainstream Western feminism is conditioned by its a priori relation of subordination to a 'man', doesn't fit Nigerian experience. 'The fundamental category "woman"' she says, 'simply did not exist in Yorùbáland prior to its sustained contact with the West' (1997, ix). By this she doesn't mean to say that 'males' or 'females' or 'masculinity'/'femininity' did not exist, but rather that the meanings that these terms have gained in Western contexts don't fit the pre-colonial Yoruba situation. Butler and Oyewùmí agree to the fact that the commonsense Western male/female opposition, which is based on interpretations of bodies as either male or female, takes far too much for granted.

Seniority, age and contingent bodies

In Yoruba contexts gender is not an a priori indicator of social hierarchy, Oyewùmí says. Sometimes social hierarchies work along gender lines, often they don't. A more frequent indication of social hierarchy in Africa (according to Oyewùmí) is seniority. Male/female in commonsense Western understand-ings is based on bodies: male bodies, female bodies. However, from a Yoruba stance, 'the body appears to have an exaggerated presence in Western thought and social practice, including feminist theories. In the Yorùbá world ... the "physicality" of maleness or femaleness did not have social antecedents and therefore did not constitute social categories. Social hierarchy was determined by social relations' (Oyewùmí 1997, 13). Oyewùmí criticizes mainstream femi-nist assumptions of a priori gender hierarchies (male dominance/female subor-dination) for being essentialist and misleading, a critique which is parallel to Butler's critique of mainstream feminism as 'a colonizing epistemological strategy'. Unlike sex/gender, which is rooted in bodies, seniority is per se a social relation: older than, younger than. Seniority is always contextual; it is not based on chronological age. [5] For instance in a polygamous relationship, the 'older' wife is the one who was first married to the husband, even if in years she might be younger than the second wife.

   Caroline Bledsoe's concept of contingency captures this contextuality, carrying it further into thinking about bodies in different ways. Bledsoe talks of

[5] In my view it is too narrow to say, as Oyewùmí actually does, that seniority is based on chrono-logical age, even if, of course, there is often correspondence. Such as, for instance, among siblings.

two visions of time and the body (Bledsoe 2002, 16): the usual chronological one (as years go by you grow older), and the other one, the logic of contingency, which means that age depends on context and social relations. She discusses how age is not simply chronological (as demographers would like to think), and how social action *produces* age. Bledsoe writes about fertility and aging, and through her concept of contingency she turns Western commonsense notions of the relation between the two upside down. In Western thinking one is likely to presume that childbearing stops because the woman grows too old; in rural Gambia women see things the other way round: many childbirths produce bodily ageing, a process that in turn precludes further reproduction (ibid., 25). 'Becoming pregnant, bringing the pregnancy to term, and giving birth to a healthy baby (not to mention doing so multiple times) – and undergoing a process of contingent aging – all these are not simply biological processes that occur within a given window of time. They are *products of action* in a precarious social and physical world' (ibid., 25; emphasis added, SA). Thus acts produce not only gender (Butler) but also age.

To support her argument that events other than chronological age produce age in Africa, Bledsoe reminds us that 'chronological age draws virtually no interest throughout rural sub-Saharan Africa, a fact to which generations of frustrated census takers and surveyors can attest' (ibid., 10). This is also true in Mozambique. In order to tell about age counted in years you rely on the language of the state; when in my early interviews I asked this – in a Western context innocent – question: 'What is your age?', people would show me their identity cards, produced by census-takers.

Bodies are produced by wilful social action, in terms of their gender, and in terms of their age. This is what the female initiation rituals are all about. You are not just *born* a woman, you do not just *grow* into adulthood. Through the chain of ceremonies described below, the young girls, previously seen as children, are produced as adult members of the community (the dimension of age), and they are produced as marriageable women (the dimension of gender).

Female initiation rituals in northern Mozambique

Female initiation rituals, as practised in northern Mozambique, are in themselves multiple events, comprising a string of sessions, performances, happenings etc. They vary from one place to another, each particular *namalaka* (*conselheira* in Portuguese; the one who directs and monitors the ritual sequence) having her own style. Furthermore, the rituals have been changing over time. In pre-war, pre-Independence days, they had a longer duration, the seclusion period could last for months. When during the first Frelimo period – 'the time of Samora' as this period is now often called, named after Mozambique's first president Samora Machel, who died 1986 – the initiation rituals were campaigned against by the Party and by the OMM, they retreated and went underground. Now, when they have re-emerged they are generally condensed to take place during a weekend only, from Friday to Sunday. The seclusion period has been cut out. This edition of 'initiation rituals light' is more easily accommodated with schoolwork, or whatever else is occupying young women.

In the details the sequence of female initiation rituals may vary quite a lot, even within a small geographical area, depending on the particular namalaka. But in the broader picture all ritual sequences share some basic elements. The first important event or process to be mentioned is actually not part of the initi-ation rituals as such; it is/was supposed to have taken place for a period of years before initiation. When time for the rituals arrives, the result of this process is/was checked by the namalaka. I am talking about the work young girls are/were supposed to engage in, pulling their *labia minora* in order to produce the elongated labia (*ithuna*). When during my second fieldwork period in the late 1990s/early 2000s I discussed this with rural women my own age (+/-) it was clear that elongation with a subsequent check was a shared experience. It is however my impression that this particular aspect of the female bodily prepa-ration for adulthood is no longer as widespread as it used to be. During the various ceremonies of female initiation in which I participated (as an observer) check of ithuna was absent.

Previously, however, the vaginal lip-elongation preceded the rituals proper. The girls were instructed regarding this pulling of vaginal lips years before they reached puberty and the age for initiation. They would be instructed by an older female relative – never the mother – regarding how to prepare a special pomade, made from the oily seed of a particular bush plant (*npichi*). The container, in which this pomade was kept, was considered a very secret and female item, a kind of extension of the personality of this particular woman. The girls were instructed how, with two fingers on each hand and by applying this pomade, gently to pull the small lips of the vagina, in order to make them longer. Some-thing like the length of a finger was the desired result. When in the early 1980s I worked in the national office of the OMM, preparing (on behalf of Frelimo and the OMM) nation-wide popular discussions about what in the political language of the time was called 'women's social problems', female initiation rituals being one, this practice of elongation was much debated in countless public meetings throughout Mozambique. Generally the practice was highly praised by women as well as by men, as a contributing factor to a pleasurable sexual life. The extended vaginal lips would prolong the sexual foreplay, the women explained, they were a pleasure for men as well as for women. 'You have the kissing,' one woman told me, 'we have the ithuna.'

Previously, when initiation rituals included a period of seclusion, this would typically start at or around the time of the first menstruation. There are stories about how expert women could detect when the first menstruation was about to occur, thus taking their precautions in advance of the actual event. Anyhow, at the time of the first menstruation (*wula*) the mother of the girl in question will call old expert women for giving initial instructions to the girl. These instruc-tions will often be given in a scary atmosphere, the menstruating girl is seeing and feeling the blood, but she doesn't know what is happening to her. I was once present at such an event; the poor girl cried all the time, the old women abusing her for being so timid.

Generally a menstruating woman cannot cook for others, and she cannot have sex, these being some of the more important among a number of compli-cated rules and prohibitions, which must be observed by menstruating women. The reason for seclusion to start at the time of menstruation was control of reproduction. In parts of northern Mozambique rules for sexual play between children were quite permissive; however, once a girl starts menstruating, strict control applies. Not in order to censor sex, but in order to make sure that reproduction takes place under controlled and institutionalized conditions, that is after marriage. If at the point of entering initiation a girl would already have a fiancé, he would also receive instructions.

Throughout the seclusion period the young initiates (*amwali*) would stay in a specially built hut in the bush, the length of the period depending on the time of year and the wealth of the parents. This location would serve as a favoured meeting place for the adult women of the area, a place in which they would be entitled to behave in particularly licentious ways, quite different from normal, controlled, subdued female conduct. Present-day rituals still serve as this kind of meeting place for women, even when the seclusion period has been cut out. The three day event, to which the rituals nowadays have been reduced, more or less corresponds with what used to be the coming out ceremony, ending the seclusion.

This ceremony was/is a dense sequence of sessions and events, during which the young initiates are told and shown how to behave as adult women, including how to show respect to older people. They are exposed to long sequences of chanted instructions (*ikano*) given by the namalaka in a singing tone of voice while her helpers beat the rhythm pertaining to this particular ikano. Parts of the instructions are given verbally, other parts are acted out by the namalaka and her helpers in a kind of instructive theatre, in which also the initiates take part. Usually a group of young girls will go through the ceremonies together, building close relations to each other based on this shared experience. A key point in the ceremonies on the last day are the instructions about how to conduct sex in marriage, how to move during intercourse with the husband, how to wipe and clean his penis after sex, and also about what to expect from the husband afterwards (for example a gift, or money). The namalaka is under her *capulana* equipped with a clay penis, which she has tied round her waist in a string, and using this penis she plays the male part during the instructions, first performing 'coitus' with one of her helpers, then with the initiates one by one.

The kinship structure of the people of northern Mozambique is matrilineal: The women remain with their own family at marriage, and children belong to the mother's lineage. Marriage thus is no big deal, and fatherhood has no great importance. The maternal uncle (mother's brother) will be the man responsible for/with authority over his sister's children. Women are – through the initiation rituals and beyond – educated in the arts of lovemaking; they must rely on their capacity as seducers, since they need the men for getting pregnant, thus being able to give continuity to their lineage.

Making sense of the rituals; initial analysis

In the early 1980s the initiation rituals were supposed to have been eradicated, and travelling at that point as an employee of the OMM, there was a limit to what the women would show me. However, when in the late 1990s/early 2000s

I returned as an individual researcher, the times as well as my position having changed, I had the chance to be present during the celebration of several of these ceremonies. A very strong impression was the division in demeanor and style of behaviour between on the one hand the young, scared girls with downcast eyes, and on the other hand the rowdy, uproarious women. But there are also exercises, tests and trials, in which the young initiates have to take part, such as sessions of dance competition, testing the girls' agility of hip-undulation and other similar movements. In other sessions the namalaka would dress up as an old frail woman, whom the initiates were expected to treat with helpfulness and respect[6]. The whole thing felt like a piece of participatory theatre, going on non-stop from Friday noon and finishing Sunday morning, through two nights without sleep and almost two days of scorching sunlight.

Obviously the rituals are about the creation of women. Simone de Beauvoir's famous dictum: 'One is not born, but rather becomes, a woman'[7] (de Beauvoir 1949/1997, 295) – is particularly true in the context of female initiation. The *anamalaka* (older, professional women in charge) are creators of women: From the raw material of the pubescent girls entering the rituals, the amwali, they create young women ready for marriage. The Western common sense notion that a girl child turns into a woman mainly as a consequence of physical and biological changes taking place in her body at a certain age does not hold true; here adult women are created by the anamalaka through trials and tests, dances, performances and passing-on of secret knowledge. Centrally positioned in this creation of adultness is the importance of respectful behaviour towards elders and other adults; respectful behaviour also dignifies yourself. Through male and female initiation rituals dignified respectful men and women are created; and accordingly, not having been through the rituals you cannot be considered a person, you do not count. Here Bledsoe's concept of contingent bodies applies: age and position depend on context and social action, not on a number of years. In one of the ritual sessions, where I participated, one of the initiates was actually a middle-aged woman. Having been of pubescent age during 'prohibition time' in the 1970s and 1980s however, she never had been through the rituals, and thus she was/had been excluded from participation in the repeated reproductions of womanhood on community level. This lack had by now become unbearable, and she had opted for going through the rituals in spite of her advanced (biological) age.

The case of this woman also points to the importance of being aware of what one might call the double aspect of the initiation rituals: the fact that the importance of the rituals is not only for the initiates, but also very much for the female community as such, that is for all the women participating. This double aspect is crucial. The same occasion, which for the initiates is a frightening and harrowing event focused on the serious business of introduction to adulthood, for the older women is an opportunity for unending childishness and types of exalted behaviour, which under normal conditions they would never allow themselves.

---

[6] The sequence of events is further described in Chapter 7.

[7] That Simone de Beauvoir did not in her own work follow this insight is another issue. *The Second Sex* is full of passages lamenting the ways in which women are chained to their difficult, leaking, reproducing bodies, cf. Chapter 4.

The division between amwali and already initiated older women carries meaning in many different ways. There is the aspect of different bodily styles or demeanour, which also reflect a relation of domination. The older women are in charge, and they are free to use the occasion for harassing and castigating the young. The amwali can only suffer and endure, talking back is unthinkable. There is also the aspect of repetition. I was first taken aback by the density and speed of the chanted instructions of the ikano. Until I remembered that individual women participate many times. The different bodily styles have also another implication, beyond the power relation. The behaviour of the older women breaks clearly with female bodily styles in normal Makhuwa life. The rituals create a space and a time where other rules apply. Similarly with the spoken/chanted ikano. Here the namalaka often uses particular words which belong only here in the space and time of the rituals. To use such words in different settings, in other spaces and at other times, would be a shocking transgression, an obscenity. By sharing secrets – a particular language and particular behaviour – the women create a bond and a community. Being part of this knowledge and this behaviour is part of womanhood, Makhuwa style.

At initiation rituals particular (normally forbidden) speech and particular (normally forbidden) behaviour are permitted. It was my impression that this carnivalesque license is part of the fascination and attraction for the female community of initiation rituals. In the course of the rituals, besides codes of conduct you are also taught particular words. This secret, esoteric knowledge gives you away, or rather: If you show that you are familiar with this secret knowledge, with these particular words and ways of talking, people will recognize that indeed this young woman has been though the initiation rites. Sometimes it works like a password: If when asked a particular question you can give the proper answer, this shows that you have been 'taught'. Much of this secret knowledge is not real knowledge in any Western sense, it is rather like being introduced to a certain code of speech, particular secret words, which attain a certain power, exactly because they are secret.[8] In a Western context this power and fear of certain words has eroded a lot over the last decades, but still particular words connected with sex and defecation are not supposed to be uttered publicly – and if they do, it is a particular act of protest or demonstration; thus even in a Western context certain words are powerful, in this sense of being obscene or repugnant. In the Makhuwa context as a child, before initiation, you rarely hear these words, and if you do, you sense their forbidden meanings.

An example of such change of vocabulary is the name of a sanitary towel. This thing has got a neutral, modern name: *Modess*, after the first brand of factory produced sanitary towels to appear on Mozambican soil. The ritual name is *nakhapa* – a loaded word with a strong impact. Other loaded words are *wula*, menstruation, and *ithuna*, small lips of the vagina. These words are not used in public. They are strong and secret words. But in the context of initiation rites the rules are different. Here speech is free, and the women indulge in using these powerful words.

[8] Cf Audrey Richards on female initiation in Zambia in the 1930s: 'What seems ... to be the most mumbo-jumbo and useless aspect of the whole affair, may actually constitute one of the most prized items to the people concerned' (1956/1982, 127) cf. Chapter 9 this volume.

The female initiation ritual is an occasion for chat and gossip and merrymaking on the part of the participating women. The women display their adornments: tattoos and missangas [strings of glass beads round the waist]. There is also a sexual initiation: Accompanied by drumbeats and chanting the women will show the initiates how to perform the particular lascivious and erotic movements, [which are part of the female education for intercourse]. With a piece of wood in the shape of a penis the girls are taught how to cleanse their husbands after intercourse. The language is obscene, which means that the women call the things by name, and only rarely they will recur to euphemisms, like saying *bicho* (worm) when referring to the male sexual organ. (female informant quoted by Sá e Bonnet 1996, 58)[9]

Thus the initiation rituals are about creation of gender, not just in terms of the nondescript initiates being produced as women, but in a wider sense also in terms of Makhuwa womanhood being produced on these occasions.

On bodies, performativity and disciplinary practices

The Butlerian notion of performativity works well as an analytical approach to initiation rituals. It overlaps partly with the notion of the rituals as 'participatory theatre', a notion which came to my mind in Ribáuè, without thinking of Judith Butler. The description as 'participatory theatre' refers to the many 'pieces of enactments' of which the rituals are composed. For instance the competitive dancing sessions mentioned above, lessons regarding how to show respect to older people, the lesson regarding sex-in-marriage, as well as other more weird pieces like 'the hunting of the *onhipi*' which consists in one of the namalaka's helpers being disguised as roaring wild animal, frightening the initiates (this goes on at night), or 'the search of the *nshileiyamwali*', which is about a particular plant, which may have a single or several roots. Each initiate must select a growing plant, the number of roots showing if the girl is single (one root), has a lover (two roots) or multiple lovers, which is considered no good, and about which she'll be forced to confess.

The basic modus of all performance is, however, the timid, frightened demeanour of the initiates: downcast eyes, no talking, no overt signs of pain or pleasure being allowed, in stark contrast to the unbridled, sexually daring behaviour of the participating crowd of community women. The whole thing looked to me like enactment of gender in two extremes: on one hand bodies which are very controlled and subdued; on the other hand bodies let loose in forms of behaviour, far beyond decent femininity in gender-mixed public life.

In order to be able to go more into detail with the different kinds of bodily disciplinary practices and techniques at play during initiation, I have taken a point of departure in Sandra Lee Bartky's categories as developed in her paper "Foucault, Femininity and the Modernization of Patriarchal Power" (1988/1998). Bartky criticizes Michel Foucault for not being aware of gender distinctions in his analysis of the ways in which modernity through a variety of institutional disciplinary techniques produce the 'docile bodies' which fit smoothly into the given society. 'Where is the account of the disciplinary prac-

[9] João Alberto de Sá e Bonnet is a Mozambican scholar; *Aspectos pedagógoicos da socialização da criança durante os ritos de iniciação da puberdade* (1996) is his MA thesis.

tices that engender the 'docile bodies' of women?' she asks (1988/1998, 27) proceeding to distinguish three categories of disciplinary practices which produce feminine bodies (in Western contexts): (a) a body of a certain size and general configuration (including dieting practices), (b) a specific repertoire of gestures, postures and movements (such as ways of sitting, walking, getting in and out of cars), and (c) the body on display as an ornamented surface (skin-care, makeup, dress etc) (ibid., 27–33).

All categories would be relevant in Mozambique, but not necessarily the taken for granted premise for Bartky's analysis that all of these practices have to do with bodies on which an inferior status has already been inscribed (ibid., 33). 'Woman lives her body as seen by another, by an anonymous patriarchal Other,' Bartky says, universalizing her analysis by talking about 'woman'. It is important to note that this paper was written in 1985, published 1988, i,e. before Butler's *Gender Trouble*, and at a point when postcolonial feminist analysis was less known than it is today. In Bartky's exceptionally clear and inspiring analysis there is no hint that the subordinate conditions of Western women are not the subordinate conditions of women everywhere. In fact she even says that 'the larger disciplines that construct a 'feminine' body out of a female one are by no means race- or class-specific' proceeding to give examples from a race- and class-divided USA. Bartky does refer, however, to sub-cultures of resistance, such as women in radical lesbian communities struggling to develop new female aesthetics (ibid., 43).

The feminine disciplining practices to which Bartky refers are so pervasive in Western contexts that they may be hard to see. Like the air you breathe – you take them for granted. Much of the accomplishment of the paper is that she makes this invisible 'air' visible. Bartky sees Western femininity as constructed under a male gaze, where the man is the subject, woman the object, the 'other' (as analyzed by Simone de Beauvoir 1949/1997). She also acknowledges a certain ambiguity to be at play in so far as dieting, make up etc are often keenly practiced and defended by women themselves, perceived as crucial parts of their respective identities, while at the same time they must be understood as 'aspects of a far larger discipline, an oppressive and inegalitarian system of sexual subordination' (Bartky 1998, 37). 'To have a body felt to be feminine – a body socially constructed through the appropriate practices – is in most cases crucial to a woman's sense of herself as female, and since persons currently can *be* only as male or female, to her sense of herself as an existing individual' (ibid., 39). In this analysis she captures how subjection and female subjectivity often go hand in hand, a point later elaborated by Butler in her notion of 'the paradox of subjectivation' (Butler 1997).

Beyond the general premise of male domination/female subordination, which in my view cannot be taken for granted in the Mozambican context, particularly not in the matrilineal north, Bartky's categories make good sense when applied to what takes place during the female initiation rituals:

(a) *general configuration.* What is the ideal shape of a woman's body in northern Mozambique? A striking difference, compared to Western ideals, is the lack of a feminine ideal of slender, not to say thin, female bodies. In rural Mozambique a certain roundness is considered attractive; a woman should rather be round than square. The skin should be smooth and light. In the old days, particularly in the coastal areas of northern Mozambique, during the long seclusion period the faces of young initiates would be smeared with *msiro*, a white substance made from the ground weed of a certain tree, mixed with water. This in order to make them beautiful. In the old days an ideal woman's body should also have the elongated labia minora. The exercise of pulling may be considered as a body-sculpting endeavour, parallel in a way to dieting, but of course very different. The pulling generally started well before puberty, initially under the instruction of an older female relative, after which the girls would go on by themselves, pulling more or less on a daily basis, generally in groups, at a secret location in the bush. Implications of vaginal lip pulling (which by colonial missionaries and anthropologists was considered deeply repugnant, see Chapters 2 and 5) are likely to be young women's familiarity with and acceptance of their own sexual potentials and capacities. The elongated *labia minora* and the subsequent instructions during initiation rituals regarding how to conduct proper sex in marriage may be seen both as a particular aspect of body sculpting and as sexual capacity building, particularly crucial for women in matrilineal contexts, whose task it is, with Karla Poewe's phrase (from her study of the matrilineal Luapula in neighboring Zambia) through their sexual powers 'to engulf male strangers and convert them into kin' (Poewe 1981, 68).

(b) *gestures, postures, movements.* Also in Mozambique as a woman you are supposed to sit in a certain way (sitting on the ground, legs together, stretched out in front of you), to walk in a certain manner, and generally to behave in certain ways. Subdued, controlled, respectful. You must lower your eyes when talking to a stranger. This has to do with showing respect, which again indicates adulthood. Children may behave in whichever way, but adulthood is shown by appropriate respectful behaviour. Sometimes by foreigners this kind of proper female behaviour has been interpreted as female subordination. This is a misunderstanding. Rather, by being respectful to others (particularly to men and elders) a woman shows herself as worthy of respect. As a woman you are also expected to be able to dance in certain ways. A special hip-undulating dance (very popular) is trained through girlhood and capacities are checked, when one gets to the initiation rituals. As already explained, also during the rituals young women are instructed regarding how to move during intercourse, and how to behave with husbands after sex.

(c) *the body on display / the body as an ornamented surface.* Interestingly the body as an ornamented surface is not necessarily on display. Female body ornaments – body tattoos and *missangas* – tend to be hidden away beneath the clothes. Body tattoos were previously very popular, less so these days. But still they are carried by many middle aged women in Mozambique. Body tattoos – at the stomach, low at the back, at the thighs – are produced at various points in time, starting at initiation. They are considered very erotic and have important functions during erotic play. Body tattoos are rarely seen, they are supposed to be felt by the caressing hands of the sexual partner. Similarly the missangas carried around the waist; are also not seen, but rather heard by the men walking by, as ever so slight a tingle, causing irresistible sexual arousal. The importance of invisible assets, things which are not to be seen, brings to mind an observation made by Oyèrónké Oyewùmí, in her point regarding the priority often given in the West to vision, the gaze. Westerners, she says, speak of knowledge as illumination, knowing as seeing, truth as light (1997, 15). 'A concentration on vision as the primary mode of comprehending reality promotes what can be seen over that which is not apparent to the eye' (ibid., 14). As against the Western predominance of the gaze, Oyewùmí points to hearing as a central sense in many African contexts

This makes sense also in a broader context in northern Mozambique, where many important things (such as large parts of the initiation rituals) take place at night, under more or less pitch-dark conditions. Sometimes you may get the feeling that the most interesting things takes/took place at night, when (in the colonial days) the generator producing light for the Westerners had stopped, and when missionaries and colonialists had gone to bed. This was when the dancing and the drumming started.

Repeated ritualized enactments, body disciplinary practices and male/female power relations

Young women in Mozambique – strictly speaking young persons not yet women – are created as adult and marriageable women through a series of bodily disciplining practices which are monitored, confirmed and expanded during the female initiation rituals. Through the rest of their lives these women continue to conduct themselves along the lines laid out at this occasion. As an aspect of this continuation the women participate again and again in new enactments of female initiation rituals, with new *amwali*. The female initiation rituals are thus repeated enactments or performances producing adult womanhood in this particular context.

As for the power relationships in this production of gender, these are more about seniority – older women commanding and controlling younger ones – than about male dominance. Men have no place in the female initiation rituals; gender hierarchies don't seem to play a role, but age hierarchies certainly do. Young women are harassed and castigated by older women with no possibilities of talking back. The old women are the owners of the ceremony. Even where, as in some places in colonial days, ritual intercourse was a part of the proceedings, it would always be in the hands of the namalaka: the namalaka would indicate a suitable male to act on her behalf.

The 'anonymous patriarchal Other', who in Western contexts – according to Bartky – pre-inscribes female bodies with inferior status, seems absent in northern Mozambique. This has to do with matriliny, where men gain status through women, rather than the other way round, but according to Oyewùmí this absence is also found in non-matrilineal parts of Africa, such as in Oyewùmí's native Yorubaland. In female initiation rituals in northern Mozambique the male gaze is not directly active in the sculpting of female bodies, at least it does not appear to be so. This corresponds to Oyewùmí's observations that gender hierarchies should not be taken for granted, and that relations of authority more often follow seniority than gender. The difference, also pointed out by Oyewùmí, is (among other things) that unlike gender hierarchies, which tend to be fixed and stable, hierarchies of seniority are context bound, and changing over time: the young woman who is today a powerless *mwali*, will tomorrow (or some years ahead) be one of the harassing old women in command. It is true that subjection and subjectivity also here go hand in hand – the process of becoming a woman goes through subjection to older women's power – but seen in a larger context it is also possible to see the rituals of female initiation as a collective female stronghold, uniting young and older women vis a vis male power. The fact that even during 'prohibition days' women in northern Mozambique were very reluctant to give up on their initiation rituals points in that direction.

7 Moonlight & *mato*[1]:
Women's initiation rituals in Ribáuè (1999)

During the after-harvest period 1998 to 1999 in Ribáuè there had been several celebrations of female initiation rites. The 'festive season' – with sufficient supplies of grain for beer-brewing and food for feasting – starts in September or October and goes on until January. The celebration on which this account is based took place early February and was the last one of the season. The rains were approaching, and with them a new cycle of agricultural work.

I had just arrived to Ribáuè for the second round of fieldwork, when I was informed that a session of initiation rites — the last of the season — was due to take place the following weekend, and that I was invited to attend the proceedings.[2] This particular session of female initiation rites took place in the compound of the *namalaka*, Arissa, in the mandioca fields behind her house, and in a nearby *mato*, close to the mountains, beyond a small stream. Arissa's house is situated a few kilometers outside Ribáuè town, at the other side of the river. Arissa is a *curandeira* (traditional healer), a *conselheira* (counsellor) and a remarkable woman. During the whole sequence of the rites that went on continuously from Saturday morning to Sunday noon, Arissa was in charge; she was the organizer, the speaker, the chanter, the performer, untiringly for 30 hours non stop. Arissa works in close collaboration with three other conselheiras, they are her permanent assistants, together with the *batuqueira*, the woman that beats the drum. Arissa and the three assistants chant and play *chocalhos* (gourd-rattles on sticks; shaking this kind of rattles is one way of attracting the attention of the spirits). The proceedings move between chanted advice/instructions: *ikano*[3], interrupted by drums and chocalhos, and enacted pieces of practical instruction. The chanting itself is not unlike the way a Catholic priest will chant the holy text at Mass in church on Sundays: The words follow each other very fast in a chanted, monotonous tone.

When the whole thing is over, and I am back in my guestroom in Salama's house in Ribáuè,[4] nurse Olinda joins me at tea. She knows that I have been to the initiation rites. 'Are you sure that the girls grasp all what is said, when the words are spoken so fast?' she asks. No. I would be surprised if they did. She goes on: 'Do they get a chance to ask, if there is something that they don't understand?' No, they don't. The girls are not supposed to utter one single word, not even to move a muscle of the face. Their role is to sit down with downcast eyes and listen when authority speaks. Of course Olinda has got a point: The teaching which takes place at initiation rituals does not conform to modern pedagogical principles. Not at all. Rather the manner of instruction transferred

[1] 'Mato' is Portuguese for 'bush'.
[2] I owed this invitation to my self-appointed fieldwork manager, interpreter and as time went by also my friend, the District Director of Culture in Ribáuè, (henceforth DDC). Being a long-time Frelimo supporter DDC was nevertheless vividly interested in traditional culture. He is a Makhuwa himself (although from another part of Nampula province), and according to himself he always speaks Emakhuwa when addressing the population, unlike some of the other District Directors, who use Portuguese as the language of power, and a means of marking a distance between themselves and the people. DDC for these reasons had very good connections to exactly the kind of people I wanted to contact: Female traditional authority (*mapwiyamwene*), *curandeiras* and *conselheiras*.
[3] *ikano* is the plural form; in singular it is *ekano*.
[4] *Salama* is a local NGO working in the field of community health. Salama very kindly offered me a room in their small house for my work in Ribáuè.

to a modern context would be traumatizing. These issues are complex, and I shall return to them below.

But first a record of the happenings during this very eventful weekend, based on my Ribáuè field notes.

Saturday morning

DDC and I arrive to Arissa's compound at 7 o'clock on Saturday morning, together with several other guests, and two of the girls walking with downcast eyes and stripped to the waist. As they approach the compound they are pushed and insulted by some of the older women. Fortunately some other women – their *madrinhas* – protect them.[5] The atmosphere among the women –excluding the initiates – is joyful and exalting. At this point there are some twenty women gathered, apart from Arissa and her assistants. These other women are having great fun. It strikes me that initiation rites, along with being the introduction of the initiates to the serious business of adulthood, is simultaneously a legitimization of continued and unending childishness. These old and grown up women behave in ways, which women of that age would otherwise never permit themselves.

There are three girls, *amwali*,[6] to be initiated. One of them has already got a *noivo* (fiancé), a young boy, around 16 or 17 years of age. The first session of instructions and advice (ikano) is aimed at this boy. The girls are ushered into the hut. He remains outside with the row of conselheiras (Arissa and her assistants) and the other women. He is ordered to take off his tattered T-shirt and sits on a low stool stripped to the waist in front of a row of women (Photo 7.1). He keeps his head bent down, and listens as Arissa chants a series of instructions, and she and the assistants beat the drum and shake the rattles. DDC translates in a whispering voice. The instructions are among others the following:

> The advice that we'll give to your wife you too will have to follow. At the place where you go to marry, you'll have to obey the rules of that place, taking the good with the bad. A man must assist his in-laws. The man is the one that works in the fields and the one that gives capulanas. If one day your wife returns late at home, you must not beat her; ask first where she has been, and why she is back so late. When you approach the house of strangers, you must cough to announce your presence, in order not to surprise the inhabitants while they are having sex. When you have sex with your wife, do it at night, not during the day. And do not have sex too often, as in this case your wife will grow thin.[7]

The boy also has to drink a certain mixture, and to jump over the body of one of the women, who is lying on the ground. This is supposed to be something

---

[5] Most of the madrinhas in fact are only slightly older than the initiates themselves. The role of the madrinha is to support her protegee, and help her through the trials. The madrinhas also take part in the fun and games of the other women present.

[6] Here the singular is *mwali*, plural *amwali*.

[7] Producing this data material has been quite laborious. I did not tape during the actual ritual, because I wanted my presence to be as little felt as possible. But I got an agreement with Arissa and her *conselheiras* that we should later make a session where they would chant the *ikano* and beat the rattles and the drum for my tape recorder. This resulted in several hours of tapes, which I had translated from Emakhuwa to Portuguese first by the DDC, and later by two different persons for greater reliability. What appears here is my edition in English, based on these translations.

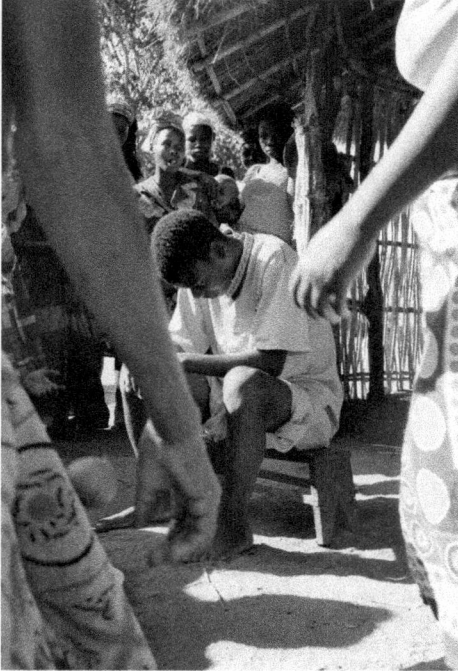

7.1 If a girl to be initiated is engaged to be married, her fiancé too will receive instructions. He does so in a humble position.
(All photographs in this chapter © Signe Arnfred, taken between 1999 and 2005)

about how to behave if you see a sick person or stumble upon a dead body: You'll have to look at the face in order to be able to inform the family. There is more abracadabra which I do not understand, and which does not seem to have any specific explanation. The atmosphere, however, is unmistakable: Here sits a row of authoritative women, giving instructions to a half-naked boy about how he should behave as a married man. Later, in the evening on Saturday, this noivo and another one, who has appeared in the meanwhile, are instructed to stand behind Arissa and put their arms around her neck, one by one, after which she starts carrying them as you would carry a child. The boys do not look very pleased, but they have to obey orders.

Later in the morning, still Saturday, the conselheiras have finished with the noivo, and the three amwali are called forward from the hut. Now it is their turn to receive instructions. Among other things they are told how to behave when menstruating, and how to deal with the *nakhapa* (the piece of cloth you use for collecting the blood). Also this session is full of weird events, things that the girls have to do, like drinking a mixture from a gourd held behind the split legs of a conselheira. All of a sudden the gourd falls to the ground, and the girl now has to sit down upon it hard, so that it breaks into pieces. After this she must collect the pieces with her lips. At the end of this session, each of the girls rides back into the hut, sitting astride a *pilão* (mortar) behind another woman, with a third one to push the pilão.

I later understand more of the meaning of this particular session. The mixture in the gourd is made from an asparagus-like plant, which grows in the mato. The name of the plant is *nshileiyamwali* , and apart from being the major ingredient in this essential mixture, the nshileiyamwali also appears later on in one of the mato-sessions/trials. The one responsible for the making of this mixture is the *pwiyamwene*. Even in the Christianized initiation rites,[8] the pwiyamwene is called in order to give this mixture to the girls. The mixture is made in and served from a gourd. The gourd is a feminine implement, as is the pilão, utensils which are only used by women. The girls have to drink the mixture bent down, with their heads put through the split legs of another woman. This is in order to teach them respect for the elders: This position does not combine well with a haughty air. When afterwards the girl has to break the gourd to pieces by sitting down hard on it, this symbolizes her breaking of all her bad habits from her younger days.

The advice given to the girls this morning, I am told, is not yet the heavy stuff – the things on sexuality and esoteric knowledge. This morning it is mostly regarding how to deal with menstruation, and about how to behave in society at large. The menstruation advice focuses on the importance of washing the nakhapa – the piece of cloth which they are shown how to use as a sanitary towel – and of keeping it out of the sight of men and children. Menstrual blood is a powerful thing, and great care should be taken that nobody sees it. When you are menstruating, do not sit at your father's chair; you might leave on it marks of blood. The word 'nakhapa' is in itself a powerful and secret word. It is not used in daily speech. Another part of the teachings regarding menstruation is the taboos you have to observe: Not having sex with your husband, not cooking for your father, not putting salt into food. The actual wording goes something like this:

> Whenever you are menstruating, you'll have to wash your nakhapa in the morning. If you don't do that, it will soon start to smell. You must take care not to let it be seen, neither by children, nor by your father. You must put it to dry in a hidden place. When menstruating you cannot sit on your father's chair, in order not to leave on it marks of blood. Further when menstruation you cannot cook for your father, and you cannot put salt into food. You must never have sex during menstruation, this is very dangerous indeed.

The ikano regarding general behaviour talk about respect for the elders, for authority and for your parents; by showing respect to others you show that you yourself are worthy of respect.

> If you happen to meet the *régulo* (chief) on your way, you must kneel down and clap your hands; he will then know that you are a grown up (i.e. that you have been through the initiation rites). Respect for your parents is very important. If you are not respectful, whichever person that would like to marry you, will soon change his mind. Also work is important, in the house and in the field: Even if you are married, you must rely on your hoe. Don't think that beauty is all that matters. One day your mother will die, and you will be left with the task of feeding the children.

Strangers should be helped, sick persons should be looked after, and children with no parents should be taken care of.

At the end of the morning the atmosphere changes. Together with their

[8] The Catholic church as well as the various Protestant churches all have their own 'reformed' editions of the initiation rites, in which the *ikano* to varying degrees are replaced by readings from the Bible, along with other modifications.

7.2 The *namalaka*'s helpers beat the rhythm, while Arissa chants the *ikano* (instructions). One beats the initiation drum, the others shake their rattles (*chocalhos*).

madrinhas and the majority of the women present – predominantly the younger ones and excluding the conselheiras – the amwali go through the cassava field behind the house, to a clearing out of sight and earshot of people near the house. This is a women-only event. I joined the women, but DDC was left behind, to entertain himself with Arissa's husband and another man, who turns out to be the father of the mwali with the noivo. What goes on in the clearing of the cassava field is called dances; in actual fact, however, it is more like competitive games. The women are almost naked, their capulanas and blouses stripped off, dressed only in what at the time I supposed to be home made briefs: a piece of an old capulana between the legs, attached in front and behind to a string round the waist. I later learn that these 'home made briefs' are in fact nakhapa; only women in town wear briefs. When not menstruating countryside women wear nothing belneath their skirts. Most, but not all, of the women, have elaborate tattoos on their breasts, bellies and thighs. The 'dances' are all rather physically demanding. You have to be more than usually fit, compared to Western standards, to be in on this. In one of the dances the women are jumping round, hands and feet on the ground, their backs turned downwards. In another they do the jumping sitting sidewise with their legs bent up at the side; sitting like this you are supposed to jump round in a circle. A third dance is more cossack-like: jumping in squatting position, stretching in front of you now one leg, now the other. The amwali participate along with the other women, and it is noticed how well they do. Another 'dance' has the form of a kind of duel, two women wrestling with a kind of staff or rod between them.

7.3 The *amwali* (girls to be instructed) have to sit with downcast eyes, legs stretched out in front, saying absolutely nothing.

The madrinhas and the other women fight among themselves, and they also challenge the amwali. The general attitude of the madrinhas towards the girls is supportive, not the more vengeful and spiteful attitude of (some of) the older women. The girls get no sanctions when they do badly, and they are cheered when they do well. The amwali are supposed not to bat an eyelid. Nevertheless, one mwali, who in the staff-battle did particularly well, cannot help looking proud, just for a moment. When the girls are seated they sit with the legs stretched out in front of them hands resting on the legs with the palms turned upwards and heads bent with downcast eyes (Photo 7.3).

In one of the squatting dances the women mime the exercise of pulling their *labia minora*, and also in other dances the atmosphere is sexual. In the beginning they cast me sidelong glances, but as the general atmosphere becomes exhilarating, they seem to forget about my presence. To me the dances and games reveal an atmosphere and feelings of play and sex, of fun and games with sexual overtones. Play and sex are interlinked, in a women-only setting displaying sexuality as a female way of expression and enjoyment. The women obviously have a good time, they are in their element, all in high spirits – apart from the amwali, who have to keep their faces straight. The initial mutual embarrassment of the women's almost-nakedness soon disappears, and before long I see their breasts and tattoos as parts of their personalities, much more expressive, in fact, than the usual outfit of worn-out capulanas and tattered t-shirts.

The dances and games go on for a couple of hours. The atmosphere is heated and nobody wants to stop. No sooner is one dance over before a new one begins.

Obviously most of the women excel in one or the other of the exercises, and they all want to expose their particular skills. A message is brought through the cassava field that DDC requests my presence, so I leave the women in order to drive DDC back to town.

Saturday night

Later in the afternoon I rejoin the women. This time in the company not of DDC, but of his wife, who very graciously has volunteered to be my translator during the evening and the night. This is for women only, and DDC after all is a man. The evening, the night and the following morning entail the most essential parts of the rites. The whole thing is like a piece of theatre, a continuous string of sketches, organized and orchestrated by the namalaka, Arissa, and including the amwali and madrinhas as participants as well as some of the older women. In between the 'sketches' the girls are given instructions and advice in the same manner as in the morning: chanted texts interrupted by drums and rattles. The idea, as I later learn, is that the same message is given in text and in action. It is 'learning by doing' to a certain extent: learning through the body.

For the evening, night and morning sessions four more amwali take part, making the number of initiates seven in all. Apparently the four latecomers have been subjected to the first part of the teachings at another occasion. During the evening and night one more noivo is present, besides the one who was already there in the Saturday morning session. The two young men, with another two men and Arissa's husband, sit by themselves at a small fire behind one of the houses of Arissa's compound: close enough to be called when they are needed, far enough not to follow what is going on.

The most spectacular event during the late evening is the *cobra* (snake). Arissa commands all the amwali – some of the madrinhas join in as well, making it nine persons in all – to lie down on their stomachs, number two placing her head between the split legs of number one, the head of number three between the legs of number two, and so on. The nine of them make up a long, winding kind of snake-like figure. Night has fallen, all is dark apart from a small fire which some of the women keep going. But during the snake-session the moon comes out. Even if it is not quite full yet, its light makes a lot of difference, as it is catching the white patterns – painted with the finely ground and very white flour of *mapira* – that Arissa makes on the backs of the recumbent women. Arissa's 'painting' grows into a work of art, the 'snake' itself barely visible, while the white flour patterns – diverse and changing down the line – stand out in the light of the rising moon. When the snake-painting is finished, the noivos are called forward. Their task now is to identify their fiancés among the nine women lying face down in the dark with painted backs. None of them is able to do so. All the women look alike, and besides it is dark. When later I ask about the significance of the cobra, I am just told that this is for the men. To me, however, the session with painted 'snake' in the moonlight was the poetic peak of the whole experience.

Another event during the night is the hunting of the *onhipi*. The amwali are taken away from the compound, into the mato in the middle of the night. In the meanwhile Arissa 'paints' – with white mapira-flour – *a peneira* (a flat round winnowing-basket) like a mask, and puts it in front of a crouching woman with a capulana cast over her. The capulana-covered woman with the 'mask' is supposed to be the onhipi, an animal of the mato, which when pursued gives out a bad smell, similar to the animal which in English is called a skunk.[9] When I asked Arissa about the meaning of this part with the chasing of the onhipi, the answer was that this was just a *divertimento* (entertainment) with no specific meaning. What happens in the night is that the amwali, who have left in order to search for the onhipi, suddenly return shouting and screaming in a frightful way when they catch sight of the 'animal' (i.e. the mask). The screaming (which may be the screaming of the accompanying women?) at least frightens us, who have been left behind, close to where the onhipi is situated. Presumably the amwali are frightened as well. It is night, and very dark in spite of the moonlight.

Also other things take place in the dark of night. At one point the fire is put out, we go indoors in the hut. It is pitch dark. Everybody is given two stones from a bag. We all start banging the stones, which give out sparks that light up the dark. This is quite a show, like fireworks, almost.

Sunday morning

Things go on happening all through the night. When the first light of dawn appears in the horizon, the girls are let out of the hut, capulanas over their heads, and disappear with their madrinhas on the path leading to the mato. The rest of us stay behind for another hour. During this time nothing in particular goes on. People chat in low voices or sleep on the ground. In due course we too leave the compound. The mato in question is just a ten minute walk away, across a couple of fields, a small stream and a patch of woodland. We find the girls and their madrinhas in a clearing.

Then the next round of lessons take place. One of the first things to happen appears to me to be particularly odd. A low but long small hill or mound is made from grass and branches. The girls all in a group have to run towards this mound, to jump over it, subsequently letting themselves fall down on the other side, lying stretched out, their faces to the ground, they are all covered with a number of capulanas. According to the explanation I was given by the consel-heiras when later I asked what it was all about, it is in order to show the girls that when they are menstruating they are not supposed to jump over hunting traps that men might have set in the mato. If they do so, they'll ruin the traps. Their falling down and being covered with capulanas is just for dramatic effect, I was told (Photo 7.4).

A central item on this Sunday morning is the *procura do remédio*[10], the search for nshileiyamwali which may have one or two or several roots. Each of the girls has to find and pull up one of these plants. If it has one root it means that she is single, if it has two roots she has a lover. Both of these are OK. If the plant has three roots or more it means that the girl has several lovers, which is bad. In this

---

[9]   According to Eduardo Medeiros onhipi is also the name of the vagina when it gives out a bad smell (1995, 229).
[10]   The Emakhuwa name for this trial is *otipeliya murette*.

7.4 Behind the drum the *amwali* are lying, covered by *capulanas*. This is one of a series of events during the last day of the rituals.

case the girl has to confess with whom she has had relations. In this particular session only plants with one and two roots are found, scandal thus being avoided. When a good root is found the madrinha of the girl and another woman fling off their capulanas and for a moment dance naked. It is clearly felt that total naked-ness – as distinct from the almost-nakedness of the day before – is different: powerful and embarrassing.

Another central item is the demonstration regarding how to behave when making love to your husband. Arissa suddenly has a penis, quite a big black one. Afterwards I see that it is fixed to a string round her waist, under her capu-lana. This penis is a secret and sacred item, kept wrapped in a cloth in a basket together with other sacred objects under the exclusive care of the namalaka. Some weeks later, when interviewing a group of male conselheiros, together with the master-circumciser for the male initiation rites, I was shown, in deep secrecy and with great awe, the sacred objects of male initiation: the circum-cision-knife, the tassel of hair from an animal's tail used in the dances, a buck's horn for keeping certain remedies etc. Also the initiation drums and rattles are sacred. In the case of the boys there were four different drums, in the case of the girls only one. The penis-session is a kind of summit of the whole sequence of initiation rites. I had been told of this 'clay penis' session and of its lessons countless times during the preparation of the OMM Conference. Now for the first time I was able to set eyes on this famous 'clay penis' and to se a live enact-ment of the sex-with-your-husband instructions of the initiation rites.

It all happens in a clearing in the mato. The seven girls are sitting on the grass, legs stretched out, palms up, downcast eyes, dressed in nakhapas only.

7.5 A key point of the girl's initiation rituals is the demonstration regarding how to conduct sex in marriage, including how to move during intercourse and how to clean the husband's penis after sex. The photo shows Arissa equipped with a penis for the purpose of these instructions.

7.6 The *amwali* listen with downcast eyes, heads bent down, to Arissa's instructions, here regarding medical uses of different wild plants. Drums and rattles in the foreground of the picture.

Arissa squats in front of them. The women, myself standing among them, form a narrow circle around the scene. For an initial model-instruction Arissa, with her penis embodying the man, uses one of the other women. Both are squatting, Arissa is embracing the other woman, partly throwing her back, making it evident that coitus is taking place. The instruction itself is focused on post-coital behaviour. The woman takes the penis in her hands and cleans it with both hands, wiping off the semen. Afterwards she washes her husband's hands and gives massage to his fingers, arms and shoulders, one arm after the other, finishing off with a light kiss on both of his cheeks. The whole thing lovingly and caringly performed. This being done the woman opens her legs – she is sitting with bent legs in front of her husband – and starts pulling her labia minora, the way that she has learnt to do it as a girl, and the way that as a married woman she is supposed to do it, inviting her husband to sex on appropriate occasions. After a short while her husband takes over the pulling, for a few moments only – a kind of acknowledgement, as I see it, of her attributes and her capacities – after which he closes her legs, and gives her some money. Here in the mato the penis is not a real penis, the husband not a real husband, and the money is not real money, but just some leaves, which as the closing act of the seance are pressed into the woman's hand. After the initial instruction, this scene is repeated seven times, with each of the amwali in turn playing the wife, Arissa being the husband with the penis (Photo 7.5).

The chanted ikano, given the night before, that match this instruction, go something like this:

> When you are going to have sex with your husband, then wash your vagina with luke-warm, salted water, for your husband to feel more pleasure. Having sex you have to move and wag your body. To remain motionless, like a dead person, is no good. When your husband wants to have sex with you, you should receive his penis in the proper place, and not in other places. And afterwards, don't forget to clean his penis with your hands or with a towel, according to his taste. If you use a towel, take care to keep it close to the bed, as otherwise the sperm will congeal on the penis. A person should never sleep after sex without having (been) washed. Also before you go to bed, do not forget to wash your sexual parts. If you know that your husband have not had sex for days, you should not refuse to have sex with him when he wants it. The sperm in his body may kill him.

One of the rules of sexual life is that the man as well as the woman should keep their sexual parts free of hair. Thus the girls are told that if they see that their husband has not taken care of this, they may post a broom high on the roof of the house, for passing persons to see that the man of this house did not maintain sexual hygiene.

The part of ikano referring to married sexual life is long and diverse. The advice given to the wife is about how to be nice to the husband, how to treat him well, sexually and otherwise. For instance:

> A man feels two kinds of need: the need of the stomach for food, and the need of his penis for sex. If you take care to meet these needs to his satisfaction, he will say that in you he found his second mother, and that even if he has had to leave his mother 's house, he still is a lucky man.

Obviously the boys in their initiation rites are instructed regarding corresponding male behaviour in this kind of situation. The boys are told that they should

7.7 The *amwali* in the stream, ready for the ritual bath. The girls with T-shirts are *madrinhas*, helpers to the *amwali*. Arissa chants her *ikano*.

7.8 When it is all over the girls, covered in brand new *capulanas*, are led back to the village.

only marry a woman who has been through the initiation rites, and that even when they marry and move to a different place, the one to whom they owe the most respect is their own mother.

But back to the amwali in the clearing in the mato. In another session they are tested as to their abilities regarding hip-undulating dancing. These are some of the movements they must apply when making love. Just as in the competitions in the cassava-field the day before, the good ones are cheered, while the bad ones are passed over in silence. There is also a session when the girls have to make faces: wrinkle their noses and twist their mouths, wag with the ears etc. One of the girls doesn't seem to be able to do this kind of thing at all; she is also the least capable one regarding the hip-undulation.

In some of the sessions the instructions have the form of live enactments. Others rely more on oral instructions. One of the oral ones is a long session where Arissa is holding up for the girls one medicinal plant after the other (previously collected in the mato by her assistants) explaining about its proper use for curing this and the other illness (Photo 7.6).

At one point the party breaks up from the clearing where most of the above described sessions have taken place, and moves to the small stream we crossed very early in the morning. Here Arissa – still going strong after more that 24 hours on end of intensive work – disappears for a short while, and reappears dressed up as an old woman, in tattered capulana and with a walking stick, stumbling along, hardly able to walk. She approaches the girls and ends up falling dead in front of their feet. This, I am told, is an illustration of the instructions given during the night regarding how to treat old and disabled persons.

Here at the stream the final ceremonies of this session of initiation rites are taking place. The girls are all placed with their feet in the stream (which is very small, with a bit of an effort you can jump from one side to the other). They stand in line, dressed in their nakhapas, and Arissa goes up to each one in turn, loosening her nakhapa so that it falls into the stream (Photo 7.7). Obviously the difference from being nakhapa-clad to being stark naked is very great. Even if there are only women around, the girls look very embarrassed, and cover their sexual parts with their hands. To ease their embarrassment they are given old capulanas in which to cover themselves from the waist down during the next hair-cutting session. Obviously nakedness has to do with the vulva. Nobody is bothered about exposing the breasts. The hair-cutting is only partial, symbolic. All of the girls seem to have had their hair cut fairly recently anyway.

Finally there is a name giving ceremony – each girl receives a new name – and a re-dressing in brand new capulanas. Dressed in these new capulanas, with other capulanas over their heads, the girls in jubilant procession are led back to Arissa's compound and from there to their homes in the village (Photo 7.8).

At this point, I too go home, dog tired after 30 hours of initiation rites.

8 *Wineliwa* – The Creation of Women:
Initiation Rituals during Frelimo abaixo *Politics*   (1990/2000)

Woodcut by Matias Mtundu Mzaanhoka

Wineliwa – Emakhuwa for initiation rites – actually means 'to be danced to'. When in the early 1980s on behalf of the OMM, *Organização da Mulher Moçambicana*, I was collecting data in northern Mozambique regarding female initiation rituals and other related issues, I found the women insisting on the importance of their daughters being danced to.

Nowadays, one woman said – this was in 1982 – Frelimo wants us to dance at district headquarters on national holidays, but they prevent us from dancing to our daughters:

> We have stopped performing the initiation rites, but still more frequently we will be called for to dance with no gain for us, and not knowing why. We are going off to the District Headquarters dancing on the twenty-fifth of September, on the third of February and on other days [these days are new national holidays of Independent Mozambique] but we do not know the significance of those dances. In the old days, when we were beating our drums, it was in order to educate our children, it had an important meaning for us. But today we are dancing on all these festive days without knowing why. One day we could refuse. The population could refuse saying: You[ie. the Party and Government structures, who demand the dancing] are enemies of the drums. But today we are not able of saying so, because we have respect for our Government. But it doesn't let us do what we want to do. We feel very inhibited. The Party prevents us from dancing when we feel the need to dance, and at the same time we have to dance at every occasion without any meaning for us.

These words were spoken by a peasant woman at a large outdoor women's meeting in Montepuez, southern Cabo Delgado. I vividly remember the massive applause, showing that she expressed shared feelings.

At that time, in the early 1980s – at 'the time of Samora' as the first period after Independence is now called in rural Mozambique[1] – Frelimo campaigned strongly against the continued existence of female (and male) initiation rites. Female initiation rituals were seen as woman oppressive, remains from the dark traditional past that henceforth would be replaced by Frelimo modernity and enlightenment. In the foundational documents of the OMM (adapted at its Second Conference in 1976) it was said that the women's organization, among other tasks, should 'organize the combat against old ideas, which act as an obstacle to the full participation of the women in public and social life as a citizen, in economic life as a free producer, in family life as a true companion and a revolutionary educator' (OMM 1977, 78). And more specifically on initiation rituals it was explained how the woman through the cruel and humiliating practices of these rituals 'from childhood onwards is violated and traumatized to a passive being without capacity of initiative' (ibid., 91).

Here in the matrilineal north of Mozambique, however, Frelimo and OMM met astonishing resistance to their *abaixo* campaigns. *Abaixo* means 'down with' and *abaixo*-slogans were shouted at the beginning and end of each political meeting: *Abaixo lobolo, abaixo poligamia, abaixo ritos de iniciação*. Following the *abaxio* slogans you shouted *viva*: *Viva Presidente Samora Moises Machel. Viva Frelimo. A Luta Continua.*

The women of northern Mozambique wondered about the abaixo slogans. 'Frelimo has done so many nice things for us,' they said,' why does it want us

---

[1] Samora Moises Machel – was the first President of Independent Mozambique. He died in a mysterious plane crash in October 1986.

to stop performing our initiation rites? They are our tradition. We have always taught our daughters in that way.' And I wondered too. Many of these women had participated in the liberation struggle, many were much more eloquent than the average peasant woman. If they defended the initiation rites, surely there had to be more to the story than the OMM tales of humiliation and oppression? During the whole campaign for preparation of the OMM Extraordinary Conference[2] – of which my 1982 data collection was a part – the hottest issue of debate was the initiation rites.

I have later speculated on the reasons why. There are, I think, three different reasons for the spellbinding effect of the initiation rituals:

One is the central position of initiation rites, male and female, in Mozambican rural cultures, particularly in the north. It was only later, during my 1998–1999 fieldwork that it became clear to me just *how* important they were and continued to be, 'the ceremonies that make us human' as it is put by one of the women who spoke to Carolina Nordstrom (1997, 180): If you have not been through the initiation rituals you are not a person, you cannot be taken seriously, even with fifty years of age you are still considered a child. People in rural areas in northern Mozambique, who had lived with missionary and later Frelimo campaigns against initiation rituals had pretended to comply, while secretly, in school holidays and at night, they went on with their rituals and ceremonies as they used to. The OMM Conference preparation process was the first chance of discussing in the open the issue of initiation rituals.

The second factor which gave energy and fascination to the OMM conference preparation discussions was, I think, the fact that even in a pre-colonial, pre-Frelimo Mozambican cultural context the initiation rituals were not an issue for debate. On the contrary, a lot of what the rituals are about is secret, esoteric knowledge, transmitted in an authoritarian way in order to be received and adhered to, not to be debated. In the enthusiasm of the OMM discussions on initiation rites I saw a creative mix of 'modernity' with 'tradition': In the 'modern' context of Frelimo, calling for reflection, it now happened for the first time that issues usually tabooed could be openly discussed. During these countless discussion meetings in *bairros* and villages, I sometimes had the feeling that tied-down psychic energy had now been released: People talked and talked, just for the sake of talking about what had previously been unspeakable.

The third reason is additional to the other two. It has to do with the contradictory character of the initiation rituals being on the one hand strictly authoritarian, and part and parcel of the 'old society' – in this aspect Frelimo/OMM was right – but on the other hand they were necessary institutions for civic education: If the kids were not submitted to the initiation rituals, how then should they learn about life and love, and how to be decent people? Teaching in

---

[2] After OMM's 3rd Conference in 1980, which was not very significant in any way, OMM was asked to arrange an Extraordinary Conference, specifically for debating 'women's social problems'. This conference – which eventually took place in November 1984 – was prepared by a nation-wide campaign of discussion and data-collection regarding what was called 'women's social problems' and among which 'old customs' like initiation rites, *lobolo* (brideprice), polygamy and premature marriages were seen as important aspects. The Extraordinary Conference preparation process also meant the end of *abaixo* politics. On the agenda now was debate of positive and negative aspects of old norms and customs, followed by discussions regarding how in the future to deal with these issues.

school does not replace initiation rituals – this was a clear outcome of the OMM Conference preparation discussions: 'If we abandon the initiation rites, we'll have to replace them with something else' – was a common opinion.

The opening in terms of the political legitimacy of discussion of 'traditional norms and customs' initiated with the OMM conference preparation campaign, has grown in later years. One positive effect of donor-pressure for multi-party so-called democracy has been a much more open climate of debate in the public sphere, and a much more relaxed acceptance of norms and customs of people's daily lives. The push for a coerced creation of *o Homem Novo* (the new man) which characterized Frelimo politics in the 1970s and early 1980s ('the time of Samora') has receded. The government – which is still 100 per cent Frelimo – now shows a much greater acceptance of (or maybe indifference to?) the enormous cultural diversity, which is so characteristic of Mozambique.

Changing valorization of initiation rites

The change in political climate vis a vis initiation rites over the last decades that I myself have witnessed is, however, only part of a longer story, starting with the onset of effective Portuguese colonialization and Christian missions in the late nineteenth/early twentieth century.

The initial attitude of the Portuguese colonial power was a strong condemnation of initiation rituals, which were seen by the colonial administration as well as by the Catholic church as 'immoral and offensive to the human nature' (Medeiros 1995, 5). The attitude of the Protestant missions, which had their strongholds in the southern provinces of Gaza, Maputo and Inhambane, was no more permissive. Henri-Alexandre Junod, of the Presbyterian Swiss Mission, considered customs relating to female sexuality so 'vile and immoral' (Junod 1912/1974, 176) that they could only be described in an appendix for 'doctors and ethnographers' written in Latin.

From around the 1950s a new approach is launched by the Catholic church. This is in the heyday of forced cotton cultivation, and the colonial regime is depending on the collaboration of traditional chiefs. Mozambican anthropologist Eduardo Medeiros gives the following reasons for the change of politics at this point:

> On one hand it was necessary for the colonial administration to give more power to the *régulos*[3] and allow them to exercise their traditional power regarding the organization and control of certain customary institutions ... On the other hand the church had come to realize that its missionary work could not continue in the ethnocentric way that had until now been the norm. The church came to see it as important to know local customary ways of life, not in order to eliminate them, but in order to integrate them into a Christian context. It is from now on that the missionaries start making systematic ethnographic investigations, and producing liturgical and biblical texts in local languages (Medeiros 1995, 5–6).

[3] *Régulo* is the Portuguese word for chief. The régulos were installed by the colonial power, as parts of a system of indirect rule. Sometimes they coincided with the real lineage chiefs, sometimes not.

This permissive style on the part of the colonial power was further accentuated in the 1960s and early 1970s when the armed struggle between Frelimo and the Portuguese army developed into a battle to conquer the soul of the Mozambican peasant. Too harsh an attitude against the ceremonies and rituals that were close to people's hearts could push them into the arms of *'o inimigo'* – the enemy, which seen from Portuguese side was Frelimo. Similarly, and for the same reasons, in the phase of the armed struggle, Frelimo refrained from a clear ban on traditional customs like initiation rites.

After Independence, however, a more unambiguous Frelimo discourse took over. These were the years of what has later been termed 'the abaixo politics'. The performance of customary ceremonies was not directly criminalized, but strong political campaigns were waged against any such performance. Customary belief and practice was seen as obscurantist, oppressive and an obstacle to progress and modernity. Central in all of this was the oppression and humiliation of women, as epitomized by the female initiation rites.

Frelimo had to realize however – like the Portuguese before them – that head-on politics just did not work. There was good participation in the shouting of slogans at political meetings, with fists pointing down or up exactly as they should (for *abaixo* you hammered your fist downwards; for *viva* and *a luta continua* it went up into the air) – but once the political brigade had left the place and night fell upon the village, *batuques* (drums) and *chocalhos* (rattles) could be heard, dancing went on and ceremonies were held in the darkness. The kids were taken secretly to the bush and initiation rites were performed in school holidays. Frelimo realized that things were more complex, and that deep-rooted customs could not be changed by slogans. Thus it was decided that OMM should undertake a participatory preparation for an Extraordinary Conference, debating what was called 'women's social problems' – but what were in fact problems of tensions, clashes and lack of conciliation between 'traditional' and 'modern' in Mozambican social politics.

Eduardo Medeiros points to the 1984 OMM Extraordinary Conference as the decisive dividing line, introducing a more balanced, and even academic way of talking about traditional customs and ceremonies (Medeiros 1995, 3), among these the initiation rituals. Still, however, on the part of Frelimo/OMM the approach was one of positive versus negative aspects, and still with the Party as the ultimate authority of good and bad. As it was put in the General Resolution resulting from the OMM Extraordinary Conference regarding initiation rituals:

> The Extraordinary Conference recommends that the local bodies of OMM, in coordination with Education and Health, should go deeper into the study of context and practice of initiation rites, in order carefully to concretize which are their negative and which their positive aspects. These bodies should submit their considerations to the Party leadership in order for it to have appropriate foundation for issuing directions as to what should be combated and what should be maintained.[4]

This approach is problematic in so far as (a) the value base for making this kind of judgment remains implicit, and (b) the overall context and meaning of the initiation rites as 'the ceremonies that make us human' are *not* taken into consideration.

---

[4] *Resolucão Geral da Conferéncia Extraordinária da OMM*, Diario Notícias 16 de Novembro 1984.

Since then, however, and particularly since the more or less official acknowledgement and rehabilitation, of *autoridade tradicional* (traditional authority)
from the mid–1990s onwards, the political atmosphere regarding initiation
rituals as a part of Mozambican reality has advanced even further.[5] In the mid-
1990s several volumes of analysis of traditional authority (Lundin & Machava
1995) and two works on Makhuwa initiation rituals appeared in Mozambique,
written by Mozambican scholars (Medeiros 1995, Sá e Bonnét 1996). It has
now become legitimate again to openly celebrate initiation rites.

Matriliny and female initiation

Nevertheless, in spite of these ups and downs during the last 100 years, in a
place like Ribáuè in the interior of Nampula province, where I conducted fieldwork in 1998–99, initiation rituals have been practised all along. It was my
impression during the OMM conference preparation that the same thing was
true more or less all over in northern Mozambique, with the Makhuwa as well
as with the Makonde and the Yao, the three major ethnic groups of the north[6].
These groups all celebrate female initiation rituals, not necessarily, however, in
exactly the same way.

Significantly these peoples of northern Mozambique all have matrilineal
kinship systems. In her book *Chisungo*, on girls' initiation ceremonies among
the Bemba of Zambia (based on the author's fieldwork in the 1930s) British
anthropologist Audrey Richards has a discussion of the distribution of female
puberty rites in Central Africa. She comes to the conclusion that 'the correla-
tion between girls' individual puberty rites and matrilineal organization is very
marked' (Richards 1956/1982, 185). Jorge and Margot Dias, Portuguese
anthropologists working in Cabo Delgado 1956–61, i.e. in the years just before
the outbreak of the liberation war, make a similar observation, connected
however specifically to the event of 'ritual defloration' which according to Dias
& Dias used to be a part of Makonde female initiation. The point of ritual defloration is, as it was explained to me during the OMM conference preparation
campaign, 'that the girl does not come back to her parents still a virgin' (SA
iw). Ritual defloration, when practised, was almost always symbolic. In some
areas of northern Mozambique, young people's sexual playing, including intercourse, is considered normal; it is even believed to be a necessity in order to
make the breasts grow, and in order to call forth menstruation. Ritual defloration, when it did occur, was always commanded by the *namalaka*, the female
conductor of women's rituals. Dias & Dias see an interconnection between this
female control of female sexuality and matrilineal kinship systems. They write:

> Even if it is a fact that the ritual defloration is related to certain beliefs, frequent among
> African as well as non-African peoples, who consider it dangerous for the man to

---

[5] In the municipalities Law, passed shortly before the General Elections in 1994 'traditional authorities' are recognized, even if their official roles are in no way specified. Cf. Jocelyn Alexander 1997
and West and Klock-Jensen 1999. Decree 15 of 2000 gives formal recognition to community
authorities, cf Buur and Kyed 2007. See also West 2005.

[6] The Makhuwa is the largest ethnic group in Mozambique, inhabiting all of Nampula province,
and parts of Cabo Delgado, Niassa and Zambezia provinces. The Makonde is the major group of
Cabo Delgado, and the Yao live mainly in Niassa.

deflorate the woman he marries, it is also a fact that when this defloration is practised by the women themselves, by doing so they demonstrate their sexual emancipation from men, at least as far as the pre-marriage life is concerned ... It is a
symptomatic fact that ritual defloration, practised by women, is related to matrilineal
societies. (Dias & Dias 1970, 245)

During the OMM conference preparation period this difference between the
matrilineal north and the patrilineal south of Mozambique became clear from
the collected material. The female initiation rites were obviously much more of
an issue in the north than in the south. There are indications that on the whole
matriliny is more resistant to change than patriliny. The power structures of
social groups accustomed to patriliny are more compatible with the patriarchal
power of colonialism and Christianity, as well as of Frelimo socialism. They are
more easily invaded and transformed. Matriliny, however, does not fit. Uncle-
power appears messy and confusing from a Western point of view, but the
uncles, the matrilineal lineage chiefs, defend their power. And so do the powerful
women. Characteristic for the Makhuwa of the interior of northern Mozambique is a system of parallel male/female traditional authority: Each lineage
chief, the *mwene*, has at his side a *pwiyamwene*: his sister, cousin or aunt. In the
past the pwiyamwene had considerable authority, and important decisions
could not be taken without her consent (Medeiros 1995). According to my
observations during fieldwork in Ribáuè this situation still prevails.

Another factor in this context, is the uneven development, in modern
economic terms, between Mozambique north and south: In the south people
had been accustomed to male wage labour in the South African mines, and on
European farms and plantations from the late nineteenth century onwards,
whereas the colonial system of exploitation in the north took place through
forced cotton cultivation on family plots, maintaining the socio-economic structure of small scale family farming more or less intact.

Regarding the differences between the Yao, the Makonde and the Makhuwa,
it became clear during the OMM Conference preparation that the Yao saw their
way of running female initiation rites as part and parcel of Islam.'Our Islamic
religion taught us the initiation rites, and we follow this Mahometan principle'
as they said in Lichinga, Niassa in 1983.[7] For the occasion of the OMM
Extraordinary Conference the women of Lichinga had even made a song. The
chorus went like this: *Papa Samora, autorize-nos lá, queremos unhango* (Father
Samora, give us permission, we want *unhango* [*unhango* is the Yao name for
initiation rites]). Also Makonde as well as Makhuwa women were insisting on
the great importance of the continued practice of female initiation rites. It
appeared to me, however, that the Makhuwa women were more determined in
just practising the rites, in spite of Frelimo's disapproval. More of the Makonde
women seemed give in to OMM/Frelimo directions, however with great frustration.

At that time I saw the difference as having to do with the greater involvement of Makonde men and women in the liberation war: They were more
attached and felt more loyal to Frelimo. In Frelimo historiography the Maconde
is the ethnic group which more than any other contributed to the armed

[7] Islam took root among the Yao in the end of the nineteenth century (cf. Alpers 1972) and as elsewhere in Mozambique African custom and Muslim religion seem to have merged well.

struggle. And for a long time, during the build-up of the Frelimo/Renamo conflict it was believed that the Makonde, at least, would be able to keep out the enemy, i.e. Renamo (at that time called MNR: *Movimento Nacional de Resisténcia*). Feelings of loyalty to – and identification with – Frelimo projects and strategies may indeed have played a role in this context. Another factor, of which I am more aware now than in the 1980s, may however be the continued existence in Makhuwa contexts, of the female traditional authority, the mapwiyamwen*e*.

Living in Ribáuè I got the impression that all the dramatic changes from colonialism to liberation war, over Frelimo '*abaixo* politics' to Frelimo/Renamo war, etc., had influenced but not really shaken people's way of life. The war had been very violent and Ribáuè town had suffered repeated attacks. By the end of it half the town was in ruins. People had fled to the mountains nearby; many men and women had been killed or captured. When I was interviewing the principal Ribáuè pwiyamwene[8] on the issues of the dramatic socio-polit- ical changes over the last 20 to 30 years, she said that the difference in her work at 'the time of Samora' as compared to now was not much. There were never serious obstacles to the pwiyamwene's work – among which was the ceremonial launching of female as well as male initiation rituals. The major difference was that during 'the time of Samora' she did not work with the régulo, but rather with the Frelimo district secretary. This bears witness to the fact – also observed during the OMM conference preparation process – that in many places Frelimo secretaries, without making too much fuss about it, stepped into the ceremonial shoes of *autoridade tradicional*. In those days the pwiyamwene was also herself a member of the district secretariat of the OMM. She was in charge of *assuntos sociais* (social issues) – which implied that she was doing more or less what she always had been doing: preparing special mixtures for the girls during female initiation, pouring *makeya* (flour of *mapira*) for rain ceremonies and the like. The pwiyamwene's tales confirmed my impression that daily life, particularly in Makhuwa areas, has been able to continue more or less as usual, and presumably more uninterrupted than else- where, thanks to the invisibility of female traditional authority. Frelimo went out hard against the régulos, and banned them all from office, no matter whether they had been for or against Frelimo during the liberation war. But nobody banned the mapwiyamwene; being women they were invisible to Frelimo eyes. Thus, thanks to the mapwiyamwene, rituals and ceremonials of daily life could proceed more or less as they used to.

Variations in context and ritual sequence of female initiation rites: a jigsaw puzzle picture

At the time of the OMM conference preparation, piecing together what the initi- ation rites were all about was indeed a challenge. Politically these rituals were frowned upon. Nothing was written about them apart from the derogatory description in the OMM documents, and a handful of scattered anthropological

---

[8] This pwiyamwene was pwiyamwene of the area of Ribáuè town and vicinity, but she was not the only one in the district of Ribáuè.

and missionary records. The following is an account of what at that point I managed to put together.

All the time during my 1982 stay in Cabo Delgado I was very keen to find out what the initiation rites were really about. I asked about it whenever I found it appropriate, but it was not always easy to get an answer. Mixed meetings with men and women were no good. It had to be all-women's meetings, or individual or small group interviews. Middle-aged or older women were the best inform- ants. I once made the blunder of trying to interview two newly initiated young girls about what happened in the initiation rites. I thought that since they had just been through it, they would know. It was a very awkward scene. The girls were feeling unspeakably embarrassed, they were cringing on their chairs. Not a word passed their lips.

Eventually, gathering information from many sources: My own interviews; notes from meetings and group discussions, and reports from local conferences during the OMM Extraordinary Conference preparation period, newspaper contributions during this same period, and anthropological and missionary writings – I managed to construct a picture of what the initiation rites in northern Mozambique were like. At times I felt very confused. I felt I was getting so many different stories. The practice of the female initiation rites seemed to change from one district to the next somewhat like celebrations of Christmas in Denmark. Each family has its particular way of doing things, its own set of traditions that must be followed and yet there is a shared framework and an overall pattern of events.

The following description is a jigsaw puzzle picture, pieced together from a variety of sources as well as places. Mostly from Cabo Delgado and Nampula provinces, that is from Makhuwa populations with supplements from the Makonde. The resulting picture thus does not claim to be the initiation rites of this or that district, or of the Makhuwa or the Makonde. It will be based on my judgement and feeling regarding the quality and significance of the particular pieces of the jigsaw chosen for the composition of the picture.

Apart from the amalgamation regarding space (bits and pieces collected from different places in northern Mozambique) a certain amalgamation regarding time is also taking place. Since a majority of the women I talked to in Cabo Delgado, as well as the majority involved in the OMM meetings and discussions were grown up women thirty to fifty years of age, the rituals they are referring to (as far as their own experience as initiates go) will have taken place in the 1940s to 1960s. But for this account I am not so much concerned neither with exactly where or when, as I am concerned with the spirit, the context and the atmosphere of the female initiation rituals.[9] What kind of experience were the initiation rites, seen from the point of view of the initiates, and from the point of view of the older women? And what do they tell us about gender identities and gender relations, and about hierarchies of age?

---

[9] The data material by which I am piecing together my account not only originates from a variety of sources It is also rather diverse in kind and quality. This is true for instance of the data. gath- ered in the context of the OMM during the Conference preparation period. Two types of data pre-dominate. Type one is direct transcriptions of interventions in meetings and interviews; what is recorded here will be women talking from experience, basically it is the women's own

Ceremonies of the first menstruation

The following case history is an account of an experience, seen from a young girl's point of view. It gives an acute feeling of the hierarchy and the cruelty of this particular story of the initiation rites.[10] The time is the beginning of the 1960s, and the place is the rural interior of the province of Nampula:

> Some days ago Sáfia, a girl of 12, had her first menstruation.
>
> Her mother knows about it, as she has been holding the girl under strict observation lately for this very reason. Sáfia doesn't understand why she is bleeding, and her mother says nothing. Sáfia is bewildered and afraid.
>
> Some days pass by in which the girl tries in vain to find the answer to the problem. Then one afternoon she finds herself surrounded by old women, accompanied by the mother, and by her aunts and older sisters. One by one the women enter the hut in which Sáfia is sitting, preparing food for a lunch which is never consumed. Her surprise is so big that in order to plead the visitors to sympathy, she displays humble respect and total submission.
>
> 'You are ill!' one of the old women exclaimed in a tremulous and solemn voice, pointing at the same time to Sáfia. 'What do you feel?' The girl felt relieved. After all her mother cared for her, as no doubt it was her who had called for the old women. Sáfia was convinced that the old women, whom she did not know, were curandeiras (traditional woman healers), and she answered: 'Blood is emerging'. But then at once she was terrified for not understanding why that was so very funny as to make all the women laugh.
>
> 'Exactly where did you see that blood?' the old woman went on.
>
> 'Here' said Sáfia, pointing to the place between her thighs.
>
> 'Here, where?' shouted the old woman, now furious. Sáfia thought that it would not be necessary to be as direct as to say the name. She looked to the faces of her mother and sisters for help, but immediately she was reproached and accused of being 'restless and with no idea of decency in her head'. Sáfia gave up finding out what it was all about, feeling very ashamed and confused. Most probably by then she had guessed that the visitors were not at all curandeiras, but for lack of experience she could not know that in fact they were *mankossi*[11], counsellors of the female initiation rituals. But the old woman went on shouting: 'Where does this blood come from?' And Sáfia, now in tears for feeling totally bewildered and lost, repeated: 'Here'. The old woman went mad with rage, the mother too lost control of herself, and the sisters ran to fetch one of the uncles (mothers brothers) in order for him to give her a thrashing 'to set the things right'.

The problem is that the answer of the girl to the question of the mankossi should be: 'The blood comes from my vagina,' in order to show that she knows the name. If the girl does not give exactly that answer, if she does not say the name, she is accused of stubbornness and obstinacy. In Sáfia's case she receives

stories told and retold. Another type of data is the reports from district and province conferences (discussing and adding to the data gathered in meetings and interviews). Here more generalized statements may occur. At each quote by which in the following I'll illustrate my account, I have indicated type and location (province). 'SA iw' is material gathered by myself. 'OMM iw' is OMM data type one, 'OMM rep' (report) is OMM data type two. The story of Sáfia is a newspaper cutting. During the Conference preparation several newspapers carried contributions and discussions on initiation rituals, *lobolo*, polygamy, etc., in support of the Conference preparation.

[10] The story appeared in the Sunday newspaper, *Domingo*, as one of a series of articles in early 1984, contributing to the OMM Extraordinary Conference discussions.

[11] In other parts of Nampula province these women, counsellors of initiation rituals, are called *anamalaka*.

a thrashing from the uncle, and eventually the proper word comes out of her mouth.

Now the spirit of the event turns to the exact opposite:

> The mother rejoices, the sisters embrace one another crying for joy. The old women shout:'Sáfia wula' (Sáfia has become a grown-up), crying out *ululus* [a special female joy-sound, a kind of trill made by the tongue and in a loud and high-pitched voice] as they all stream out of the hut where they have been questioning the girl. Sáfia alone stays behind in the hut, her head bending down. She is sitting on a mat with a capulana covering her from head to foot. In the meanwhile the women outside are celebrating her 'growing up'.
> In the whole of the following night Sáfia does not sleep. She spends the whole night listening to the significance of *wula* (growing up). According to the leader of the mankossi, 'wula means blood by every moon'. This is why this phenomenon is known simply as *mweri*, moon. The mankossi guarantee that in normal circumstances the mweri cannot happen twice in just one moon. This same night Sáfia learns how to treat the 'moon' without calling the attention of children. They threaten her with all the disastrous consequences that will follow from simple carelessness in letting be seen any indication of her state. But above all the mankossi tell her that she is a woman and nothing more. 'A woman is a woman' they emphasize. According to them a woman does not have the right to deny the man, her husband, anything at all.' (*Domingo* (weekly newspaper) Maputo, 15.04 and 22.04.1984)

It should be added here that sexual life as such is not new to Sáfia, as she has a fiancé (in Portuguese: *noivo*) with whom she has had sexual relations for more than a year. Furthermore, from the age of nine or ten, Sáfia has been taught to prepare herself for adult sexual life by daily manipulation of the small lips of her vagina, *labia minora*, in order to pull them longer. In the old days this was usually done by a group of girls sitting together in the bush – in a place where no man would pass. The actual work is done with two fingers of each hand, adding previously prepared oil from rícino, or *npichi* (a particular plant). In the OMM Conference preparation discussions these elongated labia minora were much debated: Was it good? Was it bad? Did it increase the sexual pleasure of the man? Of the woman? Of both? Points of view were diverse, the debate heated.

Thus Makhuwa girls are acquainted with their own bodies and their potential for sexual pleasure years before they reach puberty. What is new at puberty is the fact of menstruation. Menstrual blood is powerful and dangerous. In order to protect her surroundings, the menstruating woman must take great care not to let it be seen, and not to get too close to anybody, as one woman from Cabo Delgado tells:

> I entered the rituals when I had my first menstruation. My mother arranged persons to teach me, that I could not show it to children, or to men. I was told that a girl when menstruating had to take care not to sit on all layers of her capulana when seated. This was in order to make sure that bloodstains should not be seen on her skirt. A woman who is menstruating should not go close to other people, she must keep apart. The piece of cloth that is used for the blood must be well washed in order not to smell. (SA iw, Cabo Delgado province)

After a girl's first menstruation she must stay in isolation, ideally in a ceremonial hut built for the occasion, and most frequently together with other girls in the same situation; if she does go out, she is covered by a big black capulana head to foot. She is not supposed to be seen by any men, not even by her noivo. And she is only allowed to talk in a whispering voice. The local OMM official with whom I travelled in Cabo Delgado recalled how difficult it had been, after months of whispering – when you had to call somebody's attention you would clap your hands – again to talk in a normal voice.

The severity of the girls' isolation differs. Sometimes they are allowed to go out by day, and sometimes only at night, but they are not to have sexual relations with their noivo or anyone else in this intermediate period between the first menstruation and the initiation rites proper, that is the final celebrations, as it is considered disastrous for the girl to be pregnant before the rites. If this happens the belief is that many people in her family will die.

Practical arrangements for the final celebrations

The end of the girls' isolation depends on when the final ceremony of the initiation rites can be held. And that again depends on a series of factors, one of them being the available quantities of food and drink. I was told of this by Rosa in southern Cabo Delgado. Rosa is Makhuwa.

> The duration of the rites, that is to say the length of time that the girls would stay in the house [i.e. the ritual hut], would depend on each family. I myself stayed just one month, but my niece stayed secluded for six months. There are other families whose girls stay for a whole year. The parents had to prepare for the feast. Three to four sacks of maize (*milho*) would be needed, with millet (*mapira*), chicken, beans. All had to be pounded, you made millet flour (*farinha de mapira*). There would be a great feast lasting for three days. You also needed money in order to pay the *régulo* (the chief) the *sipaios* (the colonial sepoys) and the old *conselheiras* (the women heads of ceremonies). This was the reason that many girls had to stay secluded for a long time, in order to give the family time for all arrangements. The daughters of powerful families would stay for just one month. Others would wait for the cashew-season, so that they could sell cashew and get money. We stayed some girls together in the hut. Only small girls under five years of age could enter, and adult women. No men.
>
> On the first day there would be given advice. They would say: Now you are grown. You'll have to stay here. You may not speak in a loud voice, and you may not be seen by men, not even by your own father. You may not change your clothes, not until the day of the ceremonies. The clothes we were wearing was a black capulana four meters long, it served for covering the whole body, and also the face. The face must not be seen. On the day of the ceremonies when we were getting out, the *madrinha* would take care of that capulana. In the meanwhile the family would have prepared other clothes, new capulanas etc., for the coming out ceremony. (SA iw, Cabo Delgado province)

Another factor determining the length of time that they had to spend in isolation would be the number of pubescent girls in the area in question. Preferably a group of girls should be initiated at the same time. As the final celebration is a huge feast, it is advantageous for group of families to arrange it together: With a smaller effort for each one you have a bigger party.

Autoridade tradicional (traditional authority) plays an important part in the realization of the initiation rites, female as well as male. The *régulos* are the ones that mark the time and place for the final celebrations, and they have to sanction the entry of every girl (or boy) into the rituals. The application of the parents for their son/daughter to enter the initiation rites would always be accompanied by a gift of some sort, a chicken, a goat or some money. And of course the colonial administration did not lose this opportunity for imposing an extra tax, as shown by the following statements from Nampula Province:

> The one that was paid was the régulo, he should have 30 escudos for each one to pass the rites, because nobody was authorized to arrange the ceremony in his own compound. It had to be in the compound of the régulo; that was because he would control how many heads would be passing the rites. (OMM iw, Nampula province)
>
> In colonial times, before the initiation rite ceremonies of the boys as well as those of the girls could be performed, the régulo would communicate to the colonial administration that now in his zone there would be young people for initiation. The administration would authorize provided they received a certain sum of money as a tax. You also had to ask for the Padres [the Roman Catholic mission fathers] for permission. Normally the requests for permission would be accepted and authorization given for the period after the harvest in order not to interfere with the production of cotton and other crops. (OMM rep, Nampula province)

That in some places the new Frelimo officials were stepping into the shoes of the old power structures is witnessed by the following comment, also from Nampula:

> For the initiation rites there will always be a payment in money, or in food products, chicken, ducks, etc. In colonial days this payment went to the régulos, their corporals and captains and all of their assistants. Today (i.e. 1982–83) you pay to the secretaries of the Dynamization Groups. (OMM rep, Nampula province)

But not only the régulos had to be paid (and the Administration etc.), also the conselheiras, the *batuqueiras*, (drum beaters) *dancarinas* (dancers) etc. necessary for the festive celebrations:

> The families of the candidates for the rites had amassed great quantities of flour of maize, *mapira* and cassava, not to mention astronomical financial reserves, chicken, goats, ducks. The money was for the payment of the mankossi, and also for paying the dancers and singers invited in order to animate the feast during the three days it normally lasted. (The story of Sáfia, cf. above)

Master of the rituals would be one or more old women, professionals for that task. They must themselves be past menstruating age. In the different languages of northern Mozambique they are called different names: *namuku, namalaka, namungo, nalombo, mankossi*, in Portuguese: *conselheira*. Frequently there will be one *conselheira mestra* in charge, with three or four assistant conselheiras, women with whom this mestra is always working, her group or court, so to speak. In Makhuwa context these mestras are powerful women, whose advice is often sought. Furthermore each girl will have a *madrinha*, (a young woman relative or friend who has passed the rituals, and who is still menstruating). Each one of the mothers will chose a madrinha for her daughter.

Ceremonies of final celebrations

Part of the ritual programme takes place in the *mato* (the bush), this part being strictly women only. Another part takes place in the ceremonial hut; in most cases this part too is women only, but sometimes the noivos will be present for some of the instructions about married life given by the conselheira. Exactly what kind of rituals are performed in the mato will differ from place to place. One recurring aspect, however, seem to be the punishment of ill-mannered girls, showing the rituals, among all the other things, to be a means of control and discipline of the younger generation. This is Rosa's description:

> If a girl doesn't want to do what her mother tells her, when she reaches the initiation rites this girl will be punished. The mother will ask the old women to punish the girl in order to make her listen. This girl will be beaten and they'll force her to make apologies to the mother. I was beaten in the initiation rites. One day my older sister was pounding and I was playing. My sister asked me to help her, but I didn't want to, and my sister told my mother about it. Because of this, when I arrived at the last ceremony, I had a tough time. The punishments are all in the last ceremony, that's where you're suffering. I had to carry sand and burning hot embers from the fireplace in my hands during one whole hour, because I had refused to help my sister pounding.
>
> Every thing that a girl may do has its own punishment. If you don't want to go and fetch water, the mother will tell the old women, and you'll have to carry a large pot full of sand on your head singing and dancing until you are dog tired. If you have insulted your mother or your older sister you'll be punished as well. They would take a branch from a mango-tree and three to four people would beat you with that branch. The girls that had been well behaved would not be punished.
>
> If, however, there was a girl who had not wanted to help in the kitchen, they would bring a pot and firewood, and they would tell her to cry in order to fill that pot with tears. This girl would not be allowed to eat before that pot was filled with tears. In this way everything would have its own punishment. (SA iw, Cabo Delgado province)

Dias & Dias tell of a ritual flogging taking place in the mato during the final celebrations. This may very well be one of the punishments mentioned above. They note the contrast between the young initiates (who are being beaten) and the adult women enjoying themselves. The girls have to run the gauntlet of two rows of women beating them with sticks:

> Altogether the girls have to submit themselves six times, three times back and forth, to this ritual flogging. The women find all of this great fun. To them it is a kind of liberation, some sort of revenge for the self-control they have to maintain in their daily lives, in their coexistence with men, and from respect to custom. Their exhilaration mark the most striking contrast to the candidates, who remain very calm subdued and obedient through the whole trial. (Dias & Dias 1970, 229–30)

This image of the older women insulting and humiliating the younger ones also appears in the account of Silvano Barbieri, a Catholic missionary working in Nampula in the 1960s:

> Afterwards they would start again dancing naked and insulting the girl, humiliating her, and if her vaginal lips had not been well elongated, they would shout at her that she was good for nothing and that she would never get a man to marry her, and they would tell her many other things. (Silvano Barbieri, n.d.)

Sexual life in the context of marriage

After the trials and punishments taking place in the mato, the girls are subjected to a ritual bath, after which they will be dressed in new clothes, and each girl will be given a new name. Her transformation from child to grown up is now completed, and she can re-enter social life in her new capacity as a grown-up woman. The exact way in which the rituals are performed differ from one place to the next. In Rosa's case not all of the girls initiated together had *noivos*:

> If in a group of girls some have fiancés and others not, they will be instructed sepa-
> rately. I was instructed separately together with another girl; we were two with fiancés,
> and four without. The feast was the same, we only were separated for the instructions:
> 'Don't be afraid, don't cry, and don't tell about this to anybody else.' The feast of the
> ceremony isn't always also the feast of the marriage. Some make it all together: when
> they are finishing the feast of the initiation rites, they'll start the feast of the marriage.
> This is when the girl has already got a fiancé. If she hasn't got a fiancé the girl cannot
> leave the parents' house. She doesn't have to stay inside the house as such, but she
> cannot leave the compound. At this time she is already taking responsibility for the
> house: she cooks and she looks after the small children when her mother goes to the
> *machamba*. All of this sort of things. When a fiancé turns up, there'll be made a feast
> of marriage, and at this point the girl will be instructed regarding sexual life. During
> the feast of the initiation rites the girls themselves don't participate when the others
> are feasting outside. They'll stay inside the house [ie. the ceremonial hut] where they'll
> be instructed. Afterwards their pubic hair will be removed somewhere in the mato;
> when this has been done they'll take the girls to a well where they can wash and dress
> in new clothes. It is the madrinha who will remove the pubic hair. It hurts a lot. I
> myself I hadn't got courage, I had to scream. But they won't let you scream. It really
> hurts very much.
>   If the girl hasn't got a fiancé the pubic hair won't be removed. She only goes to her
> parents' house and stays there. This is only done on the day of her marriage. After-
> wards the woman has got to remove this hair regularly. Some do it with a razor blade,
> others do it just like that, with the nails. (SA iw, Cabo Delgado province)

For the girls with noivos the initiation rites will end with a wedding ceremony and ritual intercourse with their husband. Generally the wedding is no great occasion, the marriage is rather seen as a practical thing without too many rituals around it: if it works it is fine, and if it doesn't work, there will be no great fuss to dissolve it. There is no demand for virginity – obviously, the norms of pre-puberty sexuality taken into consideration.[12] On the contrary, who is tested on the wedding night is the man, in order to see if he gives good promise as a procreator, the offspring in the context of matriliny belonging to the woman's lineage. This is what Rosa told about her wedding, which was also, at the same time, the end of her initiation rites:

> On the wedding night the madrinha will stay beneath the bed. The young people will
> have sexual relations. If the man doesn't succeed in having intercourse, the madrinha
> will say so to the parents. If he does succeed she'll tell them that the man is complete.
> The parents of the boy and of the girl will be satisfied, they will feast and dance: Our
> daughter has got a husband and the husband is good. Here nobody is concerned about
> finding out if the woman is a virgin or not. Here you just want to find out about the
> man.

---

[12] This is different in the coastal Islamic areas, where female virginity is the ideal at marriage.

The madrinha will stay with the young couple for seven days. She'll teach them all of these things. The man too will be instructed about sexual life and about how to behave as a married man: 'You must not beat your wife in front of the family.' The girl will be instructed about how to show the husband respect: 'If you have something about which to ask your husband, then don't ask him outside, you'll have to wait until you are both in the bedroom, and you'll have to respect the husband when you are asking.' After 1–2 months the newlyweds may begin to make their own house. They'll stay at the house of the woman's parents for them to see what he is like, and how they behave together, so that they should not move to their own house and then not get on. If they don't get on well, they'll separate. 'This man is no good, we don't want him in our family'. (SA iw, Cabo Delgado province)

Summing up

Based on the OMM investigations I was able to discern a series of basic elements of female sexual socialization in northern Mozambique, a recurrent pattern behind the variety of ways in which the ceremonies and rituals were carried out:

- The initial preparation of the girls for female adulthood starts well before puberty, when the girls are 8–9 years old. The girls are instructed regarding how to proceed in order to achieve a certain elongation of their labia minora.
- Pre-puberty sexual play between girls and boys is not prevented. It is believed that sex is good for making the breasts grow, and for producing menstruation.
- When menstruation actually does occur, the mother calls conselheiras to scare the girl, and to tell her how to wash, and the importance of observing the menstrual taboos. Ideally this first session would be followed by seclusion – particularly in the old days it was important that from then on there would be no more sex before marriage.
- When a sufficient number of girls have been assembled, a date is set for final celebrations. This should preferably be after harvest time, when there is enough of food for a party.

The richness of data on initiation rites from Makhuwa areas, combined with the fact of the matrilineal kinship system of the Makhuwa, were decisive factors in my choice of Nampula Province for further fieldwork, when after the end of the Frelimo/Renamo war it was again possible to conduct fieldwork in the Mozambican countryside. This fieldwork, which eventually took place in 1998 and 1999, made it possible for me to be present at the actual celebration of female initiation rites, something which had never happened when I worked as a part of the OMM 'in the time of Samora'.

9 Female Initiation & the Coloniality of Gender
(2000/2010)

Woodcut by Matias Mtundu Mzaianhoka

The fieldwork on which this chapter is based, started in the early 1980s when I was working as a sociologist in the Mozambican national women's organization, *Organização da Mulher Moçambicana*, the OMM. At that point Mozambique had just emerged from a successful war of liberation against Portuguese colonialism. Then, Mozambique was a one-party state. Frelimo, the previous liberation front had transformed itself into a socialist party and was firmly in power. The general atmosphere of the country was one of optimism, enthusiasm and hopefulness. This was in spite of sanctions and boycotts by the donor world (except DDR, Russia, Bulgaria and Cuba) and economic hardship. Among Mozambican intellectuals, there were some misgivings regarding the monopolistic political style of the Party, which left little space for civil society discussions of and engagement with politics.

In the meanwhile much has changed. Mozambique has been through civil war, internationally-supervised peace negotiations, constitutional change to multi-party so-called democracy, World Bank invasion, and structural adjustment politics. In the early 1980s, Mozambique was a very special country, with a very special history – and a very special setup of expatriates: there were the Cubans, Eastern Europeans, and a bunch of left wing people from Europe and Latin America ,including a handful of Scandinavians. Today, Mozambique is just another poor African country, playing along the lines of the Washington Consensus, the Paris Declaration, the Millenium Development Goals and anything else the donor world has constructed to the supposed benefit of poor, underdeveloped countries.

The replacement of state socialism with neo-liberal economic policies also implied, however, the emergence of a so-called civil society in Mozambique. Frelimo, in the one-party days was quite harsh on certain aspects of so-called 'tradition', among which were male and female rituals of initiation. Frelimo saw itself as a force of modernization, and its visions, in the early 1980s, for rapid change were quite utopian, to put it nicely (cf. Hanlon 1984). The multi-party state and the neo-liberal setup introduced a more relaxed attitude to certain aspects of daily life, such as initiation rituals. Nowadays, the state does not interfere in this kind of issues, and female initiation rituals, which during the days of one-party rule were not performed or were performed clandestinely, have re-emerged in community life of rural northern Mozambique.

This change has greatly facilitated the study of initiation rituals in Mozambique, and for the same reason the bulk of the data on which this paper draws, are collected in the more recent period of post-war, neo-liberal multi-party Mozambique, mainly from a fieldwork period 1998–1999, with updates in 2003 and 2005. Over the years, I have struggled with framing the presentation and analysis of this body of material, in a way that is able to bring forward what I see as crucial aspects of the rituals and the reason for their survival and continuation against all odds. The forces banning and condemning initiation rituals (particularly the female ones) have been many and powerful, from Catholic and Protestant missions to the modernizing endeavours of the Frelimo one-party state. However, women of northern Mozambique continue to cherish their rituals and go on performing them.

Anthropological studies of female initiation are few and far between; presumably because anthropology has often taken a male point of departure. I have collected the data with socio-anthropological methods, and it is my ambition to interpret the material in contexts of post-colonial theorizing regarding gender and sexuality. In this chapter, I will establish a dialogue with two important contributions to the scarce anthropological literature on female initiation. These contributions are both based on ethnographic data from Zambia, bordering on northern Mozambique, some 1000 kilometers further inland (to the west) from my own fieldwork location in Ribáuè district, Nampula province, northern Mozambique. The first work is the classical study: *Chisungo*, published 1956 by Audrey Richards, British anthropologist of the social-functionalist school, connected to the Rhodes-Livingstone Institute in what was then Northern Rhodesia. Richards' book was published in the 1950s, but based on fieldwork among the Bemba in central Zambia in the 1930s. The second body of work with which I will engage, is much more recent. It is Dutch anthropologist, Thera Rasing's *The Bush Burnt, the Stones Remain (2001)* and two papers (1999, 2004) published from her fieldwork in the urban part of the very same area of Zambia (now named the Copperbelt).

Audrey Richards, who studied female initiation in the 1930s, expected the rituals to disappear in the face of modernity and rapid social change (Richards 1956, 133). Thera Rasing found to her surprise in her first fieldwork in Zambia in 1992 that initiation rites were still very important even in Copperbelt towns. She also established that the rituals were conducted in a manner very similar to that described by Richards (Rasing 2001, 1). This was the reason, in fact, for her selection of this theme for her doctoral work, resulting in the abovementioned book and papers. Rasing chose an urban setting for her study, the small mining town of Mufulira in the Copperbelt, collecting her data among middle-class women with some education, generally belonging to the Catholic church. She found that even in this environment, thoroughly influenced by Christianity and globalization, female initiation was still performed, being considered very important from the women's points of view. Even Catholic nuns had to pass through initiation before joining the Church. Thus, as she states, 'the rites are a symbolic way of becoming an adult and being Bemba, irrespective of whether one is a Christian as well' (Rasing 2004, 297). This resilience is indeed remarkable, and it frames Rasing's interpretation, especially in her 2004 paper.

Many of Rasing's observations and interpretations run parallel to my own, my own baseline of understanding also being that in their respective contexts these rituals are – as expressed by Rasing – 'of vital importance in the construction of female identity, pride, autonomy, and meaning'(2001, 23). Rasing also states that 'initiation rituals express and confirm unity among women' (2004, 280). Both of these statements reflect my own experience and conception of the initiation rituals in Mozambique from the early 1980s onwards. These interpretations were clearly at odds with the OMM/Frelimo position, which saw female initiation as harmful and oppressive to women. What I have learned from many (often failed) attempts to find a conception of 'gender' relevant to an understanding female initiation in Mozambique, is that – as a precondition for further thinking – a thorough process of de-construction and un-learning (Spivak 1990) has to take place. Our commonsense mainstream notions of 'women' and 'gender' are in this context unhelpful. Exactly for this reason it makes sense to approach interpretation of the rituals in a context of post-colonial feminist thinking, which is the theme of this chapter.

Since the aim of the paper is to develop an approach to understanding female initiation rituals in matrilineal societies in central/southern Africa (part of what was in classical anthropology named 'the matrilineal belt' (Richards 1950)), I am interested in similarities between the three sets of data – Richards', Rasing's and my own – more than in differences, and particularly in similarities which support the approach, I want to establish. After a presentation of 'the coloniality of gender' as a critical analytical approach, I will embark on a description and interpretation of the conceptions of sexuality in the context of female initiation rituals in this part of Africa – not because sexuality is the only theme of focus in the rituals, but sexuality is important in the context of the rituals, and conceptions of sexuality are central for conceptions of gender, in Africa as well as in the western world. Different conceptions of sexuality have contributed decisively to the colonial – and post-colonial – misunderstandings not only of female initiation, but of male/female relations and of 'gender' as such. The purpose of 'the coloniality of gender' approach is to identify such misunderstandings, in order to open a space for more grounded interpretations and understandings of sexuality and of gender.

The coloniality of gender

'The coloniality of gender' – thus phrased by Latin American feminist philosopher Maria Lugones (2007) – expresses the fact that in many third world contexts 'gender', parallel to 'race', was created in and by the colonial encounter. As Kopano Ratele notes, writing about 'race': 'There were no black men before the introduction of whiteness in this country [i.e. South Africa], or anywhere else on the continent. In the early seventeenth century black men were other things: AmaZulu, AmaXosa, AmaNdebele, AmaSwazi, Basotho, Batswana, Khoi and San and so on. Before that they were other things. They were bound together by explicitly cultural bonds (which themselves are fluid) rather rather than yet to be defined by blackness' (Ratele 1998, 38).

Applying a very similar logic, Nigerian sociologist Oyèrónké Oyewùmí argues that there were no 'women' in Yorubaland prior to colonization. 'I came to realize,' she says, 'that the fundamental category "woman" – which is foundational in Western gender discourses – simply did not exist in Yorùbáland prior to its sustained contact with the West' (Oyewùmí 1997, ix). 'Race' as well as 'gender' in Africa, Asia, Latin America, are colonial constructions. 'Race is no more mythical and fictional than gender – both are powerful fictions' (Lugones 2007, 202). The denaturalization of race has been more accepted in scholarship so far than the denaturalization of gender; thinking about race thus may be useful for rethinking gender. 'The invention of race is a pivotal turn as it replaces the relations of superiority and inferiority established through domination,' Lugones says. 'It reconceives humanity and human relations fictionally, in biological terms' (2007, 190). A social, political, economic relation of domination is reinvented as a biological difference, thus naturalized. What happens to 'gender' is very similar: a social relation of male domination/female subordination, brought along with the European colonial powers and supported by Christianity, is represented as a biological difference between men and women, with the 'natural' implication that women are subordinated in relation to men. In a country like Nigeria following colonization, women were expelled from the public sphere. 'In Britain, access to power was gender-based; therefore politics was largely men's job; and colonization, which is fundamentally a political affair, was no exception. ... The system of indirect rule introduced by the British colonial government recognized the male chief's authority at the local level, but did not acknowledge the existence of female chiefs' (Oyewùmí 1997, 123-4). Similarly in Mozambique under Portuguese colonization, the Portuguese administration never even recognized the double headship structure of the Makhuwa of northern Mozambique, where every *mwene* or *mfumu* (Emakhuwa for male chief) had at his side a *pwiyamwene*, a female chief. The kinship relation between the mwene and the pwiyamwene – or *mapwiyamwene*, since there might be more than one – would always be brother/sister, son/mother (or grandmother); never husband/wife, since the two would always belong to the same *níhimo* (matrilineage). An important task of the pwiyamwene was/is to take care of relations to the spirits – but to the colonizers and to the Christian missionaries political leaders could be male only. 'The very process by which females were categorized and reduced to 'women' made them ineligible for leadership roles,' Oyewùmí says. 'For females, colonization was a twofold process of racial inferiorization and gender subordination. The creation of 'women' as a category was one of the very first accomplishments of the colonial state' (Oyewùmí 1997, 124). The colonial state enforced and created a notion of 'womanhood' along European lines, part of the enforcement being the fact that the very act of creation was erased and represented as given, the notion of womanhood being conceived as natural, based on bodies and biology. This resulted in the naturalization and universalization of male/female gender hierarchies, the process which Lugones names the 'coloniality of gender'.

From a post-colonial analytical point of view the effort of denaturalizing gender thus becomes central. In order to understand what female initiation rituals are all about it is important to denaturalize and deconstruct common-sense notions of 'men' and 'women'. Gender binaries should not be taken for granted, and male/female does not necessarily follow biological sex. Ifi Amadiume, Nigerian anthropologist, highlights 'the flexibility of gender constructions in the Igbo language and culture' (Amadiume 1987, 17). Under certain conditions daughters may turn into sons, being socially recognized as male, and previous wives may take positions as husbands. Male/female is not fixed on bodies; male/female are subject positions which may be taken up or left behind by different individuals during a lifetime. In Igbo language, Amadiume says, 'no gender distinction is made in reference to males and females in writing or in speech. There is, therefore, no language or mental adjustment or confusion in reference to a woman performing a typical male role'(ibid., 17). According to Amadiume the 'rigid gender ideology of the West' (ibid., 16) thus did not apply in Igboland prior to colonization.

Oyewùmí also points to language in her attempt to conceptualize different notions of gender in Yoruba culture before the British. 'Yorùbá language is gender-free, which means that many categories taken for granted in English are absent. There are no gender-specific words denoting son, daughter, brother, or sister. ... Most names and all pronouns are ungendered. ... There is, however, considerable anxiety about establishing seniority in any social interaction' (Oyewùmí 1997, 40). According to Oyewùmí, gender binaries and hierarchies do not apply, whereas hierarchies of seniority do, as do also other social hierarchies between slave owners/slaves, different lineages etc. Yoruba language does of course have terms to describe male and female bodies, but these terms 'merely indicate the physiological differences between the two anatomies as they have to do with procreation and intercourse. ... They do not refer to gender categories that connote social privileges and disadvantages. Also they do not express sexual dimorphism because the distinction they indicate is specific to reproduction' (ibid., 34–35).

This lack of gender differentiation exists in many other African languages as well (Crehan 1997, Geffray 1990, Rasing 2001), a linguistic, conceptual and partly social indifference to gender which implies that not only male and female, but also nothing, or in between, are possible positions – unlike in Western contexts, where, as noted by Lugones, 'the law does not recognize intersexual status'. Lugones, drawing on Greenberg (2002) gives examples of how infants with ambiguous genitals are surgically reconstructed and classified as male or female (Lugones 2007, 195). Western epistemology is concerned about unambiguous bodies; bodies must be either male or female, and if they happen to be something else, this error is instantly rectified. Bodies must belong in the gender dichotomy, which is later justified by reference to these same bodies. Oyewùmí talks about 'Western somatocentricity' (1997, 3) or 'body-reasoning' (ibid., 5). According to her, bodies play far too big a role in Western thinking, including Western feminism. 'Despite the preeminence of feminist social constructionism,' she says, 'biological foundationalism if not reductionism, is still at the center of gender discourses, just as it is at the center of all other discussions of society in the West' (ibid., 9). Yoruba, Igbo and Makhuwa cultures seem to put more emphasis on *conduct* and *knowledge*. It is your social behavior, the way you act and speak/don't speak which indicate where you belong, at any given time, in the gendered or ungendered social spheres. Often gender is not important/does not apply. Rasing notes that children are regarded as gender neutral, thus closer to the genderless ancestors (2001, 48). Gender is mainly important in the field of reproduction, and as for children and ancestors issues of reproduction generally don't apply.

The coloniality of gender means that male/female, masculinity/femininity as we know and recognize the terms have been imposed on colonized societies, and that these societies were subsequently conceptualized, interpreted and governed according to this imported gender pattern characterized by bipolarity, heterosexuality, and male dominance/female subordination. This transformation is part of what feminist philosopher Gayatri Spivak, in the case of India, terms as *epistemic violence* (Spivak 1988). Acknowledgement of Western gender categories as imposed and enforced in the process of colonization, and concomitantly of the epistemic violence embedded in this process, is the first step in attempts to understand different logics of gender and different epistemologies compared to Western understandings of men and women. Gender is part of a cosmology and a social structure, where some crucial aspects are gendered while others are not. Initiation rituals as they were and are conducted in parts of Zambia and in northern Mozambique point to such different logics and epistemologies. Looking into initiation rituals thus may open our minds for de-naturalizing male and female, and for grasping different ways of conceptualizing gender.

After all, initiation rituals may not only be about the construction of women, but more in a wider sense about the confirmation and recreation of a particularly gendered sphere of powerful female sociality; women together maintaining the gendered social cosmology of a particular ethnic group. By being initiated to this universe, the initiates gain identites as Bemba or Makhuwa women. Masters of ceremonies are the older women, and in particular the figure which in Richards' and Rasing's accounts is named the *nacimbusa*; in the Ribáuè-part of Nampula province she is named *namalaka*, a woman who is often also a diviner and a midwife – a religious and spiritual expert. 'The nacimbusa had a high status and authority,' Rasing says, with reference to Richards, 'The nacimbusa was in fact a chief (*mfumu*), or at least the same rank as a chief. She was considered a priestess ... and was also a healer (*nganga*)' (Rasing 2001, 53). The special status and capacities pertaining to the nacimbusa are similar to what I saw in Ribáuè regarding the particular namalaka, Arissa, whom I followed in subsequent field visits over some years from 1998 to 2005. In addition to conducting initiation rituals, Arissa also acted as a diviner and a priestess. At one point I was present at an all night spirit ceremony in a mountain cave close to Ribáuè town, with people falling into a trance as they were visited by spirits. Both men and women were present in the cave, but the persons in charge were women (with Arissa as the master of ceremonies) and all those through whom the spirits spoke were also women. According to Rasing, and similar to what I saw in Ribáuè, women are the holders of domestic shrines, and women are mediators between the living, the dead and the unborn. Access to parenthood and to the ancestors goes through the woman (Rasing 2001, 49). The initiation ceremonies are about introduction to this powerful universe. They are also about how to behave in daily life with your husband and with other people, always respecting the spirits and forces of life and death.

Female initiation in Zambia and Mozambique: 'To make her a woman as we are'

During my post-war fieldwork in Ribáuè, I participated several times in rituals of female initiation. In the past, initiation rituals were bigger events, I was told, with months of seclusion in the ritual hut in the bush before the coming-out ceremony. Nowadays, the whole thing was a condensed affair going on non-stop from Friday noon to Sunday morning, with a small group of girls (three to seven girls in the rituals I attended) going through a sequence of sessions of different kinds. The sessions would be dancing contests and various types of performances, including tests and trials and rough treatment of the girls, as well as verbal instructions through rhythmically chanted *ikano* (instructions and advice). The event will then end with a ritual haircut and ritual bath, a new name and new *capulanas*, before the triumphant procession back to the village. (See Chapter 7 for details)

The Bemba rituals, recorded by Audrey Richards in the 1930s, were of longer duration, though already curtailed by modernity and wage work (Richards 1956, 133).The Bemba kinship system is matrilineal, however (according to Richards) with a relatively stronger position of the fathers, compared to the Makhuwa variant of matriliny. To establish the views of Bemba men and women on the importance of initiation rituals, Audrey Richards asked: Why do the rituals have to be performed? Among men, Richards records the following responses: 'No one would want to marry a girl who had not had her *chisungo* danced. She would not know what her fellow women knew. She would not be invited to other chisungo celebrations. She would just be a piece of rubbish, an uncultivated weed, an unfired pot. A fool, or just not a woman' (1956,120). In short, nothing worthwhile. Something that has not (yet) found its proper useful shape, something that had not been manufactured (an uncultivated weed, an unfired pot). The women's answers are different, but ultimately they boil down to the same thing: The girl is initiated in order to make her a woman. A girl-child does not grow into a woman on her own. The Western common-sense notion that a girl child turns into a woman mainly as a consequence of sheer biological changes taking place in her body at a certain age, is not/was not shared by the Bemba and Makhuwa. To create a woman is a purposeful and very social piece of work, performed by older women: 'It is women's magical knowledge, owned and used by women, that transforms the girls into women. Moreover, what the chisungo makes clear is that successful womanhood is taught and learned; it is not a 'natural' attribute' (la Fontaine 1982, xxxiv). In order to be acknowledged as a woman in Bemba or Makhuwa society, one has to be initiated as a member of this particular group; one must receive instructions and be taught.

Richards classified the women's answers to her question in three groups: The chisungo is danced, they say, (a) in order to make the girl grow, (b) to teach her, and (c) to make her a woman as we are (1956, 121). Below I'll comment on answers (a) and (b), first however on answer (c): *To make her a woman as we are*, which actually sums it all up. This answer points to initiation rituals as the necessary introduction to the female community and to the powerful female universe with its secret knowledge.

Understanding what this female community is about is crucial to the understanding of Makhuwa (and Bemba) gender relations. A woman is not just herself, she is part of the community of women, and this community of women is re-created and reinforced at every celebration of initiation rituals. In parts of Nampula province, female initiation is named *wineliwa*, meaning 'to be danced to', and this is much what the rituals are about: introduction through specific dances into this specific universe. Seen in this context the female initiation rituals have a double importance. At one and the same time, wineliwa is the means by which new members of this specific community are produced, and the occasion for the older members to confirm and celebrate their identities as Makhuwa women and to enjoy themselves. Each and every celebration of initiation has this double aspect: New members get initiated, and old members confirm and celebrate their way of being women – part of which has to do with the maintenance of established power hierarchies of seniority, expressed in teasing, being rough to and punishing the young initiates. The way in which the community of gender is reproduced is by means of the hierarchy of age. The older women use this opportunity to shape the younger ones in their own image, as expressed in the statement: The chisungo is danced in order 'to make her a woman as we are'.

As for the first answer to Richards' questions, 'to make the girls grow': The metaphor of growing is frequently used in Mozambique as well. The old women take the young girls through the rituals in order that they shall grow, and re-join society as grown ups. In Richards' interpretation this 'growing' is connected to the magical aspects of the rite. 'I believe' she writes, 'that the women in charge of this ceremony were convinced that they were causing super-natural changes to take place in the girls under their care, as well as marking those changes' (1956,125).

The second answer, according to Richards, was 'to teach the girls'. Teaching is a way of speaking of initiation rites which is widely used, also in Mozam-bique. In classical anthropology, initiation rites are called 'initiation schools', and also in the OMM writings, the initiation rites are referred to as *educacão tradicional* (traditional education). Richards points to the pitfalls in this way of speaking. Actually, she says, instruction is not what is going on most of the time. Regarding the patterns of behaviour expected of grown up women, the girls know most of what they need to know long time before they are subjected to initiation rites. They have followed the work of their mothers and of other grown up women of the household. The Makhuwa even expect them to know about lovemaking well before they enter into the rites. The teaching thus is not so much about capabilities as about particular aspects of conduct and knowl-edge, knowledge not necessarily being 'knowledge' in a Western sense, but more 'a secret language or rather secret terms' (Richards 1956, 127) which only pertain to initiation rituals. As Richards notes, with a certain exasperation: 'What seems to the educationist to be the most mumbo-jumbo and useless aspect of the whole affair may actually constitute one of the most prized items of information to the people concerned' (ibid.). She makes another pertinent observation that to the new initiates this is their first, but by no means their last opportunity of taking part in female initiation rituals. What the girls do not grasp this first time, they pick up later. Having attended several sessions of initi-ation rituals and having listened for hours to the chanted ikano (advice) deliv-ered by the namalaka to the accompaniment of *chocalhos* (rattles), I also realized with a certain relief that the neophytes did not have to grasp it all the first time; they get many second chances, as they are free to attend any number of initi-ation ceremonies after their own initiation.

Nevertheless, it would be possible to talk of instructions in a more straight-forward way, in two different areas, as I see it: 1) regarding menstruation, and 2) sex in the context of marriage. I will deal with these two below.

Regarding menstruation: Issues regarding menstruation are secrets to children and uninitiated girls, and an important part of the instruction given is that they must remain secrets: Utmost care must be taken that the menstruation blood does not show on your clothes or elsewhere, at all costs the sanitary towels (*nkhapa* is the ritual name) must be kept out of sight of the uninitiated. Menstrual blood is considered dangerous and powerful; the young girls have to learn how to deal with it, how to control – and how to use in proper ways – the powers from now on contained in their bodies. The initiates also learn about taboos to be observed while menstruating: You cannot have sex, and you cannot sleep in the same bed as your husband. (Rasing reports similar precautions during menstruation 2001, 181). According to what I was told in Mozambique, a woman, in order to communicate her state, doesn't use words; she places a string of red beads on the bed, and the husband will get the message. When the menstruation has passed, the string of red beads will be replaced by a string of white beads. The menstruating woman cannot cook, and she cannot put salt in the food. In Mozambique in the old days seclusion for initiation rituals started when the girl had her first menstruation, the menstruation advice thus given as a prelude to the actual rituals.

Regarding sex in the context of marriage: In pre-colonial, pre-Christian times, Makhuwa girls could well have experienced sex before marriage. In parts of Nampula province, it was even believed that intercourse would help to bring forth menstruation and help the breasts grow. Since pre-menstrual sex could not have implications for procreation it was not policed with particular zest. Sex as such was not a moral issue, as it has become later with Christianity. Sex in marriage however, was/is something special, considered as something powerful and strong. Rasing's account confirms the special status of sex in marriage – a fact which is noteworthy in this context of matriliny, where marriage ceremonies as such are not much to talk about, and marriages are easily dissolved.

A conversation with one of my women-interlocutors in Ribáuè clarified the difference for me between straightforward sex (as we would see it in a Western context) and sex in marriage. She said: Learning about sex in the initiation rituals is like learning to read in school. Before you learn how to read, letters on a page are just letters, with no meaning. Only after you have received instruction, you see what the meaning is. Sex is similar. Before initiation, sex is just *brincadeira*, playing around, it has no meaning. It is only after initiation you see the meaning and the context. It is only after initiation you understand what it is all about. From this point on, sexual relations have to be done in a particular way *com toda a cerimónia* – with the whole ceremony of the woman cleaning of the penis after intercourse, the man giving gifts to the woman etc. (cf. Chapter 7). It is this explanation, and others along similar lines, which has inspired the distinction below between 'sex-heavy' *com toda a cerimónia* and 'sex-light', which is just *brincadeira*.

Sex in the context of marriage: 'Sex-heavy' and 'sex-light'

The special character of sex in marriage has to do with the ancestors. Marriage and reproduction belong to their domain, sex as such – on its own so to say, sex as brincadeira – does not. Based on the data I collected on initiation rituals, from translations of the chanted ikano given by the namalaka during the rituals, and from interviews with knowledgeable women and men, I'll suggest an analytical division of sexual activity in 'sex-heavy' and 'sex-light'. I have previously worked with a division in *sex for procreation/sex for pleasure* (Arnfred 2004b), but I think 'sex-heavy/sex-light' may be more appropriate to express the distinction I want to make, first because 'sex-heavy' is not just about procreation, but also adherence to rules and taboos of many kinds; proper 'sex-heavy' can only take place in marriage. Second because 'sex-heavy' is also delightful (if you ask Makhuwa men, which I did). 'Sex-light' may take place in marriage and also outside marriage, where 'sex-heavy' cannot occur.[1]

Through my interviews in Ribáuè, I got the feeling that whereas the men praised 'sex-heavy', some women preferred 'sex-light'. I talked quite a lot with a woman school teacher, some fifty years of age, who was also active in the Catholic Church, and who was a very good informant on Makhuwa ways of life. On her own account, however, she was not happy about the traditional approach to sex in marriage (i.e. 'sex-heavy') with its emphasis on active female seduction as a prelude to sex. Presumably, as an educated Christian woman, she felt less at ease with the role as active sexual agent – a role which young as well as elderly rural women in Ribáuè seemed very explicitly to enjoy (cf. Chapter 13).

The discipline in which the girls are instructed during initiation rituals is 'sex-heavy': the codes of conduct, the taboos etc. of sex in the context of marriage. What the girls may know about beforehand is 'sex-light' – sexual play with boys their own age, and maybe also with girls in the context of the shared sessions of *labia* elongation in which they are instructed well before the onset of menstruation, from 8–10 years of age, so that the work may be finished, the small lips of the vagina having reached a proper length, when they enter initiation (on labia elongation see Arnfred 1988, Tamale 2005b, Bagnol and Mariamo 2008a, 2008b and Chapters 2 and 6, this volume). The extended labia (*ithuna*) are an important ingredient in the sexual foreplay; not just because of their role in 'sex-heavy' as described below, but also in other ways. During the OMM collection of data material in the early 1980s the elongated lips of the vagina were much praised by men and women for their contribution to sexual pleasure, for women as well as for men.

Pleasurable or not, 'sex-heavy' is the serious business, in which the girls are instructed during initiation. They have to learn how to behave in bed with their husbands, how to invite him to lovemaking by squatting in front of him while pulling their ithuna, how to move during the sexual act, and how to cleanse his penis after intercourse. The husband is also instructed to behave in particular ways. This codified lovemaking is particularly necessary in specific situations when sex between husband and wife has ritual functions. This is the case for instance of the first sexual relation after a period of abstinence, be it abstinence during menstruation, during childbirth and breastfeeding, during the initiation rites of a son or a daughter, or during the mourning period for a relative. Other occasions for ritual intercourse between spouses are first fruit celebrations: As an inauguration ceremony before you can start to eat the first

---

[1] I must confess that I am not quite sure here. Also, I have a feeling of rules and norms in this area undergoing change, maybe particularly in urban settings, cf Groes-Green 2011. My main point is to argue for an analytical distinction between 'sex-heavy' and 'sex-light'.

products of the harvesting season, the wife should invite her husband to sex in this prescribed ritual way. Also when she wants to thank him for having cleared a large *machamba* – or for inducing him to clear an even larger one. This kind of codified sex is a customary way of expressing gratitude – also if/when the husband comes back from town bringing his wife a capulana – and a way of persuading the husband to do as the wife wants him to do. A piece of advice given during the initiation rites is the following: If your husband wants to take a second wife, you should not quarrel; seducing him to lovemaking is a much wiser approach. The *ikano* go as follows:

> If your husband wants to take another wife, then you should undress, open your legs and invite him to sex by pulling your small lips of the vagina. In this way you tell him that you don't want him to take a second wife. After having had sex with your husband you should cook him a meal. The following day he will say that you are his mother.

During the initiation rituals I attended, Arissa – equipped with a clay penis in a string around her waist hidden under her capulana – would first enact pretended sexual intercourse with one of her helpers playing the woman, then invite the initiates to play the woman one by one. The initiates are instructed regarding how to move the pelvis during intercourse (a body movement in which they have already been trained) and how afterwards to clean the husband's penis with their hands, rinsing the hands in a bowl of water. The initiates are also instructed how to give a gentle massage to the husband's arms and body after the act, and to expect to be rewarded by a gift or by money. The clay penis part of the ritual is regarded as a high point of excitement, and the body movements of intercourse are repeated again and again by the older women, to great acclaim and enjoyment of the other women participating in the ritual event – excluding the initiates, who maintain solemn faces, having no fun at all.

Sex in marriage – the ritualized aspect of sex in marriage – is serious business in front of spirits and ancestors. Sex in marriage is connected to possible repro-duction, which – even if the children belong to the mother's lineage – is also of some consequence for the father of the children. Daughters are particularly important, since they bring in sons-in-law. But sex in marriage may also be 'sex-light', and it was my impression that this version was most priced by the women. Marriage is the framework for ritualized sex – but also for spontaneous lovemaking. Once, when in Ribáuè I asked about women's sexual pleasure, this was the answer I got:

> The joy of sex in marriage depends on the man and the woman. If the woman feels like making love, she may take the initiative, be it when they are both working in the field or when they have gone together fetching firewood. As a married couple they are entitled to lovemaking anywhere. Sometimes lovemaking in the bush is particu-larly nice.

Sex outside marriage

There are rules which apply in marriage (eg regarding ritualized sex and ritu-alized abstinence), but the marriage relationship is also a space for absence of rules. Normally a woman should not be seated with her legs apart – but in the bedroom with your husband this rule does not apply: you may put your legs in whichever position, because this man is your husband. Thus 'sex-light' may take place in marriage. But 'sex-light' also – and maybe most frequently – takes place outside marriage. In Ribáuè extra-marital affairs were not uncommon, even if the women of this inland district of Nampula province often spoke wistfully of the women of the coast (still Makhuwa) who took sexuality much lighter and who had many more extra-marital affairs. The basic rule regarding extra-marital affairs, inland and at the coast, is the same: discretion. As long as such an affair is not known/spoken about, it does not exist.

Sex and money

A further aspect of sexual intercourse in marriage, which I noted in Ribáuè, is also confirmed in Rasing's account: having been seduced and pampered sexually by his wife the husband is expected to give something in return: money or a present. The money bit is particularly interesting from a Western/Christian point of view, where sex and money are like oil and water: the two do not mix – and if they do it is beyond the pale of decency and moral: then it becomes prostitution and what is worse. Not so in the contexts here under discussion. Rasing writes:

> A man should respect his wife. This is expressed in the wedding ceremony by teaching him that he should give her money in exchange for services. For instance on the wedding night the husband is required to pay when entering the room where his bride is waiting for the marriage to be consummated. He has to give money when the bride is placed on the bed, and after intercourse. In addition he has to give money or a present, as a token of respect, when his wife washes him and shaves him. (Rasing 2001, 170)

An important part of the instructions on sex in marriage is what takes place after the sexual act itself, including cleaning of the husband's penis, giving massage to his fingers, arms and shoulders , the whole session ending with the husband giving money (or some other gift) to the wife. The husband will not necessarily be expected to pay every time after sex with his wife, but the woman will feel turned off (*fechada*) if a long time passes with the husband giving nothing. This, according to my women interlocutors in Ribáuè, is the case in relation to sex inside as well as to sex outside marriage. 'For women the basic capacities of life are her sexual powers and her work on the land, for men the basic capacities of life are their strength and their money,' they said. Taken slightly further one might say that sex is female business, while money is male business, woman/man sexual relations being based on sex/money exchange. This of course is interesting from a Western point of view, from where sex/money relations between young urban women, *curtidoras*, and their sugar-daddies, *patronicadores*, are classified as prostitution (Groes-Green 2011). Seen from a rural Mozambican point of view things look differently; the young curtidoras get help and advice from sisters, aunts and curandeiros regarding how to use their sexual powers and how to cast spells for keeping their patron-icadores under control. In spite of the fact that in these relationships the men of course command a certain economic power, the gender power relations at play cannot be described simply as male dominance / female subordination (Groes-Green 2011).

Respect and seduction

But back now to the instructions during rituals of initiation: beyond codes of conduct regarding menstruation and regarding sex – sex in the context of marriage, and sex outside marriage, where rules of discretion apply – young women also are instructed regarding codes of conduct in society in general, and particularly vis a vis their husbands. To show respect is extremely important. When in the early 1980s – increasingly bewildered by the OMM denunciation of the rituals as woman-oppressive – I asked very open questions regarding what then these rituals were about, respect was the most frequent answer: the young people must learn how to show respect. Respect is recognition of the dignity of others, including awareness of one's own position in a hierarchy, as shown in the ikano regarding how to greet the *régulo*, that you must kneel down and clap your hands when the régulo passes by. Surely this appears somewhat extreme, nowadays. I heard about this type of greeting from colonial times, but I never saw it. The point however is the importance of showing respect for authority and age, and that respectful behaviour also dignifies oneself. A child may fool around, you cannot expect too much of a child in terms of adhering to codes of conduct. But as a grown up you show your dignity and position in the way that you respect the dignity and position of others. It is simply a matter of being well behaved, and following the rules of etiquette. As a woman, one of the ways of showing respect is not to look directly at a stranger; the good-mannered way of behaving is to maintain downcast eyes. Generations of observers have mistaken this for female submission. In my view it is just following the code of conduct for being well behaved as a woman. Similarly the code of conduct for not talking back has been misinterpreted. In the ikano the girls are told that they should not 'discuss' with their husbands: 'You should never discuss with your husband and never insult him. This is bad.' Words are potentially dangerous, they should be applied with caution. 'Not discuss with your husband' does not imply that the wife should follow the husband's command. Far from it. But roundabout ways of settling issues are recommended. The wise thing to do will be to wait until the bedroom privacy, and to settle the matter through seduction, not confrontation. If your husband does something you do not like, then make love to him; prepare him a nice meal. 'The following day he will say that you are his mother'[2] – which means: He will pay you respect, and follow your lead. In the male initiation rites the boys are told that the one they must show most respect of all is their mother: 'Who is the oldest and the greatest [i.e. the highest authority, the one that deserves most respect] is your mother back home.'

Of course this education against 'discussion' clash head on with what the school tries to teach girls as well as boys. Initiation rituals are about an intro-

---

[2] Cf the quotation above, the *ikano* of Ribáuè female initiation.

duction to and acceptance of existing norms, not criticism, opposition and individual points of view. The girls are taught to be women and to handle their gender power in the ways prescribed by tradition – which is largely through seduction by sex and cooking. The man feels two kinds of hunger, or desire, they are told. One of the stomach, and one of the penis. If the woman knows how to care for these two types of male desire, the husband will be at her beck and call. Looking after one's husband well – and abstaining from having lovers – is an advisable long-term strategy:

> If you will be the wife of only your husband, you may look forward to much enjoyment in life. He will always think of you; he will buy you clothes, and he will make you a good house and a large *machamba* [field]. He will give to you all the game that he manages to kill, and almost all what he has got will also belong to you. You will get much love from your family. All of this will happen if you choose not to be the wife of a thousand men. (male informant quoted by Medeiros[3] 1995, 232)

Monogamy is not a moral issue. It is an issue of strategy.

The 'two kinds of hunger' referred to above also point to the overlap and fluid boundaries between sex and cooking. Rasing, based on Richards, states that in the past 'a husband and wife never shared a meal, except perhaps late at night when they were in their own house. It was considered shameful to eat with the opposite sex. For a woman to eat with men was almost the equivalent of being a prostitute. ... the introduction of sharing a meal with the family, as part of the Christian teaching, has been heavily criticized' (Rasing 2001, 58).

Several interesting issues are at play here. (a) a woman's way to manoeuvre a man is through sex and cooking. Sex and cooking are vital areas, where men depend on women.[4] (b) in Western patrilineal contexts, with (previous) ideals of female chastity and virginity at marriage, expertise and initiative in sex has shifted from women to men, and eating has become de-sexualized. In some Muslim countries eating is still considered an intimate act: women are not supposed to eat in public. (c) the ideal position of a wife in relation to her husband seems to be that he should consider her 'his second mother' – in terms of respect and reverence. There may be many interpretations of issues such as these – but interpretations rooted in a priori perceptions of male dominance/female subordination do not suggest themselves as particularly relevant.

Initiation rituals from a 'coloniality of gender' perspective

The coloniality of gender perspective on initiation rituals does not focus on the girls to be initiated (cf. the Audrey Richards focus on 'teaching' and on 'making the girls grow') or on behaviour they learn from the rituals (cf. Bagnol and Mariamo 2008a, 2008b). The coloniality of gender perspective focuses on the meanings of 'gender' and 'women', pointing to the very particular colonial and Christian roots of the notion of male dominance/female subordination, which has for a long time, mistakenly, been considered a universal condition for womanhood (de Beauvoir 1949/1997; Young, Wolkowitz, McCullagh, 1981).

---

[3] Eduardo Medeiros is a Mozambican scholar; *Os Senhores da Floresta* (1995) on Makhuwa male initiation is his PhD dissertation.

[4] More on sex and cooking in Chapter 13.

Investigating female initiation rituals from a coloniality of gender perspective implies asking questions regarding the character of possibly gendered social spheres. In my study of the Makhuwa I have found that through initiation rituals young girls are introduced to a powerful female universe with special links to the spirits. Communication with the spirits takes place in various ways, one of them being through sex in marriage, and young women are educated to be capable and responsible in this area. Women are expected to be experts on sex and food, thus able to satisfy the two types of hunger of their husbands, while also possessing the keys to vital areas of human life.

Frelimo/OMM misunderstandings

In a coloniality of gender – or post-colonial – interpretation, introduction to the powerful female universe is a lot of what the initiation rituals are about. Female initiation rituals have, however, been persistently misunderstood, by colonialism and Christianity, by socialism (Frelimo/OMM) and by contemporary development agencies. Not surprisingly, since all of these very different social forces subscribe to very similar conceptions of gender, namely a male/female dichotomy with a hierarchy of male domination/female subordination.

In 1981, when I started working in the OMM, the lead document was the conclusions from the 1976 Second National Conference of the OMM (*Organização da Mulher Moçambicana* 1977). In this document's narrative of initiation rites, the elements of scaring, derogation, punishments and beatings were strongly emphasized. And surely hierarchical power structures are at play with the young initiates firmly placed at the bottom. But even if these scary and derogatory events do take place, the Frelimo/OMM interpretation was wrong on two counts: first it did not understand the state of limbo into which the girls are purposely placed, in order for them to change identities from girls to culturally competent women. The point of what in classical anthropology is called the marginal phase or the liminal period is precisely the creation of a space beyond normal social contexts, ruled by a very special social structure of its own. Complete authority and complete submission in the relationship elder/initiate, and complete equality among the initiates themselves (Turner 1967, 99). According to Turner:

> The authority of the elders is absolute, because it represents the absolute,the axiomatic values of society in which are expressed the 'common good' and the common interest. The essence of the complete obedience of the neophytes is to submit to the elders but only in so far as they are in charge, so to speak, of the common good and represent in their persons the total community. (Turner 1967, 99–100)

The character of this liminality accounts for some of the aspects that Frelimo/OMM criticised in the initiation rites, the very fact that the girls (this is similar in the case of boys) are treated like nobodies, with bent heads and downcast eyes, stone faces, and no reactions in any personal, individual way to what is going on around them. Frelimo understood that this does not in any way match modern ideas about development of individuality and personality, but they did not understand the ritual context. Second, Frelimo/OMM misunderstood the character of the power hierarchies at play: They saw them as hierarchies of gender: Men's oppression of women, where in actual fact they are hierarchies of age: Older women confirming their authority – on behalf of matrilineal society – vis a vis the younger women as well as their potential husbands. The Makhuwa female initiation rites (contrary to the Frelimo/OMM interpretation) may indeed be interpreted as celebrations of female power, a manifestation and re-creation of a powerful female universe. Within this universe hierarchies of power are also reproduced, but they are hierarchies of age, not gender. Women are in control, and if men appear at all, they obey to the woman/women in charge.

The issues, particularly regarding what one could call educational style, are complex. Considered as experience the initiation rites must be quite a violent affair – the effect of course exacerbated by the fact that the girls know nothing beforehand and thus all along fear the worst. Maybe looking back they will realize that it was not that bad after all – but how could they know? As long as they are in it, anything might happen, and they are perpetually scared. In modern psychology, this kind of learning process would be called traumatizing. Not much milder than some kinds of torture, and sharing with torture the uncertainly about what comes next, the de-individualization and the total submission to power. As such the clash with modern pedagogy is head on, as is the clash with any idea of individuality, equality, democracy etc.

I was thus very surprised that when interviewing a bunch of secondary school girls from the renowned Frelimo Secondary School of Ribáuè,[5] I found that a majority of these girls had gone through female initiation rites, and also wanted the same thing for their daughters.[6] Talking about ideals and visions of life, love and work, and what they wanted to do after having finished school, many said that they wanted to become nurses, but otherwise they wanted to be like their mothers. This was not at all what I had expected. Here were first generation female secondary school leavers, and they wanted to follow the lead of their mothers! They themselves phrased it like that. I tried to probe for mother/daughter conflicts, but I found none. So unlike my own society, where the mother/daughter conflict is almost the way in which you grow up as a woman! Remembering my own years as a teenager I recall protracted conflicts with my own mother, and I don't recall any same age woman friends who couldn't tell the same kind of story. With my two daughters the experience remains the same; the way to individuation seems to go through breaks, ruptures and conflicts. Talking to these young Mozambican women (most but not all from Makhuwa backgrounds) it struck me that maybe the female initiation rites have rendered the Western mother/daughter conflict superfluous. In the female initiation rites the breaks and ruptures are institutionalized, replacing the years of struggle that our daughters have to go through on their own.

[5] After Independence, the Frelimo Secondary School of Nachingwea in Tanzania was moved to locations immediately outside Ribáuè town, in buildings which previously had been Portuguese army barracks.
[6] I first conducted a one-hour meeting with 30-40 girls from grades 9 to 11, posing a series of questions. Later I met with 12 of these girls for a whole afternoon of talk and discussion.

Resilience and resistance

The contemporary version of female initiation rituals, which I attended in Ribáuè, is a very condensed affair, the whole sequence squeezed into one single weekend: Friday–Sunday, no more. This abbreviated version makes it more manageable in terms of supplies and in terms of time off from other necessary pursuits. For schoolgirls, it is possible to be back at school on Monday.

Reduced as they are, nevertheless the crucial thing is that female initiation rituals take place, and that women – young and old – are keen to join. The fact that initiation rituals are still performed in northern Mozambique, in spite of missionary bans, OMM/Frelimo campaigns, war and Structural Adjustment testifies to a remarkable resilience of the rituals, in northern Mozambique as well as in the Zambian Copperbelt studied by Rasing. A factor, which works positively in the direction of maintaining female initiation is, I think, the continued existence in inland Makhuwa contexts of the *mapwyiamwene*, The mapwiyamwene, acting as focal points for links with the spirit world, facilitate a continuation of customary cosmology – including homage paid to ancestral spirits and performance of initiation rituals. In a place like Ribáuè this cosmology exists along with and beneath various editions of Christianity. Almost everybody in Ribáuè belong to some church – in colonial days there was the Catholic Church, which is still dominant, and two Evangelical mission churches; today a plethora of new African Independent and Pentecostal churches have established themselves in Ribáuè district, competing for devotees.

I had the feeling in Ribáuè that there was a long tradition of these kinds of overlapping identities, or simultaneous existence in different worlds: You go to church on Sundays, listen to the prayers and to all the prescriptions regarding things that you are supposed or not supposed to do. Especially some of the Evangelical Churches in Ribáuè were full of prohibitions: No dancing, no drums, no ancestor worship, and of course no initiation rites. This is one side of the double existence. But along with this there is another side, where these prescriptions and prohibitions don't really apply, and where life goes on as before. Also during the Frelimo one-Party days, in 'the time of Samora', this capacity for double existence proved its worth: People joined in on the *abaixo* slogans ('down with initiation rituals', 'down with polygamy' etc.), but tacitly and when the Party people had left the village, they went on with their lives as they had always done. Also in Rasing's study 'women overtly adhere to Christianity, while at the same time they perform rituals that belong to the traditional religion' (2004, 291). In Mozambique missionaries and Party people have been much frustrated by this state of affairs, but from women's points of view it signifies a great capacity for survival. Survival not just in terms of physical existence, but survival in terms of identity, in terms of ways of being women. Thus even if the initiation rites – which are central issues in this matter of identities – have been campaigned against, with varying intensity, for a hundred years, Makhuwa women have their own agendas and just go on performing their rituals.

Rasing conceptualizes the persistence of initiation rituals in terms of women's resistance towards increasing male dominance. Seeing modernity and male dominance as two sides of the same coin matches the coloniality of gender perspective. The very idea of a general subordination of women was introduced

by colonialism and Christianity (also shared by Islam, however in a slightly
different way). Female initiation rituals should be seen as a space for different
conceptions of gender, and as a possible point of departure for alternative
conceptualizations, notions and politics of women, men and gender in Africa
and elsewhere. The coloniality of gender approach shows the limitations of
Western notions of women and gender relations. Further studies of female initiation rituals might lead to different, more inclusive ideas regarding both women
and gender.

10 Situational Gender & Subversive Sex?
African Contributions to Feminist Theorizing (2007)

Woodcut by Wesa Maliva

Since the 1980s, feminist thinking has been challenged by feminists of colour and/or from post-colonial backgrounds. They have felt excluded from mainstream feminist concerns, and conceptualizations with implicit points of departure in Western middle-class norms and lifestyles have been seen as irrelevant or insufficient for understanding gender dynamics in different settings. This critique has highlighted weak points and blind spots in mainstream feminist thinking, paving the way for broader, more inclusive theorizing.

The particular focus in this chapter is on African contributions to feminist theorizing, with a special interest in the ways in which African feminists have taken African 'tradition' and 'culture' as points of departure for novel thinking regarding men, women and gender. This interest is spurred by my own investigations into gender relations in matrilineal northern Mozambique. My findings here – or rather my puzzlements, meeting gender identities and gender relations which did not fit my pre-conceived theoretical understandings – sent me searching for reinterpretations of so-called 'African tradition' from feminist points of view.

Re-mapping 'African culture'

In much ethnographic research on Africa, and certainly in colonial and missionary interventions, 'African tradition' is seen as patriarchal and woman oppressive. This general approach has been extended into contemporary development thinking, where notions of gender are often based on assumptions of Africa as 'underdeveloped' and 'behind', and of 'African tradition' as inherently patriarchal: cultures where women are perpetual minors, with little or no rights of their own to land or property, and with little personal freedom.

Such assumptions are increasingly being questioned by African gender scholars. They acknowledge that present gender relations of power in most African contexts are patriarchal and male dominated – but they suggest a different historical trajectory, compared to the mainstream notion of 'African women oppressed by traditional culture and harmful practices'. Rather than seeing the roots of contemporary African patriarchal structures in 'African culture', these scholars point to 'the new and growing patriarchal systems imposed on our societies through colonialism and Western religious and educational influences' (Amadiume 1987, 9). In their eyes, much of what is claimed by development agencies and by African leaders to be 'traditional African culture' is in fact invented tradition. Where development discourse sees gender oppression in the past and gender equality in the future, these feminists say: No, this is not how things are. Gender oppression in its present form has been imported to Africa from the West through colonialism and Christianity, and from the East through Islam. Before these interventions, gender relations were different, not oppressive – at least not in the same way – or maybe gender was actually not very important? As far as gender goes, they say, the past cannot be understood through the conceptual lens of present-day gender-and-development thinking. The challenge is to understand the past in different ways, in order to be able to point to new strategies for the future – to reconceptualize the past, and 'African culture-and-tradition', from a gender point of view.

Reanalysing old ethnographic texts and criticizing the (generally white, male, Christian) authors' patriarchalizing interpretations of African societies, scholars like Ifì Amadiume, Oyèrónke Oyewuùmí, Nkiru Nzegwu, Charmaine Pereira, Sylvia Tamale and many others come up with alternative conceptualizations, which challenge not only colonial anthropology and development discourse, but also Western feminist lines of thinking. Aspects of this critique will be discussed below.

This chapter is divided into two sections. In the first section, I discuss ideas of 'situational gender'. This is basically social constructionism taken further than the well known Simone de Beauvoir dictum: 'One is not born, but rather becomes, a woman' (de Beauvoir 1949/1997, 295)[1]. In this respect, I found the thinking of Ifì Amadiume and Oyèrónké Oyewùmí particularly useful. They both take a point of departure in pre-colonial Nigerian society (Igbo and Yoruba, respectively) reinvestigating and reinterpreting the ways in which pre-colonial social structures have been depicted by colonial anthropologists and others. As a result of these investigations they claim that 'gender' is not a foundational category, and that notions of gender are flexible and fluid, rooted in social positions, not in 'biological sex'. I have dubbed this line of thinking 'situational gender' in an attempt to stress the fact that in these conceptualizations, gender differences are not rooted in bodies. Gender is volatile, changing, depending on social relations; gender is given by the context, bodies are fitted in. This may look like social constructionist thinking, well known from much contemporary feminist theorizing, but it is more radical, going beyond male/female bodies. According to Oyewùmí, Western feminist claims to social constructionism cannot be taken seriously. How can they subscribe to social constructionism, she asks, and still take their point of departure in fixed man/woman binary hierarchical oppositions? Following social constructionist thinking, matters of power and subordination should be investigated, not assumed. However, in Oyewùmí's view, bodies, a priori categorized as either male or female, are far too prominently placed in Western feminist thought. She criticizes Western somatocentricity, or body-reasoning, as she calls it (Oyewùmí 1997, 5). 'Situational gender' means gender ad hoc, delinked from bodies, depending on social relations.

I have called the second section 'subversive sex' on inspiration from Sylvia Tamale. Summing up a paper given in 2005 at a conference in Gothenburg, Sweden, she said:

> While women's gendered bodies and sexualities constitute a crucial target for maintaining their subordination, they paradoxically also form an important tool in the informal systems of negotiating structures and systems of inequality. As women navigate through the maze of gender politics, reclaiming their bodily integrity and autonomy, they engage a variety of tools ranging from subtle sexuality and eroticism to unrestricted subversive sexuality, from passive to assertive. (Tamale 2005a, 18)

The notion of 'subversive sex' offers an entry point for talking about sexualities from women's (and in some cases also from men's) points of view, rather than

---

[1] This quote from *The Second Sex* actually does *not* match major lines of thinking in Simone de Beauvoir's work. Generally in *The Second Sex* Simone de Beauvoir sees women's cultural roles as linked to women's bodies, see Chapter 4.

from a position which reduces women to sexual objects. Sexuality studies is a fairly recent phenomenon in the context of African feminist writings. Sylvia Tamale is one of the pioneers, and according to her, it is the HIV/AIDS pandemic which has 'flung open the doors on sexuality. In particular, it has forced into the open the myths and secrets in relationships and identities that are often silenced or taken for granted' (Tamale 2005a). African feminists show that marriage and sexuality are not necessarily interlinked in the ways the Bible and African patriarchs preach, and that same-sex practices, far from being a Western import, as alleged by homophobic African leaders, have existed under specific circumstances in pre-colonial societies all over the continent. As pointed out by Jessica Horn:

> Homophobia is less an 'African' tradition than a patriarchal tradition that has been hijacked into local cultural discourse. ... What is bemusing is that moral condemnation and persecution of non-heteronormative behavior is often supported by allusion to two texts: laws criminalizing 'unnatural' sex and the Bible. Both were introduced via European colonization of Africa, and in the case of the latter, carried in again by a new wave of US-driven Pentecostal evangelism. (Horn 2006, 13)

Section 1: Situational gender

Ifi Amadiume (1987) and Oyèrónké Oyewùmí (1997) both make the point that gender is not a foundational category in many African contexts. Male and female are relational categories, depending on social positions. Often, but not always, female positions will be occupied by women, male positions by men. Amadiume talks of 'the flexibility of Igbo gender construction' which implies that daughters can become sons, and consequently male, just as women can marry wives and thus become husbands – i.e., male in relation to their wives (Amadiume 1987, 15). 'In Igbo grammatical construction of gender, a neuter particle is used in Igbo subject or object pronouns, so that no gender distinction is made in reference to males and females in writing or in speech. There is, therefore, no language or mental adjustment or confusion in reference to a woman performing a typical male role' (ibid., 17). Gender is located in social positions, not in bodies per se.

'The flexibility of Igbo gender construction meant that gender was separate from biological sex.' (ibid., 15). Oyéwùmí makes a similar point when she says that what was important in Yoruba society were not bodily characteristics (e.g., as man or woman) but social positionings, which are always relative and situational. 'From a Yorùbá stance, the body appears to have an exaggerated presence in Western thought and social practice, including feminist theories. ... The principle that determined social organization was seniority, which was based on chronological age. Yorùbá kinship terms did not denote gender, and other non-familial social categories were not gender-specific either' (Oyewùmí 1997: 13). Molara Ogundipe joins the critique of fixed and binary gender categorizations: 'We need to move away from the dichotomous evaluation of the woman's identity in diametrical opposition to a man's that occurs in Western studies. We need more refined and perceptive analytical tools' (Lewis/ Ogundipe, 2002). The Western male/female opposition based on interpretations of bodies as either male or female works as a mental block to further insight.

According to Oyewùmí, even if Western thinking declares itself not to be embodied (cf. the Cartesian notion of a disembodied mind), embodied is exactly what it is, all the time. Similarly, Western feminists busily criticizing Freud's dictum that anatomy is destiny (when it comes to women), are themselves thinking along those very lines. In Western dichotomous male/female thinking, womanhood is inescapably linked to bodies. The sex/gender distinction was introduced into feminist thought exactly in order to argue the point that gendered destinies are socially constructed and not bodily determined, but mainstream Western feminism has not managed to disentangle itself from bodies being interpreted as either male or female. Thus, according to Oyewùmí, 'the distinction between sex and gender is a red herring' (1997, 9). 'Despite the pre-eminence of feminist social constructionism, which claims a social deterministic approach to society, biological foundationalism, if not reductionism, is still at the center of gender discourses, just as it is at the center of all other discussions of society in the West,' Oyewùmí says (ibid.).

The concept of 'woman' overloaded with implications
Another recurrent point of critique focuses on the concept of 'woman'. What does it mean? What is implied when one talks of somebody as a 'woman'? Which are the dangers of generalized, universal, cross-cultural conceptions of womanhood?

Oyèrónké Oyewùmí confused her readers and sent waves of shock through African intellectual circles – feminist and non-feminist – when in her 1997 book she declared that 'the fundamental category "woman" – which is foundational in Western gender discourses – simply did not exist in Yorùbáland prior to its sustained contact with the West' (Oyewùmí 1997, ix). From Oyewùmí's point of view, the very concept of 'woman' in Western thinking is so overloaded with implications and associations which are irrelevant and disturbing in African contexts, that analysis with 'woman' as a conceptual tool inevitably will lead investigations off on wrong tracks, at the same time as important aspects of the subject matter remain unseen.

Judith Butler also criticizes the concept of "woman", but from a different point of view. 'To what extent,' she asks, 'does the category of woman achieve stability and coherence only in the context of the heterosexual matrix?' (Butler 1990, 9). The 'heterosexual matrix' in turn is closely linked to presumptions regarding a male/female binary, 'a hegemonic discursive /epistemic model of gender intelligibility that assumes that for bodies to cohere and make sense there must be a stable sex expressed through a stable gender ... that is oppositionally and hierarchically defined through the compulsory practice of heterosexuality' (Butler 1990, 194).

'Woman' as understood in the context of Second Wave feminism is not only in relation to a heterosexual matrix, but also in relation to a notion of a universal patriarchy, producing 'the universal subordination of women'. Writing in 1990, Butler is critical of this idea: 'The notion of universal patriarchy has been widely criticized in recent years for its failure to account for the workings of gender oppression in the concrete cultural contexts in which it exists' (Butler 1990, 6). However, she says, that 'although the notion of universal patriarchy no longer enjoys the kind of credibility it once did, the notion of a generally shared conception of 'women' the corollary to that framework, has been much more difficult to displace' (ibid., 7). Such destabilization is, however, according to Butler, an important challenge for contemporary feminism: 'To trace the political operations that produce and conceal what qualifies as the juridical subject of feminism is precisely the task of *a feminist genealogy* of the category of women' (ibid., 9, author's emphasis).

As I see it, Amadiume and Oyewùmí are meeting this challenge in their critical probing of the concept of 'woman' in African contexts. Seen from Oyewùmí's vantage point, a whole series of ideas – among these, first and foremost, the idea of 'universal subordination' – is embedded in the concept of 'woman' (1997: xii). This is what she is hinting at when she says that 'the woman in feminist theory, is a wife' (Oyéwùmí 2000, 1094). In Yoruba as well as in Igbo contexts, a position as wife is a subordinate position. But 'women' are more than wives, and not all 'wives' are women. In actual fact, across Africa, the category generally translated as 'wife' is often not gender specific, but it does indicate relations of subordination (Amadiume 1987, 90; Oyewùmí 2000, 1096). The distinction between Yoruba terms *oko* and *iyawo* (usually translated as 'husband' and 'wife') is not one of gender; it is a distinction between those who are birth members of a family/a lineage and those who enter by marriage (Oyewùmí 2002, 4). In a matrilineal society, any married man will be a 'wife' in this sense. The relation of subordination is conditioned by being insider vs outsider to the lineage; it is not conditioned by gender. If 'wives' are subordinated – as is frequently the case – this subordination is linked to the position as outsiders to the lineage, not to sex/gender per se. In patrilineal contexts, the women who are daughters of the lineage will often have different (and more privileged) positions, compared to the women who join the lineage as wives. In Emakhuwa – the language of the major population group in matrilineal northern Mozambique – the term for the person we would see as a 'father' literally translates into 'male stranger married into the lineage'.

Deprioritizing gender

Yet another line of criticism of Western gender-thinking is a critique of the automatic priority often given to gender in front of other structures of (possible) subordination, such as race, class and age. Ifi Amadiume, in the fierce critique of colonial anthropology and Western feminism, which prefaces her 1987 book: *Male Daughters, Female Husbands*, points out that Western feminism – at least until the mid-1980s – persisted in foregrounding gender, and remained blind to race (Amadiume 1987, 3). Indian feminist Chandra Mohanty makes a similar point: 'The universality of gender oppression is problematic, based as it is on the assumption that the categories of race and class have to be invisible for the category of gender to be visible' (Mohanty 2003, 107). Further along these lines, Mohanty also criticizes the Second Wave notion of Global Sisterhood (cf. Robin Morgan 1984):

> Universal sisterhood defined as the transcendence of the 'male' world thus ends up being a middle-class, psychologized notion that effectively erases material and ideological power differences within and among groups of women, especially between

first and third world women ... In Morgan's text cross-cultural comparisons are based the assumption of the singularity and homogeneity of women as a group. This homogeneity of women as a group is, in turn, predicated on a definition of the experience of oppression where difference can only be understood as male/female. (Mohanty 1993, 112, 116)

The concept of *intersectionality* was introduced into feminist studies in order to make it clear that gender relations of power will always be mediated and conditioned by other dimensions of power along the lines of, for example, race, class, and age. Even so, in Western feminist analysis, and also in development work, dichotomous notions of male/female will often prevail or be given priority.

Reconceptualizing motherhood: the wife/mother distinction

A further point of divergence and critique pertains to the concept of motherhood. In Ifi Amadiume's anger and disappointment vis-à-vis classical anthropology as well as Western feminism, with which she was confronted as a young student in England in the 1970s, the anthropological and feminist lack of understanding of African motherhood looms large: 'At no period in the history of the patriarchal cultures of Europe has motherhood been accorded the same status and reverence as it has had in African cultures' (1987, 3). Ifi Amadiume shows that even in patrilineal Igbo societies, the mother-focused matricentric unit of mother and children has great importance; the relation to one's mother and to one's maternal siblings – 'children of the same womb' – are the closest kinship bonds. This is a general phenomenon, across many African cultures (Amadiume 1997, 19). According to Amadiume, a major reason that the centrality of motherhood has not been acknowledged is the racialized and patriarchalizing gaze of (Western) observers, men as well as women, anthropologists as well as feminists.

The problem for Western feminists in acknowledging motherhood as a locus of power and autonomy is that in the patriarchal societies of the West, motherhood has been linked unilaterally to wifehood, cf. the concept of 'illegitimate children' if the mother is not a wife. In Africa, motherhood and wifehood are not linked in this way. On the contrary, a mother is a central person, and mother-child ties are crucial:

> In all African family arrangements, the most important ties within the family flow from the mother, whatever the norms of marriage residence. These ties link the mother to the child and connect the children of the same mother in bonds that are conceived as natural and unbreakable. ... The idea that mothers are powerful is very much a defining characteristic of the institution and its place in society. (Oyewùmí 2000, 1097).
>
> The mother is the pivot around which familial relationships are delineated and organized. (Oyewùmí 2002, 5)

Amadiume tries to capture this in formulations like 'the logic of motherhood' and 'the motherhood paradigm'. Her point, by talking of the motherhood paradigm, is to raise awareness regarding the often implicit patriarchal paradigm in social science: 'The recognition of the motherhood paradigm means that we do not take patriarchy as given, or as a paradigm' (1997, 21). In 'the motherhood paradigm' the focus is not on 'women' as such, but on the mother-child relationship. Amadiume proposes an analytical model which is shifting between the *obi*, the male-focused ancestral house, on one hand, and the *mpuke*, the mother-focused matri-centric unit at the other (ibid., 71). In doing so she decentres the male subject, moving the focus not to a female subject, but to a social relationship.

Thus, where subordination is embedded is in this positioning as an in-married wife, not in being a woman as such. Motherhood, in an African context, is certainly something different from wifehood. Where the position as wife denotes subordination, the position as mother denotes power. When Western women see subordination also in motherhood, this is because in Western patriarchal societies, the ban on motherhood outside marriage – motherhood independently of wifehood – has been quite fiercely policed. In fact, it is only in the most recent decades that, even in enlightened and presumedly gender-equal Scandinavian societies, unmarried motherhood has ceased to carry a stigma. According to Oyewùmí (and I agree), this implicit link in patrilineal/patriarchal settings between 'motherhood' and 'wifehood' has not been sufficiently challenged: 'Within the feminist literature, motherhood, which in many other societies constitutes the dominant identity of women, is subsumed under wifehood' (Oyewùmí 2002, 4). This is the reason why for Oyewùmí, 'wife' is the relevant concept with which to characterize the 'universally subordinated woman' of Western feminism. In the specific patrilineal/patriarchal settings of the West, wifehood and womanhood tend to overlap, but conceptual separation is important: subordination is linked to wifehood conditioned by patriarchal marriage, not to womanhood as such. In African settings, the possibility of motherhood (social and/or biological motherhood) is not necessarily linked to wifehood. You can be a mother without being a wife – an option which (under present conditions of distress) is chosen by an increasing number of African women. While wifehood in many African contexts indicates subordination, the position as a mother is central and respected, in patri- as well as in matrilineal settings.

Summing up 'Situational gender'

I find the theoretical contributions of Ifi Amadiume, Oyèrónké Oyewùmí and other African feminists inspiring and eye-opening regarding limitations and blind spots in much Western feminist thinking, including my own. In the discussion above, I have focused on my own points of fascination, paying less attention to flaws and limitations in their thinking. Amadiume can, however, be criticized for essentializing African-ness; while she is undermining gender dichotomies, she is constructing other dichotomies between 'Africans' and 'Europeans' (cf eg Amadiume 1997, 110). They have both – Oyewùmí in particular – been criticized for drawing conclusions from language to social structures (Bakare-Yusuf 2004, Matory 2005) and for creating a nostalgic image of an ideal past (e.g. Matory 2005). Parts of this critique I find justified, parts of it I don't. For example: Oyewùmí does not hide the fact that social relations in pre-colonial Yorubaland were indeed hierarchical – only not particularly along gender lines.

From the way in which I write about Amadiume and Oyewùmí, one might suppose they were collaborating. This is not at all the case. Even if Amadiume wrote her *Male Husbands, Female Daughters* in 1987, ten years before Oyewùmí's *The Invention of Women* (1997), there is hardly a reference to Amadiume in

Oyewùmí's book. Oyewùmí has been criticized by other African feminists for pretending to have invented it all herself, not acknowledging or misrepresenting the work of her predecessors. In a panel debate at the African Studies Association meeting in Washington 2002, chaired by Molara Ogundipe, the critique of Oyewùmí from African feminists was massive; ironically Oyewùmí's work was more welcomed by Nigerian male scholars participating in the debate than by the African women present. The Nigerian men seemed to be happy that Oyewùmí emphasized the non-hierarchical character of Yoruba gender relations, thus absolving them (they felt) from the general feminist critique of their patriarchal scholarship and style. In spite of the critique, however, I insist on the illuminating aspects of the thinking of both Amadiume and Oyewùmí. Where Amadiume as an anthropologist, writes in dialogue with anthropological scholarship, Oyewùmí, trained as a sociologist, has the profile of a gender scholar, challenging feminist thinking in a more direct way. Reading the works of them both has helped me to put critical question marks to my own thinking, and to be more open minded than I would otherwise have been, trying out new interpretations of unexpected empirical findings.

I also find it interesting that certain lines of this thinking run parallel to the work of Judith Butler – without much direct connection, as it seems.[2] What these authors have in common is that they approach Second Wave feminist ideas from subject positions different to those of white heterosexual middle class women. Part of Butler's motivation for critique is the marginalization and 'othering' of persons with different sexual orientations (LGBT, queer, etc.) in Second Wave feminism. Similarly, Amadiume's and Oyewùmí's motivation is the marginalization and 'othering' of non-Western women. The similarities and differences in these positions are reflected in the resulting theorizations. As an example, 'sexual orientation' is not featured at all in Amadiume's and Oyewùmí's work[3] – and issues of motherhood are absent in Butler's work.

Section 2: Subversive sex?

Sexuality has for a long time been a no-go area in African feminist thinking (Arnfred 2004b). Over the last few years, this situation has changed, presumably, as suggested by Tamale, provoked by the new interest in sexuality caused by the HIV/AIDS pandemic. Since everybody is now anyhow digging into 'African sexuality,' Africa feminists cannot leave this entire field to external investigation – and concomitant misunderstandings. In recent years, the African feminist body of writing on sexualities has been rapidly expanding. The South African feminist journal *Agenda* has published a series of issues on sexualities (issues 62, 63 and 67, 2004–2006), and the pan-African feminist journal *Feminist Africa* (edited from the African Gender Institute, Cape Town)

---

[2] Amadiume's first book *Male Daughters, Female Husbands* from 1987, precedes Butler's first important book, *Gender Trouble*, from 1990. Oyewùmí in her first book, *The Invention of Women* (1997) refers to Judith Butler only once (regarding critique of the sex/gender distinction).

[3] On the contrary Amadiume earns a rebuke from Saskia Wieringa and Evelyn Blackwood for strongly denouncing the idea that the institution of female husbands in Igboland should have anything to do with lesbianism (see Wieringa and Blackwood 1999, 4).

has published two special issues on sexualities, issues 5 (on Sexual Cultures) and 6 (on Subaltern Sexualities) in 2005 and 2006, respectively.

In African gender scholarship, sexualities have been first and most extensively debated in terms of masculinities and in terms of (male) same-sex relations, particularly in southern Africa (cf. e.g. Murray and Roscoe 1998, Morrell 2001, Reid and Walker 2005, Morrell and Ouzgane 2005). But work on female sexualities is emerging. An exciting field of feminist scholarship is opening up with great promise of reconceptualization, which may be useful also beyond Africa. As was the case of the concept of 'woman', which had to be deconstructed in order to get rid of pre-given assumptions of little relevance for social analysis in African contexts, also the notion of sexuality, particularly female sexuality, calls for deconstruction. For example, often in studies of women's conditions in Africa, sexuality and fertility have been conflated, both presumed to be under male control in the context of marriage. Patriarchal religions, including Christianity and Islam, have done nothing to destabilize this conflation, since male control of female sexuality and fertility are crucial prerequisites for patriarchal power.

An African feminist take on sexuality, which I have found most striking, follows lines of thinking from the 'situational gender' critique of colonial anthropological misunderstandings, and of shallow universalized gender-and-development conceptualizations. As noted in the discussion of the wife/mother distinction above, the critique of the centrality of marriage for the understanding of women's lives looms large when the focus is on sexuality. Did marriage actually control sexuality in pre-colonial Nigeria for example? Or was marriage more an institution through which children would be allocated to certain lineages? What are the implications of woman-woman marriages seen in this perspective? And, focusing on sexuality on its own, does it make sense to make an analytical distinction between sex for pleasure and sex for procreation? Where do same-sex practices fit in, and how should they be understood?

These are some of the questions which have been grappled with in this more recent work, much of which is based on reinterpretations of African 'culture' and 'tradition'. In the following pages, I discuss selected contributions to this growing body of work. I focus on notions of female sexuality as active and assertive, and thus potentially 'subversive' in relation to certain moralist social/cultural/religious norms.

Subversive transmarital sex

Nkiru Nzegwu's 2006 analysis of what she calls 'transmarital sex' – transmarital in the sense that sexual relations go beyond marriage – belong to the line of scholarship which reinterprets 'African culture' from feminist points of view. In a critical analysis of Igbo patriliny, she shows that even if patrilineal kinship systems are supposed to be based on patrilineal bloodlines, with husbands as biological fathers to offspring produced by their wives, such is not necessarily the case. Certainly according to the norms of Christian monogamous marriage, sexuality as well as offspring are supposed to be controlled by the institution of marriage[4] – but again, realities in Africa (and presumably elsewhere) prove

---

[4] The Ten Commandments, pillars of Christianity, state that adultery is not allowed; sex outside marriage and procreation is an issue of morality and sin, female sexuality in particular.

otherwise. Like Tamale, Nzegwu contributes to debunking the image of 'African women as helpless victims of oppressive patriarchal systems', showing how patriliny and patriarchy have been undermined and subverted all along by the sexual autonomy of wives. Marriage regulates offspring, yes, but not sexuality. Nzegwu reports from Igboland, Nigeria, how previously Igbo women engaged in transmarital relationships. Often these relationships would be tolerated by the community, for example when one of the following circumstances would apply (the list is remarkably long):

> when for professional reasons spouses, such as Awka blacksmiths and Nri ritual specialists, undertook journeys that kept them away from their conjugal units for months on end; when a wife married other wives and the male genitor was not the husband (male) of the husband (female); when a husband had difficulties producing sons and a wife had relations with a man known to have a propensity for having sons; when the wife in the previous example of a woman-woman marriage, in turn, married her own wife; when a groom died without the birth of a male child to continue his line, and the widow selected a paramour with whom to produce an heir and continue the line; when young widows with little children chose to have more children in their husbands' name; when the groom was impotent and was unable to father a child, and the aid of an obliging male surrogate was elicited; when the mother of an infant male child married a mature woman for her son and the wife engaged in sexual relations with paramours; when pregnancy did not occur within one year of marriage, and the wife returned to her natal home for 'medicinal treatment' that included sexual liaisons with other male partners; when a bride conceived between the *post-uri* and *pre-ina uno* period [i.e. the period between engagement and the formal relocation of the bride to her marital home] and arrived pregnant to her marital home; when a much older husband is unable to satisfy the sexual needs of a much younger wife and the wife elicits the services of a husband helper; when a spouse was mentally unbalanced and sexual relations were ruled out for the safety of the wife; when there were ritualized grounds for a bride or a wife to take on a lover and she exercised that right; when there was a desired physical trait that a wife or the couple saw in some man and wanted to bring the traits into their conjugal unit; and lastly when couples were estranged, but not yet formally separated, and the wife engaged in sexual relationship with other partners. (Nzegwu 2006, 45–6)

The point here is that, according to Igbo norms, 'the question of which pater constituted the line of descent was irrelevant because the collective view was that a husband of a bride is the father of the wife's children, regardless of how they were begotten' (Nzegwu 2004, 7). Similar arrangements are reported from elsewhere in Africa. Obviously in this situation, even married women command quite a measure of sexual autonomy. Often, transmarital sexual liaisons would be tolerated, even when they were not entered into for issues of procreation, but rather for sexual pleasure. Particularly in such cases relations should be conducted with a certain level of discretion. According to recent research, in colonial Zululand, married women's secret lovers were called *isidikiselo*, 'top of the pot', while name for the lawful husband would be *ibhodwe*, 'the main pot' (Hunter 2003, 15).

The above accounts are rendered in the past tense, because the steep increase in fundamentalist Christian churches – in Nigeria as well as elsewhere in Africa – is changing social norms in patriarchalizing ways. Nevertheless, it is important to realize that subversive sexuality, in terms of female sexuality not conforming to Christian and patrilineal/patriarchal norms, has been prevalent until fairly recently. As for parts of Africa where contemporary culture is dominated by Islam, also here changes have occurred from more permissive to more restrictive attitudes vis a vis female sexuality. In Islam, both men's and women's sexuality are seen as naturally active, but 'women are thought to have a greater potential for sexual desire and pleasure, nine times that of men' (Ayesha Imam, quoted in Chi-Chi Undie and Kabwe Benaya 2005). In recent times, however, Sharia law has been known to come down heavily on women who have been known to exercise that sexuality out of wedlock, cf. the Amina Lawal case in northern Nigeria 2002–2003.

Same-sex relations as subversive

One African president after another has declared same-sex relations un-African (Ratele 2005, 34) – which in a sense makes such relations, when they are practised, subversive vis a vis state ideologies. Along the same lines, the performance in Kampala of Eve Ensler's *Vagina Monologues* was banned early 2005 by state authorities, claiming that the Monologues 'promoted and glorified acts such as lesbianism and homosexuality' and that 'a stand against foreign influences undermining Africa's traditional values and culture should be taken' (Arac de Nyeko 2005, 100). Sylvia Tamale provides a long list of research references testifying to a history of various forms of same-sex relations in Uganda. 'Trends both in the present and in the past reveal that it is time for Africans to bury the tired myth that homosexuality is 'unAfrican'. ... Ironically, it is the dominant Judaeo-Christian and Arabic religions upon which most Africa anti-homosexuality proponents rely, that are foreign imports' (Tamale 2003, 1).

Same-sex relations are considered subversive not only in relation to state power, but also in relation to patriarchal power. 'What is particularly threatening to patriarchy is the idea of intimate same-sex relationships where a dominating male is absent, and where women's sexuality can be defined without reference to reproduction,' Tamale says. 'Sexuality therefore becomes a critical site for maintaining patriarchy and reproducing women's oppression' (ibid., 2). Analyzing gay/lesbian *kuchu* culture in Uganda, she underscores the importance of sub-cultural identification: 'Because homosexuals in Uganda do not feel a sense of belonging to the dominant culture, they have had to reconstruct affirming identities for themselves. ... The self-definition of lesbians and gays ... involves their subversive performance and statement-making as gender outlaws in society' (ibid., 2). Importantly, Tamale also notes that in spite of implicit lesbian critique of patriarchal gender power relations 'the kuchu subculture among Ugandan lesbians is entirely disconnected from the women's movement' (ibid., 2). 'Many of us in the women's movement,' Tamale says, 'still find it difficult to rid our consciousness of the "taboo web" that dims our understanding of the intrinsic link between sexuality and women's oppression and subordination' (ibid., 2). However, 'the process of disentanglement has begun' mainly caused by the HIV/AIDS pandemic which has forced gender activists and scholars to reflect on issues of sexuality.

For a long time, same-sex relations in Africa, particularly female same-sex relations, were hidden from the view of missionaries and anthropologists, partly because they were not classified as 'sex', and partly because they were not perceived as identities, but rather as practices, irrelevant to marriage and Christian/Muslim morality. A point of departure for African feminist analysis of female same-sex relations has been provided by Kendall's work from Lesotho, first published in Murray and Roscoe (1998), and later in Blackwood and Wieringa (1999). Kendall reports from Lesotho how sex is understood as what men have – with women or with each other (1999, 164). The suggestion that two women should 'share the blankets with each other' (the Lesotho euphemism for having sex) was perceived as uproariously funny: 'It's impossible for two women to share the blankets' Kendall was told, 'you cannot have sex unless somebody has a *koai* (penis)' (ibid., 162). Similarly *'No koai, no sex* means that women's ways of expressing love, lust, passion, or joy in each other are neither immoral nor suspect' (ibid., 167). They hardly exist, escaping the gaze of morality and of science. In his discussion of 'Proper sex, bodies, culture and objectification' Ratele says:

> A practice of sex as what happens between male and female was turned by dominant science into something dictated by nature's laws, something given by the constitution of the sexes. In other words, here as elsewhere, one could not call what happens between two women sex, just as one was disallowed from seeing what happens between two males as natural, just as one was persuaded that only a male organ penetrating a female organ is sexually and scientifically 'normal'. (Ratele 2005, 36)

Further, and importantly in many contexts, until recently, these relationships were not alternatives to marriage, but supplementary (cf. 'the top of the pot'). 'There is no tradition in Lesotho that permits or condones women or men remaining single; single persons are regarded as anomalous and tragic. ... A respectable adult is a married adult' (Kendall 1999, 163). However, the kuchu culture described by Tamale is obviously a different, presumably more 'modern', phenomenon. Gay and lesbian associations, based on acknowledgement of gay/lesbian identities are gaining ground in Africa, in a movement initially dominated by white Africans (e.g. in South Africa and in Zimbabwe), but such is no longer the case. By now, several gay/lesbian organizations have been established outside South Africa and Zimbabwe, such as for example the Coalition of African Lesbians (CAL)[5] in Namibia.

The power of the erotic

'The erotic as power' is a quote from Audre Lorde (1984, 53). In Lorde's understanding, 'the erotic' is an inherently subversive force, a source of mobilization against oppression: 'In order to perpetuate itself, every oppression must corrupt and distort those various sources of power within the culture of the oppressed that can provide energy for change. For women this has meant a suppression of the erotic as a considered source of power and information within our lives' (ibid.). Audre Lorde is/was an African-American feminist (and a lesbian). She died in 1992.

'The erotic as power' may be structured differently in African contexts. Nevertheless, Patricia McFadden argues forcefully for the power of the erotic along the lines of Audre Lorde:

> As women from every walk of life we have the resources, the knowledge, the insight and the political acumen to reassert our ownership of the problems and challenges

[5] See www.mask.org.za

generated by the virulent combination of the HIV/AIDS pandemic and misogynist violation. By reclaiming our sexual energy and power, we can discover reservoirs of personal and political courage that can equip us to envisage and to fight for what lies beyond the prison of life-threatening and oppressive social systems and circumstances. Audre Lorde conceptualized this vital link between political power and deep inner strength when she made her celebrated claim that it is only as self-loving individuals that we are able to reach into our depths and find the power within us. (McFadden 2003, 1)

This force is necessary, McFadden says, in order to counteract the dominant trends of present times, with the HIV/AIDS pandemic having generated 'a powerful resurgence of patriarchal dominance. ... Without a discourse that enables women to step beyond the bounded, limited notions of sexuality as being either tied to reproduction or to the avoidance of disease or violation, we cannot begin to imagine ourselves in new and profoundly life-transforming ways (ibid., 5).

Strangely, however, McFadden's argument is based on assumptions of 'the systematic suppression of women's sexual and erotic inclinations' (ibid., 1) and of dominant constructions of women's sexuality as "bad', 'filthy' and 'morally corrupting" (ibid., 2). These assumptions are questioned by Charmaine Pereira in her reflections on and response to McFadden's paper. Pereira shows how McFadden's assumptions as quoted above are rooted in ideas of 'the universal subordination of women,' including a generalized notion of 'African women'. 'There is no suggestion in McFadden's article that African women's sexualities may vary across space and time and across regions' Pereira says. Most importantly she shows how 'it is possible to argue for the need to enhance the value of female sexuality and to promote basic sexual freedoms *without* assuming the universal suppression of female sexualities' (Pereira 2003, 1, emphasis added, SA). According to Pereira, the notion that sexuality is 'bad' or 'filthy' is a relatively recent phenomenon, which has been introduced to Africa through colonialism and Victorian interpretations of Christianity. In the religious doctrines of Islam, Pereira says, women's sexuality is viewed as a powerful force that needs to be controlled, rather than as derogatively 'dirty'.

Pereira goes on to quote research from different African locations, showing women's sexual autonomy and initiative. Thus, based on such information it does seem as if 'the power of the erotic' would be more within reach in certain African locations compared to many other places – in spite of current setbacks caused by HIV/AIDS, emerging patriarchal cultures, etc. Regarding the need for visions and imaginations beyond patriarchal images of/restrictions on female (and male) sexualities, Pereira and McFadden do not disagree. In another paper, Charmaine Pereira writes about feminist futures and the necessity of vision and imagination:

It seems to me that there is an intimate connection between what it is possible to know and what we dare to imagine. There is no way to create knowledge that is not circumscribed by the oppressions of our times if we cannot imagine a better future, if we cannot dream of a way of life that does away with the domination that is part of our everyday realities, if we cannot envision other ways of being. (Pereira 2002, 1)

'The power of the erotic' is in itself a vision of this kind.

Ambiguities and Contradictions

'Subversive Sex?' is written with a question mark, because of all the ambiguities and contradictions. Sylvia Tamale highlights the paradoxes, women's bodies being at one and the same time a target for their subordination, and a means for assertive sexuality (Tamale 2005a). Analyzing the *Ssenga* institution in Uganda, Tamale finds even more ambiguities. The *Ssenga* is, in Baganda contexts, the paternal aunt, entrusted with instruction of young nieces, preparing them for adult womanhood. The Ssenga's primary responsibility, Tamale says, 'was to groom her nieces to become 'good'subservient wives or co-wives. A husband who was dissatisfied with his bride's behaviour, particularly her 'bedroom etiquette', would blame it on the laxity of her Ssenga, even returning the bride to the Ssenga for 'proper' training' (Tamale 2005b, 17). However, this tutelage also included some empowering messages. The Ssenga would make it clear that a wife did not have to tolerate an abusive spouse; if she felt abused, or if he failed to satisfy her sexually, she had the right to return to her parent's home. 'Sexuality featured prominently in *Ssenga*'s tutorials, which would focus on erotic skills, sexual para- phernalia and aphrodisiacs in the form of herbal perfumes, sensual oils, sexual beads *(obutiti)* and so on' (Tamale 2005a, 6). According to Tamale, young women are instructed to use sex for seduction and as a tool of manipulation. Ssengas 'encourage women to use sex to undermine patriarchal power from behind a façade of subservience' (Tamale 2005b, 24). Tamale makes interesting note of the ways in which such sexually empowering instructions, rooted in 'tradition', meet young women's demands for 'gender equality' rooted in notions of women's rights. She sees here possibilities regarding how 'African women can inherit and shape traditions of their own that go beyond the discourse of rights imposed from above' (ibid., 30),

In many other places in Africa beyond Uganda, young women are also well educated in sexual arts. In my material from northern Mozambique, for example, there are a lot of erotic tattoos and tantalizing glass beads around women's waists. In northern Mozambique, young women are educated as seducers – sexual proficiency is a women's capacity. But should this be seen as subservience to husbands, or as a basis for sexual power and autonomy – or both? Tamale highlights the ambiguities: 'The institution of Ssenga facilitates and reinforces patriarchal power, she says, while at the same time subverting and parodying it' (ibid., 12). Seen with Tamale's eyes, the fact that Ssenga as an institution has survived, and is even thriving in Kampala, in commercialized and professionalized versions, invests the institution with new scope for chal- lenging subordination and sexual control. 'While the patriarchal agendas and discourses embedded within *Ssenga* are unmistakable, women's subversive and counterhegemonic 'silent struggles' allow them to negotiate agency,' she says (ibid., 30).

Conclusion

In my view, the fields of investigation being opened by the type of research to which I have referred in this chapter, have great promise. These studies challenge established positions on several fronts, political as well as academic. In their insistence on reinterpretations of 'African culture' from feminist points of view, these studies challenge both development establishments and Western feminist analysis, not to mention African male elites, who tend to interpret 'African culture' in decidedly patriarchal ways. African feminists point to interpretations of 'culture and tradition' as a contested terrain. They suggest a potential 'liberatory value of indigenous institutions', thus representing 'a very different perspective to their idyllic or nostalgic portrayals ... often seen in mainstream patriarchal Africanist thinking' (Tamale 2005b, 30). They further question simplified notions of 'gender equality' exclusively rooted in 'modernity'. The idea of reinterpreting the past in order to find new strategies for the future is crucial.

The African feminist writings discussed in this chapter provide inspiration for reconceptualizing social structures and power relations in Africa gender research, as well as to rethinking basic notions of feminist scholarship in general. Thus, their contributions have implications beyond the borders of the African continent. In line with Chandra Mohanty's arguments for 'feminism without borders' – learning from differences rather than glossing them over (cf. the discussion of 'Global Sisterhood' above), I see north/south collaboration and cross-border exchange between feminists, gender scholars and activists as indispensable for the further development of feminist thinking and struggle. Contributions from African feminist scholars are very important in this regard.

Part III IMPLICATIONS OF MATRILINY IN NORTHERN MOZAMBIQUE

11 Male Mythologies
An Inquiry into Assumptions of Feminism & Anthropology (2005)

Woodcut by Matias Mtundu Mzaanhoka

Implicit or explicit belief in the universal subordination of women ... continues to obstruct efforts to understand both other societies and our own. (Mona Etienne & Eleanor Leacock, 1980)

The point of this chapter is to identify and make visible some persistent assumptions, active in anthropology as well as in feminism (and elsewhere). I call them 'male mythologies', not because they are produced and maintained by men only (this is far from the case) but because they naturalize and legitimize male power. I believe that a critique of these assumptions will help to clear a space for different concepts and lines of thinking, better suited for grasping realities of men's and women's lives.

I am not alone in this endeavour. Feminist anthropologists and African feminists have at various times in various ways been chasing the same assumptions, struggling to develop new conceptualizations. After an introduction explaining my personal stake in the matter at issue, I'll proceed to section 1, briefly introducing work by feminist anthropologists/sociologists Eleanor Leacock, Pauline Peters, Kate Crehan, Ifi Amadiume, Oyèrónké Oyewùmi and others, who have all made important contributions regarding the matter at issue. In the main body of the paper (section 2) I'll go back into the history of anthropology in an attempt to clarify the genealogy and subsequent configurations of the master mythology of male dominance/female subordination, as it has unfolded in anthropological analysis of matriliny. In the course of this discussion I'll show how Second Wave feminist thinking, through its foremother Simone de Beauvoir, is linked to structural anthropology. Finally in section 3, I'll sum up the critique in a discussion of 'the battle of matriliny' and alternative analytical approaches: how to be able to think beyond these persistent assumptions.

My personal stake

From Simone de Beauvoir onwards a firm belief in the universal subordination of women has characterized large parts of feminist thinking. This is particularly the case where feminist lines of thinking are applied in relation to countries in the global South (cf. Mohanty 1984/1991), and prominently in the large body of writing known as Gender-and-Development (GAD) theorizing (cf. Arnfred 2001). In this chapter I'll pursue the assumptions of male domination and female subordination as they surface in the particular area of anthropological writings which deal with matriliny. The focus on matriliny is rooted in my own concerns and needs, when as a sociologist and working in the early 1980s in the national secretariat of the Mozambican Women's Organization (OMM) I was sent off to the matrilineal north of Mozambique in order to investigate how the recent war of liberation (1964–1975) from Portuguese colonial rule, had affected and been experienced by women. The war veteran women's devoted adherence to their initiation rituals, rituals which by the OMM had been described as woman-degrading and humiliating, made it clear to me that OMM's – and my own – a priori assumptions regarding gender relations and gender hierarchies needed thorough revision. Assumptions of male dominance/female subordination were widely shared at the time in feminist as well as in anthropological circles. The universal subordination of women was a foun-

dational idea in the new women's movement (later baptized 'the Second Wave')
of which I was an active member before departing for Mozambique. Trendset-
ting groups of feminist anthropologists, such as those linked to the Subordination of Women (SOW) workshop in the UK (cf. Young, Wolkowitz,
McCullagh 1981) took this as their point of departure. As feminists of course
the SOW anthropologists – and the rest of us in the women's movement – were
critical of female subordination, they/we wanted to analyze precisely 'the
universal subordination of women' in order to fight against it, and ultimately
to change it. Like Simone de Beauvoir we had a vision of modernity as an ally
in our struggle against age-old patriarchal relations of power and for a society
with equality between men and women. But as a social condition at the outset
the paradigm of male domination/female subordination was taken for granted.
In this conception female subordination was rooted in the past, in tradition,
while gender equality and women's emancipation were embedded in the
future, in (socialist) 'modernity' and – for women of the global South – in
'development'.

1 Feminist anthropology/sociology

Eleanor Leacock's critique: Myths of male dominance

As a follow up to my bewildering experience in northern Mozambique, when
some years later I was back in university in Denmark, I embarked on a tentative
inquiry into anthropologocal literature on matriliny. Initially I was stunned by
the insensitivity of anthropologists, male and female, to the (to my eyes) quite
obvious facts of different gender balances of power evidenced in matrilineal
settings. Later it dawned on me that this was part of a pattern, which ran deeper
than what was visible to the naked eye. The name of this pattern is 'the assumption of male dominance/female subordination'. Anthropologists and feminists
who in the 1980s questioned these assumptions were few and far between. One
of them was Eleanor Leacock. In her 1981 collection of articles – *Myths of Male
Dominance* – she wanted to show that the idea of universal male dominance is
a myth, and that female subordination – instead of being located in ancient
primitive patriarchal dominance of women, which would in the course of evolution be replaced by modernity and equality – to a certain extent, in certain
places had been introduced by modernity, in the shape of colonialism, missionaries and a market economy. A sociologist and feminist with a similar position
was/is Maria Mies. Writing about the European witch hunts in the sixteenth
and seventeenth centuries, Mies points out that unlike the general assumption
that the witch hunts were indications of a lack of civilization in the dark, pre-
Enlightenment Middle Ages, this systematic persecution of 'wise women'
should rather be seen as a manifestation of the rising modern society (Mies
1986, 83). [1] Mies discerns a tendency, from the Enlightenment onwards, of

[1] 'Millions of women, mostly of poor peasant or poor urban origin, were for centuries persecuted,
tortured and finally burnt as witches, because they tried to retain a certain autonomy over their
bodies, particularly their generative forces. The attack of church and state against the witches was
aimed not only at the subordination of femal sexuality as such, although this played a major role,
but against their practices as abortionists and midwives' (Mies 1986, 70).

deeming female wisdom irrational and daemonic: 'The persecution and burning of the midwives as witches was directly connected with the emergence of modern society: the professionalization of medicine, the rise of *medicine* as a 'natural science', the rise of *science* and of *modern economy'* (ibid., emphasis in original).

A major problem with Leacock's argument was, however, that she leaned too heavily on Friedrich Engels (*The Origin of the Family, Private Property and the State*, 1884), that she got stuck in Engels' ideological visions regarding 'egalitarian society',[2] and that she did not have the conceptual tools to go beyond this line of thinking. But her hunch was right – that power relationships between men and women need rethinking, that the very concept of 'men' and 'women' needs rethinking – and that assumptions regarding universal subordination of women/universal male dominance are particularly unhelpful in this respect. Leacock's questions need reformulation and her answers should be rethought – but many of her in-between observations are insights to be retained, such as her beautiful work on the Montagnais-Naskapi Indians of eastern Labrador, partly based on her own fieldwork, and partly on the writings of a Jesuit missionary, Paul Le Jeune, who during the winter of 1633–1634 lived with a Montagnais band of hunters. Le Jeune's frustration of the lack of male authority over women is rendered in detail by Leacock, who reads Le Jeune's data as indications of female autonomy and balanced male/female power relations – a situation which gradually changed in subsequent centuries, due to European ideological and economic influence, through missionaries and through the increasingly important fur trade (Leacock 1980, 1981).

African feminists destabilize myths

Some years later, in the 1980s and 1990s, concerns similar to Leacock's but from somewhat different inroads, were taken up and developed first by Ifi Amadiume (1987, 1997) and later by Oyèrónké Oyewùmí (1997) and others. Amadiume's critique of classical anthropology is scorching and her statements regarding the patriarchal influences of colonialism, mission and market economy are as outspoken as Leacock's. In her deservedly acclaimed work *Male Daughters, Female Husbands* (Amadiume 1987) – selected as one of the 100 top African books of the twentieth century – Amadiume destabilizes the male dominance/female subordination paradigm by pointing to the importance of motherhood in terms of social power in Africa. Furthermore – well ahead of Judith Butler's *Gender Trouble* (1990) – she introduces the idea of gender as not rooted in biological sex. A Second Wave foundational idea in the 1980s was the sex/gender system, where 'sex' stood for biology, nature, the unchangeable, while 'gender' was perceived as a kind of superstructure, socially constructed, but based on biology/bodies. In Amadiume's thinking social relationships are the points of departure, bodies are fitted in. Amadiume further shows how in patrilineal Igbo society there is no 'universal subordination of women': male and female hierarchies of power coexist. She even talks about 'a missing matriarchal structure in African studies' (1997, 19), making it clear, however, that

[2] For a thorough critique of ideologiocal notions of 'egalitarian society' see Yanagisako, Sylvia J. and Jane F. Collier (1987)

when she talks in these terms it is in order 'not to take patriarchy for given, or as a paradigm' (ibid., 19). In doing this she explictly refuses to take male dominance/female subordination for granted.

Following Amadiume, an increasing number of feminist scholars writing on Africa now refuse to subscribe to these standard mythologies, pointing instead to the ways in which general concepts of feminist theory fail to grasp salient characteristics of African social life. An important example of this line of thinking is Oyèrónké Oyewùmí, who criticizes the concept of 'woman' on the grounds that connotations of gender hierarchy, rooted in the notion of female subordination, are embedded in the very concept (Oyewùmí 1997). Such connotations, Oyewùmí maintains, are misleading in African settings. According to her, general feminist theory's concept of 'woman' refers implicitly to woman-as-wife, that is to a woman who gets her status from her relationship to a man (Oyewùmí 2000, 2002). This indeed is also the concept of 'woman' applied by colonial anthropologists. In classical anthropology marriage is a pivotal institution. Under conditions of patriliny male access to offspring goes through marriage. That might be the reason why it is seen as so important?[3] The fact that under conditions of matriliny a man's access to offspring goes through his sister, stable marriages thus being of less importance even from a male point of view – this fact has been (and is) difficult to get across in Western contexts. That furthermore the position as mother, in and of itself and independently of marriage, is crucial and central in many African contexts (Amadiume 1987; Oyewùmí 2000) only adds to the clashes of comprehension.

Feminist anthropology on matriliny

As already noted my own special concern was matriliny, matrilineal societies in Africa to be more precise. An attempt at one point to try to get an overview of where to find matrilineal societies in Africa – in addition to the ones I knew about in Mozambique, and in some neighbouring countries – did not succeed at all. Matriliny is registered nowhere, apart from in anthropological studies of individual societies. 'Matriliny' doesn't figure in any statistics, nor in any encyclopedia on Africa (at least none of those I could put my hands on).[4] As a phenomenon, yes, but there is nothing in terms of geography or dispersion. This is partly for good reasons: 'Matriliny' is a composite phenomenon, not easily defined by a single measure. But it is also for bad reasons: 'Matriliny' is uninteresting in the eyes of decision makers. Matriliny where it occurs is most frequently considered an abnormality, a remains from earlier stages of development, and a characteristic which anyhow is bound to disappear (Rogers 1980; Davison 1997; Peters 1997).

In Mozambique, however, matriliny is a socio-cultural characteristic, which it would be foolish to ignore. More than 40 per cent of Mozambique's 15 million population consider themselves part of matrilineal lineage groups. This figure is based on the 1997 census count of the rural population in the northern provinces of Cabo Delgado, Niassa, Nampula, Zambézia and the northern half

---

[3] Evelyn Blackwood (2005) provides a profound critique of the ways in which classical anthropology and theories of kinship have taken marriage for granted and as a given point of departure.
[4] Precisely because of this general lack I find the list provided by Yolanda Aixelà (2005) very useful.

of the province of Tete,[5] combined with the knowledge that the population in these provinces belongs to the Makonde, Yao, Makhuwa, and Makhuwa-Lomwe ethnic groups (Rita-Ferreira 1975). All of these groups, living to the north of the Zambezi River, count descent along matrilineal lines. In the neighbouring countries, and elsewhere in Africa, there are many others. Nevertheless, the anthropological literature on matriliny is scarce and scattered.

Precisely because one could imagine societies based on matrilineal kinship systems to be particularly rich in examples of alternative male/female power relations, providing an empirical basis for arguments against male mythologies, one would think it particularly important for feminists to scrutinize matriliny. Feminists have certainly been working with and on matriliny (Poewe 1981, Vuyk 1991, Moore and Vaughan 1994, Crehan 1997, Davison 1997, Peters 1997 and others) – but actually surprisingly few of them. And even fewer with a direct focus on the type of critique, which after my experience in Cabo Delgado I felt that I needed.

The best contributions, from my point of view, was/is Kate Crehan's writing on communities in North-Western Zambia (1997) and the overview of previous critiques of classical anthropology regarding matriliny provided by Pauline Peters in a special issue of 'Critique of Anthopology' (1997) to which Crehan has also contributed. Based on insights produced by feminist anthropology, and on behalf of the contributors to this particular collection of papers, Peters writes in her introduction: 'We argue on the basis of our own and other studies that the conventional anthropological view that the only difference matriliny makes is that authority runs through the mother's brother rather than through the father, *is untenable*' (Peters 1997,141, emphasis added SA). Evidence of the difference which matrilineal organization can make for women and gender relations is too strong. The 'matrilineal puzzle' – so named and defined by Audrey Richards (cf. the discussion below) – is rooted less in the subject matter itself than in gender stereotypes and ideologies in the minds of the observers. 'The particular animus directed against matriliny,' Peters notes, 'is because of its different gender patterns, especially its association with more social independence and political authority for women' (Peters 1997, 141). As I see it, this is exactly what it is all about. A deeper study of matriliny, on its own terms, threatens to destabilize the cherished mythologies of male domination /female subordination. Not that this is not what feminists should aim for. But knowing how deeply these mythologies are rooted also in feminist thinking itself, it is after all not that easy. For anthropology in general I'll venture the hypothesis that a deep-running fear of chaos and disorder (cf. the discussion of Lévi-Strauss below) is active when anthropological conclusions regarding matriliny generally end up with business as usual, that is male domination/female subordination.[6]

---

[5] Calculation based on *II Rescenceamento Geral da População e Habitação* 1997, *Instituto Nacional de Estatística*, Maputo.

[6] Cf. for a good example of this, the passage from A Richards, quoted by Aixelà: 'Matrilineal and patrilineal descent groups are precise mirror images of each other, identical in their structure, except for the superficial point that in one group membership is obtained through the father, in the other group through the mother... the roles of men and women are identically defined in both groups, men having authoritative roles and women having responsibility for child care' (Aixelà 2005, 83)

2 Matriliny in the history of anthropology

Evolutionary approaches to matriarchy and matriliny
In anthropological studies of matriliny one could expect to find attempts to come to grips with variations in the forms of and the relation between male and female authority. Such is however not the case. Since the late nineteenth century, when J.J. Bachofen and Lewis Henry Morgan were blacklisted by the British pre-historians and evolutionists (Fee 1974), the accepted wisdom has been that matriarchy is a myth, and that male authority is paramount. Generally such authority is vested in the father, but under the allegedly rare and exceptional conditions of matriliny, it may be vested in the mother's brother.

J.J.Bachofen's *Das Mutterrecht* was published in 1861, and is referred to with due respect by David Schneider in the preface to his influential volume (co-edited with Kathleen Gough) on 'Matrilineal Kinship', published in 1961, precisely one hundred years after Bachofen's book. Bachofen launched the idea – based on among other sources Greek myth and drama, like e.g. Aeschylus's *Oresteia* – that a previous social system of mother rule, matriarchy, in the course of history had been replaced by the patriarchal systems which are better known today.[7] Bachofen's work was not popular in Britain, and John McLennan, influential British pre-historian in the time of evolutionary thinking, argued forcefully against it, particularly against the improbable assumption that women should ever have been in any position of power. According to Elizabeth Fee (1974) it was McLennan, who introduced the clear distinction between matriarchy (= myth) and matriliny (*Studies in Ancient History*, 1876). Matriliny was too frequently evidenced in anthropological field material to be discounted, but McLennan took care to show that matriliny was perfectly explicable without the absurd idea that it should have anything to do with social power or authority of women (Fee 1974). According to McLennan the possibility 'that the children of a man and a woman living together as husband and wife should be subjected to the mother's authority and not to the father's, be named after her and not after the father, be her heirs and not the fathers, *is simply incredible*' (McLennan 1876, quoted after Fee 1974, 92, emphasis added, SA). In order, however, to save the fundamental assumption of universal male dominance/female subordination, the authority of the father had to be sacrificed, and replaced with the authority of the mother's brother. At the same time McLennan takes care to point out that matrilineal societies are all to be found at the primitive end of the scale of evolution.

Like Bachofen, and like the British pre-historians and anthropologists of the time – John McLennan and Sir Henry Maine (*Ancient Law* 1861) among others, Lewis Henry Morgan (American lawyer and spare-time anthropologist) thought in evolutionary terms. This was the time of the publication of Charles Darwin's works (*The Origin of the Species* 1859) and questions of evolutionary developments characterized the scientific agendas of the day. But unlike all of the others, Morgan's works (*Systems of Consanguinity and Affinity* 1871, *Ancient Society* 1877) were based on actual fieldwork among native Americans with matrilineal

[7] Bachofen's ideas have since been supported by archeological finds in the Balkans and the Middle East, cf. Gimbutas 1974 and others.

kinship systems. And even if Morgan's theory in the style of the day followed an evolutionary scheme, he left this scheme open-ended, allowing for future change towards greater sexual equality (Fee 1974, 97). This was very unlike his contemporaries, who all – as a matter of course – saw their own patriarchal form of monogamous family as the peak and culmination of social evolution.

Neither Bachofen as a German, nor Morgan as an American, enjoyed much esteem in the British establishment of Oxford professors and knighted social anthropologists. Nevertheless, through Friedrich Engels' frequent references to their works, their names are more familiar today than those of Henry Maine and John McLennan. In *The Origin of the Family, Private Property and the State* (1884) Engels developed Bachofen's and Morgan's ideas to suit his own ideological scheme, making the emergence of private property the pivotal point for the change away from mother right and thus the reason for 'the world historical defeat of the female sex' (Engels 1884, 92). Through this work Engels influenced a line of feminist anthropolgical thinking, prominently in the works of Karen Sacks (*Sisters and Wives*, 1979) and Eleanor Leacock (*The Myth of Male Dominance*, 1981), which did not subscribe to 'the universal subordination of women'. Sacks and Leacock tried to establish alternative patterns of analysis (such as a focus on women as sisters rather than as wives) and to be explicitly aware of the specific patriarchalizing influences of colonization and Christianity, cf. the seminal volume on *Women and Colonization* (1980) edited by Mona Etienne and Eleanor Leacock. A problem in the works of Sacks and Leacock is, however, their uncritical adaptation of Engels' not very sophisticated thinking. Neither of them challenges his evolutionary scheme, nor his romantic rather than analytical vision of 'egalitarian society'. These and other flaws from Engels' work thus also hampers the otherwise important and insightful contributions by Sacks and Leacock.

Matriliny = primitivity

In British social anthropology a new approach took off in the 1920s with the works of Bronislaw Malinowski and A.R.Radcliffe-Brown. The evolutionary thinking of previous 'armchair anthropologists' was condemned, and a new style of social analysis based on long-term fieldwork, and focused on functional connections between social institutions, was introduced (cf. Schneider's preface to *Matrilineal Kinship* 1961). Audrey Richards' work, which I shall presently discuss, is a product of this new line of thinking.

In France, Claude Lévi-Strauss was a prominent spokesperson of a similar turn away from speculations regarding possible lines of historical evolution and into a very different focus on analysis of social structures. In *Les Structures élémentaires de la Parenté*, 1949 (translated to English in 1969 as *The Elementary Structures of Kinship*) Lévi-Strauss launches his analysis as explicitly anti-evolutionist: 'We have been careful to eliminate all historical speculation, all research into origins, and all attempts to reconstruct a hypothetical order in which institutions succeed one another' (1949/1969, 142). Nevertheless, the two idiosyncrasies noted as a characteristic of McLennan's work: (a) the basic and unquestionable assumption of if not paternal then at least male authority, and (b) matriliny as indication of primitivity – these two idiosyncrasies reappear in the writings of Lévi-Strauss, thus demonstrating that polemics at one level do not prevent – at another and deeper level – basic assumptions to be carried on.

To Lévi-Strauss male authority is beyond questioning. It is the very basis of his model of exchange. Lévi-Strauss sees exchange, like language, as inherent in the human condition. And the basic form of exchange is exchange of women. To Lévi-Strauss this is not just a model; this is the way empirical reality is working: 'The total relationship of exchange, which constitutes marriage is not established between a man and a woman, where each owes and receives something, but *between two groups of men*, and the woman figures only as one of the objects in the exchange, not as one of the partners between whom the exchange takes place' (1949/1969, 115, emphasis added, SA).

Male power thus is unquestioned. This basic asymmetry between the sexes – that men control and women are controlled – is to Lévi-Strauss a premise beyond discussion; those who are not aware that such is the case are guilty of severe misapprehensions. Matriliny is not and cannot be a mirror image of patriliny. To Lévi-Strauss it is of prime importance to point out that

> matrilineal groups cannot be substituted for patrilineal groups, or vice versa, for apart from their common characteristic as unilineal classes, the two forms are not equivalent, except from a purely formal point of view. They have neither the same place nor rank in human society. To be unmindful of this would be to overlook *the basic fact that it is men who exchange women, and not vice versa* . (1949/1969, 115, emphasis added, SA)

Lévi-Strauss does have to admit that matrilineal systems do exist, but first, 'in such systems – and there is scarcely need to recall it – it is the brother or eldest son of the mother's family who holds and wields authority' (ibid., 116), and second he insists that examples of 'systems with matrilineal descent and permanent and definitive matrilocal residence ... are extremely rare' (ibid.). Acceptance of matriliny and matrilocality would disrupt his entire system. 'Consequently,' he says, 'the only alternatives are, on the one hand patrilineal and patrilocal systems, and on the other matrilineal and patrilocal systems. The exceptional cases of matrilineal and matrilocal systems, *which are in conflict with the asymmetrical relationship of the sexes*, may be assimilated into the latter' (ibid., 117, emphasis added, SA). In this move Lévi-Strauss manages to make reality fit his model, instead of letting reality challenge his model, which would have been a more scientifically justifiable line of argument. [8]

But to Lévi-Strauss, like to so many anthropologists before and after him, the very idea of female authority is deeply repugnant. Letting go of paternal power is bad enough. Even if under conditions of matriliny the husband may take his wife to live with him in his village, she will 'bear children, who will never be his. The conjugal family is broken up again and again, incessantly. *How can the mind conceive of such a situation? How can it have been devised and established?*' (ibid., 116, emphasis added, SA). In my reading Lévi-Strauss is afraid of matriliny because it threatens to upset what he perceives as *order*. Lévi-Strauss himself tries to explain matriliny away as 'dramatic', with 'complicated social organization, rich in strange institutions, imbued with an atmosphere of the dramatic, and very different in this regard from what is to be expected of a society with father-right' (ibid., 117–18). Exotic, in other words. And primitive.

---

[8] In northern Mozambique matriliny *and* matrilocality is the general pattern.

Even if Lévi-Strauss disavows evolutionary thinking, it is evident that he sees matriliny as less developed. There was a hint in the above-quoted passage regarding systems of matriliny and patriliny respectively as having 'neither the same place nor rank in human society' (ibid., 115). And later, in a discussion of political authority, this evolutionary ranking becomes more explicit: 'It is true that in societies where political power takes precedence over other forms of organization, the duality which would result from the masculinity of political authority and the matrilineal character of descent could not subsist. Consequently societies attaining this level of political organization tend to generalize paternal right' (ibid., 116). Political authority, or simply social authority, which can only be male (according to Lévi-Strauss) may adapt itself to bilateral or matrilineal forms of descent, or it will impose its model on all aspects of social life, 'as is the case in more developed groups' (ibid., 117).

Thus the implicit – and partly explicit – assumptions in Lévi-Strauss's thinking are more similar to the idiosyncracies of the old evolutionists than he himself would like to admit. The major points: Man = subject; woman = object; and matriliny = primitivity reappear as basic figures of thought in Simone de Beauvoir's *Le Deuxieme Sexe* (1949, translated to English in 1953 as *The Second Sex*). Throughout *The Second Sex* de Beauvoir refers to Lévi-Strauss, always with great respect and acclaim. Like Lévi-Strauss Simone de Beauvoir takes 'universal female subordination' for granted: Woman *is* the second sex. Unlike Levi-Strauss she protests against this state of affairs, but the fact that she shares all Levi-Strauss's basic assumptions, including his distinction between 'culture' and 'nature', with women connected to 'nature' – makes her (like him) blind to possible forms of female authority. The nature/culture theme (further developed in Sherry Ortner's famous 1974 article: 'Is Female to Male as Nature is to Culture?' – an article explicitly dedicated to Simone de Beauvoir) runs through most of Simone de Beauvoir's conceptual constructions such as immanence/transcendence, as well as her persistent view of the female body as a handicap and motherhood as an impediment in women's struggle for equality (cf. Chapter 4).

'The matrilineal puzzle'

An important set of variables at play in Lévi-Strauss's work is the relationship between the 'rule of residence' and the 'rule of descent' (Lévi-Strauss 1949/1969, 493). This relationship is taken up by Audrey Richards the following year in her important paper: 'Some types of family structure among the Central Bantu' (1950). Unlike Lévi-Strauss, who only deals with matriliny unwillingly, so to speak, Audrey Richards is an expert in this field, having conducted lengthy fieldwork in the early 1930s among the matrilineal Bemba, in what was then Northern Rhodesia, now Zambia. Furthermore she is a woman. Neither factor, however, induce her to be concerned with possible forms of female authority. Like any other anthropologist of her day, Audrey Richards' point of view is firmly placed in the male subject. She like everybody else sees anthropology as a question of 'conceptualizing variations in relations between men'; the position of men as the dominant sex is taken for granted. Also in her book on *Land, Labour and Diet in Northern Rhodesia* (1939/1995) with long and detailed descriptions of daily life among the Bemba – descriptions through which the central positions of Bemba women become quite explicit – Richards persists in talking about 'the Bemba housewife', thus calling forward an image of head-of-family husbands and dependent wives, an image which does not correspond very well with her own descriptions.

Richards' concern in her 1950 paper is through a comparative analysis of different matrilineal societies in the so-called 'matrilineal belt' of Southern Central Africa, to locate the crucial variable of difference between these different matrilineal groups. All the societies concerned trace descent along matrilineal lines, where they differ is regarding rules of residence: The crucial point is, as Richards sees it, the husband's right to determine the residence of the bride or, as she decides to phrase it, 'the husband's right of bride removal'. 'For this reason,' she says, 'I have found it better to use the phrases "marriage with immediate right of bride removal" or "marriage with delayed right of bride removal" or "marriage without bride removal"' (1950, 209). The implicit assumptions of this terminology is in the first place that the variations are from a male point of view, with a male agent: the bride in this terminology is very much the object; she is not just the one being married, but also the one being 'removed'. Second, by talking about 'rights', subtle connotations are implied of 'bride removal' somehow being the husband's moral right; something must be wrong if such 'rights' are delayed or denied. It is taken for granted that the husband will find an obligation to live in his spouse's village 'irksome' and that he will try to escape from it (1950, 246), whereas the opposite situation of a wife having to live in her spouse's village as a matter of course signal a stable and durable state of affairs. Thus it is the implicitly chosen male point of view which, more than anything else, creates the famous 'matrilineal puzzle', defined by Richards herself as 'the difficulty of combining recognition of descent through the woman with the rule of exogamous marriage' (1950, 246).

Matriliny in terms of relations between men
Anthropological studies of matriliny are carried from the 1950s into the 1960s by David Schneider among others. In his preface to a sizeable volume, *Matrilineal Kinship*, 1961, co-edited with Kathleen Gough, he praises Richards' 1950 paper for being a major step forward in the analysis of matrilineal descent groups, and for providing the immediate stimulus for the 1961 volume, which as a consequence is dedicated to Audrey Richards (Schneider 1961, xiii). But Schneider also pays homage to Bachofen and Morgan, more for the questions they raised than for the answers given. In his short chronology of studies of matriliny the peak is reached with Richards, who is lauded because of her comparative cross-cultural research, reaching beyond the normal monographs and social anthropological case studies. Schneider's own prime contribution to the volume – the introductory paper titled: 'The Distinctive Features of Matrilineal Descent Groups' – has a similar comparative analytical ambition. Schneider sets out 'to develop an initial theoretical rationale for certain features of matrilineal descent groups which distinguish them from their patrilineal counterparts' (ibid, 1). The focus is on descent groups, and the challenge is to develop analytical inroads for the identification and study of supposed problematic relationships between matrilineal descent group men and their in-marrying affines.

In his introduction Schneider demonstrates sharp analytical abilities –
combined with pretty much the same idiosyncrasies as his predecessors.
Schneider takes it as a basic premise that 'the role of men as men is defined as
that of having authority over women and children' (ibid., 6). It is simply taken
for granted that authority is a male issue. Entirely in line with the consensus of
his time Schneider, in his previously mentioned historical preface to the volume,
has done away with female authority: 'It became clear that the generalized
authority of women over men, imagined by Bachofen, was never observed in
known matrilineal societies, but only recorded in legends and myths' (ibid., viii).
By doing away with the generalized authority of women over men, Schneider
– like everybody else – is doing away with female authority altogether, never
pausing to think that partial, limited – or entirely different forms of authority
may be issues worthy of consideration and investigation. This is so much the
more striking as variations and nuances of *male* authority are considered and
discussed at length in the paper. The discussion concerns the relations between
descent group men and in-marrying affines (also men). Much care is taken and
many possibilities are considered, but the possibility that women might have
some say in one area or another is left out of consideration right from the start.
Schneider's discussion, developed in detail, deals with relations between men.

3 The battle of matriliny: a battle of analytical approaches

What it all boils down to is matriliny being problematic, an aberration, something difficult, confusing, illogical, full of puzzles, tensions, etc. One is reminded
of the complicated charts with which pre-Copernicus/Kepler astronomers were
struggling in order to picture the trajectories of the planets, on the premise that
as a matter of course the earth (where *we* live) was the centre of the universe.
As soon as the same data could be interpreted in a system where the sun was
seen as the centre, a great number of previous difficulties disappeared, and the
trajectories of the planets – including the earth – could be drawn nicely and
neatly as circles/ellipses.

The battle of matriliny is similar: As long as it is taken for granted that men
exchange women (Lévi-Strauss), that men have authority over women and children (Schneider), that a man is the ego and point of departure in kinship
systems (Richards), and that kinship express relations between men (them all)
– matriliny becomes complicated. Once the analytical lens is shifted, taking a
point of departure in the position of women, the whole thing appears very differently. It is a question of 'shifting the centre', as put by Patricia Hill Collins (1994)
– looking at the same data but from a different point of view. This would mean
investigating male authority instead of taking it for granted and posing new
questions, which emerge and become relevant in this new perspective. Such as,
for example, investigating *female* authority and the kinds of authority vested in
women as well as other fields of social life which might be important, beyond the
economic and political concerns of male-focused kinship analysis.

Shifting the centre of analysis is important, of course, not just for the study
of matriliny, but for gender sensitive studies in general. Shifting the centre is
actually what Amadiume is doing, when she talks about 'matriarchy' or 'the

motherhood paradigm'. The term 'matriarchy' has been misunderstood and demonized in social science from McLennan onwards. Instead of investigating variations in male/female balances of power, 'matriarchy' has been interpreted as absolute female power, and promptly discarded and relegated to the realm of myth. By taking up the term 'matriarchy' and applying it in serious argument, Amadiume disturbs the age-old agreement that 'matriarchy' is ridiculous and absurd. Her courageous act – to theorize 'the vexing concept of matriarchy' (1997, 71) – exposes the connections between the fear of 'matriarchy' and the cherished assumptions of male dominance/female subordination. What Amadiume does is (a) to introduce 'a shift of focus from man at the centre and in control, to the primacy of the role of the mother/sister in economic, social, political and religious institutions' (ibid., 152), and (b) to insist on under-standing matriarchy 'not as a totalitarian system – that is, the total rule governing a society – but as a structural system in juxtaposition with another system in a social structure' (ibid., 71). Amadiume has developed this line of thinking from her own analysis of Igbo society, which is patrilineal when seen from a point of view of kinship and descent, but where nevertheless the unit composed of a mother and her children is of no little importance. Amadiume thus juxtaposes what she calls 'the male-focused ancestral house' with 'the mother-focused matricentric unit' constructing an analysis which makes visible both of these distinct and different structures (ibid, 18).

Lesson number one from this discussion is to shift the centre or focus of atten-tion from men to women, or rather from fathers to mothers; to see what things will look like if mothers (or mother-child relationships, cf. Amadiume 1997) are taken as the point of departure for social analysis.

Lesson number two is to investigate areas and forms of female power. Instead of just taking for granted that authority is always male, to pose questions regarding forms of female power and to investigate gender power relationships, including possible patterns of male dominance/female subordination. How to conceptualize forms of female power is in itself a challenge.

Lesson number three concerns questions regarding notions of gender. One point to be made is that perhaps gender – man/woman – is not always and everywhere a decisive difference? Seniority, for example, might be more impor-tant (Oyewùmí, 1997). Or maybe the very clear gender distinctions that are usually taken for granted, are somehow linked to patriarchal power and male mythologies? Adrienne Rich (1976) showed how assumptions regarding heterosexuality are part of a patriarchal power system and Judith Butler (1990) talks of the very category 'woman' as rooted in the heterosexual matrix. Floating and uncertain gender systems tend to upset male power. Thus ques-tioning and investigating what is usually taken for granted – such as clear and dichotomous notions of gender – is often a good idea.

Conclusion

As initially announced one point of this chapter was to make visible and thereby to undermine some persistent assumptions in anthropological as well as in feminist thinking, the prime assumption being the one about male dominance and female subordination. During the last decades parts of feminism have moved away from such assumptions, decisively pushed by queer theory, which is characterized by refusing to take established gender categories (and concomitant assumptions) for granted. Anthropology of course has also moved. Nevertheless the assumptions here discussed are still going strong in far too many contexts, Gender-and-Development theorizing being but one.

Another point of the chapter has been to lift forward contributions to new lines of thinking in anthropology as well as in feminism. The intention has been by this type of discussion to promote elaboration of conceptual tools, which will make it possible to study and to understand social life in general, and matriliny in particular, without the obstructions created by a priori assumptions regarding male domination and female subordination.

12

Ancestral Spirits, Land & Food
Gendered Power & Land Tenure in Ribáuè   (1999)

Woodcut by Matias Mtundu Mzaanhoka

Post-war ruins in Ribáuè town

Ribáuè town is situated on the main road crossing northern Mozambique, more or less midway between Malawi and the coast, in Nampula Province, some 140 kilometers to the east of the provincial capital. The road is national road number 8, and it goes from Nacala, the major port of the north, eastward to Nampula city and further east into Malawi, passing district towns Ribáuè, Malema and Cuamba. Living in Ribáuè town from 1998 to 1999 it took some time before I realized that the town's main street was in fact this national road. Few cars were passing; in the dry season the road was bad, and in the rainy season it became almost impassable. While I stayed in Ribáuè the landcruiser I had borrowed from a Danish NGO considerably increased the car park of Ribáué. Apart from this car there were only four other cars in town: The district administration had a car, the hospital had one, Salama had one (Salama is a local NGO working in community health), and the fourth car belonged to the Catholic sisters, recently installed in a newly built dormitory for secondary school girls.

Like many other district towns in Mozambique, Ribáuè appears to have been a small but neat and tidy centre for colonial administration. Nice whitewashed buildings for hospital and district administration, a police post, a few other administrative buildings, two shops, a football field, a country club and beautiful veranda-houses for the district administrator and two hospital doctors. There are whitewashed pebbles along streets and pathways, and in front of the district administration building a flagpole in a bed of flowers. Ribáuè town is situated at the foot of a range of picturesque and dramatic mountains, the *inselbergen* so typical of this part of Nampula province (Photo 12.1). In colonial days until well after Independence there was a picnic site in the mountains right above the town. Mountain streams were used for a swimming pool, shady patios had been constructed and the whole place had magnificent views over the plains.

In 1998–99 much of this was in ruins. During the war Ribáuè had suffered a series of attacks, destroying most of the town's stone buildings. Due to aid donations from the Netherlands, the hospital and the district administration headquarters had been rebuilt. These few shining and freshly painted buildings could not conceal the fact, however, that Ribáuè was a town of ruins.

Healing the war wounds of Ribáuè people

Considering this, and knowing that Ribáuè town had been attacked by Renamo forces no less that five times between 1984 and 1989, it struck me that whereas the marks of war were still very visible on the buildings, the people's wounds seemed to have healed. Demobilized soldiers from Frelimo and Renamo respectively were living side by side and drinking together on Fridays. People seemed to be getting on with their lives and enjoying peace and years of good rain and harvest. In the hearts of the population the agony of war and killings seemed to have disappeared, leaving no marks and no traumas.

Inquiring into the reasons for this, I learned that everybody returning from the war, from combat or from captivity, had been through cleansing and

12.1 In the outskirts of Ribáuè town. Maize fields, sandy roads, and in the background the mountains.
(Photo © Signe Arnfred)

12.2 One of the major roads in northern Mozambique, in the rainy season. The road runs from Nacala, the major port of the north, inland through Ribáuè town, all the way to Malawi. The car was borrowed from Danish NGO, MS. I am on my way to Nampula city; 140 km on this road is a challenge.
(Photo © Signe Arnfred)

reintegration rituals, organized by local *curandeiros* or *curandeiras*, male/female traditional healers. Individuals who participated in war, who killed or who saw people being killed, are believed to be haunted by the spirits of the murdered people. Returning home they become the vehicles through which these unsettled spirits might enter the community, spreading havoc and despair. Cleansing and reintegration ceremonies are thus a necessity not only for the individual who returns, but for the whole community also. In the cases I recorded in Ribáuè, the ritual treatment itself had not been very elaborate, the important factor was that it took place. Typically it would run like this: The clothes the person had been wearing at his/her return to home would have to be burned, and the person would be 'vaccinated', that is: through incisions made with a razor blade a medical paste would be rubbed into the person's body. Sometimes he/she would also, with a blanket over his/her head, have to inhale the smoke of certain remedies prepared by the curandeiro/a. Family and friends would be present and assist proceedings by singing and clapping. Finally a ritual meal would be prepared, taking care also to offer food to the family's ancestral spirits, informing them of the return and reintegration of the family member.

Similar post-war treatments are reported by Carolyn Nordstrom from a conversation with a group of older women in a village that had seen a great deal of devastation during the war: 'The curandeiros cut the person off from any holds the war has on him or her, they scrape off the violence from their spirits, they make them forget what they have seen or felt and experienced in the war, they make them alive again, alive and part of the community. ... The curandeiros take the war out of them. They uneducate their war education' (Nordstrom 1997, 210).

Nordstrom highlights the tremendous importance of Mozambican civil society, and especially of the curandeiros/as, in the whole peace building process. The President and the politicians got the praise for the success of the Mozambican peace process, but in actual fact the peace was created and constructed from below. According to Nordstrom (ibid., 212), 'Few have documented the sophisticated countrywide peacebuilding system these people forged day by day, from the ground up. Yet without these people's work, the peace accord that was finally reached in 1992 would never have been possible.'

This remarkable achievement of peace from below and the strength and creative forces of the curandeiros/as, is inextricably linked to the presence of ancestral spirits in daily life in rural Mozambique. In this chapter I'll investigate links between people, ancestors and land, with a special focus on food and on gendered power. Land in Ribáuè is inherited down the female line, from mother to daughters (and sons), food production is crucial, and women have key positions in the control and distribution of food, while men tend to be responsible for cash crops and money. Increasingly, however, a 'logic of subsistence' rooted in food production and land as a basis for life, is being confronted with a 'logic of the market' rooted in cash crops, money and commercialization. This chapter looks at the implications of such changes for gender power relations and also investigates whether these changes seem to affect (or not) the system of matriliny.

Links between people, ancestors and land

Land in Ribáuè district is not just a material good, not just a means of production, and not at all a commodity. Land is the basis of life. In Makhuwa culture certain territories 'belong to' certain lineages, in principle to the ones believed to have arrived first on the land in question (Martinez 1989, 62; Geffray 1991, 20; Medeiros 1995, 47). The male head of these first arrivers is an important ancestral spirit, and one to whom his successor, the present grand *mwene*,[1] along with the present *pwiyamwene*, should pay homage in the annual rain ceremonies. There is a hierarchy of spirits just as there is a hierarchy of lineages and of people. The highest chiefs of the most important lineages become the most important spirits. However, to become an ancestral spirit is the ultimate goal for any member of Makhuwa society (Martinez 1979, 246). All Makhuwa people, who lived a proper life, and who died a proper death, are transformed into ancestral spirits. Living a proper life implies giving life to children, and dying a proper death implies performance of the proper burial rituals. The crown of life is its aftermath: becoming an ancestral spirit. Ancestral existence takes place on a grander scale; as an ancestor you command extraordinary powers. 'Human life is greatly enhanced by the ending of it' as it is put by David Lan, writing about Zimbabwe (Lan 1985, 32).The ancestors have no material form, and so they can be in many places at the same time; yet they still have feelings, emotions and desires. They demand a certain attention from their descendants. If treated well, they are benefactors of the living; the welfare of their descendants is their sole concern; they become the source for fertility of the land, supplying rain for the fields and protecting the crops as they grow (ibid.). The people, the land and the ancestors are thus closely connected, an interrelation which is crucial in Makhuwa cosmology. 'The relation to the land is lived in a religious way' says Catholic father Elia Ciscato, who has studied Makhuwa society for a lifetime (Ciscato 1995, 95). Religion, in this context, refers to a cosmological totality, not just to things that happen in a church.

Like other representatives of traditional authority, after Independence the *mamwene* were put out of office by Frelimo, and replaced by Party people in new state power structures. Frelimo never saw and never respected the crucial unity of land, people, ancestors and traditional authority. On the contrary: To Frelimo traditional authority was part of the repressive 'feudal' power structure of traditional society, and besides they were suspected of having collaborated with the Portuguese. Any reference to ancestral spirits was condemned as superstition and obscurantism. According to Geffray (1991) this ignorance and disregard of traditional authority and cosmology was an important part of the background for the war. 'The state agents and specialists of development saw the rural population just as a series of separate a-socialized individuals ... somehow just waiting for Frelimo to endow them with a social organization' (Geffray 1991, 53). One consequence of this 'tabula rasa' political approach (Adam

---

[1] *Mwene* is the local name for lineage head or 'chief' in this part of Nampula. In other parts of Nampula province the word for lineage head is *humu* (Medeiros 1995, 49). There are *mamwene* (plural of mwene) at different levels, depending on the importance of the lineage. The mwene also has territorial responsibilities like allocation of land. Every mwene has a female counterpart, the *pwiyamwene*.

1996, 2005) was that crucial aspects of rural society went underground. Traditional authority and ancestral spirits became invisible. Unofficially however they remained in office, just as in many places rituals and ceremonies were still performed, but secretly, hidden from the view of the Party and the state. Another consequence was traditional leaders taking sides with Renamo during the war (Geffray 1991).

Now, after the war, traditional authority had re-emerged. Now again aspects of society were visible, which during 'the time of Samora' had been hidden from view. The links between the land, the people and the ancestors had reappeared in new and impressive ways. It is my experience from Ribáuè that these links are still very strong, and that it was this strength, these forces of identity and belonging, that lie behind the remarkable peace-building achievement recorded above. Thus I see it as important in dealing with questions of land tenure, to do so in a cosmological context.

Gender aspects of Makhuwa cosmology

Women have a central position in Makhuwa cosmology. The essential link between the dead, the living and the as yet unborn members of the lineage is maintained through female powers. The Makhuwa way of entering into communication with the ancestors is to pour *makeya* [2] in an appropriate place: a sacred tree or a graveyard. Makeya is the finely ground flour of *mapira* (sorghum), when used in a ceremonial context. Sorghum is a female crop; cultivation, weeding, harvesting are exclusively done by women, as is pounding of the grain (three times over) and its subsequent grinding between two stones. Even the ceremonial pouring of makeya is a female affair. This doesn't mean that men cannot do it, but for pouring the makeya of large and important ceremonies, female assistance will be requested. For the grand communal ceremonies, like the rain ceremony, and for male and female initiation ceremonies, the woman pouring makeya must be the *pwiyamwene*. The pwiyamwene is the female counterpart to the mwene, for each mwene, grand or small, there will be a pwiyamwene. The mwene and the pwiyamwene will never be husband and wife; they belong to the same matrilineage, thus they are brother and sister, uncle and niece, or aunt and nephew (Medeiros 1995, 61, 65). Among the responsibilities of the mwene are the allocation of land, the resolution of conflicts and the representation of the lineage in relation to the state and to visitors. The responsibilities of the pwiyamwene are of a more spiritual and ceremonial kind.

The grand pwiyamwene of 'my' part of Ribáuè district, counterpart to the *régulo*, i.e. the grand mwene of the area, lived close to Ribáuè town; she was called for every initiation ceremony taking place in the vicinity, including the ones that were celebrated in the Catholic and Protestant churches. Nowadays it has become normal for the churches to take over the initiation ceremonies, mixing the traditional teachings and prescriptions with lessons from the bible; but Christianity or not: the pwiyamwene must be there to pour makeya.

---

[2] *Makeya* is also called *ephepa* or *mukuttho*, depending on the area (Martinez 1989, 271).

12.3 My first trip ever to Mozambique was in 1979, as part of the Denmark-Mozambique Solidarity organization. The delegation travelled to Zambézia province, and this photograph is from Zambézia. I remember the powerful women (who did not speak Portuguese) and the man in Western clothes, with shoes, who was the formal village representative. Later I have come to see this photo as an image of matriliny: women in control of many matters, but men the ones who speak to foreigners.
(Photo © Jan Birket-Smith)

It was evident from living in Ribáuè that women more than men are the ones with a 'direct line' to the spirit world. Of the curandeiros, many of whom are working in close collaboration with the spirits, a large majority are women (and thus curandei*ras*).[3] In an all night spirit-ceremony which I attended in the mountains, both men and women were present, but all those in charge of proceedings were women, as were all those who fell into a trance and through whom the spirits spoke.

Women have key positions in Makhuwa cosmology, and in Makhuwa society as well – the two being closely interlinked. Women are providers of life and nutrition; descent and inheritance of land pass through the female line, as does identity and belonging to a matriclan, a *nihimo*, and a family name. 'Mirasse, Lukadje, Lapone, Munrekoni, Male, etc. are the *mahimo* (plural of nihimo) which are at the same time the names to express the belonging, the words in which to frame it, and the laws by which it is established. ... The nihimo is a spiritual and esoteric entity, *exclusively transmissible by women*' (Geffray 1990, 66–67, emphasis added, SA).

It was Portuguese colonial policy to co-opt the major chiefs, enrolling them as *régulos* to function as tax collectors, forced labour recruiters, etc. on behalf of the colonial regime. The Portuguese succeeded in this only to a limited extent; often the régulo was just a lesser member of the chiefly lineage, and sometimes

---

[3] According to AMETRAMO, the Mozambican association of traditional medicine (*Associação de Medicina Tradicional de Moçambique*) as many as 89 % of the registered *curandeiros* in Ribáuè district are women.

he was not a member at all (Medeiros 1995, 62). Furthermore, the Portuguese colonial powers never grasped the importance of the mapwiyamwene; like the British in Nigeria (cf. Oyewùmí 1997) they were blind to female power. Thus to a large extent traditional authority, male and female, continued in their social and ritual roles throughout the colonial period. According to Medeiros 'the ancestresses and the lineage chiefs continued to reproduce the social organization in a system parallel to the system of the régulos (and hidden from the eyes of the Portuguese). ... It was the hierarchical succession of the 'mothers of mothers' that maintained traditional power alive' (Medeiros 1984, 8–9).

After Independence all chiefs were put out of office by Frelimo, and replaced by Party people in newly created state power structures. In some places, however, old traditional authority secretly maintained the upper hand by posting men of the chiefly lineage, controlled by the dethroned chief, as Frelimo secretaries of communal villages etc. (Geffray and Pedersen 1985, Medeiros 1995). Frelimo only had eyes for male power, and thus they did not ban the mapwiyamwene. On the contrary, according to Medeiros (ibid., 62) in some places the male village secretaries were paralleled by female mapwiyamwene.

During and after the Frelimo/Renamo war traditional authority re-emerged – with ambiguous implications. Such revitalization is always dangerous; what in the context of a subsistence economy was part of a generally beneficial state of affairs, may turn out very differently in a situation of increasing market relations.[4] Traditional chiefs are not democratically elected. On the other hand, however, their power does depend on popular support. In the present situation, in a place like Ribáuè, the local mamwene are widely trusted, as exemplified by the following quote:

> The one who knows the land of the area is the mwene. He is the one that knows which area belongs to the family[5] Remane, and which to the family Mutumuque. He knows that at the time of the floods a son was born in the house of the family Remane, and he knows that that cashew tree was young when the grasshoppers were around. It is important that the mwene comes back into office because he is the one that knows all that goes on in the area: who are the children born, and which land belonged or belongs to whom. He doesn't know how to read and write, but he has it all in his head, more reliably that in a written document. (Casas & Camata 1996)

However, this kind of power is open to manipulation. Many of the mamwene I met in Ribáuè district were the old ones from colonial times, and the rest were nephews of the old ones. In appearance they looked just as barefoot and ragged as any other peasants of the area. But – along with other members of the local community – they took a special responsibility in the supervision of land issues and in solving local conflicts.

---

[4] Regarding a 'logic of subsistence' with land as a basis of life vs land as a scarce commodity with cash value, cf. Susana Lastarria-Cornhiel 1997.

[5] The passage is translated from Portuguese, translated from Emakhuwa. Presumably the term in Emakhuwa has been 'nloko' which means 'matrilineage'. The quote originates from a Ribáuè seminar in 1996 debating the new land law.

12.4 This line of women are the *mapwiyamwene* (female chiefs), the *curandeiras* (female traditional healers) and the *conselheiras* (masters of female initiation rituals) of Malema in Ribáuè district, Nampula province 2003. The woman with shoes is Mama Rosita, a nurse working with Salama, a local NGO. Mama Rosita was the translator in my conversations with the women. The man (also with shoes) is the chief, the *mwene*. He is a grandson of one of the *mapwiyamwene*. The women didn't think much of him; he was later replaced.
(Photo © Jan Birket-Smith)

Female gender power: Control of food

Life, food and family name are transmitted through female lines from mothers to offspring. The Makhuwa name for the family unit at household level is *erukulu*, which means womb: the female procreative powers. The erukulu is grouped around a 'mother of mothers', with her daughters, their husbands, and her grandchildren. Unmarrried sons and grandsons live with their (grand)mother until marriage, when they will move to join their wives. Christian Geffray (1990) provides a description of Makhuwa household life in the 1930s, based on the memories of old men and women of life before the colonial push for forced cotton cultivation. Sixty years have passed since then, and life keeps changing. Nevertheless Geffray's descriptions[6] offer valuable insights for understanding contemporary life in Ribáuè. The Makhuwa social structure, where women hold key positions as the providers of food, has survived because to this day, the economy in a place like Ribáuè is still largely subsistence, with production of food as its highest priority. Processes of commercialization – already under way in late colonial years – broke down in the post-Independence period, and were further halted during the recent war. People's capacity to survive from subsistence production had to be reinvented.

Makhuwa life, as depicted by Geffray, is centred around the 'mother of

[6] Geffray's fieldwork area is Erati district, to the east of Ribáuè, but before you reach the coast.

mothers'. Young men are brought into her household from other families to marry her granddaughters, as 'begetters and producers' (Geffray 1990, 46). Their offspring, as well as the produce of their work in the fields, are kept beyond their control; the children born of their wives belong to a different lineage, and the bulk of the food they produce on the land, is stored away in the granary of their (grand)mother-in-law. For the first years of marriage, the young couple does not even have a house of their own, and the (grand)son-in-law has to work on his (grand)mother-in-law's fields, in addition to performing tedious household chores: fetching water and firewood, sweeping the courtyard, etc. (Geffray 1990, 45). If the sexual life of the young couple doesn't produce offspring, the man is the one to blame, and if his performance does not improve, he'll be sent back to where he came from. Similarly his abilities as an agricultural producer will be tested; if he turns out to be lazy, or disobeys his in-laws, the marriage will be dissolved. Only when their wives give birth to their first child are the lives of these young men eased; better still when their wives become mothers of mothers, which may happen when they are only 35 to 40 years old, as marriage at puberty is/was the norm for the young women.[7]

In the household of the (great)grandmother, she is the one who receives affection and respect as the nourishing mother. The bulk of the produce of all of her (grand)daughters and (grand)sons-in-law ends up in her granary and, in return, she is the one who will feed the children of the entire household. According to Geffray, even as he wrote in the 1980s, women had total and exclusive control of the granaries. If a man wanted some produce, to offer or to sell, he would have to ask his wife.

The same applies to Ribáuè district in the 1990s: women control the food. In Marremo, some 30 kilometers north of Ribáuè town, where I carried out most of the interviews for this chapter, the largest plots of land and the greatest labour investment are dedicated to food production. The important thing is to have food enough for the whole year, including the lean months of January and February, before the new crops bear a yield. Obviously, it is a source of pride to be able to say, like one grandmother I spoke to: 'All this cassava, maize and beans I eat with my grandchildren. The only crop we ever sell is cotton. Here in this household we never had problems of lack of food.' Otherwise scarcity in the months of January and February is the general condition: 'The ones who during this period have enough of food is the minority; the majority are the ones who don't.'

In this situation the control of food is crucial. The consumption of food must be very carefully calculated; the wellbeing of the whole family depends on this. That control is in the hands of the women. As told by one of the other grandmothers of my sample: 'Things to do with food are decided by me. I am the one who knows the life of the children and the number of visitors during the year. So I'm the one in control.' And if the husband wants to sell part of the food crops – maize, beans, cassava or groundnuts – he has to ask permission from his wife. 'My husband will speak like this: "My wife, I want to sell this amount of maize; I am asking you for permission."' And in the words of another woman: 'We will discuss if we need money for clothes or for the *curandeiro*. If my husband

---

[7] Working in southern Cabo Delgado in the early 1980s I found similar characteristics of the gender relations of matriliny, cf. Chapters 1 and 2.

wants to sell this amount, and I think that that is too much, he will listen to my advice.' The questions of how much of each food crop to grow, and how to divide land and labour between food crops and cotton (the major cash crop of Ribáuè area) are often decided jointly. As one male informant said: 'The man who wants a good relationship with his wife, will grow a limited amount of cash crops compared to food.'

In general, women control the food, and men control the money resulting from cash crops, even where women participate in the actual cultivation. But as shown above there are norms concerning male/female consultation regarding money use. Husbands cannot just do as they please. They have to negotiate over the spending of income from cash crops. One woman explained in detail how the money from cotton sales would be divided between husband and wife, with the woman getting the larger share, because, as she said, 'I am the one to look after the needs of the children.'

Women and land: Matrilineal dilemmas

Land and food are closely connected: The food derives from the land. Land, like women, contains invisible creative powers. This is how it was put by a Makhuwa peasant woman:

> The land is like a woman, because when we sow a piece of land, the seed will germinate and grow just like a pregnant woman. First she waits for a while, hoping that the germination has succeeded, and then she is pregnant until her time has come and she will give birth. And thanks to God she will give birth, just like the crops sprouting from the sown land. When the child has been born we do everything for it to grow well. And here again there is no difference: For the crops to grow we weed and then we harvest. (Casas & Camata 1996)

Men have access to land only through their relationships with women. Inheritance of land follows the female line, from mothers to daughters. 'This is what my mother said to her daughters' one peasant woman told me: 'You who are women, you will get children. Here is your land.' 'Land follows the blood of the mother.' Young men get access to land through their wives, at marriage. As described above, the daughters remain on the family land of their mothers. The sons move out from home, in order to join their wives. The children belong to their mother's matrilineage. For all these reasons, girl babies are valued more highly than boy babies are. Whenever I asked the women what made them most happy, to give life to a boy or a girl, the answer was: a girl. 'The greatest joy is when a baby girl is born. A woman gives continuity to the family.'

In the first years of marriage the young men live and work in the household of their in-laws 'in order for the girl's family to see if he is well behaved, and whether he is a good worker'. If this period of trial works out well, after some years the son-in-law may ask the wife's parents for permission to settle with his wife on his own family land, i.e. close to his parents, and to his sisters.[8] In

---

[8] This virilocal settlement seemed to be quite common in Ribáuè, and similar patterns have been recorded by Anne Pitcher, doing fieldwork in 1994 in the district of Monapo (Pitcher 1996, 99), and by Liselotte Staehelin et al. working during 1994 and 1995 in the district of Mecuburi (Staehelin & Müller 1997, 38).

Marremo, I came across quite a few family settings where a grandmother/a set of grandparents were living surrounded, not only by their daughters and the daughters' husbands and children, but also by their married sons with families. In these cases, obviously, the sons are granted land along with the daughters, but only during their lifetime. When they die, the land goes back to the sisters and their children. The children of the sons belong elsewhere – in the matrilineages of their mothers.

The advantage of this virilocal arrangement[9] is that, in this way, brothers can live close to sisters, whose offspring – their nephews and nieces – they are supposed to be responsible for. In matrilineal society the uncle/nephew link is the important one; much more important than the link between father and son. The disadvantage is that their own wives and children are likely to suffer – living in foreign territory, away from their own matrikin. If the wife outlives her husband she'll move back to her own folks; alone, she doesn't feel comfortable in the husband's family, and her children don't belong there. When the daughters grow up and marry, they'll have to look for land at their mother's place of origin, which is also where the sons belong (even if they may marry and get land elsewhere).

In a classic article on variations of matrilineal marriage patterns, Audrey Richards discusses this matrilineal dilemma, namely 'the difficulty of combining recognition of descent through the woman with the rule of exogamous marriage' (Richards 1950, 246): If the woman leaves her own group to join that of her husband (as in the example above) her matrikin will have difficulty keeping control of the children, who are legally identified with them. If, on the other hand, the woman remains with her parents and her husband joins her there, she and her children remain under the control of her family – even if her brothers, the uncles of her children, are living elsewhere. Her husband, however, has few chances of enacting *his* uncle-authority, being separated from his nephews. One way of solving the dilemma is through what Richards calls 'the detachable husband' (ibid., 248). This signifies a situation where husbands come and go, meaning marriages are not very stable. This was, to a certain extent, the case in Marremo. Many of the women whom I interviewed individually had been married more than once. Another solution is shifting uxorilocal and virilocal residence, as described above. Importantly, however, temporary virilocal residence should be seen as a way of solving matrilineal dilemmas, and not as an indication of emerging patriliny.

Land tenure flexibility: A logic of subsistence

One major point about land tenure in Marremo is that all have access to land. The phenomenon of landless men or women does not exist. Another major point, also observed by the 'Centro de Estudos Africanos' (CEA) of the Eduardo Mondlane University, when they collected data on family agriculture in Nampula Province (Monapo, Erati and Meconta districts) in 1979, is the flexibility of land tenure: 'There are different, rather flexible forms, of access to land.

---

[9] Virilocal *vs* uxorilocal stands for settlement with the family of the husband *vs* the family of the wife.

During his active life a man generally will move several times, from one residence and piece of land to another. Thus a permanent and exclusive relation between a certain producer and a certain piece of land is not established' (CEA 1980, 18). According to CEA this flexibility is partly due to the low technical level of family agriculture: all work is done by hand (hoes and machetes), and no permanent investments in improving the land are undertaken. The only exception is planting of cashew trees (CEA ibid.). Cashew was introduced as a cash crop in the 1960s, and cashew, like other cash crops, is generally controlled by men. Unlike land, cashew trees tend to be inherited through the male line, from fathers to sons (Medeiros 1995, 57).[10]

Working in Marremo I found the flexibility of the local land tenure systems very impressive. Each of the matrilineages had their own land, and everybody knew where his or her family land was located. But that did not necessarily mean that this was where you lived and cultivated. Loans and borrowing of land were very common. Most families possessed more land than they actually used. If people who were not family members – neighbours, friends or strangers – asked to borrow a piece of land for cultivation, you didn't refuse: 'They need to produce and to eat just like we do. They shouldn't be turned down.' This is subsistence logic put into everyday words.

Of the twelve women in Marremo with whom I conducted individual interviews, most were involved in lending/borrowing land, as either lenders or borrowers. Some were living on their own family land, or the land of their husbands; but parts of this land would be lent out, for use by strangers. Others were living themselves on borrowed land. The reasons people gave for why they were not living on their own family land were diverse. Some claimed that the family land was 'tired'; they moved in order to till on more fertile ground, while the family land recovered. Others had moved away because of 'distaste' for the family land: During the war they had seen their loved ones being killed in this place, and did not want to go back. In another case, a 'traditional midwife' had borrowed a piece of land close to the road, to be more accessible for the women who might need her services.

Lending and borrowing is dealt with directly by the parties involved, but the mwene has to be informed. A newcomer will often apply directly to the mwene, who then, from his knowledge of the people and the area, will indicate the person to whom the applicant can carry his/her petition. It is a condition of borrowed land that the owner may claim it back whenever he/she wants it. Usually, nothing is paid in return for borrowed land, no crops must be delivered; but if he/she feels like it, the borrower may give occasional gifts to the owner. In the immediate vicinity of Ribáuè town, however, all of this worked differently. Here land could be bought, or rented, in which case a portion of the crops grown should be given as rent to the owner. Around Ribáuè town all land belonged to somebody. But this was not the case in Marremo. Not at all: vast tracts were 'no man's land', and sometimes young couples preferred to go off and make their *machamba* (field) in 'no man's land' beyond the mountains. Most people, however, preferred to borrow land that was already under cultivation, fearing unknown spirits and ghosts in the wilderness.

[10] Marremo is not an area of cashew commercialization, so I have not been able to corroborate this statement.

The general feeling in Ribáuè was that land is abundant: 'We people are few in numbers compared to the vastness of the land.' In Marremo conflicts over land were virtually non-existent. 'This thing of claiming right to land through money has not yet occurred with us,' people said. Throughout Ribáuè district, commercial farms were few. The vast majority of cultivated fields were worked by peasant men and women, with machete and a hoe. No oxen, no ploughs, no tractors. This family farming is mainly for subsistence, with a small surplus of food crops for the market, and one or two cash crops (generally cotton) for sale. When the national 'Land Campaign' (*Campanha Terra*) reached Marremo, telling people about the new Land Law[11] and advising them to register their land, it was hard from a local perspective to make sense of it all. Most people saw the campaign as addressing a problem which wasn't relevant, yet, in their area: 'When this thing of the new law begins, they will come and tell us. ... ' It is not easy to see how the extreme flexibility and adaptability of the present land tenure system in Marremo could be maintained, under conditions of titled land, or private property.

Labour power and social differentiation

Land being plentiful, the bottleneck for production is labour power. Yet, here too, the resources available are used in a flexible way, with labour power fluctuating between families and different forms of reciprocal help schemes in operation. In Ribáuè, the most common form of recruiting labour power from other families, to help in peak periods, is *olimiha*: work in exchange for food, or goods. The household which owns the field in need of weeding, or harvesting, makes a lot of *otheka* (beer) and/or *fava* (cooked beans). Then they invite people to give up a day's work, in return for a drink and a meal. Occasionally, other food products (dried cassava, sugar cane) will also be offered. I did not hear of anyone doing such work for money, the nearest case being one woman, who performed olimiha work so as to sell the food she got in return. This woman was a single mother and needed cash for her children's school fees and other needs. She was the only person I met who could be called desperately poor. Translated, 'olimiha' means 'mutual help' and most of the women in my sample of twelve had participated in, as well as organized olimiha. Obviously, however, the possibilities for arranging olimiha are unequally distributed, favouring the families which already anjoy a comfortable level of production. A certain surplus of food and drink is a precondition for inviting people for olimiha; some families are just too poor.

An awareness is also important, however, of the fact that wealth at this level is likely to fluctuate from one year to the next, depending on hazards of the weather and of pests, as well as on the physical health of key members of the household. With production reliant on labour power, the prolonged illness of just one person in a household may have a disastrous impact. When I asked in Marremo about being rich or poor, the answer was that 'this varies from one year to the next, depending on the rains and of the health of family members.

[11] The new Mozambican Land Law was passed 1997, The challenge of the law was to combine respect for communal tenure with individual titles and women's rights.

The traditional chiefs have no better conditions than anyone else.' This confers with the conclusions drawn in 1980 by the 'Centro de Estudos Africanos' at the Eduardo Mondlane University in Maputo: 'The type of differentiation that we observed seems to have more to do with certain phases of the life cycle and development of the households, with luck and chance of family composition, and with individual capacity and willingness to work – than with economic laws and class polarization' (CEA 1980, 26). It is to be expected that with structural adjustment and neo-liberal economic policies, these conditions are going to change, creating a more enduring pattern of social differentiation. So far, however, this has not happened, at least not in a place like Marremo.[12]

Among the women I interviewed, the ones belonging to large households seemed to be in the most comfortable position. This was not surprising since the larger the household, the more labour power. Some of the older women interviewed were living, not only with daughters and their families, but also with married sons gathered around them. Several of these women reported they were still helped by their sons-in-law, even if such help can no longer be taken for granted. 'Previously it was a rule that sons-in-law would work on the fields of their wives' mothers. But nowadays, this assistance depends on the goodwill of the son-in-law. It is not seen as an obligation.' In Marremo, however, many sons-in-law seemed well behaved, helping their mothers-in-law even on a voluntary basis – at least during the early years of marriage. Later, it is fully accepted that the sons-in-law may concentrate on their own fields. As one woman said: 'None of my sons-in-law have ever showed ill-will or bad behaviour. They were the ones that constructed my granaries, built my house and cleared my fields. Nowadays, though, they have their own responsibilities in their own homes.' Nevertheless this loosening of claims of mothers-in-law on the labour power of their sons-in-law, is one of the key indications of withering female power.

Cash crop: Cotton

Since the days when people were forced to grow cotton – under a colonial scheme initiated in the late 1930s – cotton cultivation has had a bad reputation in Mozambique. There are countless stories of protest and civil resistance to the violence with which forced cotton production was established and controlled. One reason for the hatred of cotton cultivation is the fact that it is extremely labour intensive. It is also very poisonous. Five rounds of weeding, and five rounds of insecticides are the ideal measure (Tique 1996, 142). In Ribáuè, peasant farmers talked about three rounds of weeding and pesticide-treatment; but still. According to Allen Isaacman, colonial officials estimated that rural households had to spend between 140 and 180 days a year to cultivate one

---

[12] Witchcraft (*feitiçaria*) – which is quite common in Ribáuè – may be seen as a force working against social differentiation, although in pretty malign ways. What causes witchcraft is 'ambition' (*ambicão*): Having good luck or being particularly clever. The following quote is from neighbouring district Mecuburi, but it could just as well have been from Ribáuè: 'When somebody produces more, especially when this somebody is a young man, some older family member will become envious of his riches and call witchcraft against him' (Staehelin & Müller 1997, 104).

single hectare of cotton (Isaacman 1996, 7). With less time left to grow food, famines became the order of the day. In consequence the colonial authorities now promoted cassava as a forced food-crop. Growing well on poor soils and requiring little labour, cassava was seen as the perfect food crop to keep cotton-growers alive (ibid., 164). The end of colonial occupation also saw the end of forced cotton cultivation, with the immediate effect of a steep fall in cotton production (CEA 1980, 1). The new Frelimo government of independent Mozambique tried to restructure cotton cultivation through cooperative farming and huge state-run farms, but without the desired results (Pitcher 1996, 90). Under the structural adjustment policies of present-day Mozambique, the previous state farms have been 51 per cent privatized and turned into joint venture companies with 49 per cent participation of the state. Apart from growing cotton on their own land, these companies also command cotton growing by the 'small-holder' farmers within a specific area, just as they did in colonial times. The post-1950 colonial cotton production system has been re-introduced (Tique ibid., 151).

Cotton production in Ribáuè district is entirely based on family production. A factory for cotton processing is situated in Ribáuè town and holds the monopoly of buying cotton from 'small-holders' throughout most of the district. This factory was built in the 1950s as a part of 'Compania dos Algodões de Moçambique' (CAM), was taken over by the state in 1977, and was later owned, for some years, by João Ferreira dos Santos, a Portuguese firm with long-standing roots in Mozambique. In 1993, the factory became a joint venture enterprise between another Portuguese firm and the Mozambican state. Its present name is CANAM: 'Compania Algodeira de Nampula, Moçambique'. Irrespective of these changes and in spite of the war, the cotton factory of Ribáuè has never stopped working. Nor does the way it now works differ much from the old days. Even some of the *capatazes*, colonial overseers controlling cotton growing by the peasants, have survived from pre-Independence times. The factory *capatazes* (now compared to 'extension workers') still control the areas marked out for cotton, their size and localization, timely weeding and application of pesticides in conformity with company requirements, etc. In carrying out their tasks, they collaborate with the local traditional authorities, who receive 'a compensation for their voluntary work' as one factory employee put it. This, too, repeats the socio-economic patterns of colonialism (CEA 1980, 6). The factory still supplies seed to the peasants (free of charge) and pesticides (to be paid for). At harvest time, sacks are distributed and communiqués are sent to let people know on which day and at what place the factory lorry will arrive, to collect and weigh the sacks and pay the peasant farmers.

The major and decisive difference between cotton growing under the colonial regime and today is that now it's voluntary. Before the start of the growing season, local meetings are held for the peasants to enlist for cotton growing. Once you decide to participate, the minimum requirement for a male head of household is to grow one hectare of cotton, and half a hectare for a female head, as in colonial days. A further requirement is that the cotton field should be close to the road (to facilitate supervision) and preferably the fields of several farmers should be close to one another.

Knowing the sombre history of cotton growing in Mozambique and seeing now how many aspects were in fact unchanged since colonial times, I was surprised to find that men and women alike approved of cotton cultivation. To many peasants in Ribáuè, cotton is the only steady source for a small, but necessary cash income. Moreover in recent years cotton prices had been relatively good, leaping from 1,100 meticais in 1994, and 1,500 in 1995 to 3,900 in 1996 for one kilogram of first quality cotton. The 1996 prices were still fresh in people's minds, and in spite of two subsequent years of falling prices: 3,300 meticais in 1997 and 2,900 in 1998 – there was an undying hope of reaching that 1996 peak again. One sack holds 30–35 kilograms of cotton, and in the Marremo area one hectare produces 10–12 sacks. In 1998 one peasant farmer had produced some 21 sacks of cotton on two hectares of land, fetching an income of just over 2,000,000 meticais. Looked at by an outsider, this is not very much (some 170 USD). If the previously quoted estimate is correct, that 140–180 work days are needed per hectare, it certainly does not amount to a very impressive daily wage. Yet that is not the way it is calculated in Ribáuè. On the contrary, the farmer with two hectares of cotton saw himself as fortunate and prosperous, compared to pre-war years when, as he said, he had only had one pair of trousers. 'Now I have a better life, I have a bicycle, a radio, and several suitcases full of clothes, thanks to cotton growing.'

Farmers associations for price negotiation

One major problem of cotton cultivation, of course, is that uncontrolled price fluctuations on the world market are reflected in oscillating local prices. Every year, the Mozambican government announces a minimum price for cotton, depending on the world market price. If there was not a monopoly control of cotton buying, however, as is presently the case with CANAM, farmers might be able to negotiate better prices.

Price negotiation on non-cotton crops has recently been introduced in Ribáuè, thanks to the creation of Farmers' Associations. Previously, the traders coming out from Nampula city had the upper hand, determining the terms of trade with peasant farmers, who had no other opportunities for selling. Now that situation is changing. Farmers' Associations are being created, with some 20 to 40 producers in each association. At the time of my stay there were said to be 20 associations functioning in Ribáuè district; not many compared to the number of peasants, but a good start. According to the people of CLUSA in Nampula city (CLUSA stands for 'Cooperative League USA', and is a North American NGO working for the creation of farmers' associations) there had been many difficulties in the beginning. People's negative recollections of cooperatives and communal villages from pre-war days sometimes made it difficult to convince them that this would be something different. In some places, too, the traditional authorities had caused problems, when they realized they would not receive any special gifts. But, as the associations started working, more and more people wanted to join. Through the associations, a platform of negotiation with the traders has been established. Well before harvest time, a meeting is held in Nampula city, between the representatives of each local association and the relevant traders. The associations bring information about the type and estimated quantity of crops that its members will have for sale, and proceed to shop around between traders for the best bid. Once tentative prices for different crops have been negotiated, the associations and traders together decide on appointed days and locations for the trader to arrive, weigh, pay for and collect the produce. The trader also has to make sure that sacks arrive for the peasants, in advance. On the day of collection there will be a representative of the association, along with the trader's employee, to control the weighing. According to CLUSA this is a win-win arrangement. The traders are also satisfied. They may pay higher prices than they did before, but then they save time and trouble.

Peasant associations obviously involve men, not women. In Makhuwa culture, cash crops and marketing belong in the male sphere. But as long as the money is used for family purposes, women will benefit as well. Meanwhile, CLUSA has not forgotten parallel developments for the women, organizing women's sub-groups for the establishment and running of small local shops with those few non-agricultural products that all rural households need: salt, soap, sugar, oil and capulanas.

Matriliny and changing gender power

The farmers' associations are examples of planned change. Most of the changes taking place in Makhuwa society, however, are unplanned ones. A major change is the gradual transformation of gendered power within the matrilineal context. Matriliny is changing as well, but apparently at a somewhat slower pace. The most immediately visible undermining of female gender power seems to be the withering control by 'the mother of mothers' over the labour power of her sons-in-law. In Marremo, services performed by the son-in-law had changed from being an obligation to an act depending of free will on the part of the young men. Data collected in the neighbouring district of Mecuburi show that young men elsewhere feel more tense about it: 'This kind of exploitation just cannot go on' (Venetsanou & Risoli 1998, 12).

Two dimensions are involved here: The dimension of gerontocracy – the power of older generations over younger ones; and the dimension of female (as opposed to male) gender power. To some extent, the young men's rebellion is against gerontocracy as much as it is against female power. Moving away from family land, cultivating no man's land 'beyond the mountains' is another strategy young people use against domination by the family elders. As young men in Mecuburi would say: 'An intelligent man will only use the land of his wife's family during the first two years of marriage. In the third year, he will get hold of his own independent land, and that way he escapes the control of his in-laws' (Staehelin & Müller 1997, 44). In Mecuburi young men talk about the way in which 'the war opened our eyes', pointing to an effect of the war that is contrary to that discussed earlier, where war was seen as reversing changes back to previous patterns. For these young men the war broke up traditional ways and opened their eyes to new possibilities. 'This recent war between Renamo and Frelimo opened the eyes of everyone, politically and socially. Nowadays young people are capable of solving their problems themselves, economically; now it is the old people (the uncles) that ask the young people to help them' (ibid.).

The rebellion against female power is less explicit. It is not even a rebellion – just changing trends over time, the major trend in this context being the push for money. This implies a change of focus from food, a female power domain, to money, which is under male control. Modern society – most certainly in its present neo-liberal guise – revolves around money, a message that the young men have been quick to pick up. Seen from their point of view, their present lack of money is the major obstacle to fulfilling their dreams. With money, any difficulty can be overcome: 'With money we can resolve the major part of the problems we come up against: family problems, illness, lack of clothes, lack of food. We can also extend our fields by hiring a tractor. In this way our poverty could be relieved' (interview in Mecuburi, ibid., 138). The young men's dream is to find wage work and money. According to them it would be perfectly possible and surely successful to open possibilities of wage work in the area, like factories and state farms. 'The major desire of the young men is employment' (ibid.). The development model the young men envisage is wage work and money for themselves, and agriculture for their wives: 'The young men want employment in order to earn money. But they want to "combine employment with agriculture". The responsibility for the fields is to be left in the hands of their wives' (Staehelin & Müller 1997, 3). This vision fits strikingly well with the Mozambican national plan for agricultural development, PROAGRI (cf. below). In the eyes of the young men, money is the key to the future. The streets of Nampula city spill over with young men from the countryside employing themselves as *vendedores ambulantes* (travelling salesmen) hawkers and peddlers, trying to sell anything from shoelaces through batteries to fancy kitchen equipment.

This development means an erosion of female power. The balance between food and money – which so far in Marremo has shown a priority for food – is gradually changing. The increasing emphasis on money goes along with a decreasing emphasis on subsistence food production: with sufficient money you can buy the food you need. In this context the control of the granary – a stronghold of female power – is losing importance. At the same time women's bargaining power also seems to be decreasing. In the new era where money reigns, the men can do as they please. This is, at least, the impression emerging from interviews with young women in Mecuburi district. For young women, the focus on money is not a positive thing: their husbands no longer conform to the norm of male/female joint decision-making: 'Our major concern is the fact that the young men, our husbands, do not show us the money they get from selling the agricultural products. Older men are more responsible. ... The young men sell the lot and use the money for drinking' (Staehelin & Müller 1997, 117, 119). Older people agree with the young women: 'The young men lack respect because they have access to money. Money destroys everything.'

Taken together, these processes point to ongoing undermining of the older generation and of female gender power, in a movement of protest articulated by young men. For the time being, however, these changes seem to be taking place *within* a context of matrilinal inheritance and descent. Because I expected matriliny to be changing, I made many probing inquiries regarding patterns of inheritance and descent, but as far as I could make out, it is not at this level that things are changing. For example, regarding the temporary virilocal settlement of young families: this was nothing new, people said, it had always been like that. Inheritance of land through the female line seemed also to be unchanging. One exception to inheritance through female lines was (as mentioned above) the cashew trees. But cashews are marginal in Marremo, and in interviews I did not find this to be an issue of concern. What I did encounter, however, was the impact of education. Young men with formal education move to town, taking their wives and children along. Having thus entered the context of the 'modern' world, what takes priority from a male point of view is paternal authority over one's own offspring, not the obligations towards nieces and nephews. The power and responsibilities of the maternal uncle are shifting to the father. Further to the same trend of patriliny matching modernity, according to Venetsanou and Risoli (1998, 12) from interviews conducted in Mecuburi, the new Land Law is being used as an argument against matrilineal inheritance: 'We want to be able to leave the land we cultivate to our sons.'

Conclusion

One aim of this chapter has been to broaden the scope of discussion of access to and control of land, by seeing land issues in a context of ancestral spirits and male/female traditional authority, rooted in a logic of food production. Another aim has been to highlight aspects of female gender power in Makhuwa culture, and to investigate different modes of change in matriliny, as a system of inheritance and descent, and in female gender power, respectively. My point of view is that subsistence logic, or the logic of food production, on one hand, and the market logic characteristic of 'modernity' and 'development' on the other both clash and co-exist – and that most likely they are going to do so for a long time to come in Mozambique. As exemplified in the observation that women control food while men control money, the kind of female gender power I have described tends to be undermined by the increasing importance of money, market and modernity.

As things work in the early parts of the twenty-first century, 'development' in Mozambique as elsewhere means increased involvement in the world market and the global economy. The master plan for Mozambican agricultural development 1998–2003, the so-called PROAGRI programme, states as its general strategy 'the transformation of the subsistence agriculture into one that is more integrated in the functions of production, distribution and processing, in order to achieve the development of a subsistence agrarian sector which contributes with surpluses for the market and the development of an efficient and participatory entrepreneurial sector' (Ministry of Agriculture 1998, 37). One may speculate about the sex of the imagined entrepreneurs. The important point, however, is the emphasis on production for the market. Subsistence production, from being the lifeline of society, is pushed to a marginal position. And so are the women – unless they compete on market terms and re-appear as 'efficient and participatory entrepreneurs'.

In this context of production, distribution and processing on market terms, the power positions of Makhuwa women erode and/or become invisible. In the eyes of 'development' ancestral spirits do not exist; motherhood is ambiguous: too many children are seen as an obstacle to development – if populations grow too fast the economic growth rate will suffer; food produced for subsistence is accepted as a necessity, but the focus is elsewhere: on cash crops and market exchange. At present, most strategies on 'Gender-and-Development' take the market model for granted, struggling on this basis to transform women into 'participatory and efficient entrepreneurs'. This strategy is problematic in several respects. First, to become an 'efficient entrepreneur' in market terms will only be possible for a tiny minority of women. It is a tacit understanding of the PROAGRI plan – corresponding to the visions of young men of Mocuburi – that men are the entrepreneurs involved in the market, while women remain in the subsistence sector growing food for the family and looking after the kids. Second, by following the entrepreneur-strategy, women will have to leave all previous power positions in order to start from scratch on a male terrain. This means entering the competition already with a great handicap – not to mention responsibilities for parenting and care, responsibilities which are often taken more seriously by women compared to men.

Thus there is a need for creative rethinking regarding gendered development designs. For ways of thinking about development that take the global capitalist market as a (temporary?) fact of life, but with visions reaching beyond the market model, informed by local knowledge of gendered power relations, and including the spirit world. Is it possible to imagine ways in which traditional female power positions could be maintained, transformed, enhanced? Is it possible, in a context of development, to acknowledge the vital connections between people, ancestors, food and land? Is it possible to put the Land Law into practice in such a way that it protects people, women as well as men, against the harshness of the market, rather than being a vehicle for market forces? The questions are many, the answers are few. But raising the questions is a precondition for finding the answers.

13 Sex, Food & Female Power
On Women's Lives in Ribáuè (2006)

Woodcut by Matias Cosme Tangawizi

Sexuality is often perceived as a site for women's subordination. Through the institution of marriage, a woman's sexuality is placed under her husband's control, for his pleasure and for patrilineal procreation. Food and cooking are similarly perceived as part of women's household chores, adding to the double workload impeding women's advancement in society.

From the point of view of such perceptions the title of this chapter may seem controversial: how could one argue for a perspective, in which sex and food may possibly be acknowledged as areas of female power? The chapter will proceed first by briefly discussing these perceptions as applied to Africa and in a historical perspective, and second by introducing the matrilineal context in which the chapter's discussion is positioned – a context which makes implicit androcentric assumptions in mainstream perceptions more visible. Third, the conception of 'female power' will be debated in the light of feminist theorizing. After this overture data from northern Mozambique with a focus on male–female relations as mediated through food and sex will be presented and discussed. Finally I will draw some conclusions, posing questions for further inquiry.

'Sexuality is a key site through which women's subordination is maintained and enforced in postcolonial Africa', Sylvia Tamale says (2005b, 10) proceeding to show, however, how this state of affairs has been constructed in and through European colonization:

> The colonialists' constructions and perceptions of Africans as profligate and hypersexual led to intensified surveillance and repression, of African women's sexuality in particular. Having constructed the hypersexed female body, the case was made for the strict regulation and control of women's sexuality. (ibid.)

In this endeavour, Tamale continues, 'colonialists worked together with African patriarchs to develop inflexible customary laws that evolved into new structures and forms of domination' (ibid.). I take my point of departure in this recent contribution by a well known African feminist, in order to position the following discussion in a context of feminist thinking. According to Tamale, patriarchal forms of Christianity and Islam were highly instrumental in promoting a view of women's bodies as inherently sinful and impure. Such perceptions, backed by state and patriarchal power under colonial and postcolonial rule, have unsurprisingly seeped into women's perceptions of themselves. Nevertheless, a certain ambivalence persists. This ambivalence is the focus of Tamale's article (2005b), an analysis of the Baganda institution of *Ssenga*, referring to female sexual initiation and/or to the women counsellors instructing the young initiates. 'Sexuality among the Baganda was traditionally defined along gender and class lines, with wifehood and motherhood central in shaping women's sexuality' (ibid., 15). Still, however, a wife's lack of sexual satisfaction in marriage was a legitimate reason for divorce. Also the *Ssenga* institution is ambivalent, the role of the Ssenga instructors being on one hand to turn the young girls into good and well-behaved Baganda women, while on the other hand, in the case of some Ssengas, instructions also embody a continuation of different sexual messages, destabilizing dominant patriarchal assumptions and matching more modern and radical views voiced by young urbanized women (Tamale 2005b, 24).

The subversive aspect of the Ssenga tradition corresponds well to my own findings from northern Mozambique, and supports my general view that behind a certain façade of wifely submissiveness, power relations of sexuality may well differ from what patriarchs in power might want to believe. A distinct male fear of autonomous female sexuality is illustrated in the reports about the uproar in Uganda on the occasion of the planned staging of Eve Ensler's *Vagina Monologues* in Kampala in February 2005 (see Moffett 2005). The performance was banned by the Uganda government on the grounds 'that the title was "offensive to cultural sensibilities" and that the content was "obscene" and "promoted lesbianism in Uganda"' (Tamale 2005b, 20). Similarly, according to Tamale, the university authorities at Makerere University condemned Ssenga activities on campus, claiming that these were not matters deserving the attention of 'honourable educated girls'. 'It is clear, however,' Tamale comments, 'that much of their discomfort derived from the potential that such Ssenga sessions held for young women to take control of their sexuality' (ibid., 25).

It is such undercurrents of female sexual autonomy on which I want to focus, using for the purpose fieldwork material from Ribáuè, a rural area in northern Mozambique, Nampula province, inhabited by matrilineal Makhuwa. Emakhuwa-speaking people belong to the largest population group in Mozambique. Emakhuwa is spoken all over the province of Nampula and in parts of the neighbouring provinces of Cabo Delgado and Zambézia. According to the 1997 census 26 per cent of the Mozambican population speak Emakhuwa as their mother tongue, as compared to the second largest group, the Xichangana speakers in southern Mozambique, which amount to 11 per cent of the population (Instituto Nacional de Estatística, 1999). Like other groups of northern Mozambique the Makhuwa count descent along matrilineal lines. In addition to being matrilineal, the Makhuwa are also matrilocal, that is, the usual location of a young newly married couple will be on the land of the family of the wife. Matriliny and matrilocality carry a series of advantages seen from the point of view of women and compared to patriliny and patrilocality: at marriage it is the young man, who has to move into the unknown, with an alien family/lineage, while the young woman stays put in her own context among her own kin; the land is inherited from mother to daughter, and giving birth to daughters is greeted more warmly than giving birth to sons. Conditions of matriliny constitute an important background for my argument: that mainstream assumptions regarding male/female power relationships as mediated through sex and food need to be re-thought.[1]

Female power?

My thinking about female power in the context of gender is inspired by the writings of Ifi Amadiume (1987, 1997) and Oyèrónké Oyewùmí (1997, 2002). In different ways Amadiume and Oyewùmí both destabilize the mainstream idea of a 'woman'. In mainstream feminist thinking the notion of 'woman' is inscribed in a binary opposition to 'man'. This concept does not work well in

---

[1] My focus is on male/female power relationships as mediated through sex and food, and on ways in which sex and food may be symbolically connected (cf. Dover 2005), not on erotic values or implications of food and cooking – even if these aspects are also very interesting.

African contexts where, according to Amadiume, a more flexible concept of gender is needed in order to capture situations where certain social positions may be gendered, but where these positions may be taken up by a man or a woman as the case may be (Amadiune 1987, 17). Oyewùmí makes a similar point when she argues that the concept of woman is not – or at least *was* not, in precolonial days – applicable in her native Yorubaland. 'I came to realize,' she says, 'that the fundamental category "woman" – which is foundational in Western gender discourses – simply did not exist in Yorùbáland' (Oyewùmí 1997, ix). According to her analysis, the whole idea of male dominance and female subordination is embedded in the concept of 'woman' (ibid., xii). This idea, she says, does not make sense in Yorubaland: biological women are not a priori subordinated to biological men, hierarchy depends on social relations and positions.

Certain social positions carry more power than others and, depending on the context, these positions may be occupied by biological men or biological women. A 'wife' is not always a woman; a 'king' is not always a man (ibid., 29). Some positions are female, even when occupied by a biological male and vice versa. The phenomenon of a 'female husband' (Amadiume 1987; Chacha 2004) is an example of this: by marrying another woman, a woman may put herself in a male position. The woman-woman marriage is about power and offspring: the children of the wife, biologically fathered by an anonymous man, will be counted socially as children of the male wife (or of her late husband). Whether or not the woman-woman marriage also provides possibilities for greater flexibility in sexual relations is another issue (see Blackwood and Wieringa 1999; Ampofo et al. 2004; Wieringa 2005).

Along these lines of thinking it is perfectly possible to subscribe to flexible and situational notions of gender, while at the same time talking of female and/or male positions, and of positions of power as linked to certain capacities. Some positions linked to certain capacities in Makhuwa society are ungendered. For example the word for healer/diviner, *kulukana*, is ungendered, indicating that this position may be filled by a man or a woman. Other positions are gendered. Somebody who is an expert on food and sex occupies a female position. Generally such a person is a biological woman, but occasionally it may be a man. Men who practise cooking will know all along that they are guest-performing in a female domain unless, of course, we talk about wage work, in which case the whole register of values and expectations will change.

My concern in this chapter is to explore the extent to which Makhuwa expertise in food and sex are defined as female gendered positions, and also to show how capacities in these domains go beyond conventional Western divisions of 'public' and 'private' spheres. Exactly because of the conventional division of public and private spheres, to talk of cooking as a female domain of expertise is uncontroversial in a Western context. Located in the private sphere, it is also an activity to which little power is credited. To talk of sex as a female domain of expertise and autonomy is much more controversial. Part of the package of male dominance/female subordination, which is often taken for granted in Western contexts, is the sexual subordination of women: woman as 'other', as sexual object for man as the subject. This notion is embedded in Christianity where the (sexual) initiative of Eve in the Garden of Eden is regarded as primordial sin. The Christian/Western idea of female (sexual) subordination has been read into the positions of women elsewhere, including in Africa, where women have been/are perceived as subordinated and subdued, sexually and otherwise. Also, Islam nurtures notions of female subordination (see e.g. Mernissi 1991).

When I first came to Mozambique in the early 1980s, I was told that married women could show no sexual initiative, having to heed the beck and call of the man/their husband. Later investigations have shown me that this is not necessarily the case. Realities are often more multi-faceted and complex. Mozambique has been influenced by Christianity and/or Islam and some 55 per cent and 17 per cent of the population respectively, according to the 1997 census, count themselves as Christians in one way or another, or Muslims (Instituto Nacional de Estatística 1999). Most women have adopted religious rulings in terms of male dominance and female subordination, sexually and otherwise. Nevertheless, 'obeying your husband' may also be a pretext for doing what you like, as illustrated in the story of the *União Baptista* wedding below.

On Makhuwa matriliny: The matriclan (*nihimo*)

In Makhuwa contexts descent is counted along the female line. A person belongs to the *nihimo* of her or his mother. Nihimo is not just a family, and not just a family name. Nihimo is a unit of belonging, reaching far beyond the visible world. 'The nihimo reaches from the beginning of human beings including the ones who are yet to come' as it was explained to me in Ribáuè. 'To possess the substance of the nihimo is the same as being possessed by it, considered that each single human being is just a temporary embodiment of this substance', as Soares de Castro (1960, 55) put it. To be of a certain nihimo is to be of a certain kind. The nihimo is exogamous. Young women have to go outside their own nihimo in order to find fathers for their children. The children belong to their mothers' nihimo. As said in a group interview with men in Ribáuè in 2003: 'We men support the families of the women.' The matriclans of the men are supported by men from elsewhere, fathering the children of their sisters.

The substance of a person comes from the nihimo and returns to it after death (de Castro1960). The nihimo is a spiritual and esoteric entity, and it is transmitted through women only. Often a nihimo is vast and dispersed (Macaire 1996), but its members will recognize each other by the same family name. A nihimo is subdivided into a number of lineages; certain lineages inhabit certain lands, and like the nihimo the land is transmitted through women.

> Only women know the magical techniques of sowing and harvesting, the secrets of cooking and the production of beer and alcohol, as well as the ways to make the clay pots and vessels in which food and beverages are produced and served. Since the women do not move away from the village where they were born, they keep intact the language as well as the tradition, being in permanent contact with the dead of the nihimo, who are buried in the same village. (de Castro 1960, 57)

Makhuwa society is basically matrilocal, meaning that a woman stays in her own village, among her own folks, while at marriage the young man arrives as a stranger to the village. A Makhuwa proverb runs like this: 'It is not the watermelon that searches for the wild pig; it is the wild pig that goes to find the water melon' (de Matos 1982, 136). The girls are the watermelons staying put where they are. The young men are the wild pigs roaming.

In two group interviews in Ribáuè in 2003, of men and women respectively, the vast majority indicated that the land that they cultivated belonged to the wife's lineage. The wife had achieved the land from her mother, who had it from her mother and so on: 'land follows the blood of the mother'. In the context of subsistence agriculture land and food are obviously connected. It is the task of the mothers and grandmothers to feed the offspring, and in order to do so they need the land. 'You who are women, you will get children. Here is your land', as said by a Ribáuè mother to her daughters (interview with daughter in 1999). Like the land, food is a holy entity, and the nihimo is behind it all.

The central position of women in Makhuwa culture is connected to the matriclan, and to the whole issue of descent following female lines. The womb of the mother – *erukulu* – is also the name for the closest kinship relation between 'children of the same womb' (Martinez 1989). In Luapula province, in neighbouring Zambia, according to Karla Poewe (based on work in the 1970s) womb – *ifumu* – not only indicates wombmates and matrilineal descent group; it has also larger connotations of social universe, life and abundance:

> Infused with spiritual and natural power ... ifumu guarantees the reproduction of the Luapula social order. Ifumu here stands for the Luapula universe, which is seen by Luapulans as unbounded, filled with an abundance of critical resources (especially land) to which everyone has access. (Poewe, 1981)

The *erukulu* is the nodal point and the link between the living, the dead and the as yet unborn members of the nihimo. Presumably for this reason women are considered the ones who are in the best positions to communicate with the ancestors. When in the Ribáuè area there is a need to make a ceremony for calling rain, or some other community ceremony, the *pwiyamwene* must be there to pour *makeya*. *Makeya* is the name for finely ground flour of *mapira* (millet) when used in a ceremonial context. The pwiyamwene is the 'female chief', the woman responsible for matters related to the invisible world, but also on other issues she will be consulted as the counterpart to the male chief, the *mwene*. The mwene and the pwiyamwene belong to the same nihimo, thus they are related as sister/brother, or (grand)mother/(grand)son, never as wife/husband.

The mapwiyamwene are clear examples of the kind of female authority which 'modern' systems of governance do not accommodate. Also the mamwene, the male chiefs, have links to spirits and ancestors and to systems of belief beyond the modern world. Being men, however, they more easily fit into modern systems of 'decentralization'. Due to the androcentric structure of modern society, the mapwiyamwene are not adaptable in this way; they must be either demonized or neglected. Evidence of Western demonization of female power in Africa is plentiful (see e.g. McClintock 1995). In Mozambique the mapwiyamwene have remained unseen.

A major task of the mapwiyamwene is to pour makeye whenever needed. To pour makeya is to call the attention of the ancestors. 'Makeya is our pencil' as it was put in a group discussion in Ribáuè in 2003. When you want to communicate with the government you take a pencil and write a letter. When you want to communicate with the ancestors, you pour makeya.

On food: Beer-brewing, cooking and control of food

It is not by accident that the 'pencil' for communicating with the ancestors is flour, i.e. food. Makeya is a very particular form of food, quintessential food, produced from the central crop (mapira), which also provides the essential yeast (miropo) for the brewing of otheka. Food and drink have a touch of the holy, particularly in ceremonial contexts (parallels exist with the Christian communion) and the ceremonial drink in Ribáuè is otheka. For any ceremony or celebration otheka is an essential. Otheka is also brewed and served on the occasion of olimiha: mutual help work-parties, when people are invited to give a day's work in return for an afternoon and evening of socializing around the pots of beer. As pointed out by Audrey Richards, writing about Bemba people of northern Zambia, millet beer (in Ribáuè fortified by cassava) is important for nutrition, but is also more than mere food. Beer is 'the common, and sometimes the essential way of fulfilling social obligations. Beer is the present of honour between kinsmen ... Without it tribal councils cannot be held, and marriage or initiation ceremonies do not take place' (Richards 1939/1995, 77). This description holds true also for Ribáuè.

The production of otheka takes several days, and the work is undertaken by women only. Otheka brewing is a delicate affair, depending on skill and knowledge. For production of the miropo and for monitoring the fermenting process, skills are needed that are only acquired through long years of training and experience. Only women have and transmit this knowledge. Otheka is always made in large quantities, often 200 litres at a time. This means lots of work for the women – collecting water and firewood. During the production of otheka there will be no time for women to work in the fields.

Cooking in general is a female capacity and domain. In a Western context this seems a trivial statement and may be equated with the burdensome household chores of a Western 'housewife'. In a society like the one in Ribáuè, fundamentally based on subsistence production and only marginally involved in circuits of cash crops and money, cooking and distribution of food has a different status. Food is a female domain and a basis for female authority. Men and women are both involved in the production (work in the fields), but at harvest time the products from the field are stored in the granaries of the older women, the grandmothers. They are the ones who control the granaries, deciding what to take out, when and for what purpose. A man, who wants to control the granary of his wife, gets a nickname, which is translated to avarento in Portuguese: the one who wants to have it all for himself[2] – as opposed to the women who are supposed to administer the granary for the benefits of all. Richards has a detailed description, from her fieldwork in the 1930s, of the female skill of assessing how much grain is left in the granary, and thus how much can be taken out on each particular occasion, still making sure that the granary will not be empty before the new harvest comes in (Richards

---

[2] Compare the derogatory term wakwaukanga in Shimakonde: 'those who eat alone' (West, 2005, 37).

1939/1995, 89). She cites a Bemba saying: 'Only old women know how to look after the food' (ibid., 88). This may be part of the rationale for the central position of grandmothers, which is a characteristic also of Makhuwa society. The young man, who marries into the family, must work in the fields of his mother(s)-in-law, the produce being stored in the granary of the grandmother. All of the men that I interviewed in Ribáuè (20 men aged 40 years and over), claimed to have worked for their in-laws when newly married. This was (in their opinion) how things ought to be. 'It is only today the youngsters don't want to do this work', they said, complaining that neither they nor their wives received the support from their sons-in-law to which they felt entitled.

It is a source of pride and satisfaction for an elderly woman in Ribáuè district to live with her daughters and their families around her, and to feed her grandchildren. The road to this status has been long. As a young woman, even as a married woman, you do not get your own granary right away. The food is controlled, cooked and distributed by the older women. Control of food is power, but is also an obligation to generosity. Richards has long descriptions of how mothers-in-law, commanding the labour of their sons-in-law, also consider it a matter of prestige to feed them well. Cooking is a privilege and a source of pride, also for the young wife, according to Richards: 'I noticed that young girls, recently betrothed, would intimate this fact by saying shyly: "I have begun to cook for him,"' (ibid., 129).

Christian Geffray, in his analysis of the circuits of work and food in Makhuwa contexts, makes the observation (with a touch of resentment on behalf of the young men) that the work of the sons-in-law becomes invisible: 'Every morning the young man gets up before sunrise and waits outside the hut of his 'father-in-law', hoe in hand, in a posture showing his humility, availability, his willingness to work and on the whole his wish to behave well' (Geffray 1990, 44). In addition to field work, the young son-in-law is expected to give his mother-in-law a hand with the housework, and if he 'refuses to fetch water, firewood, and to perform other domestic tasks, if he doesn't work well in the field, if he is lazy, if he doesn't respond willingly and nicely when he is summoned to work by his sisters-in-law – tensions and conflict are bound to emerge' (ibid., 46). If, however, the young man survives the trials, eventually he will be allowed to build a house for himself and his wife, and with time the household will even get the right to cultivate its own piece of land and store the produce in its own granary. For the first years the young man and the young woman both work on the fields of the older generation, and the product is stored in the mothers' granaries, or in the granary of the senior great grandmother. From here it is redistributed to the children and grand-children. Geffray describes how children more frequently eat with their grandmother or in some other house of the compound than with their own mother: 'The children are essentially fed from the produce which has been accumulated in the granaries of the older generation, largely the fruit of the work of the young men of the domestic group, the ones which are the biological fathers of the children' (ibid., 55).

Thus the social image of the grandmother is maintained as the one who feeds the children: the young men (the biological fathers) do the work, but the mother-in-law gets the credit. 'Entering the granary [of the senior great grandmother] the grain is no more the fruit of the work of the men; it becomes a good to be shared by all, but entrusted to the wisdom and discretion of the women' (ibid., 61). In this way, the work of the young men becomes invisible. The irony is produced by the fact that in modern contexts, what is usually turned invisible (by private/public divisions and by the market economy) is *women's* work. In the 'traditional', now disappearing, matrilineal set-up where sons-in-law work for their parents-in-law (so-called bride service), it is indeed the young *men's* work, which becomes invisible.

On sex: Men as genitors, women as seducers

Not only are the young men in a Makhuwa household assumed to work hard, they are also assumed to perform well as procreators. The young men provide the necessary input, the old women reap the benefits in terms of food and grand-children. Young men have to perform sexually, and there are stories from the old days about the quality of their semen which was tested by old women (Chapters 2 and 3; see also Dover 2005). The old women are once again in control. They educate young women to attract and ensnare young men. Where the men are progenitors, in Geffray's analysis, the young women are seducers. Young women are expected to be proficient in the erotic arts (they are tested in this discipline during the initiation rituals) and in return for their role as progeni-tors the young men 'at least have the right of expecting their wives to seduce them and to give them sexual pleasure' (Geffray 1990, 129). It is my impression that sexual proficiency is considered a pride and a privilege by women. Young women are instructed in the art of lovemaking during the initiation rituals, but like other areas of women's arts, the learning process starts well before puberty. In parts of northern Mozambique, in bygone days, pre-puberty sexual relations between girls and boys were accepted and it was even believed that intercourse and caressing was important in making the girl's breasts grow and for menstru-ation to emerge. Also well before puberty the girls would be instructed regarding how to pull the labia minora of the vagina in order to make them longer. This pulling of labia (*ithuna*) was – and still is – considered an important aspect of a young girls' preparation for lovemaking, and for giving and receiving sexual pleasure. Sylvia Tamale provides similar evidence from her investigations in Kampala. Tamale found the practice of labia-elongation anything but dead in the capital of Uganda; her findings reveal it to be alive and thriving in the urban and peri-urban areas around Kampala. Tamale's findings also show the prac-tice of elongation to be perceived as enhancing the erotic experience of both the male and the female: 'This practice, encoded within the *Ssenga* institution, has enhanced sexual pleasure for women and expanded their perceptions of themselves as active sexual beings,' Tamale asserts (2005b, 12).

Seniority and women's arts: Old women run the show

From my early work in Mozambique in the 1980s, I formed the impression that men were not always and everywhere potent (Arnfred 1988) in the way that men (and women) generally in my own cultural environment expect men to be. In Mozambique male impotence seems to be a well-known phenomenon to which women respond with the art of seduction. Christian Geffray's notion of Makhuwa women as seducers fits well into my general impression of Makhuwa women as not only sexually active, but also sexually competent and capable, well educated in sexual arts. Young women have been trained in cooking, and they have been trained in sex; they express themselves in cooking as well as in sex. Cooking is a necessity – vegetables, cereals, meat have to be cooked in order to be turned into food. But cooking is also an art; you can perform it well, or less well. Performing it exquisitely is a source of pride for a woman. Sex (with a man) is also a necessary function as well as an art. Doing it well is likewise a source of pride for a woman. Women show their pleasure and gratitude to their husband by cooking for him and by inviting him to have sex. In Makhuwa society there are particular ritualized ways for a woman to invite a man for sex. Conversely to refuse to cook and to refuse sex are women's weapons when they are dissatisfied with their husbands. I have always been fascinated by the tales of women's warfare in Nigeria and Cameroon, where by the sheer fact of lifting their skirts and showing their genitalia women would curse and scare men into obedience (Ardener, 1975, 1987). I have never come across similar tales in Mozambique, but they tally well with my impression of sex as female power.

In matrilineal contexts the sexual capacities of the young women are important assets, and are treated as such. In Karla Poewe's phrasing it is the duty of the young women through their sexual powers 'to engulf male strangers and convert them into kin' (1981, 68). This sexual activity is geared towards procreation, but not necessarily exclusively towards a single partner. According to Poewe among the Luapulans 'ties of intimate dependency between spouses are discouraged in many more or less subtle ways. While sexual enjoyment is valued, it is not limited to one specific partner' (ibid., 56). Mating is a question of getting new blood and new children into the lineage; it is not a question of founding new families. 'A man's 'marital' role is to sexually satisfy and impregnate the woman and to provide for her during her pregnancy. The man should not, in any way, be an object of exclusive emotional investment nor the focus of attention. Instead women are socialized to invest their emotions and material wealth in their respective matrilineage' (ibid., 67). Similarly in Nampula province the girls are instructed that *os homens é não só um* – the men are more than one. Valente de Matos, a Portuguese Catholic priest who worked in Nampula province in the 1950s and 1960s relates the following (with some apprehension) in his account of the female initiation rituals:

> The women have to give impression in talk and gesture of being shy and modest women, especially when confronted with other men, so that nobody, and least of all their own husband, should consider them women of bad reputation. Afterwards, in a low voice and taking advantage of some distraction on the part of the men present, the old woman in charge of the ritual of initiation will add that, provided they take the proper precautions, they may arrange a secret lover. (de Matos 1968, 12)

Interviewing in Ribáuè, Nampula province, from the late 1990s onwards my impression of women as masters of sexuality has only been confirmed. I have witnessed several events of women's sexualities enacted in ways totally alien to previous experience from my own culture. At a certain point (in 2005) I was conducting a group interview with elderly women – elite women of the village, in fact. There were two *mapwyiamwene*, several *anamalaka* (counsellors of initiation rituals) and *makulukana* (healers/diviners), all women. We talked about issues of land and labour, household composition, granaries and so on. When I started asking questions about initiation rituals the atmosphere of the discussion immediately changed. It was as if they had been looking forward to this moment. Some of the anamalaka had brought *chocalhos* (rattling instruments of a type used during female initiation and by certain makulukana). They started playing and chanting and before long they were performing central scenes from the rituals and dancing erotic and explicitly sexual dances while having a lot of fun. Being in the midst of this, surrounded by these old women behaving in ways that Catholic priests and colonial administrators would certainly have found most obscene, I thought of older women of my acquaintance back in Denmark and I could not possibly imagine them behaving anything like this. But here, in Ribáuè, sexuality was obviously an area where these women not only felt at home and at ease but experienced power and joy.

Woman–woman fun and games

Young Makhuwa women are instructed and trained in the art of lovemaking. The point of this training – seen from the old women's positions – is 'to engulf male strangers and convert them into kin' (Poewe 1981, 68). But sex is also, at the same time, a source of joy and pleasure for the women, young and old. Like food, sex is important as a means of survival (of the lineage), but like good food, good sex is also a source of pleasure and enjoyment. Sex-as-survival (that is, for procreation) is obviously heterosex, sex-as-enjoyment not necessarily so. I will readily agree with Marc Epprecht's statement that 'the homosexuality/ heterosexuality dichotomy is a false one' (Epprecht 2004, 11). This also links to insights provided by Stephen Murray and Will Roscoe in their collection of documentation regarding same-sex practices from all parts of Africa. They point to a remarkably different social code, compared to social codes espoused by Christianity and Islam: 'This social code does not require that an individual suppresses same-sex desires or behaviour, but that she or he never allows such desires to overshadow or supplant procreation' (Murray and Roscoe 1998, 273).

In general it seems as if Judith Butler-type notions of identities as fluid and performative rather than fixed and stable would provide a fruitful entry point for understanding phenomena of same-sex in Africa. Butler's concepts are developed in a polemical discussion with mainstream feminist notions of male/female binaries and notions of male domination/ female subordination as given points of departure. It is interesting to see, how on the one hand Judith Butler and on the other hand Ifi Amadiume and Oyèrónké Oyewùmí, from very different starting points arrive at similar points of critique of mainstream feminist thinking. According to Butler:

> Gender ought not to be construed as a stable identity or locus of agency from which various acts follow ... That gender reality is created through sustained social performances means that the very notions of an essential sex and a true or abiding

masculinity or femininity are also constituted as part of the strategy that conceals gender's performative character and the performative possibilities for proliferating gender configurations outside the restricting frames of masculinist domination and compulsory heterosexuality. (Butler 1990, 178–80)

Certainly in Africa same-sex behaviours and desires are in general not usefully studied as identities, but rather as practices or performance. Often, same-sex erotic play seems to be something in which you may indulge in certain contexts, on certain occasions. Female initiation rituals seem to be privileged spaces for such indulgence. This does not involve the initiates, who sit solemnly in a corner with motionless faces and downcast eyes. All the other women assembled for the occasion have a great time, however.

During my stays in Ribáuè I was present at several celebrations of female initiation rituals. The one described in the following was the 'wildest' one. It was not even a formal initiation ritual, but 'just' the counseling of a Protestant minister's daughter on the eve of her wedding day. The father of the young bride was an important man in the local branch of *União Baptista* (the Baptist Union). União Baptista has roots in an old mission church, at the puritanical end of Protestant churches: No alcohol, no tobacco, no drumming and dancing, no participation in traditional ceremonies, no *missangas* (glass bead belts worn by women, a highly erotic device), no body tattoos (highly erotic as well), no *ithuna* (elongated labia), no initiation rituals. Nevertheless, a 'counseling' session was held on the eve of the wedding. Between 30 and 40 women were gathered in a fairly small room, lit only by a candle. One of the women said a prayer, a psalm was sung. The women who led the song had to keep the psalm book quite close to the candle in order to be able to read the text. Once the psalm was finished, the women initiated another song. While the psalm-singing had floundered, the new song was lustily sung by all the women. They obviously knew the song very well. It had a very characteristic rhythm. The women clapped for lack of a drum (prohibited in the Baptist church) but soon a metal bucket was produced from somewhere. The bucket was turned upside-down and served as a drum all through the night. One inciting song followed another. Each song had a different rhythm and melody, and its own dance. The women danced wildly, lifting their skirts, showing their bare bottoms. All of the dances were of the hip-undulating kind. You learn this movement as a little girl, and your proficiency is checked during the initiation rituals. At a certain point a characteristically different rhythm-and-tune was initiated and two women entered the circle, starting to strip while still dancing. Before long they had done away with all their clothing and were dancing naked, grabbing each other with sexual movements, pretending intercourse from the front, from the back, while still dancing. In these dances only two women are dancing at any one time, the others are singing, clapping. Some of the couples roll around on the floor together, naked. All want to join the dance, all push for getting their turn at the dance floor. The bucket is never silent, intensely beating the rhythm. The room is dark, lit only by a few candles. The atmosphere is agitated, very erotic indeed, but also one of fun and games. As the women undress their brightly coloured missanga belts become visible, as do the body tattoos on their breasts, thighs and bellies. I am later told that the point of these dances is to instruct the initiate regarding love-making movements. Surely, however, the instructors are also enjoying themselves. The dancing continues throughout the night, only finishing when the grey light of the morning creeps into the room.

While this was taking place the men had been with the groom in a different house (groom and bride are both very young, less than 20 years). When the men arrive, about 6 o'clock in the morning, the women are dressed in their usual *capulanas*, sitting quietly and subdued along the walls of the house or outside in the courtyard. There is no indication of what had transpired during the night.

All of the women belonged to União Baptista, which prohibits dancing and drumming, and where female sexuality is only recognized as a means of procreation. The next day in church the pastor read Paul's letter to the people of Ephesus, the (in)famous letter admonishing women to be obedient to their husbands. When later I conducted a meeting with these same women, I tried to understand how these members of a strict Christian church were still able to dance as they did that night. 'It is important to adhere to the prohibitions,' the women said, 'no ithuna, no missangas etc. But if your husband wants you to do it nevertheless, then of course it is a different matter. A woman should be obedient to her husband, you know'. I suddenly saw how this talk of female sexuality in order to please the man came about. This is the word of the Church, and the women use it as an excuse for maintaining their drumming and dancing, and their sexual fun and games. They justify their actions by referring to gospel and, at the same time, conveniently ignore the prohibitory elements of the Church's messages.

Conclusion

Women and men in Africa – and certainly women and men in Ribáuè – live in many worlds. One of these worlds is ruled by the Christian proscriptions regarding female sexual subordination, modesty and morality. Yet it co-exists with a world where sex and cooking are female spheres of autonomy and potential power. Sylvia Tamale's findings, to which I refer in the introduction to this chapter, show a certain ambivalence towards the *Ssenga* tradition and its reception by young women in modern urban settings, where these different worlds converge and combine. By highlighting what I consider to be remarkable strongholds of female gender power in a not particularly 'developed' and certainly not urbanized part of northern Mozambique, I want to suggest that modern African women in their current quest for more autonomous sexual lives may find inspiration and support in certain aspects of African 'tradition'.

14 Tufo Dancing
*Muslim Women's Culture
in Northern Mozambique*   (1999)

'Estrela Vermelha', Ilha de Moçambique

It is afternoon in one of the densely populated *bairros* in Mozambique Island. A group of women gather on the veranda of a small red house in one of the sandy streets, not far from the sea. It is early April, the air is still warm, but not unbearably hot. There seems to be no fixed time for the meeting; some women pass by, others come and go, some settle down in the shade of the veranda. One woman is braiding another's hair. After a while, ten or twelve women have assembled. They move inside, and rehearsals can begin. Inside there is one big room with benches along two walls and no other furniture. The women sit down on the floor learning the words and the music of a new song for their performance on April 7 for the celebration of the Mozambican Women's Day. This year the words of the song have been written by the group's 'poet' who is one of the group's four male drum beaters. The words are written in a cheap exercise book, the kind children use in school. The characters are Arabic but the language is Emakhuwa. Some of the women have never gone to school, but most have attended the Islamic *madrasa* (the Quranic school) and thus they are more familiar with Arabic than with Latin letters. They rehearse the words along with the music, one verse after the other. Later they rehearse the choreography for the dancing. When I ask who invents the music and creates the dancing, the women say they do it themselves, collectively. Sometimes it is also one of the women who writes the words of the song.

The women are members of the group 'Estrela Vermelha' of Ilha de Moçambique. 'Estrela Vermelha' – Red Star – is one of the most famous women's dance groups of northern Mozambique. Their favourite dance is Tufo. Tufo used to be a religious dance, praising the prophet Muhammad in music and words. It used to be danced by men as well as by women – always in separate groups, never together. Nowadays men only dance the Tufo at special festive occasions linked to religious celebrations. For the women, Tufo has changed a lot in both choreography and in the song lyrics. In classical Tufo the women dance while kneeling, wringing their shoulders and arms, and bending the upper part of their bodies this way and that. That style of Tufo is still popular, but it is no longer the only one. Nowadays, the women often dance standing and moving about, gesticulating according to the content of the song. The rhythm of the four flat drums or tambourines, which now as before accompany the Tufo singing and dancing, has grown more hectic. Also the words of the songs have changed. Religious songs are still part of the repertoire, but many songs take up a variety of contemporary themes, some of them commenting upon particular political issues. 'The Tufo songs have more political impact than the speech of some government minister,' one group member said.[1]

All of this is intriguing, but most interesting of all is the fact that the women's Tufo groups are an expanding culture; new groups are mushrooming all along the coast and as far inland as Nampula city, the largest provincial capital in the north. The coastal culture is Islamic, and Nampula city itself has a sizeable Muslim population. In the 1990s, however, Tufo dancing was spreading even further inland, and Tufo groups were emerging in cultural contexts that were not Muslim at all.

[1] Where informants appear in the text, I have changed their names.

A whole series of questions is raised by this course of events. What explains the remarkable popularity of Tufo groups among women? What kind of support and reassurance do women obtain from Tufo group membership? Do women use the Tufo groups to defend and expand their space of manoeuvre at a time when male/female power relations otherwise tend to change in favour of men?

This chapter examines Tufo dancing from the point of view of the women involved, and in the socio-cultural contexts of Mozambican versions of Sufi Islam, of Makhuwa matriliny and of Swahili coastal culture. My motivation for conducting the study on which this chapter is based dates back to the early 1980s when I lived in Mozambique, working as a sociologist in the national women's organization, the OMM *(Organização da Mulher Moçambicana)*. I was intrigued by the co-existence in coastal northern Mozambique of matrilineal Makhuwa culture with patriarchal Islam, especially because it appeared that the women had succeeded in transferring aspects of their central position in the Makhuwa context to the Islamic setting. A study of the Tufo groups seemed to be a good vantage point for understanding how this cultural mix of matriliny and Islam worked out from the women's points of view. Due to the Frelimo/Renamo war which made northern Mozambique a no-go area for more than a decade, I was unable to return to Nampula province until the late 1990s.

The fieldwork eventually was conducted in Ilha de Moçambique (Mozambique Island), and in Angoche between November 1998 and May 1999. Ilha de Moçambique and Angoche are both old coastal towns, dating back to the first arrival of the Arabs before the tenth century AD. Ilha de Moçambique was taken over by the Portuguese quite early on, and until 1898 it was the capital of colonial Mozambique. Angoche was held by sultans of Arab origin, linked to local Makhuwa chiefs by kinship ties, only definitively conquered by the Portuguese in 1913 (Machado 1970, Bonate 2003). Ilha de Moçambique as well as Angoche may be considered outposts of Swahili culture, even if the Swahili language is not spoken there. The Tufo groups in those two places are very similar, but the Islamic contexts differ. As has been noted regarding Swahili settlements further up on the East African coast, the version and character of Islam differ from one place to the next (Trimingham 1964). Thus, for the sake of simplicity in this paper I shall discuss the Tufo groups only in the setting of Ilha de Moçambique.

Ilha de Moçambique is a tiny island off the coast of Mozambique, precisely at the place where the Madagascar Channel is narrowest. The town, which covers the entire island, has two distinct sections. One half is the stone-built town, which is the old Portuguese part, and the other half is the *macuti*-town, which is the Mozambican part of wattle and daub constructed houses (*macuti* is the name of the palm leaves used for thatching). There is no space at all for fields or for gardens. The island is connected to the continent by a wooden bridge almost four kilometers long. Some women have fields on the mainland, and cross the bridge by foot every day. *Dhows*[2] come over from nearby Cabaçeira (a peninsula on the mainland) selling food and vegetables to the Islanders.

The chapter is composed as follows: I will first explain about the Tufo dance itself, how the dance is performed, what the music is like, and the ways the

[2] Arab type small boats with large sails. A beautiful sight when they are approaching the Island. When there is no wind the sailors use the oars, singing to keep the rhythm.

women dress for the dancing. I will also relate the oral tradition regarding the history of the dance. The main focus of the paper is the Tufo dance group women, but first I will investigate the dance groups as organizational structures in the context of Islamic life in northern Mozambique. I will look at these issues in two parts. First I will look at the Islamic context itself, with an eye to the ways in which organizational characteristics of Makhuwa matriliny are reflected in the organization of the Sufi *tariqas*,[3] called *confrarias* (brotherhoods) in Mozambique, which dominate religious life on the Island. Second I will focus on the ways in which certain organizational characteristics of the tariqas/confrarias are paralleled or repeated in the organizational structure of the Tufo groups. The point is to show how Makhuwa matrilineal organization has influenced the organization of the Sufi orders, and how the organizational structure of the confrarias has provided a model for the Tufo groups. The organizational culture of the Tufo groups must, however, also be seen in the context of other dance and music groups on the Swahili coast, which I will cover in the following section. I will then discuss Tufo dancing as seen from the point of view of the women, answering some of the questions posed in the opening section of the paper. Finally I will present the contents of some Tufo songs, and discuss how the Tufo groups have responded to political changes in Mozambique, and how they continue to do so. Tufo culture is very rich, and much more could be written about it. This chapter is just an opening of the field.

The dance, dress and music of Tufo

For the performance of the Tufo dance the women, generally fifteen to twenty at any one time, will form a block of three or four rows with four to five dancers in each row. The leading dancers are placed in the front row, but in most cases all dancers perform the same movements. A characteristic of Tufo is the seated dancing (Photo 14.2); the ability of the women to rise up from and return down into this position during the dance is amazing. In the seated version most of the dancing is performed with the upper part of the body, with shoulders, arms and hands, but in recent years newer forms of dancing have been invented, where the women not only stand, but also move about, breaking up the standard formation of three to four rows. The group 'Estrela Vermelha' considers itself to be avant-garde in terms of inventing and introducing new choreographic styles. One mode of invention is a more expressive dancing which mimics the meaning of the song. One case in point is a song about the horrors of the recent war and the joy of peace when it ended. The gesticulation and the movements of the dancers, who pantomime crying and rejoicing, reveal the content of the song even to those who do not understand the words. 'Estrela Vermelha', like the other Tufo groups, sings most frequently in Emakhuwa, but also at times in Arabic and Portuguese.

The dancing women are all dressed alike, in similar capulanas[4] and scarves,

---

[3] Tariqa means way or path. The Arabic plural of *tariqa* is *turuque*. I will use the English plural: tariqas.

[4] A capulana is a brightly coloured piece of printed cotton cloth (1.00 by 1.85 meters) central to the female culture of the coast. Here capulanas are usually sold in pairs, one to be used as a skirt and (part of) the other as a scarf.

14.1 Tufo dancing in Ilha de Moçambique. Note the flat Tufo drums and the male players.
(Photo © Armando Alves/José Cardoso)

14.2 Seated Tufo dancing.
(Photo © Armando Alves/José Cardoso)

and in blouses of a matching colour. This uniform way of dressing is an essential aspect of Tufo. Each Tufo dance group has its own set of colours. For 'Estrela Vermelha' they are yellow and red: Yellow blouses and red/yellow capulanas for skirts. The colours of other major Tufo groups are as follows: 'Forte Amizade': Red/yellow (red blouse), 'Beira Mar': Black/white; 'Fura Redes': Green/white; 'Ausuafi Sanía': Blue/white; 'Anuar Lihassanate': Yellow/red. Even if the Tufo dance is not as religious as it used to be, the blouses must have sleeves, and the women must wear scarves. The blouses may be re-used from one performance to the next, but the norms for capulanas are more demanding. Each performance has its own capulana, and sometimes more than one. If for example the group is going to dance at a wedding in Nampula city, every member must have a minimum of three new capulanas; one for the journey going there, another one for the performance during the evening, and yet another one for the return trip. Some groups claim that no less than five different capulanas would be needed for such a trip.

In the late 1990s capulanas were plentiful in Ilha de Moçambique. It was different in the period after Independence and during the war, when there was a painful shortage of capulanas. But by the 1990s the only worry was the price. A pair of capulanas was not much more than 2 or 3 USD (30,000 – 40,000 meticais), but in an economy where few have any income at all, even such a small amount is prohibitive. Most capulanas are imported from India in designs commissioned by Indian traders in Mozambique, who know their customers and their preferences. Almost every week capulanas in new designs arrive at Mozambique Island from Nacala, the large international port of the north. When new capulanas arrive, the member of the Tufo group assigned to this task will keep an eye out, and when she catches sight of a beautiful one in the appropriate colours, she will place an order with the trader for the number of capulanas which the group will need.

The whole business of the dance group capulanas is part of a competitive culture well known on the Swahili coast (Ranger 1975, Strobel 1976, 1979, Fair 1997, 2001). In Ilha de Moçambique for national celebrations like April 7 and May 1, the Tufo groups will prepare new songs, new dances, and new capulanas, sometimes with whole new outfits including blouses especially sewn to fit the new capulanas. Before such an occasion, the groups are very secretive, as nothing must get out regarding plans for their shows on those days.

The name Tufo is said to derive from the Arabic name: *ad-duff* for the tambourine-like drums which are used in Tufo. In Portuguese this word became *adufe* or *adufo* thus Tufo (Lutero & Pereira 1980, 19). There are four flat, tambourine-shaped drums of different sizes, usually played by young men, though women may also be drum beaters. According to one of the few available texts on Tufo dance and music, the two larger drums play a rhythm which is well known from Arabic music, whereas the two smaller ones supply the Bantu rhythmic touch (ibid., 23–24). Often the rhythm will increase in the course of the dance, becoming quite hectic towards the end. All the women dancers sing, but one or two have the principal voices. Sometimes one voice will start a tune and others will join in, or two will sing to each other in a duet while the others make up the chorus. Even to the untrained ear, the music has a significant Arabic feel.

According to the legend told in Ilha de Moçambique, the history of the Tufo dance goes back to the Prophet's move from Mecca to Medina:

> When the Prophet saw himself obliged to flee from Mecca to Medina, his followers – men and women – welcomed him to Medina with tambourines and songs, showing him thus the joy that they felt and their devotion to the doctrines of the Quran that he had attempted to preach in Mecca. As the Prophet had favourably received the songs accompanied by tambourines, and as the songs invoked the name of Allah praising and exalting his Prophet, they were kept for the time to come, appearing from that day onwards in feasts and celebrations, whenever the respective groups professing the songs were called.(Carvalho1969, unpublished manuscript, quoted in Lutero & Pereira ibid., 19)

The dance of Tufo is said to have arrived to Ilha around 1932–33, brought to the island by a certain Yussuf, a tradesman from Kilwa who used to stay in Ilha for extended periods and who as late as the 1970s was said to pass by now and then (ibid., 20). The timing of the arrival of Tufo to the Ilha corresponds to what I was told when interviewing on the Island.

Tufo is an entirely oral culture, so very little is preserved in writing. The songs are written on odd scraps of paper and often lost after use. Discussing this with one of the groups, I was told, 'Oh the old songs are recorded in our heads. This is a better place to have them than in a written archive.' Nevertheless I managed to obtain the words of some songs and have them translated from Emakhuwa to Portuguese. A few of these will appear towards the end of the chapter.

Sufi Islam, Makhuwa edition, 1: Marks of matriliny

According to data collected shortly after Independence, Tufo at that time extended along the northern coast, north to the border with Tanzania and possibly beyond, and south to Quelimane, at the mouth of the Zambeze River (Duarte 1980, 28). Northern Mozambique has been under Muslim influence for centuries. Little is known of the early history of the coast, although Vasco da Gama observed in 1498 that the population was 'of the Mohammedan sect' (Alpers 2000, 304). The Arab merchants and sailors who came from across the sea married daughters of local chiefs (the Makhuwa *mwene*) thus gaining access to land and to kinship affiliation (Alpers 2000, Bonate 2003), making themselves at home. Ilha de Moçambique, Sancul, Quitangonha, Angoche, and Ilha de Ibo are some of the names of these early Arab settlements. Their culture and religion took root in the coastal population, just as it did further north, in what is now Tanzania and Kenya. The Swahili language is only spoken in the northernmost part of coastal Mozambique; further south it is replaced by indigenous languages and by Portuguese. Nevertheless the Islamic coast of northern Mozambique is part of Swahili culture.[5] The Portuguese settled on Ilha de Moçambique in the beginning of the sixteenth century, and the oldest church on the island is built in 1522. Until the late nineteenth century

---

[5] This also conforms to eg Schildknecht's (1969) definition of Swahili culture: 'The Arabs have commingled with the indigenous African population; this mixing brought about what we call ... Swahili culture: by marrying African women a new society was formed in which both African and Arab cultural and religious values were preserved.' (Schildknecht 1969, 230).

Portuguese residents *(moradores)* co-existed relatively peacefully with the Arab traders on the coast. Following the 1885 Berlin conference, however, Portugal felt its influence in south-east Africa threatened by British plans for imperialist expansion, and embarked on more aggressive colonial policies (Bonate ibid.).

The kind of Islam professed on the coast has been influenced decisively by two Sufi orders or tariqas, in the Mozambican context named *Cadiria* and *Xadulia*.[6] Both tariqas arrived in Mozambique Island around the turn of the century. According to oral tradition in Ilha, the Cadiria was brought to Ilha de Moçambique in 1904 by a *xehe*[7] who had studied in the Comoro Islands before going to Zanzibar, from where he was sent to Mozambique. A branch of the Xadulia tariqa called Xadulia Liaxuruti came to Mozambique directly from the Comoro Islands in 1897.[8] It is likely that the decisive rooting of these Sufi orders at Ilha de Moçambique is also linked to the fact that the turn of the century was a period of turmoil on the Mozambican coast. Portuguese colonialism was shifting from a benign presence into aggressive occupation (Bonate 2003). At the same time, the formal abolition of the slave trade made trading conditions more difficult, and Mozambique Island, which had earlier flourished as a port of embarkation, was overshadowed by Angoche and other ports, which were beyond Portuguese control. Also in this period (1898) the capital of what was then called the province of Mozambique (and which is equal to the present nation) was moved from Mozambique Island in the north to Lourenço Marques in the south.

The arrival of the new Sufi orders represented an Islamic revival on Ilha de Moçambique. According to old and knowledgeable people in Ilha, before the arrival of the tariqas, followers of the Muslim faith were not especially devout. According to xehe Amade

> The tariqas developed our religion. It was only through the tariqas we learned how to live as Muslims. And it was only the tariqas that started mobilizing people in the interior of the continent for Islam. When the railway in 1914 reached Monapo, the tariqas had already been there.

In this period Islam expanded inland with Muslim Indian merchants, and with the railway line, the construction of which was started 1913 in Lumbo on the mainland opposite Ilha de Moçambique (Alpers 2000). In the district of Ribáuè hundreds of kilometers inland the Muslims are few and far between, except for clusters of Muslim populations along the railway line!

Xehe Amade is an old and dignified member of the tariqa Xadulia Liaxuruti, with whom I spent several shady afternoons in Ilha de Moçambique. According to him the tariqas are religious brotherhoods (including women), but they are also organizations for mutual help. 'In the case of illness and death,' he said, 'members of the tariqa will help each other. Especially for the funeral celebra-

---

[6] In the Swahili literature the spelling of *tariqas* is diverse. Qadiriyya and Shadiliyya (Trimingham 1964) seem to be closest to the Arabic spelling. According to B.G. Martin, most Sufi orders are branches from the trunk of the Qadiriya, founded in the twelfth century by the saint Abd al-Qadir al-Jilani (deceased 1166). The Shadhiliya is named after al-Hasan al-Shadhili (deceased 1258) (Martin 1976, 1).

[7] A xehe, chehe, xeque or xeique, (Arabic: shaykh) means in Ilha de Moçambique both 'leader of a tariqa'and, used more generally, 'a very respected man of learning'.

[8] Edward Alpers calls this tariqa Shadhiliyya Yashruti (Alpers 1999, 11).

tions you can count on assistance from fellow members and from the xehe and halifa[9] of your tariqa.'

The tariqas, or confrarias, are still the context in which most people of Ilha de Moçambique live their religious lives. In some ways the tariqas operate like a kinship network with obligations of mutual help and support. Family relations and tariqa-membership interlink in complicated ways. According to xehe Amade it is the norm that all children (male and female) belong to the mother's tariqa, thus following the Makhuwa pattern of matriliny. It is always possible, however, for a person, man or woman, to opt for membership in a different tariqa. Eduardo Medeiros (1996) has recorded a different pattern of daughters following the mother's line, becoming a member of her tariqa, while sons will follow their father. Both may very well be true, reflecting the mix of Makhuwa matriliny with Muslim patriarchy which is characteristic of the coastal culture.

The oral tradition in Ilha de Moçambique records the lives of the founders of the tariqas: when and where they were born, when and where they died, how they came to Mozambique and what happened since in terms of quarrels between xehes and power struggles for leadership.[10] All are remembered in detail, which may explain why there are not two but eight different tariqas in Ilha de Moçambique, five rooted in Cadiria and three in Xadulia (cf. Morier-Genoud 2002).

The great influence of the tariqas in the first decades of the twentieth century is not limited to Mozambique, but is characteristic of a general pattern of Islamic expansion in Africa (Nimtz 1980). According to Nimtz, Sufism became the religion of the masses, or popular Islam for three different reasons: First the Sufi orders, compared to more orthodox Islam, were more tolerant of local customs; second the Sufi orders allowed for African leadership, and third they were in general more egalitarian, as one's position in the tariqas was based on piety rather than on status or on book learning (ibid.). These three reasons are all important in the context of this paper, where Islam is viewed from a gender point of view, since this opening up of Islam made the religion more accessible to women as well as to former slaves (see also Strobel 1979). Coulon goes as far as to talk about the Sufi brotherhoods as 'a more typically feminine form of religious practice' (Coulon 1988, 115). Through the tariqas, he says, women gain the opportunity to participate in Islam in their own way, manipulating it and accommodating it to their needs.

According to statistical information from 1859, up to three-quarters of the people living on Mozambique Island were slaves; the report for Ilha de Moçambique reports a total population of 4522, of which 3255 were slaves. The non-slaves were Portuguese, Mestizos (mixed Portuguese and African ancestry),

---

[9] People in Ilha de Moçambque talk of the halifa as the xehe's deputy. In Ilha the halifa will often be a woman.

[10] Most of the Portuguese-language literature available in Mozambique on coastal Islam is based on the same oral tradition (Branquinho 1969; Machado 1970; Carvalho 1988; Medeiros 1996) telling the same stories in slightly differing versions. None of these works see coastal Mozambique in the light of knowledge of the Swahili culture further up the coast. Similarly most English-language literature on the Swahili does not refer to the people south of the Tanzanian border with Mozambique. In this context the recent works by Alpers (1999a, 1999b, 2000), Morier-Genoud (2000, 2002) and Bonate (2003) represent a different approach, investigating Mozambican Islam in the context of (knowledge about) Islamic cultures outside Mozambique.

Indians from Goa, Baneanas (Hindu Indians), Arabs and non-slave Africans (Almanaque Civil Ecclesiástico Historico Administrativo da Província de Moçambique, 1859, quoted by Arkitektskolen i Aarhus 1985, 17). In other societies further up on the Swahili coast, such as Mombasa (Strobel 1979) and Lamu (Fuglesang 1994), one's slave or free ancestry was well known and was an important factor in the elaborate systems of social segregation found there. In contrast it is remarkable how the former slaves of Ilha de Moçambique seem to have vanished, or rather to have become integrated in the population at large. The fact that all traces of a previous slave society seem to have gone may be due, partly at least, to the egalitarian influences of the tariqas. Similarly the integration of women in religious life in Ilha de Moçambique may be due to the tariqas. Regarding this issue, however, it might be appropriate to interpret it also the other way round: Could it be that the tariqas took root and thrived in Mozambique Island and in the Makhuwa hinterland precisely because they were open to women? This interpretation takes as a point of departure the fact that women had certain positions of power in Makhuwa contexts, and that religious and other cultural influences had to be accommodated to this situation.

In Makhuwa daily life, especially as far back as in the early decades of the twentieth century, older women had central positions (Geffray 1990, Newitt 1995). Even today men and women complement each other at most levels of traditional leadership: 'Whenever you have a *mwene* [male lineage head] at his side you have a *pwyiamwene* [female lineage head]' (Medeiros 1985). The Makhuwa society as such is not very hierarchical. There were lineages and lineage heads, but no great chieftaincies or large-scale political organization (Newitt ibid.). The pwyiamwene was responsible for the important relations with the ancestors and the spirit world. Women in general are said to be better suited than men for these types of activities, and the majority of traditional healers and diviners among the Makhuwa are women[11].

The complementarity of male and female roles in Makhuwa traditional religion seems to re-emerge (to a certain extent) in the tariqas. People in Ilha de Moçambique say that 'always when you have a xehe (male) you also have a *halifa* (female)', a gender-duplication of religious leadership that reflects Makhuwa culture in general. According to my Ilha informants, 'halifa' means second in charge in the tariqa (the xehe being the leader) and strictly speaking a halifa is not necessarily a woman. In Ilha de Moçambique, however, when people say halifa they mean a woman; halifa has become the name for a woman with religious responsibility. The halifa directs the women's prayer and takes care of women's affairs at funerals and religious gatherings. In Ilha de Moçambique the women have their own places of worship. Sometimes called 'women's mosques' and sometimes called *zaurias* (from *zawiya*, referring to women's secluded space). Zaurias are places where women gather among themselves in order to pray, just at the men gather at the mosques. There are three zaurias in Ilha de Moçambique, and six mosques, the largest one having a separate space for women. The number of men who pray in the mosques on a daily basis, and particularly on Fridays, appears to be somewhat larger that the number of women who pray in the zaurias.

---

[11] Information from AMETRAMO (*Associação de Medicina Tradicional de Moçambique*, ie. the traditional healers' association), Nampula .

Regarding matrilineal aspects of Islamic coastal culture, interesting matrilineal influences in the direction of greater equality between former freeborn and former slaves in Zanzibar have been documented by Laura Fair (1996). In Zanzibar in the nineteenth century female initiation rituals, called *unyago* and originating among Yao, Makhuwa and Makonde peoples (all matrilineal), were widespread among the slaves, most of whom were of mainland origin. Fair sees the continued practice of this ceremony as an indication of the resilience and resistance of the enslaved populations (Fair 1996). The interesting thing, however, is that after slavery was abolished in the second half of the nineteenth century, a new version of female initiation rituals turned into a social force capable of uniting women across their class differences. According to Fair the story goes as follows: The freeborn women knew about the unyago from their domestic slaves, and they longed to join the fun and games of the women, which were characterized among other things by quite explicit sexual instructions. But the higher-born women felt inhibited by the religious and moral prescriptions of their class, as sexual purity and restraint of elite women was considered a defining mark of their social status. Thus in Zanzibar at the turn of the last century, the *mkinda* was created; it was a new kind of initiation ritual in which freeborn women could participate together with former slaves (Fair 1996). The mkinda instructions were not very different from instructions for the older rite, the unyago. The major change was that the initiation ceremonies, which had been performed in an open space, were moved indoors, thus becoming more hidden and more respectable. Furthermore, the dancers in the mkinda rites would wear identical *kangas* (the Swahili word for capulanas), the kanga itself being a new form of female dress appearing in Zanzibar only at the turn at the century, exactly at the point in time when tens of thousands of ex-slaves began to define themselves as Swahili. The identical kangas had the effect of 'visually marking the women as equals', levelling out previous class differences (ibid., 158).

Laura Fair's story of Zanzibar women creating new egalitarian female initiation rituals and dances in which every woman could participate irrespective of previous class hierarchies, is a potent story of the equalizing potential of female ceremonies, rooted (in this case) in matrilineal structures. Whether something similar has taken place in Ilha de Moçambique is unknown. I read Laura Fair's paper only after having conducted fieldwork, and it had not occured to me to ask about the history of the female initiation rituals in Mozambique Island. Certainly, however, initiation rituals on the Island differ from mainland Makhuwa rituals in ways similar to the ones described by Laura Fair. The rituals are performed indoors, in a respectable space, but otherwise with much the same kind of direct sexual instruction as is the case in the Makhuwa mainland. It is possible that in Mozambique Island, just as in Zanzibar, women from different classes were able to share matrilineal female initiation rituals and perhaps this became one of the forces that led to a rapid erasure of the status differences evident in a slave society.

Sufi Islam, Makhuwa edition 2: Other aspects of religious life

In addition to the requested prayers, a particular activity of the tariqas is *dhikr*, in Mozambique called *tiquiri*. Tiquiri is a kind of singing prayer with body movements, the performers sitting or standing in a circle, singing and swaying, sometimes for hours. 'In a *dhikr* circle the participants commonly sang hymns, recited formulas, and brought themselves to the brink of collective ecstasy by techniques of controlled breathing or bodily motion. Hyperventilation, or states of consciousness approaching the threshold of hyperventilation, could be introduced by these collective rites' (Martin 1976, 1–2). In Mozambique I saw tiquiri performed by groups of men as well as by women, always separate. I observed one male tiquiri in a city square performed by a fairly large group of men on the occasion of the feast of *Ide al-kabir*. I was told that in earlier years the crowd would have been much larger. In the 1990s the people who care about celebrating the Ide tended to be older men. Trimingham's description of the dhikr closely resembles the event I viewed:

> The dhikr is the 'remembrance' of God by the repetition of His name and attributes, co-ordinated, when recited in congregation, with breathing techniques and physical movements. ... they begin the *dhikr*, chanting ... slowly, then faster, the leader indicating the change of tempo by clapping his hands. The leader then rises and all stand, the outer circle linking hands and usually shutting their eyes as an aid to concentration. Movements become faster backwards and forwards, then change to jumping. All the time the singing is going on, the shaik often leading; the singers may know from his movements what song he is changing to, but sometimes he sings the first line and they join in'. (Trimingham 1964, 96, 99)

The female tiquiri, I observed was performed in the zaurias, partly sitting, partly standing, always chanting and swaying. As noted by Nimtz (1980), because the *dhikr* is performed in groups, it may create a strong sense of group solidarity. Another aspect of religious life is the *ziaras*; *ziyyara* literally means 'visit', and it is often used in the context of 'visit to the grave of a saint'. Ziaras elsewhere on the coast, according to Trimingham (ibid.) are annual celebrations of the anniversary of the founder of the tariqa in question, sometimes coinciding with the celebration of the birthday of the prophet Muhammad. In East Africa in general, however, the devotion to the Prophet is vastly more important than any cult of tariqa founders (ibid.). This also seems to be the case in Mozambique. Ziaras in Mozambique Island indicate large religious meetings, to which members and leadership of the remotest branches of a given tariqa are invited. 'In the old days' Xehe Amade said,

> the ziara was an annual event. Since Independence, however, we haven't had any. For a ziara 3000 to 4000 people would come to Ilha de Moçambique to take part, all being members of our tariqa. The guests themselves would organize the journey and pay the dhows to take them to the Island. But we here would have to provide the food. Such an event had to be prepared a long time in advance. People would give contributions – money, rice and meat – according to their abilities. Also a collective purchase of cotton material would be organized so that all the women of the tariqa could be dressed in matching kimãos[12] and capulanas.

Halifa Àmina, now an elderly woman, talks about the ziaras: 'For the ziara the invited guests would arrive on a Friday, staying until Sunday. The hosts would

---

[12] A *kimão* is a type of woman's blouse, long sleeves and open neck with complicated applications and embroideries, which was common on the coast as late as in the early 1980s. Now it is considered old fashioned and is rarely seen. During the recent Frelimo/Renamo war a lot of cheap secondhand clothing (local name: *calamidades*) started pouring into Mozambique, women started wearing T-shirts with their capulanas, and kimãos went out of use.

serve lunch, and after that the orations would begin.' The tiquiri started in the afternoon and continued through the night. Men and women performed their tiquiri separately. The ziaras would also be occasions for the announcement of a new xehe or halifa. Halifa Àmina was nominated at a ziara in the 1950s when she was a young woman. On the morning after the all-night tiquiri there was a big meeting. Àmina recalls the event: 'In the middle of this huge mass of people my name was called. I had to go forward and stand next to the banner.[13] In this way all were informed that in the Ilha de Moçambique-section of the tariqa, Àmina is now halifa.' According to Àmina it was not the xehe himself who elected the halifa. The older halifas made the decision and gave the name to the xehe, who announced the nomination.

Tufo in the context of Sufi Islam

After having looked at ways in which certain characteristics of matrilineal organization – particularly the male/female leadership structure – are reflected in Mozambique Island tariqa organisation, I will now look into how certain characteristics of tariqa organization and religious life are reflected in the organization and activities of the Tufo groups. I will first look at the male/female leadership of the Tufo groups (a), then at similarities between tiquiri and Tufo dancing (b), and lastly I will look at the great gatherings, the *carramas*, arranged by the Tufo groups (c).

(a) My first visit to Ilha de Moçambique in November 1998 was a kind of exploratory trip in order to plan for future fieldwork. I was accompanied by Abdallah, a native of the island who had volunteered to be my guide and facilitator on the trip. Nothing was planned in advance, but my guide knew some of the patrons[14] of the leading dance groups. Thus it happened that on our walk through the macuti bairros in Ilha de Moçambique we entered the club house of the Tufo group 'Forte Amizade' just at a time when most of the group including its leadership was assembled in order to say goodbye to a sister group from Nampula city, which had been visiting over the weekend. Abdallah greeted his friends and introduced me as somebody who was making a study of the Tufo groups. There were a lot of men and women in the room, the women all dressed in red and yellow, the men in white, gray and brown Islamic gowns of different styles and with the pillbox type of cap, *cofió*, on their heads. The men present seemed to be of an older generation, the women all middle aged or young. Some of the women came up to greet me, after which they continued with whatever they were doing. The men formed a circle around me, however, ready for interview. The men were the male patrons of the dance group. They all had titles in the context of the group: The President and the Vice President, the Treasurer, the Director of Planning, and several Counsellors and Founders. In civil life they were shopkeepers, xehes and senior bank employees, people of some standing in local society. When I asked about the group leadership they said that the board of directors consisted of ten men and ten women. As for group members in general the large majority were women. This pattern, which I met

[13] Each of the tariqas has its own banner, which is brought along on occasions like a ziara.
[14] I use the word 'patron' to designate a mixture between 'leader' and 'honourable member'.

the first time in the group 'Forte Amizade', was repeated with slight variations in all of the ten different Tufo groups with whom I worked during my stays in Ilha de Moçambique and Angoche. When I first heard about the Tufo groups, I was told that they all had male leaders. Seen with Western eyes this will easily be interpreted in terms of female weakness after all: 'Women's groups, oh yes, but with male leadership, that is: Patriarchy as usual!' In my view, however, this interpretation is a gross simplification. The gender setup of the groups should be seen in its own context and not with Western patriarchalizing eyes.[15]

(b) Having discussed tiquiri as well as Tufo, it is possible to make a comparison: What are the differences, and could the Tufo dance have roots in the tiquiri? A colonial observer in Tanzania in 1923 called dhikr 'a Dervish dance' (Nimtz 1980 , 67), and certainly it does look like a dance, sharing many characteristics with the Tufo : The singing and swaying, occasional jumping, the acceleration of the rhythm. One difference is that the tiquiri, at least as performed in Mozambique, has no drums.[16] According to Trimingham using drums or not using drums for the dhikr has been one of the standard controversies among the Sunni Muslims[17] of Eastern Africa, singing or not at funerals being another (Trimingham 1964, Bonate 1998, Alpers 2000). And the Tufo dance, as explained above, took its name directly from the drums. When I asked the women about the differences between tiquiri and Tufo, they mentioned in addition to the drums the fact that for performing tiquiri you must be clean in an Islamic sense, having washed according to the prescriptions.

(c) When interviewing the Tufo groups I was told of occasional grand get-togethers, *carramas*, where sister Tufo groups would meet, not unlike the pre-Independence ziaras of the tariqas. Also, sometimes, the Tufo carramas would be Prophet's birthday celebrations. Like the tariqas, the Tufo groups have a mother group (for the oldest groups, headquarters are in Ilha de Moçambique) and sister sub-groups all along the coast as well as upcountry. The Tufo carramas seem to have taken many characteristics from the ziaras, as they include huge gatherings of people, masses of food, a uniform style of dressing, and the use of the occasion for new nominations. Other characteristics that the Tufo groups have taken over from the tariqas include some functions of mutual help and the construction of social structure in the 'de-tribalized' environment of city life. Seen from the perspective of 'social events' it appears that the Tufo groups are expanding and are taking over from the tariqas, which are on the decline. If this is the process, it is not just a process of secularization, but also of a shift in gender emphasis from male to female, reflected in an increasing female presence. The majority of participants in a Tufo carrama are women.

Daily life in Tufo contexts: Tufo group activities

The Tufo groups meet frequently, sometimes daily, as with 'Estrela Vermelha',

---

[15] *Cf.* Oyewùmí (1997) for discussions of processes of patriarchalization.

[16] Fransesca Declich reports from Somalia of dhikr accompanied – although rarely – by musical instruments, generally a tambourine (Declich 1995, 198).

[17] According to the Swahili literature most East African Muslims are Sunni; this is true of Mozambican Muslims as well.

or two to three afternoons during the week. The female members meet regularly while the male patrons only show up on specific occasions. In some groups the assembly – which is everybody – meets every two or three months. In the assembly the group decides on future performances, outings and celebrations. The three major types of activity of the group are (a) performances close to home, where no travelling is involved,(b) outings, that is performances in other places, necessitating travel, and (c) hosting celebrations with invitation sent to sister groups. All of the groups have membership fees (5,000 – 10,000 meticais a month), but the scarcity of money means that dues are rarely paid. When paid, the fees are used for *esteiras* (large straw mats on which to dance), maintenance of the club house and similar group expenses. Costs of capulanas and transport will normally be covered by the members themselves.

The standard way of celebrating national holidays such as April 7 and May 1 is with (more or less competitive) Tufo dancing. The local government also calls upon the groups to welcome important visitors (a minister, an ambassador, a official delegation of donors) by Tufo dancing. The songs for these visits are composed for the occasion, as when the Minister of Health visited Mozambique Island and the groups sang about the bad management of the local hospital. Other local assignments are performances at weddings or initiation feasts. Normally the groups are not paid for their performances, but spectators may pay tribute for good dancing, and at private parties the dancers will be fed.

Outings are an important aspect of group life. A group from Mozambique Island may be invited to perform at a wedding in Nampula city, or in another town necessitating travel. Sometimes the group will travel to a celebration, carrama, held by a sister group. The rules regarding outings are that the travelling group pays the fare of transport, while the host group, family or individual provides food and lodging, as was the case for the tariqa ziaras. I asked the groups about their outings during the previous year; often they told of impressive travelling programmes that included ten to twelve outings (normally over the weekend) during the year.

The last activity, hosting celebrations, is the most demanding. Carrama is a matter of prestige for the groups. Carrama involves inviting all sister groups, or a calculated selection if they are too many. In 1999 'Estrela Vermelha', which is the largest and most popular of the Tufo groups, had 112 sister-subgroups all along the Islamic coast, in major towns as far away as Maputo, and more recently also in non-Islamic upcountry locations. The other major groups — 'Forte Amizade', 'Beira Mar', 'Anuar Lihassanate', 'Fura Redes' and 'Ausuafi Sanía' — have fewer, but still between twenty and fifty sub-groups each. By the 1990s, when economic conditions were growing tougher, carramas were not held as frequently as in the past. The people of 'Beira Mar' maintained that they were the only ones who still had an annual carramas in celebration of the Prophet's birthday. 'Other groups also do this, but not with the same regularity'. In previous years local groups had arranged Prophet's birthday-carramas[18] in Angoche and Nampula city. Carrama always involves religious orations and recitals, but apparently may be arranged on occasions other than the Prophet's birthday.

---

[18] Sometimes this celebration is called 'maulide' or 'brazange'. The religious terminology is rather floating; few know what the Arabic words really mean.

If a local group decides that they will prepare for carrama, they first have to contact headquarters, i.e. the mother group. All the Tufo groups in Mozambique Island are mother groups, because this was where the groups were created first. The mother group will help send out invitations to the other groups, and well in advance of the date a small delegation from the mother group will visit the host group to help with the preparations. Carramas are usually held in a time of plenty, after the harvest during the months of June to October. In early 1999 'Estrela Vermelha' was involved in a carrama to be hosted by the group in Pemba. Sixty groups, totaling roughly three thousand people, had been invited. Of course such a feast is a major undertaking.

I was given the following account by the Tufo group 'Fura Redes', which had hosted a carrama on Mozambique Island in 1997. The host group began collecting money and amassing the necessary quantities of rice, flour, potatoes, onions, oil, tea and so forth well in advance of the event. Cooking and preparations went on for days. The guests, mostly women, arrived on Friday. The celebrations started on Saturday morning, when breakfast was served and the men made religious recitals and orations. Following that, lunch was served throughout the afternoon until six o'clock in the evening. That was also the time for announcements of new appointments to leadership positions in the groups. In the evening the groups started performing, one after the other, all through the night. During carrama nobody goes to sleep. In the morning, about seven or eight o'clock, the entire party marched through the streets, dancing and playing the drums. After Sunday lunch the party was over and the visiting groups headed for home. The gist of what the Fura Redes people said when I interviewed them is as follows:

> To arrange a carrama is not an easy thing to do. It is very costly. Previously you would kill a head of cattle, as well as several goats, ducks and chicken. Today there is more rice and less meat. But still to arrange carrama is a great effort. But it is good for the group. In 1997 'Fura Redes' was the only group that arranged carrama in Mozambique Island. In 1998 nobody did.

These tales of feasts and lavish spending are a characteristic which the Tufo groups share with the *Beni* and *Lelemama* groups of Kenya and Tanzania (see below). Both Ranger (1975, 145) and Strobel (1976, 187) tell about competitive slaughter of cattle for lavish Beni or Lelemama 'picnics'. But exactly because of these great displays, the Tufo groups, just like the Lelemama and Beni groups, may be seen as schools of organizational skills:

> The mobilization of people, finances and equipment for these celebrations trained women in organizational skills and leadership. All members were informed of the time and place of the competitions, which meant notifying several hundred dancers, supporters and observers. Money was collected for the purchase of anywhere from one to twenty heads of cattle, rice, ghee, onions, and other necessities for the feast. (Strobel ibid., 183)

Precisely the same system is true of the Tufo groups. The capacity for communication, and for planning and organizing these great events, is stunning.

Tufo in the context of the Swahili coast

One frame of interpretation for the male/female leadership of the groups is provided by the mainland Makhuwa culture, which is matrilineal and where a pattern of balanced male/female leadership is the norm. Another frame of interpretation for the male/female presence and leadership in the Tufo groups is the history of other dance groups on the Swahili coast. The so-called 'Beni associations', active more or less from 1890 to 1960, were predominantly male dance groups, their distinctive characteristic being the European military inspiration in brass band and drill-like dancing (Ranger 1975). The Beni groups, however, had women's divisions,[19] and the women sometimes broke away to form associations of their own (Strobel 1976, 1979). The name of the women's dance was Lelemama. In the male/female Beni groups 'the duties of the Queen and her subordinates are with regard to the female members of the society similar to those of the King and his assistants' (Ranger 1975, 63–64).[20] Nowadays the male/female balance of the Tufo groups is uneven, because the male element has been reduced to just a small group of patrons. Previously, however, Tufo groups had a lot of male activity, including football playing and male Tufo dancing.

'Estrela Vermelha' is the oldest of the Tufo groups now active in Ilha de Moçambique. It was founded on January 2, 1931. At that time it was called 'Mahafil Islam', and it had a different range of activities. The religious aspect was more important then, and the celebrations and recitals on the Prophet's birthday were a major activity. In those days Tufo was danced by men as well as by women. All of the Ilha groups that were founded in the 1930s – that is, 'Mahafil Islam', 'Beira Mar' and 'Fura Redes' – had football teams.[21] It may seem odd to realize that organizations that began with men's football in the 1930s developed into women's dance groups from the 1970s on. But the context of the Beni groups offers a framework for interpretation. According to Ranger, football competitions were closely linked with dance societies (Ranger 1975). Lienhardt also comments on the Swahili connections between football and dancing: 'Each football team has its own dancing club, and the dance-bands compete just as vigorously as the footballers' (Lienhardt 1968, here quoted from Ranger 1975, 99). Sometimes it was not really clear whether it was a football club cum dance association or vice versa (Ranger ibid.). Football, dancing and lavish parades were all aspects of a larger pattern of competition, which seems to have been constitutive to the whole Beni phenomenon, and also very strong indeed in the Lelemama associations (Ranger 1975, Strobel 1975, 1979, Fair 1997). Competition is also a part of the Tufo culture, but nothing as devastating as what is reported from the heyday of Beni and Lelemama.

In Ilha de Moçambique football faded out during the 1960s. When I asked for the reasons for this, people referred to the lack of sponsors. Football cannot be

---

[19] The women's divisions are left unseen and unanalysed by Ranger, even if they are present in the data material he presents (eg. Ranger 1975, 63–64; 97–98). In an appendix to the book he belatedly admits this gender blindness.

[20] The Beni were copying European royal and military ranks, having internal titles of King, Queen, etc. (Ranger 1975; Strobel 1976, 189).

[21] The name Fura Redes derives from football language, meaning something like 'blow the net'.

played without equipment (balls, boots etc.), and equipment in Ilha de Moçambique as elsewhere was provided by sponsors such as wealthy firms and companies. There used to be plenty of potential sponsors in Ilha de Moçambique, the
former capital of the country and until the 1960s the major port of the north.
But all of this changed with the opening of the harbour in Nacala, which was
completed in 1964. The big firms moved their headquarters to Nacala, and Ilha
de Moçambique became a backwater town. Another reason is the general
exodus of people from Ilha, caused by the opening of the Nacala harbour, and
later by Independence. Many young men disappeared, among them football
players as well as Tufo dancers. Also many other male dances have vanished.
People in Ilha de Moçambique claim that so-called 'traditional dancing' was
much richer twenty years back than in the 1990s. In Ranger's account Beni
group dancing was replaced by European style 'dansi' much earlier (Ranger
1975, 142). Thus the relevant question seems to be not why the male Tufo
dancing has gone, but rather why the female Tufo dancing is alive and
expanding, even today.

Tufo dancing from the point of view of the women

When I asked the women what was good about belonging to a Tufo group, the
first aspects they mentioned were often entertainment and social life: 'The great
advantage is the fun we have together in the group. As a single mother you have
many concerns, life is not at all simple. But when you are in the group with the
others, the problems seem less grave.' And the group indeed does work as an
institution of mutual aid. 'The group is like a family. If one of us falls ill, the
others will come to the hospital to visit, bringing biscuits, soft drinks and fruit.
If somebody dies in the family of one group member, the others will help.' 'The
group takes notice. The group is concerned with its members.'
    Both Mozambique Island and Angoche are urban societies. People come
from elsewhere, and many women live far from their families. As one woman
said, 'The first advantage of the group is that when you die you will be treated
like a person.' Proper burial is a very important issue, and if you live far from
your own family, you must depend on friends. A further item in the list of group
advantages for its members is the traveling. 'Through the group we have the
possibility of getting to know other places.' The women acquire a mobility
which otherwise they would not have had. 'If you just stay at home your mind
gets closed. In the group things are different. You get to know other places,
and you yourself become known.' In her historical work on Zanzibar Laura
Fair has made similar observations: 'Dance groups provided individuals from
poor and socially marginalized backgrounds with avenues for achieving status,
titles and positions of authority – as well as a ritualized atmosphere in which
they could challenge superiors' (Fair 1997, 227) – exactly as the Tufo groups
are doing.
    Possibly, one may even talk of the Tufo groups as producing female identities.
There is first the issue of 'titles'. Like the men, the female group members have
titles: First, Second and Third *Rainha* or *Rais* (Queen), Chief of the Line
(dancing), Chief of Organization, Chief of Protocol, Chief of Outfit (she is the

one responsible for the capulanas), Chief of Cooking, etc. Sometimes the Raises are middle-aged women who have retired from active dancing. Sometimes they have never been dancers at all, but were active in the organizing of the group. Several of the female patrons seemed very obviously to derive their standing in the local community from their position in the Tufo group. There is also the issue of 'capability', which may overlap with acquiring status. As one woman put it, 'What happens in the groups is almost a professionalization. Through the group we acquire a personal identity as singers and dancers, as artists.' Where the Tufo group men, especially the patrons, tend to be men of some local standing who are employed, the Tufo group women are a mix of single mothers, street corner vendors, peasants and patrons' wives. Dance group membership is not a source of income, but it may be a source of identity. Through the dance group the women have a chance of acquiring a kind of profession, as 'artists', as the district and provincial Departments of Culture refers to them. They become known outside their immediate neighbourhood. Just as football playing may offer career possibilities for young men with neither family nor educational background, Tufo dancing may open the world to some extent for the women involved. They travel, they are artists, they become somebody. In this way the Tufo dancing may function as a kind of shortcut to modernity. The women participate actively in contemporary social and urban life. There are Tufo groups in the countryside as well, but Tufo as such is part of an urban, thus more 'modern' culture. Furthermore the groups offer a framework for an identity that may help reduce women's dependency on men. This is not without its contradictions, because, as we have seen, Tufo group membership can be quite a costly affair, not least in terms of capulanas, which are traditionally offered to women by men. The balance desired seems to be to *have* a man, while still not being dependent on a man.

To a certain extent the negotiating position of women of Mozambique Island vis a vis their husbands has improved. Before the Nacala harbour was built many men had been wage workers and the women were economically dependent on the men. According to social norms, women were not supposed to deal too much with money. This has changed. Most men now are unemployed and the women have taken up petty trading in the streets. At every corner nowadays two or three women will be sitting with homemade sweets or similar items for sale. Other women have fields on the mainland, traveling to and fro daily. At low tide women also go to the sea in search of cockles and mussels. Young men make a living by fishing from tiny but beautiful dhows. Life in Ilha de Moçambique is harsher than it used to be: A money-based economy with no money. But it has opened opportunities for women to earn an income. As they say, 'We women are now learning to do something.' In terms of income generation women sell homemade biscuits, sweets made of coco or groundnuts; cooked corn on the cob, or a whole meal of curry and rice. The profits of this trade are tiny, but the women are proud.

In the Tufo groups it is not a big deal whether a woman is married or not. The identity of the woman is her own; it is not derived from her possible relationship with a husband. Some of the women are married, some are single. But even the married women are never identified in terms of their husbands. Identification in terms of marriage works rather the other way round, with male group members being identified in terms of their wives.[22] Most of the male patrons are married to women of the group, and this seems to be an important part of their reason for being there. The general pattern is that in a woman's life the dance group membership is a more stable factor than marriage. The man who really wants this particular woman will have to put up with her dance group as well!

Many women in the groups are single mothers, though their marital situation fluctuates. Marriage on the coast is often a shaky arrangement. As the women say: 'It is difficult to remain married to the same man for a long time. Many of us who have husbands are in our second, third or fourth marriage. Some are single because they are fed up with husbands.'

In general, however, to have a husband is the most desired state of affairs. But husbands come and go, and divorce is frequent. When I asked about the reasons for divorce, the primary reason (as seen by the women) was the inclination for the husband to get involved with another woman. Polygamy is a part of the cultural norms of Islam, but is not much liked by women. Often their response will be to provoke divorce. Another reason for divorce mentioned by the women, was the husband's dissatisfaction with too many children. In one case the woman said that her former husband had left her because of this, on the advice of his mother. This explanation again points to the matrilineal Makhuwa context. The children belong to the mother's lineage, and seen from the point of view of the father's family, they have no particular value.

I was lectured by Abdallah regarding the norms of the coast as far as marriage and divorce are concerned:

> The men of the coast do not supervise their women too closely. As long as they behave well in public they close their eyes to what else is going on. Adultery is a normal situation, it is nothing new. The clever woman might have a lover, but in order for the husband not to notice, she will show him even more love than usual, and the husband who has a girlfriend in town will do the same thing. This is the behaviour of wise and well-behaved men and women. Discretion is an important capacity. On the coast adultery is a way of life, it is part of our culture. There is more enjoyment and more fun in these extra-marital relations, and if husband and wife behave well, it will very rarely be those that provoke divorce. What provokes divorce is the bad behaviour of man or woman. If the woman does not wash the husband's clothes, if she leaves the house without his permission, if she responds to him in a bad way – that is: if she uses bad language, if she is not nice, kind and polite in her way of communicating with the husband. Or on the part of the husband: if he gets drunk, if he does not buy clothes and capulanas for his wife, or if he is jealous.

According to Abdallah, the rules of discretion in marriage are of the highest importance, and marriages can last only if the rules are carefully adhered to. The problem with the dance groups is the demands of the women. If they don't get what they want from their husbands, they will get it anyhow: 'Some women in the Tufo groups make negotiations with their body, in order to get hold of the required number of capulanas.' When I asked the women in group interviews how they managed to arrange the necessary capulanas, they said that they got them from husbands or from 'male friends'.

---

[22] The identification of men through women is a general phenomenon of Makhuwa matriliny. However, it normally takes place through mothers and sisters, not through wives.

I did not hear of any cases where the woman's membership in a Tufo group had provoked divorce, but that might be a matter of interpretation. Several groups complained that they had lost members because of marriage. For women the value of marriage is high, and a single woman wants to marry, even if this means that she will have to leave the group. Many men set leaving the group as a condition for marriage. 'The men say like this: You cannot remain in the group. I am not going to buy your capulanas'. Abdallah would never marry a woman from a Tufo group, he said, no matter how beautiful she might be. 'I cannot afford three or four capulanas a week.' The problem with the Tufo groups, from the point of view of certain men, is not just the capulanas, however, but also the travel and the independence of the women. Some groups explained that they worked with the husbands, inviting them to take part in group celebrations, and persuading them to let their wives go along on weekend trips. But in many cases the women had to trade group membership for marriage.

Only for so long, however, as any particular marriage would last. Secretly these women will remain group members, not taking part in dancing and outings, but without the husband noticing, they will follow the life of the group and make sure to get hold of every new capulana, preparing for a possible come-back. No sooner does the marriage end than the woman is back in the group. This typical account points to the fact that membership in a Tufo group is more stable than marriage in a coastal woman's life. The women compromise between their identity and independence in the Tufo groups on one hand, and their wish to be married on the other. But in the long run the group identity seems to be the stronger one.

14.3 Dhows with passengers from the mainland arriving at Ilha de Moçambique.
(Photo © Signe Arnfred)

Life in Ilha de Moçambique: The content of Tufo songs

The golden age of Mozambique Island was in colonial days, the time before the port of Nacala was built, the time when big ships anchored at the shores of Ilha de Moçambique, the time when there was plenty of activity and waged work for the Islanders. At that time large sectors of the male population in Ilha worked as stevedores, bringing goods ashore from the ships in the bay, while others were employed as clerks and office workers in the commercial firms. The harbour facilities of Ilha have always been poor, however, with shallow water and a solitary pier, which was falling to pieces by the 1990s. In Nacala the natural conditions for a harbour are much better. When quays were built in Nacala (1951–64) all shipping activity moved there. In Ilha de Moçambique the memory of Portuguese colonialism is the memory of the golden days when Ilha was an important city. All memory of Portuguese colonial oppression, forced labour and secret police seems to have evaporated.

With declining economic activity, especially after Frelimo came to power at Independence, Ilha houses and streets fell into decay. The colonial programme of maintenance was discontinued; little by little the houses turned into ruins and the parks into wilderness. The building material in the stone-built town is coral limestone covered with lime (whitewash). Such houses need to be whitewashed once a year in order to survive the ocean climate. The process of decay initiated at Independence was accelerated by the war, when masses of people from the mainland sought refuge on Mozambique Island. Wood from windows and doors in the old colonial houses was used for fires. The paved city streets were turned into sandy roads. In the macuti town houses are built wall to wall almost like a beehive. The present island population is estimated at 13,000, and according to the City Council the maximum capacity is 8,000. Fresh water supplies are insufficient, and sewage is non-existent. People defecate on the beaches. Several of the Tufo songs touch on this topic of former splendour compared to more recent decay and government neglect.[23]

> Gentlemen visitors, now you have arrived in Ilha de Moçambique
> Today our Island is no longer the same as the one you used to know.
> Our palaces and houses are not as they used to be.
> Just look at the palace São Paulo, and look at the fortress São Sebastião.
> Look at our streets: When a car is passing the dust is everywhere,
> and when it rains there are great pools of water.
> The time has gone when all our streets were paved
> Look at our hospital, such a pity, such a shame,
> if a person is gravely ill he or she will have to be transferred from Ilha to Monapo;
> the unfortunate will die on the road.
> Oh behold, Gentlemen visitors, the great disgrace of the people of this Island.

Mozambique Island was never a Frelimo stronghold. On the contrary, during the Frelimo/Renamo war and in the subsequent general elections (1994) most of Nampula province, and especially the coastal region, supported

---

[23] Translation from Emakhuwa to Portuguese was done on Mozambique Island by Maria de Conceição Amade. The last song (How it is beautiful...) was written in Portuguese. Translations from Portuguese to English are mine.

Renamo.[24] People on the island see a connection between this fact and their experience of more recent political neglect.

Another song about former splendour is also a moving account of a great disappointment when tourists from a South African cruise ship wanted to disembark in Ilha, but were not able to do so because of the destruction of the pier. Subsequent attempts have succeeded, and Mozambique Island is now visited by several cruise ships each year.

We, the people, we feel hurt when what we are told is not true.
When long time ago the Portuguese came to this island, they came by the sea.
This was the start of the fame of the *capitanía*.[25]
In order to get things right, let us tell the story right from the beginning.
In 1996, on the 26 of November, it was on a Tuesday early in the morning,
the first cruise ship arrived in our bay.
Old people were crying, others were laughing happily,
thinking of the past and of the way things were then.
But look how we at the Island are being insulted and abused.

At ten o'clock in the morning the sea was crowded with small motor boats
and tourists waving their hands in good-bye.
They never succeeded in getting ashore on the Island.
There was not a place they could land
because of the destruction of the pier.
The pier has gone asunder, the wood has been used for cooking.

Lots of people were terribly disappointed.
So many were those who had wanted to do business with the foreigners
without being able to do so.
The Tufo groups waiting ashore to welcome the visit,
how fed up they were!
Who are those that give such false promises to the people?
How come that the City Council pretends to know about issues regarding the harbour,
when else they do nothing but quarrel among themselves?
These people who never came further than to the 5th grade at school.
Issues regarding the harbour pertains to the *capitanía*.
But nowadays the pilot goes out from the port of Nacala.
Ilha de Moçambique is defamed, even if she used to be the capital of the country.

This song is a striking critique of the Frelimo members on the City Council, some of whom obtained their jobs through nepotism and not ability, as they have passed only the fifth class. They had been informed about the cruise ship visit and had announced it to the Islanders, but neglected the practical preparations for the disembarkation.

Despite the difficulties, few want to move to the mainland. The urban atmosphere of Ilha de Moçambique is found nowhere else. Nightlife on weekends is buzzing with videos and discos. Some Tufo songs also praise these aspects of the Island:

How it is beautiful, the Island of Mozambique, in the first hours of the morning,
With the strong winds, and the fishermen in their tiny boats,

[24] Renamo is the major opposition party to the ruling Frelimo. In the 1990s, local administration, even in parts of Mozambique with Renamo majority, was staffed with Frelimo members.
[25] *Capitanía*, the port authority.

setting sail in order to eke out a living from the sea.
Even more beautiful it is at time of night,
people crowding in the streets at Hoti and Matadouro,
and also at Estrela there is lots of life.

Hoti and Matadouro are places for disco dancing and video shows in the *macuti* town. Estrela is the club house of 'Estrela Vermelha', where the Tufo group at one point ran evening video shows, as a way of raising money for the association. After a while the television set broke down, putting an end to that.

Tufo and politics

As shown by the Tufo songs quoted above, the population of Mozambique Island is very patriotic. The Islanders love their Island, and they are proud of its famous past. Those who grew up on the Island all know one another, as distinct from the newcomers who arrived during the war. In colonial days the upper class was the Portuguese colonial administrators, traders and businessmen. Today the top members of society on the Island are the local state representatives, Frelimo Party members, who form the upper layer of district and municipality administration. They are generally Mozambicans from other parts of the country, and often they only stay in the Island for a few years. Stories of corruption are plentiful. Administrators have pocketed aid money that was destined for the physical restoration of the once-beautiful stone-built town. In the early 1980s Ilha de Moçambique was declared a UN World Cultural Heritage site, and a lot of aid money was allocated to maintenance and restoration. Little of this has happened, and the money has disappeared.

The relationship between political power and the Tufo groups is ambiguous. Following Independence, the Tufo groups, along with other local dance groups, were turned into folklore by the Frelimo government: exotic entertainment to welcome important visitors in airports. The Tufo groups replied by singing about harsh realities when they greeted visiting notables, though usually they sang in the Makhuwa language, which meant that the critique might pass unnoticed. When Tufo groups today display Frelimo posters in their club houses or compose songs praising Frelimo they are likely to do so for pragmatic reasons. The wise person or group will back the political party in power. The practice has little to do with political convictions. 'When this Father dies, we'll have to look for another' they say, by 'Father' referring to Frelimo.

The story of the changing names of 'Mahafil Islam' reflects this type of position. 'Mahafil Islam' was the name of the oldest dance association cum football club on Ilha de Moçambique. An early Frelimo administrator in Mozambique Island suggested an updating of the name; 'Mahafil Islam' had a colonial as well as a religious ring, neither very pleasant in Frelimo socialist ears. The name 'Estrela Vermelha' (Red Star) had very different connotations; in addition to the general socialist touch, 'Estrela Vermelha' was also the nickname of the Frelimo security forces. The move proved a wise one, and the name 'Estrela Vermelha' became very popular. It has even outlived the recent political change away from socialism. At the time of Independence a splinter group broke away from 'Mahafil Islam'. That group also changed its name for political reasons, several times. First it took the name of 'Mahafil Camarada' (Comrade Mahafil), later – but still in Frelimo socialist times – changing it to 'Associação a Luta Continua' (The Struggle Continues). Later again, after the 1994 multi-party elections when *a luta continua* had already become a slogan of the past, it changed its name to the present 'Associação Forte Amizade' (Strong Friendship).

In Ilha de Moçambique in the 1990s these two groups had quite a close relation to the Frelimo Party, while some of other Tufo groups were blacklisted by the local (Frelimo) District Department of Culture. The crime of one particular group was that, shortly after the end of the war but before the general elections, it had danced to welcome a delegation from Renamo. Since then this group has ceased to exist as far as the local (Frelimo) administration is concerned. When I asked the District Department of Culture for a list of the Tufo groups in the Island, that group was not on the list. I found a similar situation in Angoche where Tufo groups thought to be close to Renamo were blacklisted.

A new kind of Tufo/Frelimo relationship has emerged more recently, with Tufo not only criticising political power, but also speaking on its behalf. This relationship works in particular with those groups that are 'close' to the Party, which tend to be groups with capable and eloquent men placed in central positions. As one of them said:

> Our purpose [in the group] is the transmission of messages. Messages that derive from our daily lives. Messages regarding the problems that we encounter, but also regarding our visions and our dreams. Sometimes we will criticize the Government; we are the mouthpiece for what the people want. Sometimes also, however, we will transmit the Government's messages.

In this capacity some groups were active in the information and mobilization campaign regarding participation in the local elections for city councils. In Ilha de Moçambique, as well as in Angoche, some Tufo groups did a lot of work in this context; this was not in favour of one political party or another, but rather an endeavour of civil education, commissioned by the Frelimo government. And in the same vein Tufo groups on the coast are active in consciousness-raising and mobilizing on environmental issues. Seen from the perspective of the Tufo groups this collaboration has the advantage of increasing their visibility and chances of eligibility for small-scale income-generation and savings projects. The development projects, when they occur, are channeled through local and international NGOs. In some respects this is a promising development. Tufo groups are well organized, and their members tend to be women in difficult situations – single mothers for example, and women with no income. They appear to be an ideal target group for a poverty-oriented NGO aid programme. It remains to be seen how this will work out in the longer run, and if the groups and the women will be able to maintain their autonomy and independence vis a vis economic and political powers.

Women, Tufo, Islam and politics : Winding up

Supported by traditions of female gender power in Makhuwa culture, women of the northern coast of Mozambique have developed a space of their own in the Tufo associations. Women who don't have many other possibilities because of low education, shaky marriages or lack of income for instance, get the chance through the Tufo groups of becoming somebody. The Tufo group activities take a lot of the members' time, but it is not income-generating. On the contrary, a member of a Tufo group must expect to pay a lot of expenses, for capulanas, for transport and for the monthly fee. 'Survival strategies' however, are not always just about food, but also about identity and belonging. Marriage is important for social respectability, but for a number of women the long term reliable source of identity and belonging seems to be the Tufo groups.

The Tufo dance has roots in Islam, and on the northern Mozambican coast the Tufo groups are still a part of Islamic culture. Processes of secularization are occurring, however. On one hand coastal groups are detaching themselves from religion, and Quranic songs and Islamic celebrations are of decreasing importance in the life of the groups. Likewise, upcountry Tufo groups are emerging with no religious attachment whatsoever. Thus many aspects of Tufo development display an expansion of women's culture and a renewed source of status and identity for the participating women. On the other hand a factor in, and an effect of, the general process of the secularization of Tufo is the increasing involvement in politics and 'development' as described above. Some groups have moved from being the people's mouthpiece vis a vis political power to also acting as a mouthpiece for government policies. And some groups have been targeted for small-project support by development NGOs. To a certain extent this looks like an ideal choice, and a good idea: to use these already existing and well-organized associations for small-scale credit schemes and support for income generation. Among the Tufo groups there is a high demand for this type of aid. At the same time, however, this development may be dangerous for the Tufo groups as women's groups. Research from elsewhere (Schroeder 1997) has shown how women's well-functioning organizations, once they were targeted by aid money, became dominated by men. Seen in this light the future of the Tufo groups is uncertain. Will they be taken over and run by industrious men? Or will the women be strong and visionary enough to embark on the development project, while still insisting on the Tufo groups a women's culture?

Epilogue

291

The work on this book has been carried along by two major concerns. One is about politics – in particular politics of gender and development – the other is about conceptualizations. The two concerns are closely interlinked. First on politics. As pointed out in several chapters, most explicitly in Chapter 5, political approaches to issues of women and gender have been characterized by continuities rather than radical breaks, all the way from the days of Frelimo socialism in the 1970s and early 1980s to the days of World Bank hegemony from the 1990s onwards. This is one step: to realize that in spite of remarkable changes, from a centralized socialist economy to a neo-liberal one, approaches to women and gender have remained much the same. The next step is to investigate the basic assumptions of these approaches. This is where conceptualizations come into the picture. As discussed in several chapters (Chapters 4, 10 and 11 among them) even simple concepts like 'woman', 'man' and 'gender' are far from innocent; they are rooted in often quite tenacious taken-for-granted assumptions revolving around notions of male dominance/female subordination.

A major line of argument in the book is that such assumptions do not fit realities very well, certainly not realities in northern Mozambique , and that – very simply – gender relations should be investigated, not assumed. The political implication of this argument is that policies, which are not rooted in and responding to the actual lives and concerns of men and women, are not likely to have success. They will be diverted, counteracted, used for other purposes and so on, not having the intended outcome. A more sinister implication of Gender-and Development policies being guided by die-hard assumptions of male/female gender dichotomy and hierarchy is that these lines of thinking – through the economic power and intellectual hegemony of donor forces in Africa – seep from donor-funded projects and NGOs into political activism, and from politics into research.[1] Ready-made top-down Gender-and-Development notions of, for example, Harmful Traditional Practices – which, given the sheer fact that they are conceptualized as 'harmful' have to be combated and replaced – prevent and obstruct an alternative approach of investigating what these 'practices' might be about, and which male/female or other relations and identities they might convey.

This alternative approach of investigating, reinterpreting and remapping 'African culture' has proved a rich source of inspiration for post-colonial African feminist thinkers, who have often started off by criticizing lines of thinking in Western feminism, in order to clear a space, as it were, for alternative conceptualizations.[2] I see my project in similar terms: criticizing, undermining, deconstructing existing lines of thinking, preparing and opening in this way the mind for different ways of seeing. I am also convinced that this manoeuvre is useful, not only for a better understanding of what goes on in Africa or in Mozambique, but for feminist thinking in general.

---

[1] *African Feminist Politics of Knowledge. Tensions, Challenges, Possibilities*, edited by Akosua Adomako Ampofo and myself (2010) discusses exactly these issues.

[2] Regarding this focus on 'African culture' it is important to note, that 'African culture' is approached and used by feminists in ways very different from the revitalization of 'African culture' which is and has been the project of certain African elites and heads of state, such as Robert Mugabe and Thabo Mbeki. See e.g. Sylvia Tamale 2005b.

When during my research in Mozambique in the early 1980s I first felt the inadequacy and shortcomings of my conceptual luggage for coming to grips with what I met on the ground, I was very much at a loss regarding how then to proceed. Feminist theory has developed a lot since then, and very much in the directions I felt, I needed, for critically scrutinizing implicit assumptions embedded in seemingly innocent concepts; much Foucault-inspired feminist thinking moves along these lines. It was, however, only when I came across the work of post-colonial feminist writers, that I felt some very deeply embedded assumptions in feminist thinking, such as those regarding gender dichotomies and hierarchies, properly addressed – combined with rethinkings of mother-hood in unessentialist terms. Since then I have been a happy reader of works by Ifi Amadiume, Oyèrónké Oyewùmí, Nkiru Nzegwu, Sylvia Tamale and others. Reading through the chapters these names appear a lot, particularly from 2000 onwards. Some chapters are explicitly written as a form of introduction to these strands of African feminist thinking (Chapters 4 and 10), in other chapters I try to apply their thinking in my own analysis. Ifi Amadiume, Oyèrónké Oyewùmí, Nkiru Nzegwu and Sylvia Tamale all think in different ways, and they are engaged in different issues. What they share is the approach to 'custom' and 'African culture' as possible points of departure, not only for ideas and visions regarding feminist futures (cf. Elizabeth Grosz 2000, quoted in Chapter 4) but also for grasping the mix of women's lives in many African contexts. I found throughout my fieldwork in Ribáuè and in Ilha de Moçambique that people live in different worlds at the same time, and that for men and women on the ground the past, the spirits and so-called custom is very much part of their lives. Recent research on similar issues (gender and sexuality) in capital city Maputo (Groes-Green 2011) points in the same direction – as does also Thera Rasing's research on female initiation in urban settings in Zambia discussed in Chapter 9.

This finding has theoretical/conceptual as well as political implications. Theo-retically it means that in order to understand people's lives, these kinds of multiple identities must be taken into consideration. Politically, and from a femi-nist point of view – as shown by a long list of scholars, including those mentioned above – it is well worth taking a closer look at 'custom' and 'culture/tradition'. Far from being just oppressive and harmful, as imagined by Frelimo/OMM – inspired, as it turns out, not only by socialism, but also by Protestant Christianity (see Chapters 2 and 5) – 'custom' and 'culture' may include empowering messages for young, modern women, even if sometimes in contradictory and convoluted forms. This is what Tamale and Rasing write about, and this also expires from the data material presented by Groes-Green. Seen in the context of the fact that the Frelimo view of 'custom' as harmful and woman-oppressive is shared by the mainstream of the contemporary develop-ment establishment, this kind of research, which takes up issues similar to the ones I have investigated, but do so in urban settings among young people, seems particularly urgent.

So much money and effort is invested in Gender-and-Development initiatives of various kinds in Africa. Lots of good will, and many good intentions. The sombre reality of HIV/AIDS has caused an increase of input, efforts, programmes and organizations focused on the sexual lives of men and women;

this is also the case in Mozambique. A question worth posing is, however, if all of these programmes work as intended, and if they don't, then why not?

The chapters of this book do not directly confront this question. Indirectly however, a discussion and controversy with Gender-and-Development conceptualizations are running through the pages from cover to cover. As pointed out above – and repeatedly in the chapters – regarding issues of gender, the basic assumptions of Frelimo socialism and World Bank liberalism are much the same. Thus the explicit controversy with OMM/Frelimo lines of thinking in Part I of the book (Conceptions of Gender and Gender Policy in Mozambique) is also implicitly a controversy with current development discourse. As for the following sections – Part II on female initiation, and Part III on investigating matriliny – the point here has been to take a closer look at 'custom' and 'culture', fully in line with the programme of my African feminist sources of inspiration, even if I started this work before I knew about theirs.

Regarding female initiation I try to show the empowering potential, as well as the contradictions. I see initiation as female capacity building: young women are educated in sexual arts of seduction, also with knowledge of their own pleasure and enjoyment, as a basis for faith and confidence in their own sexual powers. It all takes place in a setting of submission to established hierarchies of age. But to which extent are these hierarchies determining and limiting for the ways in which the young women can use their lessons? In one of the sessions of initiation I attended in Ribáuè in 2005, two of the young women were urban girls who had come out from the provincial capital of Nampula to go through a session of initiation, hosted by their Ribáuè based uncle. There is a rich, exciting and important field of research in further investigating if and how modern, urban, well educated girls make use of 'custom' and 'culture' in the field of sexuality.

Regarding matriliny, the implicit – partly explicit – debate is initially with classical anthropology (Chapter 11), intending to put the spotlight on implicit assumptions of male dominance/female subordination, which (in my view) define the conceptual field in ways that make particular characteristics of matriliny (as I see them) invisible. The whole matriliny-section is a debate with taken for granted notions of gender dichotomies and hierarchies, notions which also underpin development thinking, where matriliny has remained unacknowledged and unseen, in spite of the fact that in Mozambique 40 per cent of the population live under conditions of matriliny. The intentions of my analysis of life in Ribáuè has been to make visible how gender relations *not* characterized by male dominance/female subordination permeate daily life, and in continuation of this to investigate how gender could be conceptualized in this context. Obviously the next step will be to investigate how to design development projects, which take a point of departure in these female positions of power, instead of glossing them over or wiping them out.

The final chapter in the section to some extent stands on its own, being the only chapter dealing with an Islamic setting. In all of the other chapters Christian churches, Catholic or Protestant, have been implicitly or explicitly present as a part of the social setting under investigation. In Chapter 14 the co-existence of Islam with matriliny is discussed, with a focus, still, on matriliny and on the room for manoeuvre this opens for women – but the chapter is also carried, I must confess, by my plain fascination of the Tufo dance groups and their capulana culture, as a coastal women's culture of music, poetry, dance and dress, rich in history and aesthetic elaboration. The 'development' challenge here – as also suggested in the chapter – is to take this already existing cluster of organizations, the Tufo groups, as points of departure for bottom-up development work. Surprisingly, this is exactly what in the meanwhile has happened (the chapter was first published 2004). At the initiative of the Danish Embassy in Mozambique, a women's cultural association embracing almost all of the Tufo groups (*Associação Cultural das Mulheres de Ilha de Moçambique, ACUMIM*) has been formed with the aim of starting a series of projects for the improvement of Tufo-group women's lives. The Association is still young, thus the question posed in the chapter (where this type of project is suggested) remains valid: 'It remains to be seen how this will work out in the longer run, and if the groups and the women will be able to maintain their autonomy and independence vis-à-vis economic and political powers' (Chapter 14). Nevertheless, the existence of ACUMIM is evidence of the possibility of positive links between research and development practice.

References

Adam, Wenke, 1997, 'Quo vadis, gender?', *NotMoç – Notícias de Moçambique* no 99, Edição especial 7 Abril, Maputo.

Adam, Yussuf, 1996, *Trick or Treat*, PhD dissertation, International Development Studies, Roskilde University.

Adam, Yussuf, 2005, *Escapar aos Dentes do Crocodilo e Cair na Boca do Leopardo*, Maputo: Promedia, Collecção Identidades.

AIM – Agencia de Informação de Moçambique.

Aixelá, Yolanda, 2005, 'Parentesco y género en el África sahariana y subsahariana. La categorización sexual de los grupos matrilineales', *Studia Africana* no 16, Barcelona.

Agenda 62, 2004, *African Feminisms, vol. 2,1: Sexuality in Africa*, guest editor Vasu Reddy, Durban: Agenda Feminism Media Company.

Agenda 63, 2005, *African Feminisms, vol. 2,2: Sexuality and Body Image*, guest editor Pumla Dineo Gqola, Durban: Agenda Feminism Media Company.

Agenda 67, 2006, *African Feminisms, vol. 2,3: Homosexuality*, guest editor Cheryl Potgieter, Durban: Agenda Feminism Media Company.

Alexander, Jocelyn, 1997, 'The Local State in Post-War Mozambique: Political Practice and Ideas about Authority', *Africa* 67/1.

Alpers, Edward, 1972, 'Towards the History of the Expansion of Islam in East Africa: the Matrilineal Peoples of the Southern Interior', in Terence O. Ranger & Isaria N. Kimambo (eds), *The Historical Study of African Religion*, London, Ibadan: Heinemann Educational Books.

Alpers, Edward, 1999, 'Islam in the Service of Colonialism? Portuguese Strategy during the Armed Liberation Struggle in Mozambique', *Lusotopie 1999*, Paris: Karthala

Alpers, Edward, 2000, 'East Central Africa', in Pouwels & Levtzion (eds), *History of Islam in Africa*, Athens: Ohio University Press.

Amadiume, Ifi, 1987, *Male Daughters, Female Husbands*, London: Zed Books.

Amadiume, Ifi, 1997, *Reinventing Africa. Matriarchy, Religion and Culture*, London: Zed Books.

Ampofo, Akosua Adomako, Josephine Beoku-Betts, Wairimo Njambi and Mary Osirim, M. (2004) 'Women's and Gender Studies in English-Speaking Sub-Saharan Africa', *Gender and Society* 18/6.

Ampofo, Akosua Adomako, and Signe Arnfred (eds), 2010, *African Feminist Politics of Knowledge. Tensions, Challenges, Possibilities*, Uppsala: The Nordic Africa Institute.

Anuário Católico de Moçambique, 1974, Lourenço Marques.

Arac de Nyeko, Monica, 2005, 'Ugandan Monologues', *Agenda* no 63.

Ardener, Shirley, 1987, 'A Note on Gender Iconography: The Vagina', in Pat Caplan (ed.), *The Cultural Construction of Sexuality*, London, New York: Tavistock Publications.

Ardener, Shirley (ed.) 1975, *Perceiving Women*, London: Malaby Press.

Arkitekskolen i Aarhus (Danmark) 1985, *Ilha de Moçambique, Relatório – Report*, Maputo: Secretariado de Estado da Cultura.

Arnfred, Signe, 1985, 'Rapport från kvinnokonferensen i Maputo', *Afrikabulletinen* 81.

Arnfred, Signe, 1987, 'Om kvinderne i landbrugskooperativerne i Maputos Zonas Verdes', *Moçambique*, Exhibition Catalogue, Stockholm: Kulturhuset.

Arnfred, Signe, 1988, 'Könsidentitet och könskamp i Moçambique', *Kvinnovetenskaplig tidskrift* 2.

Arnfred, Signe, 1990, 'Femmes et modernisation au Mozambique', *Politique africaine* 38, Paris: Karthala.

Arnfred, Signe, 2001, 'Questions of Power. Women's Movements, Feminist Theory and Development Aid', *Sida Studies* 3, Stockholm.

Arnfred, Signe (ed.) 2004a, *Re-thinking Sexualities in Africa*, Uppsala: The Nordic Africa Institute.

Arnfred, Signe, 2004b: 'Re-thinking Sexualities in Africa. Introduction', in Signe Arnfred (ed.), *Re-thinking Sexualities in Africa*, Uppsala: The Nordic Africa Institute.

Arnfred, Signe, 2004c, '"African Sexuality"/Sexuality in Africa. Tales and Silences', in Signe Arnfred (ed.), *Re-thinking Sexualities in Africa*, Uppsala: The Nordic Africa Institute.

Arthur, Maria José, 2000, *Políticas da Desigualdade?* Maputo: Forum Mulher.

Bachofen, Johann Jakob, 1861/1980, *Das Mutterrecht*, Berlin: Suhrkamp.

Bagnol, Brigitte and Esmeralda Mariano, 2008a, 'Elongation of the labia minora and Use of Vaginal Products to Enhance Eroticism: Can these Practices be Considered FGM?' *Finnish Journal of Ethnicity and Migration* 3/2.

Bagnol, Brigitte and Esmeralda Mariano, 2008b, 'Vaginal practices: eroticism and implications for women's health and condom use in Mozambique', *Culture, Health and Sexuality* 10/6.

Bakare-Yusuf, Bibi, 2004, 'Yorubas Don't do Gender: A critical review of Oyeronke Oyewumi's The Invention of Women', *CODESRIA Gender Series 1: African Gender Scholarship*, Dakar: CODESRIA.

Barbieri, Silvano n.d., Maputo: Centro de Estudos Africanos, unpublished.

Bartky, Sandra Lee, 1988/1998, 'Foucault, Femininity and the Modernization of Patriarchal Power', Rose Weitz (ed.), *The Politics of Women's Bodies*, Oxford: Oxford University Press.

Biber, Charles, 1987, *Cent ans au Mozambique. Reportage sur l'histoire de l'Église presbyterienne du Mozambique*, Lausanne: Editions du Soc.

Blackwood, Evelyn and Saskia Wieringa (eds), 1999, *Female Desires, Same-Sex Relations and Transgender Practices Across Cultures*, New York, Columbia University Press.

Blackwood, Evelyn, 2005, 'Wedding bell blues: Marriage, missing men and matrifocal follies', *American Ethnologist* 32/1.

Bledsoe, Caroline, 2002, *Contingent Lives*, Chicago: The University of Chicago Press.

Boddy, Janice, 1989, *Wombs and Alien Spirits*, Wisconsin: University of Wisconsin Press.

Boddy, Janice, 2007, *Civilizing Women: British Crusades in Colonial Sudan*, Princeton: Princeton University Press.

Boletim Geral das Colónias, 1940, 'Sessão Inaugural do Congresso Colonial, Discurso de Sua Excellencia o Sr Ministro das Colónias', Lisboa.

Boletim Geral das Colónias, 1948, 'Entrevista no 'Oriente' com o Governador Geral de Moçambique', Lisboa.

Bonate, Lizzat, 1998, *A Demolidora dos Prazeres*, London: SOAS, unpublished.

Bonate, Lizzat, 2003, 'The Ascendance of Angoche. The Politics of Kinship and Territory in Nineteenth Century Northern Mozambique', *Lusotopie 2003*, Paris: Karthala.

Branquinho, J.A. Gomes de Melo 1969, *Prospecção das forças tradicionais no distrito de Moçambique*, Lourenço Marques: Serviços de Centralização e Coordenação de Informações, unpublished.

Butler, Judith, 1990, *Gender Trouble*, London, New York: Routledge.

Butler, Judith, 1997, *The Psychic Life of Power: Theories in Subjection*, Stanford: Stanford University Press.

Buur, Lars and Helene Maria Kyed 2007, 'Traditional Authority in Mozambique: The Space between State and Community', in Buur and Kyed (eds), *State Recognition and Democratization in Sub-Saharan Africa*, New York, Basingstoke: Palgrave Macmillan.

Carvalho, Á. Pinto de, 1988, 'Notas para a História das Confrarias Islámicas na Ilha de Moçambique', *Boletim do Arquivo Histórico de Moçambique* 4, Maputo.

Casas, Maria Isabel & Paula Camata, 1996, *Campahna 'As Mulheres Camponesas de Nampula e a Lei de Terras'*, Documento de seminarios realizados nos Distritos de Ribáuè e Murrupula, Próvincia de Nampula, unpublished.

Casas, Maria Isabel, Teresinha da Silva, Ana Loforte & Margarita Mejia, 1998, *Perfil de Género na Província de Nampula*, Maputo: Embaixada do Reino dos Paises Baixos.

Casimiro, Isabel, 2001, Repensando as Relações entre Mulher e Homem no Tempo de Samora, Centro de Estudos Africanos, Unversidade Eduardo Mondlane, unpublished.

Casimiro, Isabel, 2004, *Paz na Terra, Guerra em Casa, Feminismo e Organizações de Mulheres em Moçambique*, Maputo: Promedia, Collecção Identidades.

Centro de Estudos Africanos, 1979, *Mozambican Miners in South Africa*, Maputo: CEA.

Centro de Estudos Africanos, 1980, *A Transformação da Agricultura Familiar na Província de Nampula*, Maputo: CEA.

Chacha, Babere Kerata, 2004, 'Traversing Gender and Colonial Madness: Same-Sex Relationships, Customary Law and Change in Tanzania, 1890–1990', CODESRIA Gender Series 3, *Gender Activism and Studies in Africa*, Dakar: CODESRIA.

Ciscato, Elia, 1995, 'A Dimensão Cosmológica do Político', in Irãe Baptiste Lundin & Francisco Jamisse Machava (eds), *Autoridade e Poder Tradicional* 1, Maputo: Ministério de Administração Estatal.

Collins, Patricia Hill, 1991, *Black Feminist Thought : knowledge, consciousness, and the politics of empowerment*, New York, London: Routledge.

Collins, Patricia Hill, 1994, 'Shifting the Center: Race, Class and Feminist Theorizing about Motherhood', in Evelyn Nakano Glenn, Grace Chang and Linda Rennie Forcey (eds) *Mothering: Ideology, Experience and Agency*, New York, London: Routledge.

Constituição da República Popular de Moçambique, 1978, Maputo: Instituto Nacional de Livro e Disco.

Cott, Nancy, 1978, 'Passionlessness: An Interpretation of Victorian Sexual Ideology, 1790–1850', *Signs* 4/2.

Coulon, Cristian, 1988, 'Women, Islam and Baraka' in Donal Cruise O'Brien and Cristian Coulon (eds), *Charisma and Brotherhood in African Islam*, Oxford: Clarendon Press.

Crehan, Kate 1997, *The Fractured Community: Landscapes of Power and Gender in Rural Zambia*, Berkeley: University of California Press.

Cruz e Silva, Teresa and Ana Loforte, 1998, 'Christianity, African traditional Religions and Cultural Identity in Southern Mozambique', in James L. Coz (ed.), *Rites of Passage in Contemporary Africa*, Cardiff: Cardiff Academic Press.

Cruz e Silva, Teresa, 2001, *Protestant Churches and the Formation of Political Consciousness in Southern Mozambique (1930 – 1974)*, Basel: P. Schlettwein Publishing.

Dagnino, Francesca, Gita Honwana & Albie Sachs, 1982, 'A família e o Direito tradicional', *Justiça Popular* 5, Maputo.

da Silva Rego, A., 1960, *Alguns problemas socio-missionários da Africa Negra*, Lisboa: Junta de Investigações do Ultramar.

da Silva,Terezinha & Ximena Andrade, 2000, *Beyond Equalities. Women in Mozambique*, WIDSAA, Amsterdam: The Netherlands Government Directorate of International Cooperation.

Danida, 2002, *Review of Danida-suppported Activities in the Agricultural Sector Programme Support*, Copenhagen: Ministry of Foreign Affairs, Denmark.

Darwin, Charles 1859/1987, *The Origin of the Species*, London: Penguin Classics.

Davison, Jean, 1997, *Gender, Lineage and Ethnicity in Southern Africa*, Oxford: Westview Press.

De Beauvoir, Simone. 1949/1997, *The Second Sex*, London: Vintage Classics.

de Castro, Soares 1960, 'Breves considerações sobre 'Maimo' do Distrito de Moçambique', *Boletim da Museu de Nampula* 1/1.

de Matos, Alexandre Valente, 1968, *Cerimónias da iniciacão das raparigas, Mutuali e Malema, Província de Nampula*, Maputo: Departmento de Antropologia e Arquelogia, Universidade Eduardo Mondlane, unpublished.

de Matos, Alexandea Valente, 1982, *Provérbios Macuas*, Lisboa: Junta de Investigações Científicas do Ultramar.

Declich, Francesca, 1995, 'Identity, Dance and Islam. Among People with Bantu Origins in Riverain Areas of Somalia', in A.J. Ahmed (ed.), *The Invention of Somalia*, Trenton, New Jersey: The Red Sea Press Inc.

Dias, Jorge & Margot Dias, 1970, *Os Macondes de Moçambique, III; Vida social e ritual*, Lisboa: Junta de Investigacões do Ultramar.

Direcção Nacional de Estatística 1984/85, *Analise dos Resultados do 1 Recenseamento Geral do População 1980*, Maputo: Direcção Nacional de Estatística.

Domingo (weekly newspaper) Maputo.

Dover, Paul, 2005,'Gender and Embodiment: Expectations of Manliness in a Zambian Village', in Lahoucine Ouzgane and Robert Morrell (eds) *African Masculinities*, New York, Basingstoke: Palgrave Macmillan.

Duarte, Maria da Luz Teixeira 1980, *Catálogo de Instrumentos Musicais de Moçambique*, Maputo: Ministério da Educação e Cultura.

Earthy, Dora, 1933/1968, *Valenge Women*, London: Frank Cass and Co.

Engels, Friedrich, 1884, sixth impression undated, *The Origin of the Family, Private Property and the State*. Moscow: Foreign Languages Publishing House.

Epprecht, Marc, 2004, *Hungochani. The History of a Dissident Sexuality in Southern Africa*. Montreal & Kingston: McGill-Queens University Press.

Etienne, Mona and Eleanor Leacock (eds), 1980, *Women and Colonization*, New York: Praeger.

Fair, Laura, 1996, 'Identity, Difference and Dance: Female Initiation in Zanzibar', 1890 to 1930, *Frontiers: A Journal of Women's Studies* XVII/3.

Fair, Laura 1997, 'Kickin' it: Leisure, Politics and Football in Colonial Zanzibar', 1900s–1950s, *Africa* LXVII /2.

Fair, Laura, 2001, *Pastimes and Politics. Culture, Community and Identity in Post-Abolition Urban Zanzibar*, 1890–1945, Athens: Ohio University Press.

Fee, Elizabeth, 1974, 'The Sexual Politics of Victorian Social Anthropology', in M. and L. W. B. Hartman (eds), *Clio's Consciousness Raised*, San Francisco: Harper and Row.

Feminist Africa 5, 2005, *Sexual Cultures*, Amina Mama, Charmaine Pereira and Takyiwaa Manuh (eds), Cape Town: African Gender Institute.

Feminist Africa 6, 2006, *Subaltern Sexualities*, Elaine Salo and Pumla Dineo Gqola (eds), Cape Town: African Gender Institute.

Fialho Feliciano, José, 1982, *Alguns dados sobre Antropologia em Moçambigue*, Maputo: Universidade Eduardo Mondlane, Departamento de Arqueologia e Antropologia.

Fialho Feliciano, José, 1998, *Antropologia Económica dos Thonga do Sul de Moçambique*, Maputo: Arquivo Histórico de Moçambique.

Foucault, Michel, 1976/1981, *The History of Sexuality*, London: Penguin Classics.

Foucault, Michel, 1980, *Power/Knowledge, Selected Interviews and Other Writings 1972–1977*, New York: Pantheon Books.

Frelimo Party Central Committee, 1983, *Out of Underdevelopment to Socialism*, Maputo: Frelimo Party.

Freud, Sigmund, 1917, *Vorlesungen zur Einführung in die Psychoanalyse*, Wien: Internationaler Psychoanalytischer Verlag.

Freud, Sigmund, 1930, *Das Unbehagen in der Kultur*, Wien: Internationaler Psychoanalytischer Verlag.

Fuglesang, Minou, 1994, *Veils and Videos*, PhD dissertation, Stockholm Studies in Social Anthropology, 32, Stockholm: University of Stockholm.

Geffray, Christian, 1990, *Ni père, ni mère. Critique de la parenté : le cas Makhuwa*, Paris: Seuil.

Geffray, Christian 1991, *A causa das Armas. Antropologia da guerra contemporânea em Moçambique*, Porto: Edições Afrontamento.

Geffray, Christian & Mogens Pedersen, 1985, *Transformação da organização social e do sistema agrário do campesinato no Distrito de Erati*, Maputo: Universidade Eduardo Mondlane.

Gilman, Sander, 1989, *Sexuality, An Illustrated History*, New York: John Wiley and Sons.

Gouws, Amanda (ed.) 2005, *(Un)thinking Citizenship. Feminist Debates in Contemporary South Africa*, Burlington: Ashgate.

Greenberg, Julie 2002, 'Definitional dilemmas: Male or Female? Black or White? The law's failure to recognize intersexuals and multiracials', in Toni Lester (ed.), *Gender nonconformity, race and sexuality: Charting the connections*, Wisconsin: University of Wisconsin Press.

Groes-Green, Christian 2011, *Transgressive Sexualities. Reconfiguring gender, power and (un)safe sexual cultures in urban Mozambique*, PhD dissertation, Faculty of Health Sciences, University of Copenhagen.

Grosz, Elizabeth, 2000, 'Histories of a Feminist Future', *Signs, Journal of Women in Culture and Society* 25/4.

Hanlon, Joseph, 1984, *Mozambique: The Revolution under Fire*, London: Zed Books.

Hedges, David, 1985, 'Educacão, missão e a ideologia política de assimilacão 1930–60', *Cadernos de História* 1, Maputo: Universidade Eduardo Mondlane.

Honwana Welch Gita, 1982, *O Lobolo: Por uma estrategía adequada*, Tese de Licenciatura, Faculdade de Direito, Maputo: Universidade de Eduardo Mondlane.

Horn, Jessica, 2006, 'Re-righting the sexual body', *Feminist Africa* 6.

Hunter, Marc, 2003, *Masculinities and Multiple Partners in Kwa-Zulu Natal: The Making and Un-making of Isoka*, Paper presented at Sex & Secrecy Conference, Johannesburg.

Instituto Nacional de Estatística, 1999, *II Recenseamento Geral da População, Resultados Definitivos*, Maputo.

Instituto Nacional de Estatística 2000, *Situação linguística de Moçambique. Dados do II Recenseamento Geral da População e Habitação de 1997*, Maputo.

Isaacman, Allen 1996, *Cotton is the Mother of Poverty*, Oxford: James Currey.

Junod, Henri-Alexandre, 1912/1974, *Usos e Costumes dos Bantos*, Lourenço Marques: Imprensa Nacional.

Kelly, Joan, 1984, *Women, History and Theory*, Chicago: University of Chicago Press.

Kendall 1999, 'Women in Lesotho and the (Western) Construction of Homophobia', in Evelyn Blackwood and Saskia Wieringa (eds), *Female Desires, Same-Sex Relations and Transgender Practices Across Cultures*, New York: Columbia University Press.

Klock-Jensen, Scott 1997, *Analysis of the Parliamentary Debate and New National Land Law for Mozambique*, Land Tenure Center, Universidade Eduardo Mondlane, Maputo.

Kratz, Corinne 1994, *Affecting Performance*, Washington, London : Smithsonian Institution Press.

la Fontaine, Jean 1982, Introduction, in Audrey Richards, *Chisungo*, London, New York: Tavistock Publications.

Lan, David, 1985, *Guns and Rain: Guerrillas and Spirit Mediums in Zimbabwe*, London: James Currey.

Larsen, Wenche, 2000, 'Frihet, likhet og ...? Det annet kjönn, take two. En samtale med Toril Moi', *Kvinneforskning* 2/2000.

Lastarria-Cornhiel, Susana 1997, 'Impact of Privatization on Gender and Property Rights in Africa', *World Development*, 25/8.

Leacock, Eleanor,1981, *Myths of Male Dominance*, New York: Monthly Review Press.

Lévi-Strauss, Claude, 1949/1969, *The Elementary Structures of Kinship*, London: Social Science Paperbacks.

Lewis, Desiree/Molara Ogundipe, 2002, 'Conversation. Desiree Lewis talks to Molara Ogundipe', *Feminist Africa* 1.

Lienhardt, P. 1968, 'Introduction', in H. bin Ismail (ed.), *The Medicine Man, Swifa Ya Nguvumali*, Oxford: Oxford University Press.

Loforte, Ana 2000, *Género e Poder*, Maputo: Promedia, Collecção Identidades.

Lorde, Audre, 1984, *Sister Outsider*, Freedom, California:The Crossing Press.

Lugones, Maria, 2007, 'Heterosexualism and the Colonial/Modern Gender system', *Hypatia* 22/1.

Lundin, Irae Baptiste, & Francisco Jamisse Machava (eds) 1995: *Autoridade e Poder Tradicional I*, Maputo: Ministério da Administracão Estatal.

Lundin, Irae Baptiste, & Francisco Jamisse Machava (eds) 1998: *Autoridade e Poder Tradicional II*, Maputo: Ministério da Administracão Estatal.

Lutero, M. & Pereira, M. 1980, 'A influência Àrabe na música tradiçional', *Música Tradicional em Moçambique*, Maputo: Ministério da Educação e Cultura.

Macaire, Pierre, 1996, *L'héritage Makhuwa au Mozambique*, Paris: L'Harmattan.

Machado A.J. de Mello, 1970, *Entre os Macuas de Angoche*, Lisbon: Prelo Editora.

Machel, Samora, 1973/1980: A emancipacão da mulher, Maputo: Collecção Estudos e Orientacões.

Machel, Samora 1974, *Mozambique: Sowing the Seeds of Revolution*, London: Committee for Freedom in Mozambique, Angola and Guine (CFMAG).

Machel, Samora 1977a, 'Discurso no Acto de Abertura da 2a Conferéncia da OMM', *Documentos da 2a conferencia da OMM*, Maputo.

Machel, Samora 1977b: 'Discurso na Sessão de Encerramento da 2a Conferéncia da OMM', *Documentos da 2a conferencia da OMM*, Maputo.

Machel, Samora, 1982, 'Discurso na Província de Gaza, Março 1982', *Tempo* 600, Maputo.

Machel, Samora 1985, 'We are declaring war on the enemy within', in Barry Munslow (ed.), *Samora Machel: An African Revolution*, London: Zed Books.

Maine, Henry, 1861/1986, *Ancient Law*, Tucson: University of Arizona Press.

Mama, Amina, 1997, 'Defining Terms and Concepts for Ourselves', in Charmaine Pereira (ed.), *Concepts and Methods for Gender and Women's Studies in Nigeria*, Report of the Network for Women's Studies in Nigeria, 2, Zaria: Tamaza Publishing Co.

Martin, Bradford G., 1976, 'The Qadiri and Shadhil: Brotherhoods in East Africa 1880–1910', in Bradford G. Martin (ed.), *Muslim Brotherhoods in Nineteenth Century Africa*, Cambridge: Cambridge University Press.

Martinez, Francisco Lema, 1989, *O povo Macua e a sua cultura*, Lisboa: Instituto de Investigação Científica Tropical.

Marx, Karl, 1858/1939, *Grundrisse der kritik der politischen Ökonomie*, Frankfurt: Europäische Verlagsanstalt.

Matory, J Lorand, 2005, *Black Atlantic Religion. Tradition, Transnationalism and Matriarchy in the Afro-Brazilian Candomblé*, Princeton: Princeton University Press.

McClintock, Anne, 1995, *Imperial Leather. Race, Gender and Sexuality in the Colonial Contest*, New York, London: Routledge.

McFadden, Patricia, 1992, 'Sex, Sexuality and the Problem of AIDS in Africa', in Ruth Meena (ed.) *Gender in Southern Africa*, Harare: SAPES Books.

McFadden, Patricia, 2003, 'Sexual Pleasure as Feminist Choice', *Feminist Africa* 2.

Medeiros, Eduardo, 1984, *A Representação da Mulher nas Estruturas do Poder Tradicional*, Maputo: UNESCO/FNUAP.

Medeiros, Eduardo, 1985a, 'Evolução de algumas instituições socio-familiares', *Cadernos da História* 1, Universidade Eduardo Mondlane, Maputo.

Medeiros, Eduardo 1985b, *O Sistema Linhageiro de Macua-Lómwè*, Universidade Eduardo Mondlane, Maputo.

Medeiros, Eduardo, 1995, *Os Senhores da Floresta*, PhD dissertation, Universidade de Coimbra.

Medeiros, Eduardo, 1996,' Irmandades Muçulmanas do norte de Moçambique', *Semanário Savana* 116, Maputo.

Meillassoux, Claude, 1975/1981, *Maidens, Meal and Money*, Cambridge: Cambridge University Press.

Mernissi, Fatima, 1975/1985, *Beyond the Veil. Male-Female Dynamics in a Muslim Society*, London: Al Saqi Books.

Mernissi, Fatima, 1991, *Women and Islam: A Historical and Theological Enquiry*, Oxford: Blackwell.

Mies, Maria, 1986, *Patriarchy and Accumulation on a World Scale*, London: Zed Books.

Ministério da Justica, 1982, *Projecto da Lei da Família*.

Ministry of Agriculture, Mozambique, 1998, PROAGRI Master Document 1998–2003, Maputo.

Moffett, Helen, 2005, 'A Space in which 'Vagina' is Not a Dirty Word: The Vagina Monologues on the GWSA Listserve', *Feminist Africa* 5.

Mohanty, Chandra Talpade, 1984/1991, 'Under Western Eyes: Feminist Scholarship and Colonial Discourses', in Chandra Mohanty, Ann Russo, Lourdes Torres (eds), *Third World Women and the Politics of Feminism*, Bloomington and Indianapolis: Indiana University Press.

Mohanty, Chandra Talpade, 2003, *Feminism Without Borders*, Durham: Duke University Press.

Moi, Toril, 1994, *Simone de Beauvoir, The Making of an Intellectual Woman*, Oxford: Blackwell Publishers.

Moore, Henrietta ánd Megan Vaughan, 1994, *Cutting Down Trees. Gender, Nutrition and Agricultural Change in the Northern Province of Zambia 1890–1990*, Oxford: James Currey.

Moreira, Eduardo, 1936, *Portuguese East Africa – A Study of its Religious Needs*, London: World Dominion Press.

Morgan, Lewis Henry, 1871/1966, *Systems of Consanguinity and Affinity*, Smithsonian Contributions to Knowledge.

Morgan, Lewis Henry, 1877/1985, *Ancient Society*, Tucson: University of Arizona Press.

Morgan, Robin (ed.) 1984, *Sisterhood is Global. The International Women's Movement Anthology*, Norwell: Anchor Press.

Morier-Genoud, Éric 2000, 'The 1996 'Muslim Holidays' Affair: Religious Competition and State Mediation in Contemporary Mozambique', *Journal of Southern African Studies* 26/3.

Morier-Genoud, Éric, 2002,' L'islam au Mozambique après l'Indépendence', *L'Afrique Politique* 2002.

Morrell, Robert (ed.), 2001, *Changing Men in Southern Africa*, London: Zed Books.

Morrell, Robert and Lahoucine Ouzgane (eds), 2005, *African Masculinities. Men in Africa from the Late Nineteenth Century to the Present*, Basingstoke: Palgrave Macmillan.

Murdock, George Peter, 1949, *Social Structure*, New York: Macmillan.

Murray, Stephen and Will Roscoe (eds), 1998, *Boy Wives and Female Husbands: Studies in African Homosexualities*, New York: St Martin's Press.

Nelson, Nici, 1987, Selling her kiosk: Kikuyu notions of sexuality and sex for sale in Mathare Valley, Kenya, in Pat Caplan (ed.) *The Cultural Construction of Sexuality*, New York, London: Routledge.

Newitt Malin, 1981, *Portugal in Africa. The last Hundred Years*, London: Hurst & Company.

Newitt, Malin, 1995, *A History of Mozambique*, London: Hurst & Company.

Nimtz, A.H. 1980, *Islam and Politics in East Africa. The Sufi Order in Tanzania*, Minneapolis: University of Minnesota Press.

Nnaemeka, Obioma, 2005, *Female Circumcision and the Politics of Knowledge*, New York: Praeger.

Nordstrom, Carolyn 1997, *A Different Kind of War Story*, Pennsylvania: University of Pennsylvania Press.

Nzegwu, Nkiru 2004, 'The Epistemological Challenge of Motherhood to Patriliny', *JENdA, A Journal of Culture and African Women Studies* 5.

Nzegwu, Nkiru, 2006, *Family Matters*, New York: State University of New York Press.

OMM 1977, *Documentos da 2a Conferéncia da Organização da Mulher Moçambicana 1976*, Maputo.

OMM 1984, 'Resolução Geral da Conferéncia Extraordinária da OMM', *Tempo* 737, Maputo.

Ortner, Sherry, 1974, 'Is Female to Male as Nature is to Culture?', in Michelle Rosaldo and Louise Lamphere (eds), *Woman, Culture and Society*, Stanford: Stanford University Press.

Oyewùmí, Oyèrónké, 1997: *The Invention of Women. Making an African sense of Western gender discourses*. Minneapolis: University of Minnesota Press.

Oyewùmí, Oyèrónké, 2000, 'Family Bonds/Conceptual Binds: African Notes on Feminist Epistemologies', *Signs: Journal of Women in Culture and Society* 25/4.

Oyewùmí, Oyèrónke, 2002, 'Conceptualizing Gender: The Eurocentric Foundations of Feminist Concepts and the Challenge of African Epistemologies', *JENdA: A Journal of Culture and African Women's Studies* 2/1.

Pereira, Charmaine 2002, 'Between Knowing and Imagining – What Space for Feminism in Scholarship on Africa?' *Feminist Africa* 1.

Pereira, Charmaine 2003, 'Where Angles Fear to Tread? Some thoughts on Patricia McFadden's Sexual Pleasure as Feminist Choice', *Feminist Africa* 2.

Peters, Pauline, 1997, 'Introduction: Revisiting the Puzzle of Matriliny in South-Central Africa', *Critique of Anthropology* 17/2.

Pitcher, Anne, 1996, 'Conflict and Cooperation: Gendered Roles and Responsibilities within Cotton Households in Northern Mozambique', *African Studies Review* 39/3.

Pitcher, Anne, 2008, *Transforming Mozambique: The Politics of Privatization, 1975–2000*, Cambridge: Cambridge University Press.

Poewe, Karla, 1981, *Matrilineal Ideology. Male–Female Dynamics in Luapula, Zambia*, Maryland: Academic Press.

Ranger, Terence, 1972, 'Missionary Adaption of African Religious Institutions, The Masasi Case', Terence O. Ranger and Isaria N. Kimambo (eds), *The Historical Study of African Religion with Special Reference to East and Central Africa*, London, Ibadan: Heinemann Educational Books.

Ranger, Terence, 1975, *Dance and Society in Eastern Africa 1890–1970*, Berkeley: University of California Press.

Rasing, Thera, 1999, 'Globalization and the making of consumers. Zambian Kitchen Parties', in Richard Fardon, Wim van Binsbergen and Rijk van Dijk (eds) *Modernity on a Shoestring*, The Hague: EIDOS.

Rasing, Thera, 2001, *The Bush Burnt, the Stones Remain. Female initiation rituals in urban Zambia*, Berlin: LIT Verlag.

Rasing, Thera, 2004, The persistence of female initiation rites: Reflexivity amd resilience of women in Zambia, in Wim van Binsbergen and Rijk van Dijk (eds) 2004, *Situating Globality*, Leiden, Boston: Brill.

Ratele, Kopano, 1998, 'Relation to Whiteness: Writing about the black man', *Psychology Bulletin* 8/2, University of the Western Cape.

Ratele, Kopano, 2005, 'Proper sex, bodies, culture and objectification', *Agenda* 63, Durban.

Rebelo, Jorge, 1981, *Discurso no Conselho Coordenador Nacional da OMM*, Maputo, unpublished.

Reid, Graeme and Liz Walker (eds) 2005, *Men Behaving Differently. South African Men since 1994*,

Cape Town: Double Storey Books.

Rich, Adrienne, 1976, *Of Woman Born: Motherhood as Experience and Institution*, London: Virago.

Richards, Audrey, 1939/1995, *Land, Labour and Diet in Northern Rhodesia*, International African Institute, Berlin: LIT Verlag; London: International African Institute (IAI) and James Currey.

Richards, Audrey, 1950, 'Some Types of Family Structure amongst the Central Bantu', in A. R. Radcliffe-Brown and C. Daryll Forde (eds), *African Systems of Kinship and Marriage*, Oxford: Oxford University Press.

Richards, Audrey, 1956/1982 *Chisungu, A girl's initiation ceremony among the Bemba of Zambia*, London: Tavistock Publications.

Rita-Ferreira, António et al 1964, *Promoçao Social em Moçambique*, Estudos de Sciencias e Politicas Sociais no 71, Lisboa: Junta de Investigacões do Ultramar.

Rita-Ferreira, António, 1975, *Povos de Moçambique, história e cultura*, Porto: Afrontamento.

Rogers, Barbara, 1980, *The Domestication of Women*, London: Kogan Page.

Rosander, Eva Evers 1997, 'Introduction: The Islamization of "tradition" and "modernity"'', in David Westerlund and Eva Evers Rosander (eds), *African Islam and Islam in Africa*, London: Hurst & Company.

Rubin, Gayle, 1975, 'The Traffic in Women', in Rayna Reiter (ed.), *Toward an Anthropology of Women*, New York: Monthly Review Press.

Sá e Bonnet, João Alberto de, 1996, *Aspectos pedagógicos da socializacão da crianca durante os ritos de iniciação da puberdade*, Universidade pedagógica, Maputo.

Sachs, Albie & Teodosio Uate, 1984, 'Por que razão o conservador não registou o seu próprio casamento?', *Justiça Popular* 8/9.

Sacks, Karen, 1979, *Sisters and Wives. The Past and Future of Sexual Equality*, Santa Barbara: Greenwood Press.

Saúte, Nelson & António Sopa, 1992, *Ilha de Moçambique pela voz dos poetas*, Lisbon: Edições 70.

Schildknecht, F. 1969, Tanzania, in J. Kritzeck and W.H. Lewis (eds), *Islam in Africa*, New York: Van Rostrand-Reinhold Company.

Schneider, David M. and Kathleen Gough (eds) 1961, *Matrilineal Kinship*, Berkeley: University of California Press.

Schroeder, Richard, 1997, *Re-claiming land in the Gambia: Gendered Policy Rights and Environmental Intervention*, paper for Seminar on 'The Politics of Poverty and Environmental Intervention', Stockholm.

Spivak, Gayatri, 1988, 'Can the Subaltern Speak?' in C.Nelson and L.Crossberg (eds), *Marxism and the Interpretation of Culture*, Champaign: University of Illinois Press.

Spivak, Gayatri, 1990, *The Post-colonial Critique: Interviews, Strategies and Dialogues*. New York, London: Routledge.

Staehelin, Liselotte & Barbara Müller, 1997, *Uma vida Boa. Perspectivas Locais de Desenvolvimento em Nametil, Mecuburi*, Cooperação Suiça, Mecuburi.

Strobel, Margot, 1976, 'From Lelemama to Lobbying: Women's Associations in Mombasa, Kenya', in Nancy Hafkin and Edna Bay, *Women in Africa: Studies in Social and Economic Change*, Stanford: Stanford University Press.

Strobel, Margot, 1979, *Muslim Women in Mombasa 1890–1975*, Yale: Yale University Press.

Suttner, Raymond, 2009, *The ANC Underground in South Africa*, Johannesburg: Jacana Media.

Swantz, Marja-Liisa, 1970/1986, *Ritual and Symbol*, Uppsala: The Nordic Africa Institute.

Tamale, Sylvia, 2003, 'Out of the Closet: Unveiling Sexuality Discourses in Uganda', *Feminist Africa* 2.

Tamale, Sylvia 2005a, *Gendered Bodies, Sexuality and Negotiating Power in Uganda*, paper presented at conference organized by the Centre for Global Gender Studies, Gothenburg.

Tamale, Sylvia 2005b, 'Eroticism, Sensuality and 'Women's Secrets' among the Baganda: A Critical Analysis', *Feminist Africa* 5.

Tempo (weekly political magazine, closely linked to Frelimo), Maputo.

Tique, Cesar Augusto 1996, *Peasant Perception of Land Degradation and Conservation in Mozambique: The Case of Namialo, Nampula Porvince*, MA thesis, University of Illinois.

Trimingham, J.S. 1964, *Islam in East Africa*, Gloucestershire: Clarendon Press.

Turner, Victor, 1967, *The Forest of Symbols*, Ithaca: Cornell University Press.

Undie, Chi-Chi and Kabwe Benaya, 2005, The State of Knowledge on Sexuality in Sub-Saharan Africa: A Synthesis of Literature, presented at Workshop: Theorizing Sexuality in Africa, Nairobi.

União Geral dos Cooperativas do Maputo, Zonas Verdes, 1986, *A Experiencia do Engajamento da Mulher ca Cidade do Maputo*, paper given at Conference on Women and National Reconstruction, Universidade Eduardo Mondlane, Maputo.

Venetsanou, Emilia & Camillo Risoli, 1998, *Elementos para uma abordagem do sistema agricola familiar na Província de Nampula, Mozambique*, Cooperação Suiça, Nampula.

Vuyk, Trudeke, 1991, *Children of One Womb: Descent, Marriage and Gender in Central African Societies*. Leiden: Centre of Non-Western Studies.

Weber, Max, 1920/1930, *The Protestant Ethic and the Spirit of Capitalism*, London: Unwin University Books.

West, Harry, 2005, *Kupilikula. Governance and the Invisible Realm in Mozambique*, Chicago: The University of Chicago Press.

West, Harry and Scott Klock-Jensen, 1999, 'Betwixt and Between: "Traditional Authority" and Democratic Decentralization in Post-War Mozambique', *African Affairs* 98/393.

Whitehead, Ann, 2000, 'Continuities and Discontinuities in Political Constructions of the Working Man in Rural Sub-Saharan Africa: The "Lazy Man" in African Agriculture', *European Journal of Development Research* 12/2.

Wieringa, Saskia, 2005, Women Marriages and Other Same Sex Practices: Historical Reflections on African Women's Same-Sex Relations, in R. Morgan and S. Wieringa (eds) *Tommy Boys, Lesbian Men and Ancestral Wives*, Johannesburg: Jacana Media.

Wieringa, Saskia and Evelyn Blackwood, 1999, 'Introduction', in Blackwood, E. and Wieringa, S (eds) *Female Desires. Same-Sex Relations and Transgender Practices Across Cultures*, New York: Columbia University Press.

Wuyts, Marc, 1978, *Camponeses e economia rural em Moçambique*, Universidade Eduardo Mondlane, Maputo.

Yanagisako, Sylvia J. and Jane F. C.ollier, 1987, Toward a Unified Analysis of Gender and Kinship, in Collier, Jane F. and Sylvia J. Yanagasaki , *Gender and Kinship. Essays Toward a Unified Analysis*, Stanford: Stanford University Press.

Young, Kate, Carol Wolkowitz, Roslyn McCullagh, 1981, *Of Marriage and the Market. Women's subordination in international perspective*, London: CSE Books.

Index

www.ingramcontent.com/pod-product-compliance
Lightning Source LLC
Chambersburg PA
CBHW051952270326
41929CB00015B/2619